To Keith with [?]
you enjoy reading it
as much as I enjoyed writing the
book.
    Yours
        Bill Hayes

YOUR NUMBER'S NOT DRY

YOUR NUMBER'S NOT DRY

An unreliable and probably self-delusory progression
through a lifetime spent in
His and Her Majesties' Royal Air Force

ERIC HAYES MBE

The title is a derogatory comment offered by a long serving airman to another airman who has, in his opinion, only just joined the Service.

SERENDIPITY

Copyright © Eric Hayes 2007

First Published in 2007 by

Serendipity Publishers, Darlington, UK

All rights reserved
Unauthorised duplication
contravenes existing laws
British Library Cataloguing-in-Publication data
A catalogue record for this book is available from the British Library

ISBN 978-1-84394-213-9

To my family who look forward to blissful silence following publication of my stories

To Gitti Hayes, my long suffering wife
'I've been her cross in life'

FOREWORD

Eric Hayes has enjoyed a fascinating and remarkable career in the Royal Air Force, from his somewhat nomadic early life and his relatively humble beginnings as a Boy Entrant tradesman, through to his life as a technician, NCO aircrew and commissioned Air Engineer and his later tours as a staff officer in NATO and RAF headquarters. This equally remarkable book contains a wealth of memories; of places seen by many and remembered with great affection by those who served in the RAF during the turbulent period after WWII when the political map of the world was being redrawn. It also serves as a window on the world of Britain's colonial past and its efforts to remain on the world stage, viewed by those involved, their different social mores and the strengths, frailties and sometimes sheer cantankerousness of human nature in general. Many of the characters are instantly recognisable in almost any close knit community. The golden thread that runs through all these wonderful vignettes of Service life is a rich vein of dry, self effacing, self deprecating and often dark sense of humour that is unique not only to the author, but to all those who have served the Queen, whatever the colour of their uniform.

Squadron Leader Andrew Thomas

Contents

CHAPTER

ONE	BOY ENTRANT HAYES	1
TWO	HEMSWELL – MY FIRST POSTING	21
THREE	MY FIRST OVERSEAS TOUR	27
FOUR	HOSPITAL AND MELKSHAM	47
FIVE	BINBROOK AND THE CANBERRA BOMBER	55
SIX	THE MALAYAN DETACHMENT	81
SEVEN	THE JOURNEY HOME	95
EIGHT	MALTA AND THE SUEZ CAMPAIGN	99
NINE	MALTA AGAIN	107
TEN	DECISION TIME AND AN INTERLUDE WITH VULCAN BOMBERS	123
ELEVEN	AIRCREW TRAINING	125
TWELVE	ADEN AND THE BLACKBURN BEVERLEY	133
THIRTEEN	KENYA	167
FOURTEEN	WESSEX HELICOPTERS AT ODIHAM	185
FIFTEEN	OFFICER CADET HAYES	199
SIXTEEN	THE HERCULES TRANSPORT AIRCRAFT	213
SEVENTEEN	AN INTERLUDE AT GAN	245
EIGHTEEN	ONCE A TRAPPER NOW A FAILURE	249
NINETEEN	RAF FINNINGLEY	253
TWENTY	RETURN TO FLYING	269
TWENTY-ONE	A NATO APPOINTMENT	285
TWENTY-TWO	OPERATIONS OFFICER, BRIZE NORTON	301
TWENTY-THREE	WINTEX AND MY FINAL TOUR OF DUTY	305
TWENTY-FOUR	MESS ENTERTAINMENT	315

CHAPTER ONE
BOY ENTRANT HAYES

I looked at the eight-figure number I had just been given and thought that I'd never remember it! (I think now that a postmortem would find the number somewhere in my body.) Perhaps it might be found throughout my body rather like the lettering in a stick of Blackpool rock. Apparently this was to be my identification within the Royal Air Force. It was the 27th of September 1949 and I was now Boy Entrant E Hayes, electrical mechanic under training, and a member of the Eighth Entry. I was four feet eleven inches tall; six stone and eight pounds in weight and newly arrived at RAF Locking near Weston Super Mare. I was now one of the 'Brats', lower life than even an Aircraft Apprentice, who were similar to Boy Entrants but deemed to be of marginally higher intelligence and worthy of a three-year apprentice training rather than the eighteen-month course that was to be my lot.

A few months earlier my parents had been faced by a quandary. Employment was hard to find at the time and my Father had decided to become a gardener with the Imperial War Graves Commission. Unfortunately the War Graves, as they were known, wanted him to work at the Reichwald Forest Cemetery in Germany. My parents had seen little of each other for many years, for Dad had joined the Palestine Police in 1936. He remained in Palestine until 1942 and during his return voyage was torpedoed firstly off Durban and then again off the eastern seaboard of the US. On his return to England he worked for the NAAFI while his body recovered before rejoining the Army. He spent a short time in the Far East before returning to Germany to work for the NAAFI again. At last my parents could be together, for No. 1 son could go to University. I, however, was only fifteen years old, and most unlikely to matriculate. I wasn't thick, indeed I was pretty good at some subjects, but I had a block where maths were concerned. I thought up the idea of joining up myself, and applied to the Selection Board based at Hornchurch in Essex where I passed the medical examination and the Board. I think that a certain relief that they could once more live together again tempered my parents' anxiety. They had not had an easy life.

Boy entrant, at 15 years old.

Little did my mother know what her youngest had got himself into! It was all a far cry from Worcester Park in Surrey, and even further from Tiffin School in Kingston upon Thames. There is a Hayes on the Honours Board of that time but the initial is not E but J W. My elder brother was blessed with brains, whereas I, who had the misfortune to follow him through the same school, didn't even have brawn. James had timed his efforts well, for my parents wanted to work in Germany as civilians. This meant that I could not attend a military school in postwar Germany, nor could they afford to educate me in England, Furthermore, to matriculate, that is to pass out of school with any qualification, one had to pass Maths and English. I achieved a modest 18% in mathematics. It was said of me by one Mr Spriggs, ' His ignorance is bewildering, and, as his ignorance increases so does his bewilderment.' A truly helpful assessment of my abilities. Brother Hayes, on the other hand, had won a State Scholarship to University. What to do with Eric? I had the answer: I'll join the Air Force. I didn't fancy the Navy and I didn't care for the Army, although Dad had been a professional soldier in India and Egypt before marrying my Mother. I hadn't seen much of him in my young life, but I liked him nonetheless. So, with parents off to the Fatherland and James off to University, I too was setting out for a new life. I signed on for eight years regular service and four years in the Reserve, whatever that meant.

There were nineteen would-be electricians in my entry and we were to share a wooden hut condemned some years earlier. It was said that the place had been renovated, but everywhere there was evidence that every expense had been spared. The beds lined each side of the long room. There were two small individual rooms at one end, whilst a door at the other end led into a maze of wooden corridors that linked to washing rooms, toilets and drying rooms. The individual huts, about twenty in number, all sprouted from this central facility. There were other similar edifices about the base. The beds were of a construction I'd never seen before. They were incredibly short, measuring four feet in length. I found out later that they pulled out to a reasonable length and had three little mattresses, which when placed side by side provided a suitably uncomfortable and lumpy resting-place. Although I was the second smallest boy in the entry, I was glad that the beds extended.

Boy entrants to the Royal Air Force in 1949 were not gilded lilies. We were, I was to find, a very mixed bunch indeed. I think eleven boys in my group had fallen foul of the law and had been encouraged by a Magistrate to join up. Two had come from the Bangalore Military Academy when their parents had retreated from India following partition. A chap from a public school graced our ranks together with the Czech offspring of a former wartime ally. Of the remaining four recruits, two had been thrown out of home by stepfathers and that left me and one other boy. It seemed later, that we two were the only boys who had enjoyed a normal happy childhood.

My father told me that he couldn't offer much in the way of advice, but what little he could give would be invaluable. There were two kinds in a barrack room, the ones who laugh and the ones who are laughed at. It was important that I should be in the first group, particularly as I was on the small side. There was, he told me, only one way to start off well and that was to hit the first bloke to annoy me, be he big, little, or bloody enormous. You'll never have to do it again, he promised. Don't worry; you won't get hurt for you'll be pulled apart before any damage is done. I believed him.

On that first day at Locking, we drew our bedding and swore allegiance to the King, his heirs and successors. I think that it was four blankets, two sheets, one pillow and pillowcase, in any case quite a load for a little lad. 'Your hut's L2' the Sergeant bellowed, and we all wandered in the appropriate direction. By good fortune I was one of the first into the hut. Spying a corner bed I threw my bedding onto it. Just as quickly, a large youth threw my bedding off and replaced it with his own. Father's advice came to mind, and with a swift left and right to the stomach, I couldn't reach his face, I laid into him. It was at this point that I realised that Father could be wrong. The mountain defended vigorously, and there was no authority available to stop us fighting. Moreover, the rest of the boys egged us on. You recall the adage about a good little'un beating a bigger chap? It's lies, bloody lies! We fought happily for some minutes until the uproar brought a snarling Corporal to the scene. Now we were separated – or should I say at last. However, Father was right, I never had another fight within my entry and Stan Lewry and I became good friends. He kept the corner bed though.

Boy entrants were allowed to enlist aged 15½ years and the age limit extended to 17½. There was therefore a wide disparity in stature, physique and in experience of life. Among the Borstal or else group was a boy called Gilmore, He was about five feet three inches with a large, moon-faced head, no neck and a very stocky body. He had very sparse hair, and extremely smelly feet, which he washed four times a day. He carried an incredible aura of menace for one so young, and it wasn't due to the smell. He announced that if anything should be stolen within our hut, then the thief would not be one of 'them', meaning the Borstal or else group. He jerked his head to indicate the rest of our entry. We all believed him – and he was right. Within the entry system of boy entrants, an incredible esprit de corps developed. My entry, right or wrong, was the credo. Later I was to be most grateful for this loyalty. Especially when raiding parties of senior entry boys were looking for revenge when, promoted to authority, I charged half their entry for some offence or other.

There was one boy that I greatly admired. As we went to bed on the first night of Air Force life, he knelt beside his bed to silently say his prayers. A shower of boots fell around him. He ignored all comments. On the second night he did the same and again the boots flew. On the third day he said his prayers without interruption. I lacked his courage, if not his conviction.

Chaz, or to give his correct name, Prochazka was a youth of Czech origins. His Father had flown for the RAF during the war. Poor Chaz, I don't think that I ever heard his name correctly pronounced throughout our acquaintance. Various drill instructors tried without success, providing us with considerable amusement. Chaz became a ground electrician and did not make a long-term career in the Air Force. I believe that he now runs a winter sports shop in Aviemore.

The two boys who came from India at the time of partition were entirely at home in the regime of boys' service, for they had been pupils at a military academy. They knew how to bull boots up to a glass-like sheen. Their webbing equipment was perfectly blanco-ed and square and they took every new problem in their stride. I envied them, for there was nothing that they could not do well.

After about three months I felt confident in my surroundings and capable of holding my own if necessary. This was a delusion. As I opened a corridor door, a large Scots youth from the poorer part of Edinburgh shoved me aside. I protested. He took me by the collar and lifted me up to his face level. At this point, I thought, when he puts me down I shall hit him with a left and right to the solar plexus. He didn't know about this brilliant tactic and head butted me. This, I was to learn, was a 'Dandruff Decider' or a 'Glasgow Kiss'. As I lay on the floor with a nose that felt as though it was growing like that of a lying Pinocchio, I did not offer further offence. Instead I thought that I did not like this game, and would much rather play doctor and nurses. I didn't know about husbands and wives at this time.

Before continuing, I must say a little more about the huts we lived in. The floor was covered in brown linoleum, polished to a mirror shine by mansion polish and lead loaded bumpers with long handles. I haven't seen one in half a century. One did not walk on the floor! Instead, old blankets were torn and folded to become footpads. In this manner one moved around and polished the floor at the same time. Heating was provided in the form of a centrally mounted pot-bellied coke burning stove. If your bed was near the stove, other boys sat on it and you were too warm in bed. If you lived at the extremities of the room, you froze, but nobody sat on your bed. There must have been ten windows on each side of each hut, and every one of the windows had a brass handle and retaining strut. In addition there were the windows and brass accoutrements of our share of the wooden maze of toilets etc to polish. This meant, of course, that they must gleam at all times. The hut owned a galvanised bucket in addition to the red painted sand-filled fire buckets. This bucket gleamed like chrome, through the tireless and unpaid labour of generations of boy entrants.

My parents had little money, and it was the recognition of this that caused me to make a very serious error of judgement. My mother sent me a postal order for 5 shillings (remember that this was a week's pay to me at the time). I thought about it and returned the postal order with, what seems to me now, a rather pompous letter saying that I was trying very hard to be independent. I thanked her very much for her kind thought. Error, error, error! I never ever received another postal order. I would see my colleagues shaking the postal order from their letters and spending the money long before they actually read the accompanying letter. I had turned the tap off. I had killed the 'golden goose'. I may have hurt my mother's feelings, but I hope not. At any rate, I paid the price of false pride.

In my capacity of Leading Boy Entrant, I had been promoted after six months of service; I was required to pass a message to a member of the 6th entry. Unthinkingly, for there were no pads available, I crossed their hut floor wearing my boots, working, studded, quantity x 1pr. Not quite the ultimate sin, but this was a senior entry floor and as such forbidden and sacred ground to any member of a junior entry. I was stripped naked and suspended from the roof beams of the hut and whipped with wet towels. I tried to feign unconsciousness, but it is somewhat difficult when one's parts are attacked in this manner. Oh yes, and I was supposed to lick up tomato sauce from the floor while they were doing this. I remember all of this very well. Eventually I was released, and trying desperately not to cry, I escaped to my bunk. That night my entry raided the 6th in revenge. Clubbing anything that moved with knotted wet towels, we swept up their room overturning beds and lockers. Sand buckets of trash sullied the revered floor. Silently we had come, and silently we fled into the night. Honour had been restored.

I'm not going to tell you about the training, but rather about the personalities and a few illustrative incidents. Firstly, there was Flight Sergeant Ireland, the Squadron disciplinary NCO. Ireland was of the old school. He wore a magnificent moustache, and carried himself with the assured air of God himself. Sure, was he not as Irish as they come? Sadistic in some ways, he had an uncanny knowledge of what was going on in the Lines. He had the merciless tongue of a Drill Sergeant, the blessing of a sense of humour and the knowledge of an almanac. I liked him, despite the fact that he was a supporter of all boxing events. Did I say that I had been a schoolboy-boxing champion? Well, I had been and I certainly didn't look the part. This was a great asset when paired for a punch up in the gym during the first sports period. Paddy Ireland watched me nip across the ring punching other unfortunates at will, and deftly avoiding their attacks. A British professional middleweight champion had trained me at school and my school at that time had probably the best schoolboy team in England. Certainly we held Great Britain Championships at six weights at one time. I had had at least 50 fights of one description of another. Brother James was not good at boxing. 'Ah, young Hayes,' said Paddy, in his thick brogue, 'You can do something right.' This was the start of a love hate relationship, for Paddy would bet up to a month's pay on my performances in the Air Force and later the Combined Services Championships. He acted as my second. If I was winning, he would fan me gently, but if all was not well, he would revive me with ice-cold water down the inside of my pants and, instead of fanning me would whip me with the towel. He was a devious man, whose lady friend apparently lived in nearby Banwell village. I found this out by accident as I strolled gently in from what was meant to be a hard morning training run. I heard an enraged roar behind me, and there was Paddy, sat on a lady's sit up and beg bike. He produced a rope's end from the wicker basket on the handlebars and lashed me all the way back to camp. 'I'll have no bluidy skivers young Hayes, Y'are an idle little git – an you'll have me waste me money. Double, you little divil.'

It was the finals of the Imperial Services Championships, I can't remember where, but I remember Paddy talking to his army counterpart. Earlier, in the dressing room, he had told me, 'Just sit in that corner with your book young Hayes and look as stupid as you really are. I'm off to raise the odds.' I heard him say that the Air Force had a very good team except at my weight. Jerking his head, he indicated me and went on to say that how I had got this far he simply did not know. 'Look at him,' he said. 'Butter wouldn't melt in his bloody mouth'. With the disappearance of the Army trainer, Paddy was ecstatic and back to my side like a flash, 'Their lad'll come out of his corner like a raging bull niver thinking that you'll do one of your fancy little dance steps out of his way and flatten him as he passes. Now that's what's goin to happen boy.'

I was very proud of my Air Force Boxing Vest

I climbed into the ring and looked across at the other corner. The Army lad was a year or two older than I was. He had muscles that showed – everywhere. I had muscles, but they didn't look like his. A slight doubt crept into my mind. A confident smirk crossed my opponent's face as we touched gloves in the centre of the ring. We retired to our corners, the bell rang and a raging bull emerged, as promised. A flurry of punches sailed in my direction. As he surged forward, I parried a left and, moving to the left, hit him twice. A left jab to the solar plexus and the finest right I've ever thrown to the jaw as he doubled up. Since he was still moving forward the force of the punch was multiplied. There was a gasp from the Army supporters as their prime championship candidate continued his forward movement to hit the floor – and stayed there. A triumphant, 'Glory be, boy' sprang from Paddy's lips, as he swept around collecting his winnings. He gave me two shillings and sixpence – half a week's pay at the time! 'After all, t'was my advice that did the job, and ye didn't exactly work hard now, did yuh?' he declared. The fight had lasted 45 seconds. I was later to have an even shorter one. A lot later I learnt that Paddy had made a small fortune on that fight.

I said earlier that boy entrants were a very disparate group. There was no more disparate character than Corporal Boy Entrant Murphy. Six feet two inches of black maned Irishman, he had a devilishly uncertain disposition. He was in an entry senior to mine, but very occasionally our groups would come together for General Service Training (GST), meaning weapon training and the like. The instructor of this class was a lithe bronzed RAF Regiment Sergeant called Gillespie, who had recently returned from the Far East. He was a good instructor who contrived to make the most boring lectures interesting, largely through his stock of stories from the East. On this day he was lecturing on the Bren gun. Some ten minutes into the lecture we became aware that someone had gone audibly to sleep. Murphy, hunched in his chair, was snoring tunelessly. Gillespie kicked the chair away and Murphy sprawled on the floor. Gazing down he said, 'Perhaps you know all about the Bren, Murphy. You can give the lecture if you're that bright'. To our amazement, Murphy strode to the front desk where an assembled Bren gun lay. Supremely confident, he began, 'This is a Bren gun, muzzle velocity x, weight x, rate of fire x.' He went on to say that it was a magnificent light machine gun, and as he talked, he deftly stripped the weapon into its component parts. 'Now,' he said, 'the clever bit, the puttin t'gether agin.' He closed his eyes and reassembled the gun to total stunned silence. Gillespie, equally astonished as the class, inquired where he had learnt to do all this. Murphy's reply completed the amazement. 'Sure, was I not a gunner instructor in the Eire army before they found out me age!' On 'off' days, Gillespie would sit with the class while Murphy would give lectures on German trench ribbon grenades and other rarities used by Eirean Army of the time.

There were other, less likeable characters. Sometimes they were bullies, and sometimes the bullied. The well spoken ex-public schoolboy was among the bullied and he led a dog's life. I said that he should stand up to his tormentors just once. Just hit one, the others will lose interest if they are opposed, I promised. Well, he took my advice and, waiting until night, he smashed his fist repeatedly into the sleeping bully. This was not quite what I meant. However, since other boys woke abruptly with bleeding noses or cut lips the bullying stopped. My roommates were unsure who was the puncher, but I knew!

Justice in a barrack room is pretty savage. We were paid five shillings a week and seven shillings and sixpence in credits. Not a great deal and I think that we were paid fortnightly. We started to lose money on Friday nights and we trusted our own. I had been promoted to Leading Boy Entrant and now lived in the small room (bunk) at the end of the room. In the early hours of the Saturday morning, I heard a shrill scream. Scrambling out of bed, I switched on the barrack room lights to find that Carl Alison had trapped the arm of a would-be thief in the door of his steel locker. Given a choice of being reported or to take their punishment, he elected to take his chance with them. I managed to make it one versus one at a time, but I knew that he was going to take a beating. They avoided facial blows, because a badly marked face would cause questions to be asked. Next morning on working parade, Paddy Ireland stalked through the ranks. He paused in front of the thief. 'You look tired boy,' he said.' You should stay in your own bed at night. Off you go back to bed.' No junior or senior NCO lived in the boy's quarters – but somehow he knew. God knows how.

We really had very little time for truly leisure activities – we didn't have the money either. We made our own entertainment, often bawdy and usually crude. Dressed in our pyjamas with towels wound around our heads we held the Grand Farting Competition. One boy maintained that flatus burnt with a clear blue flame. We put it to the test by turning off the lights and attempted to ignite the gases produced. In the half-light given off by the pot bellied coke stove in the centre of the room, we lined up two beds and positioned six bare bottomed aspirants into the 'present' position. The Fireman, armed with matches, proceeded down the line. 'Fire One', 'Fire Two'. It was true, flatus burnt with a blue flame. A very high-speed camera would have revealed a positive northern lights effect as the flame developed, but it was over in a fraction of time. When the cry 'Fire Three' went up there was resounding ejection followed by a howl of agony. True, there had been a clear blue flame, but the gentleman concerned had suffered a blowback and he was, in parts, a hairy man. A smell, rather like that which emanated from a ladies' hairdressing establishment of the time, permeated the room. No further volunteers appeared. On another occasion, there was a lad who could fart to the cadence of 'God save the King'. As he marched down the room, the final note was spoilt as he followed through. Howls of derision greeted the unfortunate. Little things please little minds, you may think.

We would play 'submarines' with the innocents. A planted volunteer would lie on the floor covered by his greatcoat, peering up through one sleeve. A selection of objects would be passed over the sleeve end to be identified. After a couple of successful identifications he would fail to guess simple objects. We would then get an unsuspecting boy, preferably from a junior entry, to lie under his greatcoat. We would then repeat the identification process. A comb, a brush and then a mug would be passed across the open sleeve end. As he identified the mug, it would be turned over and a pint of water would descend through the sleeve onto his upturned face. At the same moment our galvanised bucket was beaten with a shovel close to his exposed ear. 'You've just been sunk' would be the hysterical chorus. I know it was puerile, but it was fun. One of the best things about boy's service was that you were all broke together.

After seven months at Locking we were granted leave. My parents now lived on the Dutch/German border near Kleve. Actually, they lived in a requisitioned house in Bedburg Hau. The very quiet railway station was some eighty yards from the front of the house whilst at the back was a mental hospital with a difference. The Anstalt was self-contained, with a magnificent 1920s direct current electrical generating plant. It had its own farm, dairy and workshops where many of the inmates worked. The chief engineer was a remarkable man and a drinking partner of my redoubtable father. Oskar Windenger was six feet four inches and two hundred and twenty pounds, a handsome man; a badly broken nose spoiled his beauty. I asked him once how this had happened and he said that he had been leading the advance of the glorious Third Reich through Holland on his motorcycle machine gun combination when he came across some children at a crossroads. He continued, 'I raised my hand in greeting and they thrust a pole through the spokes of my front wheel. When I recovered, I found my gunner dead and my nose broken when my steel helmet smashed it.' He went on to say that, had he found the kids, yet another atrocity would have been committed in the name of the Third Reich.

Oskar and Father enjoyed the local boxing matches. There, they would loudly state that Eric would knock seven colours of anything out of the locals. They would also place their money on the table. I was now nearly eight stone seven pounds in weight, and a pretty fair boxer. However, Germany intended to enter the 1952 Olympic Games, and it was against the best of these aspirants to the German team that I was matched. I did my best and father was satisfied with a 'draw'. Actually, I was thrashed. It crossed my mind that the judges had been nobbled!

My parents, pleased to see me I thought, took me to meet their friends who also worked for the Imperial War Graves Commission. The German wife of one greeted us and me in particular, by embracing me asking if I had had a good fart! A sixteen-year-old does not have the aplomb to deal with such question. Later, I was to discover that she had meant Fahrt (drive). There were several such misunderstandings, notably 'the cake problem'. I simply could not understand that when the cake plate was offered and I said ' Dankeschoen' (thank you) it was interpreted as no thank you, and the plate moved on before I could reach out. I remain as razor witted as I then was.

The pay of a boy entrant was in two parts. We were paid five shillings a week and this was augmented by a further seven shillings and sixpence in 'Credit'. This sum was saved and if there was any money left after barrack damages were deducted, we got this money to spend on leave. There was often a group levy to be paid, for inter entry night raiding caused undue wear and tear on the flimsy barrack structure. However, it was with incredible riches that I shot off on leave to visit my parents in Germany. My father worked on the creation of the Reichwald cemetery, which ultimately held 26,000 British and Allied graves. I never cease to wonder what brought a nineteen-year-old from Canada, New Zealand, Australia and every corner of the old empire to die in a bitter war fought thousands of miles from their homeland. Some had falsified their ages, while others had joined under assumed names. That such men should have rallied to our defence has always humbled me.

Life is frequently unfair. I rather liked the girls in Bedburg for I'd just found out what made a girl's shirt stick out. Strutting manfully about in my uniform, which had stripes and badges in abundance, I found to my horror that the chequered band on my peaked hat was exactly the same as the armband worn by the inmates of the Anstalt! (Asylum for the mentally handicapped). The girls just loved this unfortunate coincidence. I used to walk our Alsatian dog, Zabra, daily. The girls mocked the little Englander in his little blue uniform etc.

Slipping the dog's lead, I said, 'Go'. Appalled, I watched the dog go into stalk mode. I heard a 'Platz' screamed by my father. The dog sat immediately, and I was backhanded left and right about the face by an irate parent. ' You stupid idiot, don't you realise that that damned dog is a trained police dog?' I had not known, but I did now. I got my revenge on my father as I left by train at the end of my leave. Boy entrant footwear was one of two types of boot. Working boot, pebbledash and best boots, smooth leather. I had borrowed a pair of Dad's shoes and this fact eluded him until he realised that he was stood on the railway platform, waving goodbye to his best black shoes.

I returned to Locking and the ceaseless grind of parades. Our day began at 0600hrs, when the duty bugler sounded reveille. This was followed by the calls for 'Breakfast', 'Quarter Dress' and then 'On Parade'. We were like Pavlovian dogs, sent here and there by the frequently un-musical bugle calls. Lights out was at 2200hrs. We had a working parade prior to marching down to the workshops, complete with band and a boy Bandmaster who threw the mace into the sky. He even threw the beautiful silver-topped parade mace – and he always caught it. We paraded to return for lunch, which was, of course, followed by a further parade to return to the workshops. So it went on. We had Wednesday sports afternoon parades, pay parades, church parades and a parade at any time at the whim of any minor authority. I hated parades, for if the parade was ordered by the Flight Sergeant for 1400hrs, the corporal would get you there ten minutes early. You got up in the middle of the night for a Station Commander's parade. One parade that sticks in my memory is that of the Air Officer Commanding Technical Training Command's Annual Inspection. Six hundred boys in full webbing – that means big pack, small pack, water bottle, webbing belt etc – paraded for inspection. I was in the rear rank of the squadron when the order was given. ' Rear ranks, three paces to the rear, March.' This was unusual to say the least, but it was followed by, 'Rear ranks will ground arms, Ground Arms.' Something was wrong; we all knew that – but what? We soon found out. 'Rear ranks will fall out and lay out their kit on the grass verge. Fall out.' A helpless moan swept silently across the entire parade ground, for everybody, surely everybody, knew that those blue blanco-ed, immaculately squared large and small packs contained only the cardboard or wood packing. With nothing to display we formed into line at attention. The AOC and Station Commander swept by without a second glance or comment. We never heard another word on the matter. Nevertheless, I never lost my lack of enthusiasm for parades, although I greatly admire a well-executed piece of ceremonial drill.

Life was not all work and parades, although it did seem like that. On Sundays, I would join Padre Scutt, the Church of England priest, and together with about six other boys we would go caving. There are an awful lot of limestone caves around the Weston area. Padre Scutt was on excellent terms with the farmers who owned the land, and more importantly with their wives, who were under the impression that we were starved. We would emerge from a hole to be greeted with an enormous tea, served by a kind and beaming lady. I don't remember much about the caves, but I do recall the excellent cakes.

Still on the subject of food, I went to the Air show at Farnborough in company with about twenty boys. We were supposed to be programme sellers, but three of us spent our days in the cookhouse that fed the lower ranks working on various tasks associated with the show. We were shown a potato mountain, and told to peel the lot. The staff was friendly, despite viewing the square potatoes that we manufactured in vast numbers, and produced meals of a size and quality that I had never seen in my few months of service. My mother was, by her own admission, a 'plain cook'. She was the only woman I knew who, when she made rock cakes, kept her promise. Indeed, my father expressed the belief that our dog's severe limp was caused by a cake falling off the table. Mother was not amused.

The desire for food dominated the life of a boy entrant, for we rarely saw girls. We lived monastically, tied to the school by perimeter fences and lack of money. In truth, we were largely without social graces – I had never been to a dance in my life. Food however, in the form of bread and eggs removed from the cookhouse, could be acquired. The problem lay in how to cook the eggs, for we had no utensils. This was overcome by ironing the bread with an electric flat iron and frying the eggs on the base of an electric iron suspended upside down between two metal drawers taken from our lockers. Great skill was required not only in the positioning of the iron to create and maintain a horizontal surface, but also in contriving to keep the egg upon the iron's base. Should an egg hit the floor it was automatically yours.

The thought of electric irons prompts another memory. The issue shirt at that time was a collarless affair and the fashion was to wear a starched shiny collar held in place by front and rear collar studs. To maintain a fashionable appearance it was necessary to send the collars to the local Chinese laundry. Price per collar was 3d – three old pence to you – and this meant that the collar was worn for a considerable period. I decided that I might enter the market for the production of such collars. I went into Weston super Mare and visited the Chinese laundry to find out how the shiny surface was achieved. An aged Chinese held in his mouth a quantity of water and rice grains whilst he held a hot iron. Placing the collar on the table he periodically squirted a spray of chewed up rice water onto the collar. In no time at all he produced the finished article. I was certain that I could do that. So indeed I could and squirted rice water profitably for the rest of my training. They didn't look quite as good as the oriental version, but they weren't bad at 2d per collar. A financial saving of 33% was achieved by at least the blokes of my entry.

Fired with enthusiasm at the success of this venture, I decided to enter the millinery trade. Boy Entrants were issued with two hats, a forage cap, or side hat, and a service dress hat with a shiny patent leather peak. The latter was a rigid and uncomfortable affair, which had the top surface held circular by a spring wire ring. We boys favoured a variety of high fashion styles. The front vertical surface could be 'propped' by the insertion of the shaft of a toothbrush, while the back could be lowered by trimming the inner headband from over two inches to half an inch in a gentle slope to the rear. Such treatment produced the 'Gestapo' hat, much favoured by senior entries. Taller boys affected the 'guardsman' which entailed propping the front and 'spooning' or slashing the peak. The 'guardsman' involved the cutting of most of the stitches holding the peak to the hat. The angle at which the peak entered the hat could then be varied. Stroking the lower surface of the peak with a hot spoon produced a 'spooned' peak. This caused the peak to adopt the desired curved surface without cracking the upper surface. I paid Jim Dady, a senior entry boy, two week's pay to teach me the required skills. However, the production of high fashion millinery was not the object of my money-raising venture. I proposed to charge my colleagues to restore such doctored hats to parade standard! I got more than my money back from my efforts.

While I am on the subject of sartorial elegance I must remind you of the old hairy wool working uniform, which didn't take kindly to trouser creases and it scorched very easily. Many boy entrants, especially those who favoured the many crease look, augmented the crease pattern. It was not enough to have sleeve creases. They had supplementary creases across the shoulder, a crease leading to rank or service stripes and further vertical creases down each side of the back. These fashion leaders went around wearing the scorched look and left a delicate whiff of burnt wool in their passing. To avoid at least the burnt trouser look, most of us slept on them. Each night we would carefully dampen the crease area before placing the folded article under the bottom blanket of our bed. Too much dampening and body heat was insufficient to dry the trousers before reveille, too little and the desired effect was not produced. Restless sleepers could produce alarming results.

Sleep reminds of a peculiar event. As Duty Leading Boy, I was required to meet the Orderly Officer during the late evening. To my surprise, I was instructed to examine what each boy in the Wing was wearing in bed! I wandered from room to room, taking notes but not names. I was astounded, for some had every item of clothing except trousers on, while others wearing pyjamas had clearly washed only those parts visible when clothed in months. Some were in underwear, while an odd few wore nothing. Mystified, I reported back to the officer who merely grunted before moving off. I heard no more of this bizarre affair. However, their roommates, who arranged bath nights, had noted the identities of the unwashed. Such baths were usually in cold water and 'friends' using floor-scrubbing brushes and yellow bar soap administered the scrubbing. It was a painful, often humiliating lesson in personal hygiene, and rarely had to be repeated.

I recall another adolescent who woke each morning with a magnificent but painful erection. He dispersed the tumescence by banging his member on the barrack room table, crying as he did so, 'Down you Blighter, down!' I have never said that we were nice boys.

Boy's service was soon to be over and I would be promoted to this new rank of senior aircraftsman and paid forty-nine shillings a week! The final examinations were in progress and I had been selected to captain the RAF boys boxing team. Unfortunately, the match coincided with one exam and this I took separately. Years later this was to cause me major pain.

You recall Gilmore, he of the smelly feet? Reluctantly, after some fifteen months of training, he was given a medical discharge. His feet were truly anti-social. I thought I'd seen the last of him, but about eighteen months later, I met him on Paddington station looking prosperous. He told me that he'd been very lucky. He now worked for a small electrical contractor who performed repair and new work on the non-sensitive parts of several embassies in London. On his second day of work he had found the root cause of an electrical fault that had puzzled his colleagues for months. His luck had further improved when an American doctor at the embassy heard his workmates complaining about the stench from his feet. Privately, he had asked what the cause of the smell could be. The doctor had examined his feet and after consultation with a specialist in the United States produced a near instant cure. I was pleased, not only that he was gainfully employed, but also grateful that those around him would not suffer as we in hut L2 had done.

Somerset is cider country. This in turn means that apples are grown in the area. I wasn't too keen on the local scrumpy as the cider was called, but I did like apples. The entry went scrumping one night. We went fairly often, but this particular night I remember well. We located our target, a rather nice country house set in a large garden containing a walled orchard. We did the usual things by setting lookouts whilst the main body stripped the trees. The lookouts gave the warning and we duly fled. It was a false alarm given by a bored watcher. We recrossed the wall and had begun to look at the pear trees when the second lookout signalled. We ignored him. Wrong, wrong. A large red-faced character in a dressing gown waving a large stick herded us into his conservatory. It transpired that he was a retired colonel of the Indian Army. His wife, a small fine-featured woman fluttered in the background. The Colonel growled,' Who are you, damn you?' He quickly discovered our identities, writing our names down. He then gave the nine of us who were caught a choice. We could either take his punishment or he would report us to the Station Commander. I was thinking about this choice as the others chorused that they'd take his punishment. You recall the big stick that he had been waving earlier? Well he beat the backside of every boy, but he was afraid that he was tiring when it came to the last boy. He made a tremendous effort to compensate for any tiredness. I was that last boy! The lady of the house objected to the beatings and called her husband an absolute brute. She said that he had never been young and other hard things. The following Sunday, at church parade, a list of names was read out. We were to report to the main guardroom at 1530 hrs. The beaten nine looked at each other. The blighter's shopped us as well as beating us, we thought. We reported at the appointed time, to be met by a smiling Colonel's lady and a large Rolls Royce car. 'We are off to tea, boys,' she cried. We piled into the car, to find an almost affable colonel within. They gave us a perfectly splendid tea and Mrs Colonel told her husband to apologise to us. There was a pause and he said, 'No I bloody well will not – they got half my blasted apples, and in another five minutes they'd have had the bloody pears! Anyway they deserved it.' Three years later I was to meet the colonel again.

The final phase of training was airfield practice in which we were let loose on a considerable collection of aircraft that were no longer airworthy. There were Spitfires, Typhoons, Beaufighters, and Wellington bombers. Behind Airspeed Oxfords and Avro Ansons were Horsa gliders in various stages of neglect. We had just moved the entire Boy Entrant School to Cosford near Wolverhampton and there were lots of things here to play with. I distinguished myself immediately. I was stood on the mainplane, cranking the starting handle of an Airspeed Oxford's engine, when the engine fired. Startled, I stepped back and went straight through the fabric-covered wing. Received with withering scorn by the instructor, I went on to step off the walkway inside a Wellington bomber and once more put a foot through the fabric between geodetic structures. I was quite popular with the airframe instructors who were keen to find a whipping boy from some other trade group.

While we worked on the aircraft, we were taught in classrooms within the main hangars. One Flight Sergeant (FS) instructor was a pre-war aircraft apprentice who had been a Japanese prisoner of war. He wore glasses as thick as the bottom of milk bottles. We believed that the Air Force did its best to retain its injured career men, at least until pension time. He was a very quiet and good instructor, but one day in class he went berserk. Wielding a four foot ebony ruler, he lashed out, knocking two boys unconscious. Several others including me were left with hefty bruises. It took six of us to subdue him. We had some quick thinking to do. The unconscious needed stitches in their head wounds and another had a red welt across his face. After a lot of talk, we staged an accident and managed to convince the unsuspecting medical staff. The price of our silence was that the FS came to our hut every evening for a week and spoke to us about his experiences. He didn't like this solution, but the alternative was Court Martial and he knew it. We were unaware that our 'punishment' was probably a great act of kindness. We sat horrified and enthralled as he told the story of capture and captivity He spoke of the camp deaths, of how the big and strong died first, and how the city runt survived. He spoke of heroism and deceit, of gallantry and surrender. The tears ran down his face as he spoke of the lack of food and medicine. I believe that he had never previously spoken of his experience and that our 'punishment' was the finest therapy possible. Later, I was to find that other Jap prisoners had been unable to speak of their experiences either to family or friends. Such people were much more likely to have an emotional breakdown.

Before I leave Boys Service I must tell of the trivial, mindless punishments and inconveniences forced upon us by petty dictators. One such was a Police Corporal who specialised in obstruction. For the first few months of training we had to wear uniform when visiting town. In fact, I'm not sure now that we didn't have to wear uniform all the time. We had to 'Book Out' and 'In' at the Guardroom, If a boy presented himself with a belt holding up his trousers, he was sent back to wear braces. If he wore braces, he was sent back for a belt. If he wore both, he was then found lacking in some other part of his dress and sent back to change. In this way, we nearly always missed the infrequent buses. Corporal Bloggs was found half-drowned in the static water tank following our graduation. I didn't have a hand in it – but I would have helped had I known.

Missing the bus was not catastrophic, for the local people were well aware that the boys were not paid well. I was standing at the roadside looking disconsolate when I was picked up by two very well spoken elderly sisters, driving an old Morris cabriolet who, a mile further down the road, exclaimed, 'Look, there's another of your friends. We'll give him a ride too'. I looked, and my heart sank, for the boy in question was one of the most foul-mouthed people I had ever met. His gutter bred language and ill manners stood out in a society that was not noted for its charm. The car stopped; the ladies offered the lift into town, and the boy opened his mouth. He was totally and utterly different. His manners were exemplary, the choice of adjectives appropriate and the modulation of his voice reflected a gentler upbringing than his previous utterances would have suggested. Bewildered, I was silent as he charmed the ladies. Thanking them profusely we left to enjoy the blessings of Regent Street. I asked him why the change, but he just smiled and said that everyone had to survive. He had some dog rough friends in the 6th entry.

It was now March 1951 and the 8th Entry had graduated from training. My Mother travelled from Germany for the event, to be met by FS Ireland, who twirling his moustache, asked, 'What iver did a decent looking woman like yourself do to deserve a son like that.' She was thrilled to meet this charming man! Later, she was mystified when told that I had won the education prize – or at least I think I did. She was mystified because second son was not known for brainpower. My wife says that if I'm not sure, then I definitely didn't. We all have our critics.

I was now told that the electrical trade group would split into two, and that I would become an Electrical Mechanic (Air). I was reasonably pleased because I liked to work on aircraft, despite my ability to walk through fabric wings. The subsequent posting notice sent me to Mountbatten near Plymouth to work on marine craft! They were lovely Air Sea Rescue launches, powered by two Rolls Royce aero engines, but within days I was moved on to RAF Hemswell near Gainsborough, Lincolnshire, where a new life awaited me.

No.8 Entry, RAF Cosford. Sitting fourth from the left on the front row is the author, growing out of his trousers.

CHAPTER TWO
HEMSWELL – MY FIRST POSTING

RAF Hemswell was part of Bomber Command, home to two squadrons of Mosquitoes and two squadrons of Lincoln bombers. The Lincoln was a development of the wartime Lancaster bomber and had more powerful Rolls Royce Griffon engines instead of the Merlin. The station had been built during the glory period of construction between 1933 and 1939 when a startled government finally woke up to the threat of war. The Station was built to the standard layout of H block, two-storey accommodation and the magnificent large green hangars with enormous three or four section steel doors that ran on rails to open and close. I think that there were four hangars, each of which had two-storey aircrew offices to the airfield side and the ground crew rooms etc on the dull side. The exception to this was the Aircraft Servicing Squadron (ASF) hangar that had the electrical and instrument Bay Servicing workshops on the front side. Other sections may have adorned the scenic side too. The taxiway ran past the front of all hangars. On the airfield side of the taxiway, about midway between the hangars, was the air traffic control tower. It was a happy station and we took our recreation either in nearby Gainsborough or in Lincoln, which was a bit further away.

The NAAFI served as a recreation centre for the 'other ranks', and provided a separate series of rooms as the Corporals' Club. The Salvation Army also ran a seedy and dilapidated establishment beloved of the lads. We were considerably upset when the NAAFI insisted that it close shortly after my arrival. The rationale behind this was that the NAAFI paid considerable funds to all three services' sports funds and the like in the form of rebate. The Sally Ann pushed its profits into saving souls and was thus less valuable to the military purse.

The NAAFI wagon, a mobile canteen, called at various workplace locations throughout the day and sold all manner of delights. There was Fly Pie, an open tart filled with mincemeat, and Sinker MK1 that was a solid mass of something topped with white icing. On special occasions the icing was pink! There was another confection called Chinese Wedding Cake, and I enjoyed all of them and mourn their passing.

My arrival at ASF was not auspicious, and I did not receive an enthusiastic welcome. Chris Coffey, a Boy Entrant of the 7th entry, had preceded me to Hemswell. As I arrived, walking across the hangar to report to the squadron Warrant Officer, I heard a coughing noise. I looked around to see what looked like smoke emerging from all four engines of a Lincoln bomber, which was up on jacks and surrounded by aircraft servicing platforms. This was followed by howls of rage from those working on the engines. Mystified, I continued my stroll to the office. I announced myself – and was immediately thrown out. 'Not another bloody boy entrant. Do you know Coffey?' I said that I did, but that he had been senior entry to me, and asked if he was here. From all sides a torrent of abuse was poured upon his name – and upon me by association. The coughing noise that I had heard was a repetition of three weeks earlier when Coffey had blown all the fire extinguisher bottles of an aircraft. Apparently Coffey had replaced the clockwork time switches that caused a delay between the firing of the area fire bottle and the one that fired into the induction system of the engines. Dutifully he had disconnected the fire bottles, attached a test lamp to each electrical plug and had carried out a functional check on the system. He then removed electrical power and reconnected the bottles. When power was restored to the aircraft all the bottles blew, for he had not reset the time switches!

The problem this flow of fire extinguishant into the engine caused was difficult to resolve. Piston engines so contaminated must be run within 48 hours. Since the aircraft was some days from completing its major inspection, it was likely that each engine would have to have the cylinder head removed. The engine fitters did not appreciate this encore of Coffey's ineptitude. Their revenge followed swiftly. The fire bottles required replacement, and this meant that Coffey had to stand on the H crossbar of the undercarriage and work about eighteen inches above his own head. Like many of us, he would open his mouth as he did so. There are holes in the engine bulkhead (the bit where the actual engine is fixed to the aircraft). As Coffey worked away, a swan necked oil can holding perhaps a quart of engine and hydraulic oil mixed with every kind of unpleasantness was poured carefully and precisely into his mouth. He gagged, lost his footing and straddled the H bar, landing judiciously upon his marriage gear. He then spun. He had a choice, to the rear of the main wheel lay a few bits of assorted and very hard servicing trolleys, whereas to the front lay a shallow oil bath. Fortunately, he landed in the bath. He was rushed off to Sick Quarters to have his stomach pumped and to have various balms placed upon his parts. This was only my first day.

One of the Lincoln Squadrons, No 97, was short of electricians due to sickness, and at very short notice I found myself off to Shalufa in the Canal Zone of Egypt for a short detachment. I had several disappointments, the first of which was waking up on the first morning to hear birds singing. I rushed out to find that they were sparrows. I was expecting something more exotic. The second of my disappointments was the duration of my stay in Egypt. On the third day I was sent to accompany a storeman as he drove off to some maintenance unit for some spare parts. We stopped en route for base to talk to some army people who took an instant dislike to the pair of us. They threw me into the canal, or some backwater off it. Somebody told me later that it was the Sweetwater Canal. Sweet it was not. As I broke surface the inflated carcass of a long dead dog moved sluggishly by. As I turned in the water a large chunk of human excrement passed under my nose. It was dreadful, and I knew that I had swallowed quite a bit. To cut a long story short I managed to scramble out and we returned to Shalufa where I reported to Sick Quarters. There the Princess Alexandra Nursing Sister held sway. Immaculate in her whites with her neat blue half cape draped on her shoulders and her white cap stiffly starched, sat a Goddess. Gravely she listened to my story, and as I recounted the sad tale of my involuntary swim and the various animal and other life present in the water, she smiled. She smiled rather a lot I thought. She put on gloves and rolled up my sleeve. I had a jab here, another there, to a total of five. She then told me to drop my trousers and sneaking up from behind she injected a large red-hot stone into my bottom. I clutched my rear and began to move painfully about the room. Gradually I began to speed up as the stone radiated dull pain. I looked at Sister, who was paralysed with laughter as I completed yet another circuit of the room. 'It's only a penicillin jab,' she giggled. God's teeth, it was agony! As if all this was not enough, the following day I got a severe attack of the 'runs' and was returned to Hemswell on the first available aircraft. My ordeal was not over. 'Dog Cement' certainly stopped the runs after four days, but there followed the opposite problem. I was given a pill to rectify this difficulty. It was rather large but I managed to swallow it eventually. I did not tell anyone that I hadn't known that it was supposed to have been inserted at the other end of the alimentary canal. It did work though!

Life in the barrack room at Hemswell was more relaxed and although there were still working parades each morning we did not have a rigid regimen of accommodation inspections. I still lived with twenty or more men in a single room, but the rooms were centrally heated and were of a permanent nature. Much renovated and sub-divided those two-storeyed barrack blocks were still in use when I retired. Chris Coffey and I were in the same room. Like me, he was not very big, but unlike me he grew. Why did he grow? Well, five of us clubbed together as a joke and bought him a Charles Atlas course. To our amazement he did all the dynamic tension exercises and he grew and grew! I don't swear to this but I believe that he grew nearly five inches between the ages of 17 and 21 years. Coffey could get into more trouble in six months than most of us could achieve in years. Cheerful in any circumstance he was naturally mischievous. In the Canal Zone of Egypt he was out with friends when they were attacked by a large group of young Egyptians. Laughing like a drain, he produced a Luger pistol, at which point the locals prudently ran away. His Father had been, or was, a part of King Farouk's police – that must have been where he got the pistol. Returning late at night, and somewhat the worse for drink, he was unable to get into the wooden walled, tent topped, room he shared with an Instrument Fitter Corporal. He drew the pistol and shot off the lock. The camp awoke – the Corporal had a brief nervous breakdown and Coffey went to jail for six months. There, he occupied himself with his technical textbooks and emerged to pass the Corporal Technician exams (two stripes upside down). The Station Commander refused to promote him, until Coffey pointed out that the rank was not executive, but a technical qualification, and as such could not be withheld. He had style. Years later, I was to meet him as a Flight Sergeant Air Engineer flying a Britannia transport aircraft, thus proving that you can't keep a good lad down.

  You will recall that the Mosquito aircraft was built of various woods and this meant that with lots of high-octane fuel on board, it did not crash well. During my third week at Hemswell, I found that the aero modellers absolutely loved the Mosquito aircraft. An aircraft of 139 Squadron, I think, had the undercarriage collapse on landing. The port wing dropped first and the aircraft swung off the runway. The propellers stopped instantly, the now familiar cloud of fire extinguishant issued from the nacelles. A hatch popped out of the cockpit, followed by two figures that ran along the starboard main plane and dived off. The two aircrew hit the grass running and were a hundred yards away from before the aircraft had even stopped! The Official Inquiry stated that Master Pilot Bronowski and his Navigator were to be congratulated on their rapid exit! Now, during the aircraft's passage to destruction a bomb door was torn off, together with a few other bits and pieces. As soon as it was dark, two of the model makers just walked off with the whole door – it was so light and so very attractive, for it was made of balsa wood.

I developed an interest in gun turrets. In the electrical bay I serviced a thing called the gun firing interrupter drum. The Lincoln had three turrets. Nose, tail and mid upper. The mid-upper gun turret fascinated me. Two electrically fired 20mm cannon were mounted in the turret which could rotate through 360 degrees. To prevent an excitable gunner from following his target through the obstructions of the aircraft tail fins while still firing, an interrupter was fitted. Nothing posh, it was a cylinder of insulating material into which was mounted a few brass slip rings which carried electrical current into the turret. Only the gun firing circuit had little breaks in the slip rings. These little insulated gaps coincided with the fin and other parts of the aircraft when the guns were fired and stopped an enthusiastic gunner from scoring an 'own goal'.

Periodically, the aircraft were taken to the butts to fire the guns and to 'harmonise' the aim. I begged, I moaned, 'Please, can I have a go?' The Armourers were not too keen, but I wore them down. At last my chance had arrived. The turret had two speeds and, pressing the high-speed rotation button, I fired. There was a deafening noise as the canon fired. The aircraft shook like a live thing, and I realised that I had shot a chunk off the fin! The Unit Inquiry sat the next day. All the evidence had been heard and the Flight Lieutenant president of the Board recalled me to the room. 'Before I warn you under Section 1269A of the Air Force Act…' Before he warns me? That means I am deeply in the shit, I thought. My heart sank. He continued, 'In your statement, you said that you had set up the interrupter drums several times in the past, and that there had been no problem. Can you think of anything, absolutely anything, which could have caused this incident?' 'No sir, the floor would have had to move,' I whispered miserably. Authority paused for thought, 'Ask the Airframe Sergeant if the floor has been checked,' he directed, before adjourning the Inquiry for lunch. I arrived back from lunch, to find a grinning sergeant. 'You're off the hook son – the floor's peppered with urine corrosion. You can't see it until you lift the floor panel. The longeron is a U section, not a top hat and sometime in the past a gunner has dropped the pee bladder that spilt on the floor. Either that, or he had a lousy aim. The whole thing under the interrupter drum has become a cantilever. It can move about an eighth of an inch.

When the turret turns, the floor flexes, just a fraction.' The Inquiry was wrapped up within the next hour, and I was free again.

Charlie Parker, a squadron Airframe Mechanic, was posted out to Kenya. We bought a little present for him – a face mask! Charlie had some breathing problems and went around with his mouth perpetually open. We told him that he would need it because of the flies and thought him fortunate to get out of Bomber Command!

Prior to leaving Boys Service I had filled in an application to be stationed overseas, but I was very surprised to be sent for by the General Office (all the personnel office work is done there). On arrival, I was told that I had a week's leave, and that I was posted to RAF Wahn, near Cologne in Germany. I was chuffed, to say the least. I asked around,' Anybody been to Wahn?' I was immediately informed by a dozen voices that nobody, but nobody left RAF Lincolnshire. Once you were on bombers – that was it. How had I managed to escape from Bomber Command? Astonished at this, I replied that I had applied for an overseas posting. I didn't escape for long.

CHAPTER THREE
MY FIRST OVERSEAS TOUR

Wahn, apparently, was an ex Luftwaffe base, which lay in the middle of the Afrika Corps' old training grounds. It was about 14 km from Cologne. I reported to RAF Innsworth near Gloucester, from whence generations of airman have been dispatched to the ends of the earth. There, I was suitably inoculated and my kit checked, augmented or replaced as necessary. Fully dressed in best uniform, greatcoat and full webbing, I had a large white kitbag to carry. I found it to be quite difficult, but larger people appeared to have few problems with that bag. It was a hell of a performance just to get to Germany, because I had first to report to Liverpool Street Station from where I boarded the military train bound for Harwich. There, I embarked on a ferryboat headed for The Hook of Holland. Once in Holland, where it was raining of course, we boarded yet another military train. This train wended its way across Holland into Germany, passing very close to my parents' home, stopping at Cologne before continuing on to Hamburg. My parents, hearing of my posting to nearby Wahn, arranged to be moved to Kiel in Schleswig Holstein, another few hundred kilometres away, where a large British war cemetery had been created. That's not true, but it seemed so at the time. Happily, their posting north was delayed a few months.

Transport was waiting at the railway station to take some six of us to Wahn. It was now late 1951 and the war had been over for some years, but the signs of bombing were everywhere to be seen in the city of Cologne (Koln). True, a tremendous, no, an unbelievable, amount of work had been done but the scars were there. As we approached the main gate of the airbase, I was surprised to see the three-storey accommodation blocks. They were huge; they were permanent; they had good central heating; the floors were of wood parquet block and the rooms were for only 4 persons. The beds were magnificent with deep, thick, spring interior mattresses! The toilets and showers gleamed and actually worked. The windows all had a second window within and the whole place had an air of permanence. It was a far cry from Hut L2. I found then that the Germans built very fine barracks. Today they build even better ones, designed for minimum maintenance. They don't build a crew room wall of painted hardboard that gets scuffed and filthy within months, they do the job properly in the first place. And their ground crew don't work from Nissen huts. I'll bet that their facilities cost less in the long run too. It is true that the facilities the British built in Germany many years later were infinitely better than those of the past, but NATO blocks still appear to be built to much higher specifications. Wahn is now Koln-Bonn international airport.

I found myself posted to 89 Squadron equipped with Meteor MkII night fighters. This was a long nosed variant of the familiar Meteor fighter. The nose contained a large radar scanner. It was unwise, I was told, ever to stand in front of this radar, for the efficiency of one's marriage tackle could be impaired – permanently. The aircraft was equipped with a wide speed range generator. I was impressed, but all that this meant was that the fighter could warm up its electronic equipment while taxiing, and thus was ready to fight immediately after take off. The older aircraft did not generate enough electrical power at low engine speeds to run the radar, but the improvement did complicate the power system.

The Air Force was home to all types. A small obsessively tidy Instrument Fitter Corporal, named Winfield, shared one room with a continental gentleman called Stanislaus Palir. Stan was a tall, blond and blue-eyed Czech. Before the war he had been a student in Berlin. At least five times during his university days he had been asked if he wished to join the SS. His refusals looked as though they might get him into trouble, so he abandoned his studies and left quietly for England. He joined our Air Force in 1940 and, during the war years had risen in rank to become a Flight Sergeant interpreter. At the end of the war, with the Russians in Czechoslovakia, he had decided to stay in the Air Force. With vastly reduced numbers of servicemen, he was forced to accept several reductions in rank and a change of basic trade to do so.

Winfield was a fresh air fiend and an early riser. Stan was none of these things. The alarm clock trilled at 0530hrs. I heard an angry roar. The window of the first floor room was thrown open and the offending clock soared out into the darkness. 'This isn't reveille, it's a disturbance after lights out! Say one bloody word Winfield, and you follow the bloody clock.' There was silence. Winfield did not buy a new clock, as it seemed hardly worth it.

The Squadron had five electricians, no six. I forgot Brother Spooner. One Sergeant, one Corporal, two Junior Technicians, (J/T) Spooner, and me. The two J/Ts had recently graduated from Halton. They had been

Aircraft Apprentices (the superior kind of boy entrant who undertook a three-year course). In life we all have our strengths and weaknesses. Spooner and myself could actually find what caused a fault. The two ex-apprentices were not good at this, but once they knew what was wrong, they could repair the fault. The Squadron split into two parts for the duration of an exercise. Spooner and I went off with Part One to Fassberg, in the eastern part of the then West Germany. The Sergeant was on leave, and thus the Corporal and the two apprentices were left to service their part of the squadron aircraft. A braver man than me told the Warrant Officer that this division was not a good idea. He got an instant flea in his ear. We had the last laugh though, for on our return to base there was only one serviceable aircraft – all the others had an electrical fault of some kind.

The airfield that we were detached to was RAF Fassberg. This was a secret airfield built in a pine forest whose existence was not known to the Allies until the end of the war. A huge retractable camouflaged net that was electrically operated covered the runway. The main hangar complex was built in large U shape open to the taxiway and runway. A certain Group Captain Donaldson was the base commander. He was a pretty dynamic character by all reports, and had held the world air speed record for a short time. He decided that there should be an emergency take off strip to augment the single runway in emergencies. It was his belief that a Vampire Mk5 could take off across the arms of the U shape. I don't think that many of the pilots shared this view. To make his point, he actually did it himself. There was only minor damage to the air traffic control tower aerial situated at the end of one arm of the U shape. His point safely made, nobody ever tried it again – or so we were told.

I don't know how I came to forget Bill Spooner. He came from 'up north like' and did not care for petty restrictions. Everything that he didn't like constituted a petty restriction. In those days, you couldn't just walk out the gate if you fancied a stroll. There were official times. To be out of camp other than at these times constituted 'breaking out of camp'. Bill just popped over the perimeter fence when he felt the urge, which was quite often. To return to camp, it was necessary to repeat the process. On one fateful day, he shinned over the fence, to be met by a large Alsatian police dog on free run. Deftly, the dog tripped him and sat on his shoulders. He was released when the German handler eventually called the dog off.

All administration of military justice is pure theatre. There are procedures to be followed. You've all seen the cinema depiction of a military charge at unit level. It is theatrical; every person involved knows his part, and the facial expression that he must maintain. The accused, dressed in his best uniform, but hatless, is arraigned. That means that he, together with two escorts complete with headgear, (I was one) lurk outside the Squadron Cdr's office while the witness or witnesses are readily available nearby. The Squadron Disciplinary Sergeant appears and bellows, 'Escort, and Accused, Attenshun. Quick March, Left Wheel' a few yards later, 'Left Wheel. Mark Time. Halt, Left Turn. Escort, Stand at Ease.' The stage is now set and the seated Squadron Commander, with his hat on, and the telephone off the hook, views the scene. He then reads out the personal details of the accused (Number, rank and name). He determines that he's got the right chap in front of him and then the Charge is read out. 'Whilst on active service etc you are charged from being absent from your place of duty etc etc. How do you plead?' Bill said that he was not guilty. The first witness is called. In this case the German Dog Handler was asked how and when he had found the accused. The guard explained that he had let his dog off the lead while he went to the toilet nearby. He described how the dog was holding Spooner and said that the maximum time that the dog had been unleashed was ten minutes. The Boss then asked Spooner how long the dog had held him down. Bill replied soulfully, and with deep feeling, 'Years, sir'. After the laughter had stopped, the Boss said, 'Spooner, I find you guilty of the offence as charged.' He looked towards the Disciplinary Sergeant who, unseen by all but the Boss, for he stood behind the accused, raised five fingers. This told the Boss that the going rate for the job was five days Restrictions ('jankers'). The Boss considered this and said, 'Case admonished, I feel that you have already undergone a suitable period of punishment'. In plain language he was warned, which is a recorded punishment.

Jankers, I never did know where this word originated, involved early rising to report to the guardroom in one's uniform, followed by further reporting and work duties as specified by the guardroom at other times. This was then followed by a best uniform parade of defaulters at 10pm. In short, one's day was blighted. In later years the custom of defaulters was changed to a regime of monetary fines as the Air Force realised that valuable manpower was being lost. More importantly, the good boys were also being punished by having to do the culprit's work. The fines system isn't too good either. In the army, unit commanders fine their troops for offences real and imagined. I was once staying in an hotel where an Army Sergeant was also on leave. He had his wallet stolen when travelling on a bus. He was fined £100 for losing his identity card – he'd lost all his money too. In the Air Force if an identity card was lost, providing that the owner reported the matter immediately, there was no fine or charge. It was not smiled upon, but it was recognised that you could actually lose things. Make a habit of it, and the mood changed.

On my first real period of leave back to Britain, I had decided to go up to Scotland to see my various aunts. David, my roommate in Germany, asked me if I would visit his sister who worked in Edinburgh on my way to Colinsburgh in Fife. She was a nurse at the Greenbank hospital and lived in the Nurse's Home there. When I arrived at about lunchtime she was on duty. Since I did not have a great deal of time to spare, I went to see the matron. I asked that matriarch if I could see the girl for a few minutes. Matron smiled benevolently and sent for Nurse Hampton. David and I were of very similar size, build and colouring and when Wendy came into the room I was standing, in uniform, with my back to the door. Thinking that I was her brother, she whirled me round and hugged and kissed me before recoiling in horror! Not very flattering, but she had been told only that there was an Air Force lad from Germany to see her, and the only person she knew who fitted that description was her brother. In a fit of unusual generosity, I asked her out to dinner that evening.

I have always had delusions of grandeur and took her to the Royal Hotel on Princes Street. We got on well together and we enjoyed a very pleasant meal. When the bill was presented I nearly had a heart attack, for I did not have anything like the sum required. Moreover, I had no chequebook. Credit cards had not been invented, and I possessed only a Post Office Savings Book. It was Saturday and Post Offices are shut on Sundays – panic.

I excused myself, ostensibly to go to the toilet, but instead asked a waiter if the manager would meet me in the toilet. He looked surprised but shot off. The manager, a short, stocky middle-aged Scot, looked at me both cautiously and curiously. 'I don't usually meet my guests in this room!' I'm sure that this was true. Swiftly, I outlined the situation and offered several courses of action.

Perhaps I could work the bill off in the kitchen later. I explained that I did not want to involve or embarrass the girl. He smiled and suggested that, when the bill came I should pay it with what I'd got. He would brief the waiter personally. I was to take the girl back to her home and return to work in the kitchen. It worked wonderfully; the bill was presented and paid. I took Wendy back home, kissed her goodnight and returned by tram to the Royal. I trotted up the stairs to tell the manager of my promised return. He greeted me with a smile,' Come away in laddie, and have a wee dram.' He would not hear of me working to repay him. I praised his organisation of the event and the waiter who had shown no surprise whatsoever when I paid him just under half of the dinner bill Indeed, the waiter had been most gracious when I gave him the tip. 'Aye, he would be,' said the manager bitterly. 'But did ye have to tip him with my money?' The manager smiled thinly and said that his staff was well trained. The absolute absurdity of the toilet meeting and the matter of the waiter's tip dawned upon us both simultaneously and we exploded with laughter. We enjoyed several drams together and parted in the small hours. I didn't even like whisky at that time. From that time, whenever I passed through Edinburgh, I always called into the hotel. On one such occasion the manager and myself were standing in the foyer watching a group of American sailors walking down Princes Street. He looked disparagingly at the sailors and said,' thon's no a man, ye could na hang a kilt on those airses could ye?' It was true, for kilts do not hang well on those with very slim hips.

Life in Germany was good, especially for me. I had a few words of the language and I liked the people and country. It was Karneval time in Cologne and I was to learn all sorts of things. Did you know how Eau de Cologne was called 4711? Do you even want to know? Well, the French occupied this part of Germany a long, long time ago. I think that it must have been during the Napoleonic period. They numbered the houses and just guess where the perfume was made! You've got it – house number 4711.

I was accident prone in Germany; or rather I was unfortunate in that I was always the one who was caught. At this time, 1951, the German police wore an exceptionally smart helmet. It was a splendid black metal affair with a large silver badge. Five of us decided that we would steal one. One evening, when it was dark, two of us approached a suitably hatted solitary policeman. While one talked to him another whipped his helmet off and tossed it over a pile of bomb damage rubble where it was collected by a third man who in turn threw it to the two others who then ran in different directions. The plan was sound. The policeman, however, did not know that the plan was sound. We believed that, distracted, he would tear off after his hat, whilst the two who had approached him would depart in opposite directions. He did follow his helmet, but then he did something that we had not considered at all. He drew his pistol and fired a warning shot into the air! We all stopped dead. The policeman collected man A (me) and man B. The others returned to the scene to see whether or not we had been shot. He then reclaimed his helmet and we joined him in a gentle stroll to the police station where we were handed over to the Air Force police. We were, of course, brought before the Squadron Commander. He was absolutely livid with rage and refused to hear the charges until he had read us the contents of a letter that he had received from the German police commander. It was written in perfect English and I remember part of it well. It said that had he known how attractive the helmets of his police were, he would have been pleased to have given us one as a present and thus avoided a foolhardy and indeed dangerous act by five of his men. He continued, by saying how flattered his men were that five airmen were required for the attempt. This last was a red rag to our bull of a Boss. He heard the charge in a cold fury and gave each of us 14 days restrictions. The German police were informed of the punishment and added insult to injury by presenting our Boss with a splendid new helmet. He was very proud of it and it became his valued personal possession.

Two months later, I was in the local pub (Kneipe) – I think that it was called the Beenenhaus. A fight broke out at the bar and, knowing my luck, I decided to leave immediately by the front door. The main camp gate lay three hundred metres up the straight road from the pub and I saw the police vehicles rapidly approaching. Turning, I screamed that the 'Snoops' were on the way with the Provost. When the police arrived, I was the only airman there, for everyone else had left by the back door. I was, of course, taken into custody.

In my now familiar role of the accused, I stood before an unsmiling Boss who having completed the identification procedure read out the charge. I pleaded not guilty. The evidence was heard and I was then asked to give some explanation of my conduct. 'Sir', I said firmly, 'there is no charge to answer for I was not involved. I left immediately

I had that pipe for fifty years!

the fight started.' The Boss smiled thinly and remarked that the bar had been wrecked. Moreover, the German police had not apprehended the combatants, nor had the Air Force police. There was only one person in the place and that person was yours truly. Did I wish to change my story? I did not, for I was innocent of any crime other than that of being there at the wrong time. The Boss then stated that my sense of occasion and timing were suspect, to say the least, and that he had no choice but to find me guilty. I was then awarded (lovely word 'awarded') seven days restriction. I protested bitterly. The Boss looked me square in the eye and said that he could easily make it 14 days. I left the room a disappointed and embittered man with my faith in service justice destroyed.

The last few weeks before Lent, the period leading up to Easter, is an interesting time in the Rhineland. Karneval, which begins on the eleventh day of the eleventh month at eleven minutes past eleven, was originally connected with religious festival, which has adapted over the centuries to become a very great mine of economic activity. Karneval is big business, and despite the austerity of post-war Germany, it was big business then too. The final week of Karneval is almost frenetic in the sheer number and scale of activities. There are Karneval Clubs, associations and special days. One of these days is Weiberfastnacht, which is a kind of ladies' day, which takes place on the Thursday before Shrove Tuesday. No male is safe on this day. In all the workplaces and on the streets, packs of women, usually in costume, prowl around armed with scissors. Any male wearing a good tie on such a day will inevitably lose it, for it will be snipped off at the six-inch point. Thirty years later, I worked in a major NATO Headquarters, and a meeting, chaired by a very senior General, was invaded by ladies who totally disrupted the whole schedule. They only left when the last tie had fallen. That gives a fair idea of how seriously Karneval is played out. I noted that the General's tie was one of the first to fall, but that it was extremely old. Perhaps preparation of this sort was one reason that he had risen to command.

Nightfall brought no respite as the ladies took over places of entertainment. Along with two friends I was having a quiet beer in a riverside pub when it was invaded by a group of inebriated and amorous ladies. I was singled out by a very pretty young thing for 'special attention' (This alone should have made me suspicious, and remember that at this time we were still occupation troops) Koln. was not in the British zone, but was under the control of the Belgian Army. By contrast with the Belgians, we were popular, but that didn't make us friends. At midnight, the males returned, suitably tanked up. The husband or boy friend of the amorous octopus that sat on my knee took exception to my presence, and with a few stout friends proceeded to carry me shoulder high to the river parapet. Even then German youth was both taller and more muscular than the average Brit. Amid great cheers I was thrown into the Rhine. It was dark and it was cold. The river, swelled with the spring thaw of mountain snows, was in full flow, if not flood. Moreover, there was still a considerable amount of bomb damage debris in the river, especially around the buttresses of the Rhine Brucke. The river current was immensely strong and even if I could have reached the bank, I couldn't get over the six to eight feet parapet. Shedding my good shoes reluctantly, I allowed myself to be carried downstream. Yes, they were the ones I'd pinched from my Father! Spitting cold water from my lungs, I looked for a suitable landing site. I could see very little apart from darkness from where I was situated. The current bowled me on, and although I was a bit afraid, I knew myself to be a decent swimmer, but it was cold, bloody cold. I heard no cries offering help from those who had tossed me into the river, and presumed that they had drunk so much that they didn't realise that they might have committed murder. This was not a good thought. I was carried downstream, and there was no visible barge traffic, for which I was grateful. Eventually, after travelling about two to three kilometres, I was able to claw my way up a small wall. It took me quite a time to get over the wall, where I stood shivering like a dog passing clothes pegs. I'd been in the water for half an hour at least. Luckily I met some local people within a few minutes, who telephoned the German police. Safely inside a warm room, I told my story. It has always amazes me that so many continentals speak excellent English, whereas few Brits speak anything other than their own particular brand of regional English. I was given a stiff tot of schnapps, and after about an hour the Air Force police arrived and whisked me off to base. There I was informed that it was probably my own fault, and no action would be taken. How nice – but what about my shoes?

Well, Karneval was about to reach its climax on the following Monday. Rosenmontag is the Monday before Ash Wednesday. On Rosenmontag there are enormous processions in nearly every town and village throughout the Rhineland, Huge horse and motor drawn floats are dragged through thronged streets. Costumed regiments dressed in immaculate and splendid uniforms of the 1780s march eight abreast led by mounted officers. It was a memorable sight. Where all the uniforms, muskets and swords appeared from, God only knows. There were green clad regiments, powder blue clad regiments and every kind of costumed group. The army of costumed regiments came smartly to the salute as they passed the dais upon which were seated the wonderfully costumed Prince and Princess of Karneval, showing a precision and skill in drill movements that comes only from hard and long practice. We supposed that most must have been in the Wehrmacht. On every side the floats disgorged sweets and little mementos. Normally these were tossed into the air to be caught by the population, but when the floats passed the British stands at the roadside, the sweets were thrown with strength and accuracy! I was hit on the ear by a tiny sample bottle of 4711 Cologne. It was all good clean fun. All day we were greeted by the Karneval challenge of 'Kolle Alaaf', to which the jovial riposte was 'Kolle Alaaf'. In Dusseldorf the challenge is 'Helau'. Even we Brits could master that bit. We enjoyed a splendid day out and enjoyed the evening too. The Peace Treaty either had just been signed, or was about to be signed.

With the completion of the Treaty, the Control Commission for Germany disbanded. All their equipment and vehicles were auctioned off. The car auctions were 'blind', that is to say that you bought a lot of four Volkswagen cars sight unseen. You can guess what sort of cars my little syndicate bought. One that looked as though it had been run over by a tank, one badly bashed at the front, one nearly brand new and another in passable condition. We paid £100 for the lot. It may sound very little money, but remember that the pay for my rank was 49/- a week (£2.45p to you). We eventually made three vehicles, but I saw little of them. Correction, I saw nothing of them nor did I see any money back.

There were other high points in our lives, and one such was the final farewell tour of five star General Dwight D Eisenhower prior to his retirement to run as a presidential candidate in the USA. Until his retirement he was SACEUR (Supreme Allied Commander Europe). We had a parade, of course. Afterwards, he toured the station area with only one accompanying officer. He came into our crew room unannounced and chatted to us. He was a surprisingly large and stocky man, in his service greatcoat and side hat. He was very friendly, and conveyed the impression that he was genuinely interested in what was said to him. I was impressed, and glad that he became President. I wasn't quite so pleased with him when as President of the USA he screwed up the British and French Suez Canal operations some years later.

On another occasion, while lurking near the aircrew offices, I heard a loud altercation between Boss and Flight Commander. 'When

I say, medals are to worn on parade, I mean it. All of them. Do you understand?' There were reluctant noises of agreement. I thought little of this conversation until, one beautiful summer day, enjoying an interminable stroll on the parade ground with many friends I heard, 'Officers will take post, Inwards turn. Quick March'. There was a clanking noise to my right. Using my peripheral vision and screwing my head as far to the right as I could without reprimand, I saw the Man. He was decked out like a Gilbert and Sullivan character on stage. I have never, before or since, seen anything like his decorations. He had, apparently, flown for the Condor Legion in Spain during the Civil War. He returned to Britain in time to fight during the Battle of Britain. Subsequently, he was commissioned and flew bomber, Pathfinder and later Special operations. In addition to British gallantry medals, he had more from France, Belgium, Poland, Norway and Yugoslavia, He wore the insignia of the iron cross and sported one or two Orders, and a sash. The whole ensemble was topped off by a presentation dirk worn on the right side. The total effect was 'over the top'. I could now see why he restricted himself to a less ostentatious medal package on parade days. Regrettably, this pilot was killed in a flying accident on the North Sea island of Sylt.

Despite the earlier minor excursions into a life of crime I enjoyed myself. Life was not at all bad at Wahn for there were many distractions, not least the secretary to the French High Commissioner for Germany. The Commissioner kept his official aircraft in the next hangar to ours. It was a Flying Fortress, a genuine B17 bomber, whose innards had been converted into a flying office. The High Commissioner had been an officer of the Foreign Legion and his aircraft was named Bir Hacheim after the North African desert battle where the outnumbered and outgunned Legion had held the Allied line at a critical time prior to El Alamein. Small painted unit shields ran in a line down each side of the fuselage. The aircraft gleamed, but the effect was marred, for the top three feet of the fin remained dirty, as no ladder or piece of ground equipment enabled the ground staff to reach and polish the area. It was, nevertheless, an impressive aircraft serviced by French Air Force personnel who smoked Gaulloises while refuelling and laid their cigarette ends on the cylinder block of the engines during maintenance. We were appalled, and left the area during such operations, but they had no accidents. The aircraft was boarded via a stepladder, and the secretary wore exceptionally tight skirts. Clad as she was, it was an impossibility for her to board the aircraft unaided. There was considerable competition to lift this delightfully pretty and deliciously perfumed lady into the aircraft.

The hangar which housed the B17 had a small outdoor cafe, which was surrounded by a white picket fence. I remember this soon to be ex-fence well. It was the NATO Open Day in which aircraft from all over Europe congregated for a monster day of flying. This was in the days where squadrons of aircraft arrived rather than the single example of today. There were literally two hundred fighters on the base. There must have been over a hundred Vampires from Italy, Holland and Belgium alone. Sabre jets from America and Canada and the cream of the show – The English Electric Canberra that was shortly to enter service. What an aircraft! In those times, squadrons performed mass start and take off. The Vampires were arraigned in two rows, and to start the aircraft a large number of 3-wheeled trolleys containing four very large lead acid batteries were required. Normally, such trolleys were either moved by hand or towed at a maximum of two at a time by Fordson tractor. On this beautifully sunny day, we had neither the manpower nor the tractors to obey the rules. We had nine trolleys behind the tractor as we swept towards the airfield and the cafe at a much higher speed than that recommended. The two rear trolleys became detached from the group. Mounted on trolley three was me and mounted on trolley eight was Spooner. The trolleys were very heavy and were impossible to steer. Yes, we headed straight for the packed cafe and its al fresco delights. The place became a disaster area – the fence was destroyed and people threw themselves in all directions as tables and chairs were crushed and mangled. From my vantage point on trolley three, still firmly attached to the tractor, I could see Spooner's face as he approached the cafe. Horror, dismay and acceptance all showed on his expressive face as he created carnage. It was like a Tom and Jerry cartoon with Bill Spooner grinning inanely like Tom the cat as he roared through the cafe holding on to the trolley for grim death. Fortunately there were no injuries to anything other than tables, chairs crockery and cake, but there was a lot of damage. We heard more – officially – later.

The day's entertainment was just beginning, for those familiar with the old Vampire know that the engine is prone to wet starts. This means that the engine fails to start at first attempt and a pool of fuel forms in the combustion chambers. When this ignites a spurt of flame is shot out of the jet pipe. The aircraft, you will recall, were in two rows, and the ground personnel marshalling aircraft of Row Two were caught in the jet efflux of Row One. Their own aircraft were in the midst of having wet starts. Those aircraft with wet starts had airmen festooned from the twin booms of the fighters weighing down the tail so that fuel could drain from the engine. Other aircraft belched flame before the engine settled down to a dull roar. The lads were now rather short of places to go, because aircraft were taxiing out of dispersal onto the perimeter track. There was aircraft movement everywhere and airmen rushing out of their way. When viewed from the remnants of the cafe it appeared to be chaos. The audience loved the show! Service readers will know, of course, that this was not chaos, for spectators were being treated to a highly disciplined team of aircraft handlers dealing competently with each and every situation. The aircraft now congregated at the take off point in rows of four. There were about six rows per squadron. Take off was planned with three rows of Vampires on the runway at a time. The first four Italian fighters soared into the sky with Row Two roaring up behind them. As they too became airborne, one aircraft was caught in the turbulence of the preceding group and was thrown back onto the ground. The plane cart-wheeled and came to a gentle stop. The pilot emerged unscathed and standing on a slight hillock he waved. 'I'ma alla right.' However, he had clearly not learnt lesson one in 'How to survive aircraft crashes.' Move smartly away at max speed from a crashed aircraft. There was a thunderous explosion and the pilot disappeared in a plume of black oily smoke and flame. The smoke slowly cleared, to reveal the pilot, now crouched on the hillock feebly waving this time. 'I'ma stilla all right.' There was a cheer from the cafe!

There was another cheer as the fire tender skidded on fuel and hit the wreckage. (Years later at an aircraft crash site I saw the site controller run over by an arriving ambulance.) The show was not over, for the crash had unnerved a pilot in Row Four. He actually forgot to take off, and firmly on the ground, he roared into the clearway beyond the runway, coming to a stop in the sand dunes. I think that he forgot to put the flaps to the take off position. Spectators got their money's worth that day. Nevertheless, despite a couple of further incidents it was a great flying display and there were no lasting human injuries. The local press carried great photographs of both crash and cafe. Because I was senior to Spooner the cafe incident was my responsibility. I had avoided any punishments during boy's service, but I wasn't doing too well in 'real life'. However, I was becoming well known to authority.

When I reached Germany, no peace treaty had been signed and the British had the powers of an occupation force. I enjoyed hunting and the airfield area was over 40 square kilometres and overrun with game. Deer, wild pig and hares had bred in abundance. All that was necessary was to apply for a game licence and own the appropriate weapon, which had to be stored in the armoury. The game licence defined the area of 'your' shoot. I had shot with my father in the Reichwald area on many occasions. My beautiful two-barrelled shotgun was borrowed from the Control Commission for Germany who had confiscated all weapons including sporting weapons at the end of the war. It was a nice weapon; the barrels were mounted one over the other. The upper barrel was 12-bore, while the lower was a rifle firing standard German Army .793mm ammunition. It was thus a fine weapon for use against pig, for the ammunition for pig was a 12-bore cartridge containing one single pellet. A large pellet. Shortly after I began to shoot over the area the peace treaty was signed and the airfield area once more belonged to the Federal Republic. One day, some months later, I was summoned to the Station Commander's office and to my surprise I was asked to sit down on entry. Group Captain Hartley, a well-decorated war-time fighter pilot, was most affable. He had a problem, he said, that only I could resolve. He had a problem that senior aircraftsman Hayes could resolve? Mmmm, interesting. He went on to say that he had been shooting on the airfield and had been approached by a gentleman in a green gamekeeper's outfit who asked him what he was doing on this shoot. He went on to say that they had exchanged 'words' and that he now knew from an official letter that he had in fact been poaching on a licensed shoot belonging to me. On top of that, he'd discovered that the green clad individual, with whom he had been extremely short, was an important individual, quite unused to arrogant treatment. The post of Forester (Forstmeister) is not a lowly one in the Fatherland. He continued sayign that he was now liable to a substantial fine if he could not prove that he had my written permission to shoot on the airfield! I am a pragmatist and I quickly said that I would be delighted to enter him as a guest on my licence. Hartley was a real gentleman; for he went on to say that he was most grateful, and that in exchange he would invite me to accompany him on any shoot that he was invited to. This invitation would of course be as a 'gun'. He had one further favour to ask and that was that I allow him to invite others to shoots to be held on my ground. I agreed and had many pleasant days out. My colleagues at work were astounded at all this, but then so was I.

The Station Commander was as good as his word, for we often held shoots together. Many of his friends were senior officials of the Control

Commission or diplomats of one kind or another. They all had decent weapons but suffered from a common problem in that ammunition was hard to come by. Young Hayes, however, had the resources of the airbase near Kiel, and could get almost anything in the way of ammunition, which he duly sold on to his fellow guns. I really did enjoy those shoots. But all good things come to an end, and with the signing of the peace treaty the airfield returned to the ownership of the new Germany. What really changed was that the syndicates that shot over areas of land now became liable for damage caused by the animals. I resigned my shooting licence immediately, for I had seen a remarkable sight a few weeks earlier. You are familiar with the phrase, 'He tore his hair out in rage'. Well, I've actually seen a man do this. He was the superintendent of a major engineering works. A new runway was under construction on the airfield. A runway capable of withstanding the landing shock of very large future transport aircraft. In some places it was nearly four feet thick and reinforced with wire mesh. A 50-metre section had just been completed and was left overnight. During the night a herd of wild pigs had moved onto the wet concrete and had wallowed there for hours. The damage was unimaginable – and incredibly difficult and expensive to rectify. Imagine the State suing senior aircraftsman Hayes for the cost of repairs!

I still boxed, and in a match between local German clubs and the RAF I found myself in the ring against a rather fleshy welterweight. Under German rules of the time, matches were of six two-minute rounds. On the other hand, the British fought three, three-minute rounds. In reality, to successfully fight to German rules, it was necessary to change training methods. I had not really trained for any fight. I looked across the ring to the German corner where this chap in his middle to late twenties stood. I looked at his vest, which looked vaguely familiar. In fact it was the colours of the old German Navy, Kriegsmarine. I didn't like the look of him for he looked rough! I looked him over very carefully and noted that he had quite a stomach on him, and that he didn't look particularly fit either. The physical training instructor, (PTI) who acted as my second said, 'If I was you, I'd stay away from him for as long as you can, he might just fall down! He'll try to knock you out quick – I don't think he's had a fight that's gone the distance for some time'. I thanked him for this last cheerful thought and strode manfully out for battle. The PTI was right, he did try to knock me out quickly but I just back-pedalled and kept out of his way to heartfelt and derisory jeers from the crowd. As I left my corner in the fourth round, I knew that my opponent was very tired, but so was I. However, I now attacked, and my opponent took a light right to the jaw and collapsed through sheer exhaustion. Beating this particular chap earned me a reputation that I could not support. I got thrashed regularly thereafter. I stopped boxing as soon as people really started to punch me back, and I'm very glad that I did so.

You may remember, if you read Chapter One carefully, that my Imperial Services Championship fight lasted forty-five seconds. Immediately prior to my retirement from the ring, I went to Berlin to represent the Second Allied Tactical Air Force (2ATAF). The match was between all Allied Forces based in Europe and was held in a magnificent huge hall in the American Zone. The preliminary fights took place on a Friday and the championship fights were scheduled for Saturday evening. I had no trouble disposing of my Italian opponent in the preliminaries and went on to meet the winner of the bout between American and Dutch forces. The great night came. I warmed up in the dressing room and emerged to cheers from the partisan crowd on the left. I did emerge at the same time as the cheers started, but the tumultuous cheers were from personnel of the Berlin based US infantry and were for my opponent. I was proudly wearing my Imperial Service Championship vest, with its crown, wings and anchor, covered by a natty green dressing gown. Standing in the red corner, I looked across at my opponent. He was a small, well-muscled man of about 25 years. He looked strong, very strong. He wore a dark green vest with a small golden motif by the left shoulder. We strode to the centre of the ring. We touched gloves as the referee gave us the usual spiel. He wanted a good clean fight, no butting, no holding etc. I returned to my corner and asked my second what a little motif showing a pair of golden gloves meant. Half of me knew already. The Army man was a Golden Gloves coast-to-coast champion – you don't win that by looking pretty. Still, I thought, he might not be able to punch hard. We moved to the centre of the ring, and I led with a ramrod left – that's all I remember. I believe that the fight took eighteen seconds, including the count. I felt a complete fraud in attending the celebratory dinner later that night. That's really why I finally stopped boxing.

I had now spent about a year in Germany and I wanted to return to England to complete an advanced course of training as an aircraft electrician. The training was conducted at RAF Melksham in Wiltshire and was a prerequisite for promotion to Junior Technician. As usual, I applied to go on this course – you could die of old age waiting for a NCO to recommend that you be given the opportunity for further training. As for Engineering officers – I think that I spoke to one, once.

The availability of weapons was to prove my downfall, or nearly my downfall. Over the past two years, I had collected all sorts of weapons, all of which were kept at my parents' home, which was now in Kiel, Schleswig Holstein. I had a Luger, two Mauser 6.75s, a Schmeisser sub machine gun, a Walther PPK and a Webley Scott revolver. The pride of the collection was a very posh German Army rifle sleeved to fire long 6mm ammunition. I had a telescopic sight for the rifle and I loved it. The old German naval air base at nearby Holtenau had a disused rifle range and huge stocks of outdated ammunition. I used to blast away using all weapons for hours. The Royal Engineer care and maintenance group didn't mind, for they were all fellow drinkers and friends of my father who was a most gregarious soul.

According to my Father I have always been naive, and I was about to prove him right again. I was on leave in London and was staying at the Union Jack Club in Waterloo. The Nuffield Centre in the Strand provided recreational facilities, and, if you were very lucky, it was possible that you might be given free tickets to one of the London theatre shows. I think that I had been to see *Salad Days*, but I'm not sure. I was walking alone through Covent Garden on my way back to the Union Jack Club at about midnight, when I came across two men harassing a girl. They were pushing her around, and she was clearly distressed. Girding on my white armour, I charged to the rescue. With the advantage of surprise I punched one to the ground, and was about to start on the second man, when a handbag walloped me on the ear. A woman's voice screamed, 'Why don't you F-off and mind your own business!' Bemused, and nursing a bruised ear, I wandered away. When I asked my Father why this woman had thumped me – he fell about laughing, saying that only I could come between a prostitute and her pimp. There are hard lessons to be learnt in life.

In addition to our normal period of annual leave we were allowed up to two weeks 'continental' leave. I chose to go to Bad Harzburg in the Harz Mountains. The town was a leading ski resort and the British had commandeered various hotels in the town to act as a leave centre. I can't remember the name of the hotel, but it was in the centre of town and was a most impressive building. Constructed in the old style, there were very comfortable lounges, the walls of which were decorated with a variety of long dead beasts' heads. Well, only the skull and antlers in most cases.

Bad Harzburg lay on the border between the British and Russian Zones of occupation. I had never seen a Russian soldier, although I had heard a great deal about them. One very cold evening we were high up in the hills when we saw a ski patrol of about ten or twelve men on their side of the border. To my amazement, they had made camp in the snow. Thrusting their weapons inside their greatcoats they prepared for sleep in shallow snow holes. The temperature was well below zero and likely to get much colder during the night. I was impressed, for I thought that I would probably freeze to death from raw imagination.

Ski instructors did their best with poor clay. Each day we would go by ski lift up to the top of the hills and gradually work our way down by nightfall. I tried my best to learn how to ski, and by the end of a fortnight could usually remain standing for some of the time. I found that I bounced well off most surfaces, although the tree stump that I attempted to destroy with my head appeared to come off best. The local people, especially those elderly persons taking the Cure at the Spa, turned up each evening to watch the return of the ski-mounted Brits. We appeared to offer a good deal of free amusement. On one occasion a very large soldier came roaring down the slope, and fighting to maintain his balance, came off the slope onto a swept car parking area. Still upright he continued across the car park, ruining the skis, before coming to a graceless halt in the hedge. Several old ladies were nearly hysterical with laughter, and at least one was incontinent. We later observed that a lot of the patients of the Spa hotels turned up to witness the 'Return of the Brits'.

Among our squadron ground crew was one man who built model rockets. These were quite sophisticated objects, which were launched from V2-like ramps, which he built in quiet corners of the airfield area. The propellant content of broken down 20mm cannon ammunition powered the rockets. This could be quite dangerous to extract. However, I digress, because a few weeks earlier I had been telling others of my weapon collection. I was accused of exaggerating, or lying. To prove my case I returned from leave carrying a few choice pistols, showed them to the doubters and returned them to Kiel shortly afterwards. The 'Rocketeer' asked if I could get some 6.75mm ammunition, as this calibre was perfect for something in his rocket. I did not inquire precisely what. Three weeks later, when drunk, he 'fell through a jeweller's window' and when challenged by the German Police, produced a loaded automatic pistol. He did not use it and handed it over to the police immediately and peacefully. He later told the Air Force Police that I had sold him both pistol and ammunition! He felt safe to tell the police this, because I had been posted back to England some two weeks before the incident.

CHAPTER FOUR
HOSPITAL AND MELKSHAM

On my return to England, I had quite a bit of leave saved up, so I went first up to Scotland to see various aunts before returning to stay with friends in London. I remember this time because of two incidents. The first was going to the theatre with friends to see *Kiss me Kate*. While the overture was being played, I was asked to go back to the car for something or other, which was in a multi-storey park nearby. When I got there, I found that a hoist had been erected over the engine bay and that two men were stealing the engine! It was a Triumph Mayflower saloon. Isn't it amazing what one can remember? I called the police who caught the thieves in the act and I returned to watch a lovely actress called Patricia Morrison steal the show. It was a memorable night. The second incident was that I began to feel unwell. I went on to become very unwell, and was admitted to Princess Alexandra Hospital at RAF Wroughton near Swindon. Although I started off with just an inflamed appendix, I went on to have a ruptured appendix, blood poisoning and all sorts of nasty things. I was in hospital for months. I was not left in peace, for the Special Investigation Branch wished to speak with me regarding the loaded automatic pistol and my involvement with weapons.

I woke one day to find a presence at my bedside armed with a notebook. He had a friend with him. (One to read and one to write, as we used to comment.) To cut a very long story short, the policemen asked for my weapon licence, which I handed over. It was in the German language and he accepted it as a weapons licence. It was in fact a game licence, but I wasn't going to argue the point. The policeman then asked me to account for every round of ammunition that had passed through my hands during the past year. A hundred rounds to the High Commissioner, 200 rounds to the head of Intelligence, and 200 rounds to the Frontier Control Commissioner. The list was endless. As I lay in hospital, my parents, who knew nothing of my illness, were told that I had been court martialled and been given six months in military prison. It was therefore something of a relief for them to learn that I had been critically ill and was in hospital. I had not written for I was very ill. Apparently I had been in military limbo. I had left Wahn to go to Melksham but had never arrived. Therefore, I did not exist as far as Melksham was concerned. My parents were not amused at this, nor were they amused when a group of Air Force Police arrived to search the family home. Father, being an ex-Palestine Policeman, knew his rights. 'Push off,' he cried. 'That is a military search warrant, and this is a civilian house. You will have to get the Control Commission Policeman to do the search.' He did not tell them that Jimmy Weir, the Control Policeman lived on the opposite side of the road and was a bosom drinking friend. Temporarily baffled, the Air Force Police left. Father spoke with Jimmy Weir, and as a result all my beautiful weapons went into the Kiel Canal. I never heard another word about military charges against me. There were a few boxes of pistol ammunition around the house, so Father Hayes took them to work and put them in a drawer of his metal desk. I mention this only because they were there for years. One very hot summer's day, when Dad was working in the cemetery, there was a loud explosion. Returning to his Nissen hut office he found the tabletop was curled back like an opened sardine tin, and that a drawer was embedded in the plaster wall! All he could say was, 'I don't know how I'm going to explain this to the War Graves Commission.'

Continuing the domestic stories, I am reminded of Brother James who now was in the Army. He had been a member of the Territorial Army while at university and was now completing his national service. I'd seen very little of him during the previous few years except on very odd occasions. I once met him, and a tall young lady, in a London pub. The girl could sink a pint as quickly as any man, and she towered over my brother who was about 5 ft 5 inches in height. This lass had a pretty sense of humour, and used to 'Slope Arms' in the street with great precision using James' brolly. There was another girl I remember who confided in me that girls came from miles around to admire James' knees when he ran in University cross country running events. I doubted this, but she was nice. James indulged himself by buying odd pieces of old luggage and I recall an enormous leather antique Gladstone bag into which you could easily fit a body. He was something of a sight, because when carrying this relic, the bag scraped along the ground. James was not a large man and the handles were quite long.

When called into the army, James, by virtue of his superior intellect and education, was sent to Eaton Hall to become an officer. He was commissioned into The Duke of Wellington's Regiment and posted to the war in Korea. After a short period of battle training in Hong Kong he arrived in Korea to be sent to join his battalion in the line. All this had taken place while I was based in Germany. I'm glad that I joined the Air Force, although I have reflected that in the Army, the officers send the men off to die, whereas in the Air Force the men send the officers (most aircrew are officers) off to die. Strange, isn't it? I think that Naval ranks all drown together.

As I began to recover, the first casualties from the Duke of Wellington's regiment in Korea began to arrive at Wroughton hospital. The battalion had been involved in fierce fighting in the 'Battle of the Hook', during which battle the Dukes had taken heavy casualties. Rising painfully from my bed, I persuaded others to push me down to the main entrance hall of the hospital where I spent the next few hours trying to glean information about James. Eventually, I found two walking wounded who, when asked if they knew Lieutenant Hayes, said knowingly,' 'Do we know Mickey Mouse, Fred?' The pair agreed that they did and commented that he was the only bloody officer who made them clean their boots in the line. I asked if he had been hurt, and was relieved when they said unfortunately not. Feeling very weak, I returned to bed.

Life in a military hospital is quite different and unlike the life enjoyed by patients in a civilian hospital. At this time, Matron ruled the entire nursing roost, and nursing sisters ruled the wards under the strict regime imposed by her. The Sisters were responsible to Matron for the entirety of activity within the ward. Cleanliness – ever close to the military heart – was insisted upon and all patients capable of even dusting were encouraged to assist in daily cleaning operations. The loss of a limb was not considered an excuse for not participating in some form of cleaning task. Rounds took place daily, with the various surgeons and doctors touring the ward accompanied by an anxious Sister armed with up to date information on every patient. Occasionally, the tour would include Matron, and it was clear that these redoubtable Sisters were terrified of Matron. It was very odd, because the matron at the time was a petite, grey haired lady of considerable charm. She had nursed in the Japanese prison camps in Java and was something of a heroine. She was greatly loved by the nursing fraternity, but she was reputed to have an extremely nasty bite when roused.

After nearly five months delay, I finally arrived at Melksham to begin my Electrical Fitters' Course of six months duration. Melksham is in Wiltshire and is close to Chippenham and Trowbridge. The subject matter of the course was a doddle really, for I enjoyed it all. No, I didn't, for I hated the new subject of electronics. I built an amplifier as instructed. However, I shouted into the microphone in room one, and my amplifier produced a very small quiet shout that issued from the speaker in the next room!

While it was true that I had rejoined the regime of parades and yet more parades I was in company with many old friends. During my absence in Germany the fashion wear for young men had changed. Hairstyles had changed, as had clothing and footwear. I was devastated to see an old friend clad in his post office red, finger-tip drape, two-button suit jacket. Thick crepe soled green suede brothel creepers completed the ensemble! His friend, also an old acquaintance, had a similar outfit in a fetching shade of lilac. I did not see myself in such restrained fashion wear and returned to my old Harris Tweed outfit, to which I now added a pork pie trilby hat. I was now nineteen years old.

Now, I intended this book as a record for my family, but there is a snag. Susi, my youngest daughter, said,' Hard luck, Daddy, you'll put every story into the book and then we'll all say that we've all read it. Then you'll have nothing to say.' Fat chance of that sweetheart.

The pay of a senior aircraftsman did not amount to much and, if I remember correctly we paid one shilling each to a sports fund. (In Boys Service it had been a barrack damage fund,) I've never been sure that this levy was quite legal.

I had friends in London and, like most young men, I liked to get away from camp at the weekends. Dressed in uniform, it was then pretty easy to hitchhike up to London. Most civilians recognised that servicemen were poorly paid, and felt quite secure in offering a lift. Moreover, most families had someone in their family doing his national service duty. My ploy was to hitchhike up to London on a Friday night, then go to the Savoy Hotel. Yes, I went to the Savoy – but I went first to the Nuffield Centre in the Strand to volunteer my services as a dishwasher! At this time the Savoy hosted two banquets, each for up to 450 diners each Friday night. Curiously, the hotel was not equipped with an electrical dishwasher. Instead, six or eight casual labourers would be employed. We started washing up at about eight pm, and finished at about 3am. We could eat as much as we liked, and we drank whatever we could find, I used to find a corner and doze until about 7am when I would wash and stroll down to the Union Jack Club in Waterloo where I had booked a room for the Saturday night. I earned as much during the night of dishwashing as I did in a full week of Air Force life. I learnt about crockery there too. Six very casual labourers washing up for nine hundred broke perhaps six pieces each night. I thought that attrition rate remarkable and found that the crockery was hotel weight Spode. My wife loves good crockery and today I am quite happy to pay the price for decent stuff.

The hierarchy in the hotel was quite something. The Head Porter and the Head Chef dined in a room dedicated for their use. They had waiter service, of course. The main staff dining area contained designated areas for the staff of the various restaurants throughout the hotel. I particularly remember a waiter from the Swiss restaurant who, before sitting down, carefully wiped the table with a cloth produced from his tailcoat. There must have been a sort of poacher's pocket in that coat, for he produced a table napkin and his own condiments and cutlery. The bellboys dined in a corner, and a more irritating bunch of half educated little horrors I've rarely come across. They were all in their very late teen years. One particularly offensive specimen so taunted and enraged me that I clouted his ear. The conversation died and there was a deathly silence followed by a round of applause from the waiters. Later, several waiters told me that they would have loved to wallop these supercilious brats, but it would cost them their job. One of the under chefs patted my shoulder as he passed.

At Melksham, we still worked on Saturday mornings. We had 36-hour pass on three weekends and a 48-hour pass on the fourth weekend. Wednesday afternoon was traditionally sports afternoon. We were supposed to engage in organised sporting activities. A lot of people who played no football, rugby, or hockey used to slip surreptitiously out of camp by various means. On one occasion, I left camp in the boot of a friend's MG Midget car. At the guardroom checkpoint, the duty Snoop asked for the boot to be opened for inspection! It was a long walk back.

It was Coronation Year, 1953, and I was determined to see something of the event first hand. My assessment of the situation was that there was unlikely to be another coronation in my lifetime – and if there were, I'd be too old to enjoy the occasion. The School closed for two days to celebrate the event, so I set off the day prior to the coronation to hitchhike up to London. My first lift took me as far as Hungerford, and as I stood at the roadside in uniform, a Rolls Royce passed and then drew to a gentle halt some thirty yards ahead. I scrambled up to the car and was asked where I was going. I told the elderly driver that I was off to London to see the Coronation. 'Get in boy,' he said, 'I'm going up to town for the same reason.' We moved smoothly away and I looked closely at the driver who looked oddly familiar. After a few minutes I remembered. He was the same Indian Army Colonel who had beaten seven daylights out of me when I had been caught scrumping his apples at Weston super Mare. I asked him if I was right and he smiled broadly. 'The old girl gave me hell for beating you lot, you know.' He went on to say that his wife had died quite suddenly in her sleep some ten months before. I was sorry for she had been a kind and gracious lady who had fed us well in recompense for her husband's beating.

The Colonel drove me to the Union Jack Club. I doubt that many arrive there in such splendour. He was staying at the Army and Navy Club. He shook my hand warmly and wished me well. Alas, there was no room at the Inn and I set off to choose a spot on the pavement. The whole world was on the streets of London during this time. There were people from every part of the globe. Thousands, probably tens of thousands had chosen to while the night away on the street to preserve their vantage point. The humour and spirit was overwhelming, nobody slept except in fits and starts. I joined a large group of young people, all of whom were determined that the rain would not spoil their day or night. We told stories; we sang until we were hoarse and we cheered every person who was lucky enough to have found a house with a balcony to peer over. At first light the route-lining troops began to appear. Single files of soldiers marched down the gutters, to be halted by martial orders bellowed by ex-servicemen. Confused, the soldiers always halted to the chagrin of their own officers. Officers wore swords, which was unfortunate for some. One, coming to attention from at ease, sliced his ear, which bled copiously. An old dear who claimed to have served with the St John Ambulance Brigade during the war (probably the Boer War) rushed up to stem the flow of blood, only to be vigorously shrugged away by the indignant Lieutenant. On the packed balconies elegantly dressed people waved imperiously to the motley below, to be greeted with cries of 'Speech' and rapturous applause, especially if the girls were pretty. In my group, there were young people from New Zealand and Canada, a couple from Fiji and several South Africans. I couldn't understand what the 'Yarpies' were saying because they had a very thick and unfamiliar accent. They told me that they couldn't understand my English either. The day wore on, and the bladders of the populace swelled to the point of pain. There were many toilets located in the streets behind the procession route, but some fool had positioned an equal number of male and female toilets. Even I knew that females take much longer to perform the simple task of emptying their bladders than men. Consequently, there was a hundred-yard queue for the barely continent ladies and no queue for the gents. From halfway down the female queue emerged a stocky young woman brandishing a handbag who cried, 'Come on girls, let's storm the bloody place.' Led by this archetypal, jolly hockeystick maiden, the Ladies queue parted to form a flying wedge of desperate ladies, most of whom swung handbags threateningly. Storming down the street, they tore down the Gents sign to ragged cheers, while a small group of startled males shot out of the toilet exit. Having just relieved myself, I found it all very amusing. As the day wore on however, we men never achieved the numerical superiority necessary to retake our toilet.

The variety of the military contingents was astounding. I don't suppose that London will ever again see such pageantry and splendour. There were soldiers, sailors and airmen from the whole Commonwealth of Nations. Ghurkhas, Fijians, Kenyans vied with the men from India and Pakistan in their colourful dress uniforms. There were squadrons of turbaned Indian Army cavalry carrying lances. Oh, there was every kind of soldiery that you've ever seen even in books, or even on cigarette cards. Australian troops proudly wore their distinctive hats and the Mounties trotted by on magnificent black horses. National groups within the crowd became near hysterical as 'their' contingent passed. It was indeed a day to remember. Then came the sumptuous carriages of the various dignitaries. Who can forget Queen Salote standing in her open carriage in the pouring rain acknowledging the cheering crowds? Each national contingent was led by a band, blasting away, the noise of the music lost in the tempestuous roars from the crowd. The poor old troops who couldn't hear the band frequently lost step and were tormented by their SNCOs. The crowd loved it all and when the Royal coach appeared went delirious with pleasure. Our young Queen seemed serenely happy and her subjects appeared to share the mood. That night London partied! What an understatement that is. I cleaned myself up in the Union Jack Club – there was even a queue for the toilets there too – and set off on the town. I've never been kissed by so many strange young women before or since. I hitchhiked back to Melksham as dawn broke and was fortunate to get a lift virtually the whole way down the A4. I'm glad that I went to see the Coronation.

Speaking of toilets reminds me of the toilet paper then favoured by the suppliers of such things to HM forces. Known to the RAF as Army Blank Form One, it was a tracing paper like sheet with an almost glossy surface. Using such paper one did not so much clean oneself, but rather it enabled you spread the effluent around a bit more evenly.

I thought that I had one more boxing story, and I've just remembered my final entry into the ring. RAF Melksham lies close to Trowbridge where there used to be a fair each summer. With a few friends, I was wandering around trying my luck on the cheaper attractions when I saw a boxing booth that offered five pounds to any man who could last three rounds with the resident bruisers. As we walked towards the ring I saw an old friend from the Air Force Boys Boxing Team climb into the ring. One round later he was the proud possessor of their money. Talking later, he said,' Eric, it's money for old rope – easy money'. He should never have said that. I volunteered to fight. The booth operator looked closely at me and decided to change my opponent from a badly marked youth to a forty-year-old plug-ugly. As I climbed into the ring I realised that I had just spent six months in hospital and that I was not the man I thought I was. My worst fears were confirmed when the inside of the glove lacing was rubbed up my nose. Ah, I thought, Marquis of Dublin Rules and fell back into the corner with my knee up. I was sorry when he damaged his parts, but he recovered enough to kidney punch me. He then attempted in the clinches to head butt me – I knew that one too, and lowered my head a touch. It apparently hurt him more than me. I contrived to stay out of his way for two rounds and the proprietor muttered angrily to his man during the interval. We stood toe to toe committing every foul in the book. He ran his unshaven cheek up and down my rosebud complexion; I rubbed the inside of my glove up his ear and stepped down the inside of his legs tearing the hairs out. He didn't like that. Head butts, and low blows abounded until the final bell. My opponent gave me a hug and whispered, 'Where'd a nice boy like you learn all those bloody tricks?' Same place as you mate, I thought. Never again.

Newly qualified as an Electrical Fitter (Air) and promoted to the rank of Junior Technician, I received my next assignment. Damnation! I was to return to the Bomber force in Lincolnshire. I was posted to 12 Squadron based at RAF Binbrook. The blokes at Hemswell had said that you never get away from bombers!

CHAPTER FIVE
BINBROOK AND THE CANBERRA BOMBER

RAF Binbrook lay on the top of the Lincolnshire Wolds above the village of Binbrook and beneath the duty cloud that constantly lay over the airfield. The airfield, now long closed, was some ten miles from Grimsby. Binbrook opened in June 1940 and had five of those wonderfully durable C hangars and three runways. The station at the time was to become the home of what was the finest twin jet bomber ever produced by British industry. The English Electric Canberra B Mk1 was a magnificent machine in every way. Designers used to say of aircraft that if it looked right, then it was right. It looked right. The earliest models were black painted in a high-speed shiny finish. The aircraft lay low on the ground on its tricycle undercarriage and looked menacing with its tall fin and vast drooping elevators. There was not a fighter in the sky that could successfully engage the aircraft with guns. The aircraft first flew in May 1949 and was released to service in May 1951. The new aircraft was equipped with a rearwards facing radar, and when the Orange Putter radar said there was an aircraft behind, then that huge electrically driven tail plane went up and the aircraft soared upwards into thinner air. It could outmanoeuvre any fighter of the day, and fly 10,000 feet above them! There were not many fighters of the time that were equipped with decent air-to-air missiles either. The first squadron to equip with the Canberra B2 was 101 and it was swiftly joined by aircraft for 9, 12, 109 and 139 Squadrons as the production lines went into high gear. I was now Junior Technician Hayes; complete with a rank badge on my sleeve of one stripe upside down. Now began a formative part of my life.

The production of the Canberra outstripped some areas of existing technology in that the aircraft could fly at 40,000 ft plus. Each time it did so, the carbon brushes in any piece of rotating electrical equipment wore away more quickly than it would at lower altitudes. As a result, the electricians became adept in changing generators and inverters. There were two generators and five inverters, so we were always busy. In addition, the large perspex canopy and metal hatch above the

Navigator and radar operator were blown off in emergency by rows of tiny electrically fired explosive bolts to permit the exit of the crew. This entry into explosive bolts was new technology to me at least and they had to be periodically replaced. The flying control run beneath the yoke of the control column was severed by a small circular charge permitting a spring to pull the column forward into the instrument panel thus allowing the Pilot to eject without losing his legs. All of these jobs were awkward to get at, and that is an understatement, but nothing like as bad as trying to work on the periscopic sextant demister of the Vulcan bomber in later years.

My lifestyle began to change and expand in many ways; due mainly to a national serviceman called Reginald Horace Chiddick. He had extended his service by one year (known as the greedy year, it increased the pay of a national serviceman considerably) and we worked together for much of his service. Chiddick was a slim, shy man, of undoubted ability. Everything that he did, he did faster and better than the time before. He timed himself on every task, and encouraged me to keep up with him. On paper, I was his superior, but it didn't work that way in practice, indeed I learnt a great deal about standards of workmanship from him. He had a lasting influence upon me. Together, we made a formidable team. We changed generators and inverters in no time at all. The explosive charges in canopy and hatch bolts we could change in six hours, whereas it took others nearer 12 hours. Our work was always beautifully taped and cleated to factory standards. This was not due to my supervisory talent, for one occasion we had worked through the night on a detonator change, completing the job by 0400hrs. Reg looked disparagingly at the finished article and said that it was not up to standard. He then ripped it all out, starting with my bit, and we began again. You try telling an irate Flight Sergeant that, yes you finished it much earlier, but that you didn't like the finished job and you will now finish in two hours. Disbelief and a few other choice expressions show on his face. Reg and I worked on strict divisions of labour, with each of us regularly taking a set part of a job. We developed a great rapport, and on one occasion, when I slid off to meet my girlfriend in the evening, on the understanding that I would join him later to finish the job, a rather strange thing happened. I was on the bus to Grimsby, when I realised that he could be injured if he did not disconnect the snatch unit before sticking his head into a confined space. (The snatch unit was the large spring that pulled the control column out of the way of an ejecting pilot.)

I leapt off the bus and rang the hangar. After a few minutes the phone was answered and a voice said,' Yep, I did disconnect the snatch unit'. I had not said a word before he spoke! Reg's standards were forced upon me, and they were much higher than mine.

We developed our own tools to perform specific tasks. Box spanners were cut down to half an inch in length, spanners were twisted, or shortened and we employed all sorts of schemes to reduce the time expended on routine tasks.

Then Bomber Command Work-Study Group arrived – such groups were very popular in the Fifties. Men with watches and clipboards followed station personnel around for weeks, timing and logging every kind of activity. At the end of some weeks, Chiddick and I were called in front of a meeting chaired by OC Engineering and attended by all Squadron Cdrs. Our presence was required to explain to the Board how, or why, we changed electrical equipment five times quicker than the station average times. Greatly flattered, we produced our purpose made tools, which we were asked to demonstrate. We each took an inverter out of an aircraft and re-installed it watched by our beaming Squadron Cdr. Three minutes ten seconds to remove and four minutes fifteen seconds to reinstall. We then all retired to the boardroom, where the head of the work-study team confiscated our tools! Our Boss was flabbergasted, while we were speechless. Non-standard tools were dangerous, we were told. The work-study chief lectured the meeting, saying that shortly all tools used on aircraft would be centrally controlled within each hangar and accounted for at the end of each working day. There was no place for extreme efficiency based on improper procedures and non-standard tools. It seemed beyond belief that to produce more effective tools was not an option considered at any time.

Although he was a reticent and shy man, Reg could be very amusing. He enlivened our days by various means. One day, he was about to start work inside the upper equipment hatch of a Canberra. Carefully placing his tool bag on the curved upper fuselage, he bellowed, 'Reginald Chiddick pr-e-esents Chiddick on the Wurlitzer Organ'. With that he began the opening notes of 'Let's all go down the Strand,' slowly bending his knees and descending into the hatchway, grabbing his tool bag at the last possible second. When he emerged, he could be anything, but I particularly remember the day when a visiting Air Marshal was walking through the hangar in company with our Boss. A two-note Klaxon noise was heard, followed by a stentorian shout of, 'Blow Two, Blow Four'. There was a hissing noise and again the shout, 'Blow One,

Blow Six, Hands to surfacing stations' A change of voice, 'Periscope depth sir.' 'Up periscope,' cried voice one, and a large inspection mirror slowly rose to survey the scene. After one careful rotation of the mirror, the periscope descended, and the order 'Surface','Off Clips' was given. Chiddick emerged from the hatch and looked down to observe the bemused looks on the face of both Boss and super Boss. 'Dive, Dive' wailed Chiddick, as he descended in confusion into the bowels of the aircraft. 'What the hell was that, Wright?' I heard super Boss ask. 'Nothing much, sir, just one of my electricians. He's a bit of a wit.' Super Boss indicated that he would like to see that Wit and our Boss told me to get him out of the aircraft. I rapped on the side of the aircraft and told Reg to come out, 'F..... off,' he cried, 'I'm not coming out until all the Brass has gone!' The Boss then added his voice and Chiddick emerged, blushing like a rose, standing there in his one-piece green overalls and his grey kerosene boots. The Air Marshal began to speak, but stopped when he saw the row of medal ribbons on Reg's overalls. These were made of folded Spangles sweet covers. The purple diagonal stripe when folded is not unlike the Distinguished Flying Cross and the red striped sweet cover like another decoration. The Air Marshal looked down at his own ribbons and obviously reflected that Chiddick too was a hero. Pointing with an accusatory finger, he inquired, 'What's that?' A muffled response emerged, 'Kings Cross Sir'. 'And that?' 'P-p-p-paddington sir.' We were told curtly to bugger off, and we retired, shaken, to the electrician's private cubbyhole. Some minutes later a very couth looking ADC type figure appeared and told us through a plum filled mouth that we were to scrub out our tea mug (and he meant scrub) and that the Air Marshal would be across shortly. Aghast, we did as bid, and the Air Marshal appeared. A likeable and affable man with one arm, he did his best to calm Reg down, but he shook for an hour afterwards.

    A very small and slight young man joined the squadron as an airframe mechanic. Talking in the crew room, he said he was most surprised at the friendliness shown him by the entire group of senior NCOs. We exchanged knowing smiles. He went on to say that he thought that he might like it at Binbrook. An unkind soul sneered and said, 'Yeah, you're gonna be popular all right, but I bet you don't know why!' The lad looked a bit puzzled, so we enlightened him. 'Tools are dropped in aircraft, and often they are very difficult to retrieve,' we told him. 'They must be retrieved, at any cost, because they can jam controls at some later date. You, my son, are going to be the bloke that they hang by the ankles until the tool is removed from the aircraft. There are a hundred jobs for a chap your size!' He looked very crestfallen, but he recognised truth when he heard it.

We told him of Fred, who was working on an item mounted inside the engine bay. The securing bolts for the item were accessible through a small panel outboard of the engine. Fred had threaded his hand and wrist through a lightening hole in the wing rib to reach the bolt head. He had difficulty in removing his hand, and some ten minutes elapsed before he asked for help. His supervisor greased his hand and wrist and they both pulled and twisted his wrist to no avail. Fred began to go into shock, and was supported now on a toolbox with a man each side to hold him up. The medical officer arrived, and after giving Fred some kind of injection, retired to consult with the airframe senior staff. Time passed and we were still unable to release Fred, and his condition was worsening rapidly. 'Cut him out, now,' said the Medic. The airframe people were absolutely horrified, as the area contained primary structure. (We might need new wing type stuff.) The doctor however was adamant, 'Get him out now'. After some two and half-hours, Fred was finally released. We did not cut primary structure, but it was a close run thing. Fred spent a few days in Sick Quarters, before emerging none the worse. Some airframe people actually talked of removing his hand. I have always hoped that they were joking, but after a lifetime spent caring for aircraft, I know that one can become very attached to one specific machine.

I lived a carefree life, I enjoyed my work and I felt competent and valued. Does pride come or go before a fall? A modification to the electrical system of the aircraft involved the replacement of the aircraft crash switch. This is a gravity-operated device that in the event of crash or impact switches to cut off normal electrical power and arms the fire extinguisher discharge switches, amongst other things. In our normal manner we worked furiously away and completed the task in short order. Two, perhaps three days later, we received a phone call from the electrical chief technician of the major servicing base hangar saying that he had something interesting to show us, and that we should come down together. Flattered that we should be so singled out, we strolled down. We were met in a friendly manner, and pointing into the side equipment hatch of an aircraft in process of a Minor Inspection the chief said, 'Look in there, young Hayes, Can you see anything wrong?' I looked and couldn't see anything amiss. 'You, Chiddick, you have a look,' directed the Chief. Reg looked around carefully for about a minute before shooting a step backwards. 'Jeez,' he said, 'the crash switch is fitted upside down.' 'Who the hell did this, Chief?' I asked, for neither Reg or myself had noted the aircraft serial number as we came into the hangar. There was a pregnant pause before he answered,' You did,' producing the Form 700 (aircraft servicing history)!

The aircraft would almost certainly have crashed. I could have been responsible for not only the loss of the aircraft, but also for the death of three crew members. Reg was ashen and silent, for he too recognised the implications of the error. We were guilty of negligence, and criminal negligence at that. We stood there in dumb misery while I think the Chief looked us over. 'Away you go – you've learnt a hard lesson today. It's a good job for the pair of you that I've known both you and your work'. I was wholly to blame because, although I was a Junior Technician, I had over signing authority in the aircraft logbook. In effect, we did the job and I checked the job. I learnt that day that the great Hayes could not only make mistakes, but that he could endanger life. It remains a sobering thought and that incident has remained vivid in my memory. This incident and its outcome made a lasting impression on me. Many years later, this experience and the sympathetic handling saved the hides of a couple of airmen who made a serious mistake on the aircraft that I was about to fly as crew. A very chastened and surprised sergeant and his corporal lived to fight another day. I did tell them why.

Reg was a radio Ham – I remember when visiting his home in Norwich that his Mother confided that if she heard her lounge referred to as 'the Shack' again, she would kill him. On another visit, I found his Mother marooned at the top of the stairs. Reg had every tread out laying a new cable run to the shack. This interest in radio led to his creation of Binbrook Radio Services. Wired into the station tannoy system, it provided radio to each room of the accommodation blocks. Reg, helped by me in very small part, built the whole set-up of radio receiver, and record tables. It was a very popular broadcasting system, for Reg was a pretty good DJ with a fairly extensive taste in music. We were allowed to use station funds to buy new records each month. I had suffered music of the majority for years in barrack rooms, and I much preferred classical music. After some discussion, I was initially given half an hour slot a week. I recorded the programme and wandered around the rooms of the barrack block to hear myself. I was out of luck, for every bugger had switched me off! My following slowly grew as I descended into light classics and musicals.

We were a mixed bag in our barrack room, which was on the upper floor of an H block. One chap sticks in my mind, for I found him to be a pain. 'The average man', he would declaim 'should be able to lift his own weight plus fifteen pounds.' He got on my nerves so much that I went down to the gymnasium and trained myself on the weights until I could do just that. I waited until this Yorkshire lad repeated his statement and called his bluff. 'Let's see you do that then, if you're an average man,' I said, indicating that a few others could act as witnesses. At the gym, he said that I could be first to try at my own weight, I successfully lifted the weight and casually added another fifteen pounds. My practice paid off, up went the weight and I looked expectantly at him. Stripping off his jacket, he stated his weight, added fifteen pounds and hoisted it, first time, manfully into the air. Honour had been satisfied on both sides and no attempt was made by either party to continue adding weights. There was no further discussion, but we never heard 'The average man' etc again.

The squadron ground crew were a friendly bunch and we had many distinct characters. For example, there were four Smiths on the Squadron. Smith with four FFFFs because of language difficulties. Smith the Teddy Boy, Smith the Edwardian, and a Smith known as Chaz. Chaz's father was a scrap metal dealer in the East End of London. Smith, the Teddy Boy, was discovered ironing a bootlace. When I asked for an explanation, I was haughtily informed that this was no bootlace, but a Slim Jim tie! Smith the Edwardian was a different animal, for he was tall and slim and affected multi coloured waistcoats and well cut suits. He looked rather good, I thought. At the time, I still allowed myself to be seen out and about in the three-piece Harris Tweed suit topped with a riding mac! God only knows what I thought I was.

In the early fifties pay was abysmal, and very very few of those corporals and below owned their own transport. It was the era of the motor bike, and pretty few of those. The sergeants usually owned an old car, as did junior officers, but decent vehicles were usually the property of senior officers of wing commander rank and warrant officers. The Station Commanders rarely-possessed a car, because they had the use of a staff car. Reg owned an elderly Ford 8, a corporal an even older Hillman, and Chaz a 1928 Fiat, saved from the scrap heap by a generous father. It had possessed a top in its heyday, but this had long gone. The car had leather seating and when it rained the interior slowly filled with water, for the doors fitted well and there were no drain holes. The Hillman, which had wire spoked wheels, gave up the ghost climbing the hill leading from Binbrook village to Grimsby. The wheels collapsed, due no doubt to the excess weight it was invariably forced to carry. It was therefore the bus or nothing for most of us. I did attempt to buy a car myself from an airman of another squadron. It was a Singer Le Mans open coupé, dating from some time in the thirties. The car looked alright except for a pronounced dip in the centre.

The car was almost bow shaped, but it had green leather upholstery. (I liked that.) The owner claimed that the car was mechanically sound and offered a test drive. I suggested that he drove, and we roared up the perimeter track when flying had stopped for the day. As the car reached about forty miles an hour, there was a terrific bang and the car came to a halt amid ominous and serious grinding noises. When the bonnet was lifted, a piston could be seen nosing curiously about amid large pieces of crankcase. The car looked infinitely sad, as a mixture of coolant and engine oil urinated onto the tarmac. Despite this forlorn sight, or definitely because of it, I said that under the circumstances I would not buy the vehicle, but would help him to push it to a graveyard!

Chaz and his red open Fiat car got us into trouble with the police. We had motored (One did not drive in a motor vehicle of such character) into Grimsby. We were surprised to see so many people on the streets, and more surprised when some waved to us. The three of us on the rear bench seat began to acknowledge the plaudits left and right in the fashion of royalty. I later stood up clasping my hands in boxer style above my head to great public approval. Alas, our moment of glory did not last long, for an unfriendly policeman with 'friends' informed us that we were 150 yards ahead of Princess Alexandra and her motorcade! We were shown the fastest way out of town.

Our incident did not end there, because after attending the dance at the Gaiety, on our way back to camp we passed three stationary cars, standing in the darkness of the countryside. Before we could utter a word, Chaz had stopped his car, raced over to the Royal car and told the Princess that, although he wasn't too keen on royalty as a general rule, that she was OK. He must have caught the protection squad 'at their ablutions', because they were completely wrong-footed. The lady, Chaz said, just smiled and thanked him. We restarted the car and proceeded homewards in pouring rain, which steadily filled the floor pan to a depth of four inches before we reached camp.

The motorcycle continued to deplete the ranks of the Royal Air Force. There were far too many accidents and more than a few deaths.

A roommate, a Jewish lad known as Icky Plush, bought himself a motorcycle, probably to speed his way to ingest more food. He ate two breakfasts each day, cajoled the cooks into giving large portions of everything, ate two desserts and was always to be seen eating in the NAAFI. I've never known a man to eat so much without becoming obese. He was fleshy, yes – but obese – no. When all the dangers of motorcycling were highlighted yet again on Station Routine Orders, he invested in a new crash helmet. Dressed for riding, he displayed himself to a group of us. We criticised the round, old fashioned, shape of the helmet, saying that if he came off, it would probably break his neck. 'Rubbish,' he retorted, 'I'll show you.' Turning towards a wall he ran six paces and threw himself head first at said wall. Well, it didn't break his neck, but he didn't go out that afternoon and he walked with his head listing to port for a week. Icky loved his bike, and was in the habit of touring off to Ludford Magna, a disused wartime satellite air strip, where he could drive the bike at speed. One afternoon, he failed to return for the evening meal, which indicated to familiars that all was not well. We mounted a search party and arrived at the old runway just before dark. Splitting into four groups, we searched the length of the runway. We eventually found him. That's not really true, because we found the bike's wheel tracks leading into a huge patch of briar and the bike some ten or fifteen feet into the briar first. Of Icky there was no sign. We yelled like hell, and a weak cry from the centre of the briar patch told us that we'd found him. It took all of us half an hour to cut away sufficient briar and gorse to get him out. He'd hit a pothole at speed, run off the hard surface, and been catapulted over the briars to land in the densest section. We knew that he was largely unhurt, because he moaned all the way back about missing his meal.

Of all the senior NCOs I've ever known, Flight Sergeant Brisbane takes the prize. 'Dizzy', as he was not so affectionately called behind his back, was in charge of the squadron ground crew. Small, aggressive, and usually bad tempered; he was a lowland Scot from the West Coast. Dizzy was in charge, a fact that he impressed upon all those who came into contact with him. He was damned near a control freak and positively Machiavellian in the machinations of his mind. I recall one day in early spring, when the demands upon the squadron ground crew had been particularly heavy. We were operating from the dispersal area, some one-mile distant from the hangar line. A small Seco fibreboard hut complex and a large Nissen hut, surrounded by earthen berms containing wartime air raid shelters, formed our accommodation. It was possible from the Chief's office to see across the airfield and perimeter track and have all five hangars in view. The phone rang, and Dizzy spoke with our Squadron Boss, 'I ken fine that you want seven aircraft on the pan at seven tomorrow morning for the training programme – but ye'll no get them. Ah've worked these lads gey hard lately. Ye can have four, and that's ma best, Sir.' He put the phone down without waiting for any response. In the distance, he watched a figure storm out of the squadron offices, jump into a landrover and head our way. Dizzy smiled, and telephoned the station senior engineering officer (Lord of all things technical, OC Eng). 'Ma Boss is makin'' unreasonable demands on ma manpower, Sir. He's on his way tae sort me out now, I wonder if you could possibly help me out a bit and intervene now, because you know that the lads are working gey hard these days. Ah canna work them all day, and night too, fer weeks at a time.' This was pure hypocrisy, for if Dizzy felt like working us to a standstill – he'd have done just that, as long as he thought that it was his idea to do so. Peering towards another hangar, he observed with visible satisfaction that OC Eng. was on his way to the dispersal area too.

Our Boss arrived. 'A word in your office Flight Sergeant.' Together they moved into Dizzy's office and ground personnel scattered to where they could hear, and if possible see, but remain unseen. The Boss informed Dizzy in no uncertain fashion that he gave the orders and that Dizzy would do as he was told. It was at this precise moment that OC Eng arrived. There is little professional love lost between aircraft provider and aircraft operator, for there are too many constraints upon the provider and too many demands from the operator. Hearing the ground crew (provider) being addressed in such arbitrary terms by our Boss, he sprang to Dizzy's defence. The wing commander began to speak, but was interrupted. 'Excuse me, Sir,' said our devious Scot, 'if ma Boss tells me tae produce seven aircraft ah will of course, 'cos he's ma Boss,' moving to the side and slightly to the rear of our Squadron Cdr to face the engineer wing commander. Thus demonstrating unswerving loyalty in the face of foreign interference. The Squadron Cdr and OC Eng stared grim faced at one another and our Boss said,' I think that you'd better leave us for a few minutes Flight Sergeant, if you will.' Dizzy left with ponderous dignity and when out of view did a little dance and rubbed his hands together with glee. The two senior officers battled it out, leaving separately and each stiff with rage. Half an hour later, we heard our Boss thank Dizzy for his support in facing OC Eng and that he had reviewed the squadron training programme. He would now require only three aircraft at first light tomorrow!

We worked five and a half days a week. Wednesday afternoons continued to be used for organised sport and we worked Saturday mornings. There was one 48-hour pass a month. In truth, we worked all the hours necessary to complete the task in hand. I had no social skills. I could not dance and had very little contact with the opposite sex. We had a bit of a discussion amongst ourselves and decided that five of us would all learn to dance properly. We would go to the Joyce Atkins School de Danse in Grimsby! This establishment was poorly attended and unfashionable, for rock and roll was the coming thing. The formidable lady owner in person made our little group of five welcome. She was most kind, and made little adverse comment when we all trod on her toes, ripped stockings and destroyed shoes. Slowly, we learnt the quickstep and foxtrot, even the tango. We all liked the barn dance. Many more young ladies appeared at practice sessions and we became moderately popular partners. Indeed, we began to have fun. The School de Danse prospered as more of the squadron members arrived for training, attracting even more girls to the place. A new problem arose, in that main stream social life took place at dances held at the Gaiety Ballrooms in Grimsby and The Winter Gardens in Cleethorpes. There was also a lower class establishment in Grimsby dockland called the Alexandra. Dances were held on Wednesdays and Saturdays.

Reg and myself were keen to exploit our new skills and we needed Wednesday evenings free. The squadron conducted night flying exercises three, sometimes four nights a week and we attempted to 'book' Wednesday night off. This was difficult for Dizzy Brisbane ruled every aspect of squadron life. Knowing the man as we did, I didn't give much for our chances. It was then that I had a brainwave! A guaranteed way to make sure that we were free to dance. Marching into the Chief's office, I said that night flying was planned for Tuesday, Wednesday, Thursday and Friday. Chiddick and myself would do Wednesday and Thursday. There was a blast from Brisbane, 'I say who does what and when on this squadron, Hayes. You'll do Tuesday and Thursday, and like it!' Disconsolate in appearance I departed the presence, to jubilantly tell Reg that the master plan had worked. We had found the key to get what we wanted – argue for the exact opposite.

To give Dizzy his due, it's necessary to speak of his good points and they were many. His boast to us that only he buggered us around was justified, for he defended us vigorously against all comers – including the Squadron Cdr. When we worked through cold winters nights on the far side of the airfield, it was not unknown for Dizzy to appear, clutching a thermos of tea and sandwiches. 'Are youse all right, lads?' The Mess bar had closed, he was half cut and had come to check on us – but who cared. Certainly not us, for we saw it as a kindness. There are many today who will check, but few who will bring sandwiches when they do so.

We had a good bunch of senior NCOs, particularly in the engine and airframe trades, where most were either boy entrants or, aircraft apprentices from before the war. To a man they had served everywhere, or so it seemed. All were raconteurs of some merit. Among the best of them were two engine fitter sergeants and the Airframe Sergeant. When night flying was in progress it was common practice to leave a small cadre in the dispersal to look after possible early returns, while the rest of us bogged off to the NAAFI. This rarely happened on 12 Squadron, for we had story time. Huddled around the large pot bellied stove of the Nissen hut, we would listen for hours as first one then the other would speak of India, Burma and Egypt and the desert. There was never a dull moment. Taff Owen, the Airframe chap, was of course Welsh. He had a rich brown mellifluous voice with a delightful timbre. He could recite a hundred verses of Eskimo Nell in ever increasing vulgarity. His stated ambition, when leaving the Service, was to become a Beadle. Many years later, watching *Songs of Praise* from St David's cathedral on television, I believe that I recognised Taff bearing the civic mace marching before the Town Mayor in procession. I hope that it was he.

As time went by, we became concerned as to the employment prospects of the two Engine Sergeants because they were due for discharge. They could only talk about engines, their Air Force life, cricket and football in season. We need not have concerned ourselves, for both became field representatives for Rolls Royce immediately on discharge.

We had some characters amongst our aircrew. We had I think three Sergeant Pilots and the rest were officers. Flight Lieutenant Attlee added a spot of class to the aircrew room. I believe that he was some relation to the Labour Prime Minister. Tony Harris was a well spoken ex Cranwell cadet with a broad Yorkshire speaking father. It was a delight to see them together, for each was demonstrably proud of the other. It doesn't always work that way. The cream of the bunch, to me at least, was Floyd E Singleton, then Captain, and later Major, USAF. A large man, Singleton had been seconded to the RAF prior to joining the first American manufactured Canberra (Martin B57) squadron to be formed in the future. The American was a revelation to me, I had never served with an American and he constantly surprised me. Firstly, he learnt most of our names. Secondly, he always came around the ground crew rooms prior to main holidays. He wished us a Happy Christmas, and never failed to subsequently ask us if we'd had a good time. I don't know if he was interested, but he certainly gave that impression. In this, he was my model of how an aircrew officer should behave, especially now that ground crew no longer form part of a squadron. He was an above average pilot, and when he later commanded an American B57D squadron I'm told that he gave his men hell, and bored them to tears with stories of his British Air Force days. We affectionately knew him as Captain Shinglebum. He left us after a year and a half and was replaced by a Captain Cole.

Once, returning from a flying sortie, he was taxiing into dispersal where a marshaller would direct the pilot to bring the aircraft to a stop facing into wind. One Chiddick was cycling up to the dispersal at three miles an hour when Singleton, seeing no marshaller to direct him, swept around in a tight circle to stop the aircraft facing into wind. You can turn a Canberra on a sixpence, but considerable engine power is required to accomplish this with panache. Singleton had panache. Reg Chiddick's direction was radically changed as a high-speed blast of hot air reeking of unburnt kerosene struck him. Turning at right angles to his previous track he descended into and out of the ditch and into the hedgerow. It was most amusing from where I stood. Reg had yet another unfortunate occurrence when he opened the crew access door before the pilot had opened the direct vision window to release the final cockpit air pressure. Even a very small pressure above ambient can have a marked effect when bearing on a hatch of four by three feet. Mercifully Reg had his body close to the hatch and was only hurled a little way and the door was undamaged. He suffered no more than a sprained wrist, and injured dignity.

The memory of the day that we found an old steel locker containing 108 explosive detonator charges is ever with me. What could we do with these? They were obviously quite old and we could account for each and every detonator that we had ever replaced. Therefore they were 'gash'. We decided that we should stage a test piece. Behind the dispersal, beyond the shelter berms (and out of sight of Dizzy) was an old tree root. It was about ten inches above ground and some 35 inches across. We bored 25 holes around the circumference and inserted an explosive charge into each. Carefully, we wired them into a whole and retired to find a means of ignition. All we required was a battery or two because we needed 24 volts. We laid out the firing cable to a corner of the berm, so that we had some protection from any blast. Cautiously we completed the wiring and we were ready to fire. I climbed to the top of the air raid shelter and confirmed that all was clear. As I ducked down, Reg fired the charge. Joy of joys, a wedge-shaped section of tree root rose four feet into the air in a puff of thin white smoke, accompanied by a sharp crack of noise. Marvellous, now what could we do, for we'd only used 25 detonators?

Somehow we decided that these tiny charges were not quite what we wanted. We needed a more spectacular event. Could a slow burning Canberra engine starter cartridge power a rocket? It was a working weekend, and it was Sunday afternoon and all was quiet with no flying in progress. We created a rocket by fitting a broom handle with cardboard fins. The brass starter cartridge casing was strapped to the broom handle, which was weighted to place the cartridge at about the point of balance. We found a large earthenware drainage pipe of about the right calibre and set all this lot up behind our dispersal huts. Again the charge had to be electrically fired, but we couldn't have the rocket ascending while still connected to the battery cable. The problem was quickly solved, by boring a hole in the drain and inserting a brass plate, upon which rested the cartridge electrical connection. With most of the squadron ground crew watching, we staged a countdown and fired. The broom rose slowly into the air. There was very little wind and the contraption rose nearly vertically to about two hundred feet before it toppled, bereft of further power, to descend striking Dizzy's office roof. He emerged, looked around and returned, puzzled, to his place of work. However, two minutes later the Air Traffic Control tower rang to ask what, or if, anything was going on at our end. Dizzy gave them short shrift, 'Dinna waste ma time.'

I had now been a Junior Technician for nearly two years, and this was far too long. Why had I not been promoted? I'd had good assessments and I had held the over signing authority of a corporal for eighteen months. I stormed into Flight Sergeant Brisbane's office and demanded an explanation. 'Oh ma God, did ah no send it off?' He rummaged apologetically in a drawer and pulled out a paper. He looked at it in horror. 'Hell, ah shoulda sent it off ages ago – ah thought ah had,' he said miserably. I snatched it out of his hand, read the date and went berserk. Holding the paper, I stormed into the Squadron Cdr's office and slapped it down in front of a startled Boss. 'Look at this,' I shouted indignantly,' I should have had my tapes a year ago.' The Boss was reading the letter when Dizzy arrived. I was asked to leave. Ten days later, I was promoted and it was backdated and paid for six months. The Boss explained that this was the best that he could do (His elder brother was Director of Personnel at Innsworth). I don't think that could be done in today's Air Force.

In every form of activity there are accidents. However, there are no accidents in the Air Force. Instead, there are incidents caused by people, or failures of equipment attributable to an individual's shortcomings. One day it was necessary to remove the starboard wing tip fuel tank from an aircraft in the hangar. I disconnected the explosive charges from the bolts that held the tank in place and went off to ask the airframe Chief Technician if the tank was empty before rejoining the team to lower the tank to the ground using a lightweight red metal cradle. Two men at the back, two at the front and the fifth man slowly undid the bolts on the upper surface of the wing tip. The tank could hold 450 gallons at 7.2 lbs weight per gallon. As the bolts were loosened the tank fell upon us. The two rear men jumped clear but the front two, of which I was one, were left to hold up the best part of a ton, for there was still a substantial amount of fuel in the tank. The tail section of the tank struck the ground first, which probably saved us both from serious injury. It then split as the weight of the tank bore down on us. We fell to the ground, badly twisting our knee joints and the cradle ripped a half-inch long tear in the outer chest of the other man holding the cradle. We lay in about 250 gallons of kerosene. We had it in our eyes, in our anus and scrotum. The other chap had his wound 'salved' by kerosene and he didn't like it. We were whisked to sick quarters where I was cleaned up and discharged to bed. The next day I was picked up by car and taken to a country house for a week's rehabilitation. I could walk, but my knees were badly swollen.

On my return to the squadron I demanded to know what was happening about the accident. It's all over,' they said, 'Sandells, a national serviceman, took the blame.' Absolutely flabbergasted and outraged at the injustice, I set out for Dizzy's office. I roared in, told them it was a great miscarriage of justice and that Geordie the Chief Technician had specifically told me that the tank was empty before we started the job. Sandells, I nearly screamed, had only undone the securing bolts as instructed. To my astonishment, Dizzy smiled with pleasure and self-satisfaction. Turning to the bevy of senior NCOs in the room he declaimed, 'Whit did ah tell youse? Ah told youse that if we got rid of Corporal Hayes we could save Geordie's BEM (British Empire Medal).

Ther widna be a chance if that lad with his ideas of justice wis around!' There was general agreement from around the room. I wasn't having any of this, and demanded to know why Sandells should be punished for something that he hadn't done. Brisbane looked indulgently at me, and gently explained that the Unit Inquiry had accepted the squadron story in which Sandells had agreed to take the blame. He was due for discharge in two months time and the punishments had been left to the squadron. He, Flight Sergeant Brisbane, had agreed a series of restrictions and additional duties, none of which Sandells would perform. Geordie would go to the Palace for his medal and Sandells would drift quietly towards Civvy Street. Did I not think that this was a fine solution? No, I bloody well did not. What about my knees, what about the chap with the torn chest, what about his legs? Why hadn't he given evidence – or had he too been got out of the way? 'Dinna fash yourself, he's alright and so are you. The Doctor himself told me.' He was not totally correct, for I have had weak knees ever since. I religiously mentioned this fact during every annual medical inspection for the next 35 years – just in case!

The good Flight Sergeant was a mass of conflictions. Peering out from his dispersal office he saw an aircraft taxiing into dispersal with a brake fire. Swiftly, he picked up a fire extinguisher and ran full speed for the aircraft. We gaped in horror, for he had picked up the wrong type of extinguisher. If he were allowed to spray the wheel area with it, an explosion would be the probable result. A large airframe corporal sprinted out behind him, calling as he ran. Dizzy ignored him and was about to set off the extinguisher when the corporal laid him out cold. It was the only way that he could have been stopped. Dizzy was carried to his office and on his recovery was told why he had been attacked. Standing, he gazed up at the burly corporal and said, 'It's a court martial charge tae strike a superior. Ah'll let you off this time!' He did not utter a single word of thanks, or recognise that he could have caused a 'Nasty.'

I was part of a small group of tradesmen who were sent off around the world to 'recover' unserviceable Canberra aircraft. I went to all sorts of places and had just returned from Idris, once Castel Benito, an airfield just outside Tripoli, when I was asked if I would turn around and return there the next day. I told the Boss that I would like to think about it for a bit. As I left his office, I met Reg. He looked very uncomfortable when told him that I'd been asked to return to Tripoli the next day. He asked if it had to be me that went and when he heard that I had an option to decline, he really brightened up. 'Tell them someone else can go, Eric, you've been away three weeks already'. Puzzled, I returned to the office and said that, on reflection, I had a lot that needed my attention at base. The engineer officer said that was perfectly OK by him. The next day, the aircraft that would have taken me out to Tripoli, somersaulted on take off. The aircraft careered off the runway and blew up near our dispersal, the largest part of the fuselage coming to a halt about a hundred yards from our dispersal area. A huge plume of black smoke and flame marked the funeral pyre of our squadron commander and my replacement. On this day the good Brisbane earned every penny of his pay. It was as though he had waited for this event all his life. Within minutes he had restored order to a chaotic situation. All the right things were done in a timely manner. He was in charge. The Inquiry praised him too.

Every Station has its black sheep and one of ours was a driver of the Mechanical Transport Squadron (MT). He was always in one sort of trouble or another. On the day of the crash he was on the airfield near the red and white painted vans of the radar site. As WD891 crashed, the ruptured wingtip fuel tank sprayed fuel all over the site, which burst into flames. Into this inferno drove the black sheep, rescuing the staff and driving the undamaged vehicles and trailers to safety. I believe that he was awarded some medal or other. Curiously, he never seemed to get into trouble again and was promoted some months later. Perhaps we need black sheep.

The Canberra was a brilliant aircraft and it was shown off by the Air Force all over the world. There were sales tours all through South America led by Air Vice Marshal Dermot Boyle, and there were detachments in India, Pakistan, and every other country where sales might be made. English Electric built a great number of aircraft in many shapes and variants and sold them throughout the world. Australia bought the aircraft, as did Venezuela to mention just two countries. I believe that both India and Pakistan bombed each other using the Canberra. Just as an aside, motoring through the near outback, north of Adelaide, South Australia in 2004, I found a Canberra sat in a field outside farm buildings! The owner had a fabulous private air museum. He had a P51 Mustang too. Among his treasures was a mid-upper gun turret from a Lincoln bomber. My day was made. My wife was bored to tears and said so.

The war in Korea was over, but the RAF felt that it needed to retain technicians. Accordingly, they offered a bounty of £100 for an extra year of regular service. I didn't read the small print, which said that it was payable on discharge from the service. However, years later when I was an officer cadet, I was reading a copy of Queen's Regulations (As one does, at this stage of life) when I realised that I was being '*Discharged* to commission.' I successfully extracted the long awaited £100 from Pay Accounts. Now, of course, it was worth a great deal less in real terms. It would have been worth a great deal less by 1992 when I finally retired aged fifty nine!

It was about this time that we were told that the squadron was to be presented with a new standard. A squadron standard is in itself a work of art and God only knows what they cost for they are individually made – I think by the Royal College of Needlewomen. They are never touched other than by persons wearing gloves. They are carried on ceremonial parades with, of course, great ceremony, and guarded. I digress, for I want to tell of the preparations for the Presentation of the Squadron Colour. As every good officer knows, there are two kinds of parade – an outdoor parade or an indoor parade. The latter kind ensures that should the heavens open, the rain will not totally ruin the occasion. We opted for the indoor version, which required a clean parade ground.

Our hangar was deemed ideal for the parade, but the condition of the floor reflected its normal usage. Some bright spark produced large barrels of caustic soda. And with the hangar floor cleared, we began to wash the area mixing the soda as we went. We wore our normal working dress and overalls. Some of us had the new fangled grey rubber kerosene boot, but most of us wore normal footwear. We started cleaning on the Thursday and finished late on the Friday evening. By this time we had discovered that hats that dropped into the 'mix' fell to pieces within hours and boots went first a soggy grey colour before they too disintegrated. Trousers and overalls were eaten from the bottom up and airmen complained of vicious looking red patches on exposed skin. Those old hairy working uniforms could stink at the best of times, but caustic soda amplified the odours. When all the scrubbing was completed, we opened both sets of hangar doors and washed the whole floor area with fire hoses before departing for the weekend. On arrival at work on Monday morning we viewed the floor. It seemed like a miracle, for the floor was almost perfectly white. It positively glistened in the morning sun. We were amazed and grateful, for we had visions of a second attempt and most of us had ruined clothes.

In parallel with all the cleaning, we were of course practising our drill. I hate drill, and I hated having to stand still for protracted periods of time even more. We practised quick march and we practised slow marching too. We marched in columns of three and we marched in line abreast. The Colour party drilled in private using a rag on a broomstick to simulate the new standard. Oh, it was fun. We painted everything around the hangar that did not move and we enjoyed lots of little organised outings into the hangar area to scour the place for litter.

The great day arrived, and I was quite nervous, for above the fire doors hung a large squadron badge, which has a fox's head as the main motif. The eyes of the fox appear to look directly at you wherever you look. I know that this may sound daft, but when the parade is formed up this damned fox looked me square in the eye. I was very conscious that this 'evil eye' affected my sense of balance. I was afraid that I would fall over. I didn't, but good old Reg Chiddick was the only man in step as we passed the saluting base during the slow march past. His frantic efforts to regain the step reminded the irreverent of a red faced dancing bear. Poor Reg was painfully aware that he was out of step, but could do nothing to remedy the situation. It was a great day, all the good and great came for the day. As the comedian Tony Hancock would later say, 'A load of beribboned buffoons!' Not really an apt description, for there were some very good men there that day.

The families and various girl friends attended the parade too and they were shown around the squadron buildings and dispersal areas. There was a small chap called Merritt on the squadron who was unusually well endowed in the genital region. As our visitors entered the ground crew room they saw a wanted poster bearing a photograph of Merritt. 'Wanted for carrying an offensive Weapon' was the caption. Merritt's young lady observed the poster with interest. 'What sort of weapon?' There was a suggestive snigger from his roommates. Realisation slowly dawned on the poor girl and a rising red tide swept over her face, 'Oh!' she cried and departed at speed. It's quite amazing what memories I retain!

During the preparations for the presentation of the colours we had painted everything in sight, including some strange large green tanks mounted on the hangar wall. At the time, we thought nothing of this, but I was curious. Fetching a ladder I attempted to open the cap. I was very hard to open but the tank was nearly full of a thickish liquid. I found a thin stick and pushed it into the tank. The liquid on the stick tasted sweet. Suddenly I realised that I had found about 250 gallons of glycol! Glycol is anti-freeze and had been used when the Station had been home to piston engine bombers. Cars use anti-freeze and it costs money to buy. We sold quite a lot before the Boss found out. Thereafter the squadron fund benefited from all transactions.

The squadron was issued with a new Bedford 1-ton truck fitted with air brakes. Among our band of qualified drivers was one Miller. He distinguished himself on day one of the truck's new life. Sweeping into the squadron dispersal he turned the right hand corner into the small concrete square parking area outside the office building. As he turned the corner, he switched off the engine and stamped on the brakes. Alas, for some reason or other – no brakes. The vehicle struck the fibreboard side of the Seco hut knocking a six-foot mousehole out of the flight sergeant's office wall. The side of the hut fell away to reveal Dizzy, sat at his desk. Miller leapt from the driver's seat, trotted through the new door up to the desk. In a single fluid movement he produced his driving licence and airfield-driving permit and placed them both in front of Dizzy. 'You'll be wanting these, I think.' I believe that this was one of the few occasions that Dizzy could think of nothing caustic to say.

I remember moments of great sadness too. An aircraft had crashed during the weekend, and I was one of a large party of airmen sent out to search the area for human remains. This is a most unpleasant job, particularly if you were acquainted with the crew. We were searching a wooded area into which the aircraft had plunged at high speed. There was very little that was recognisable amidst the wreckage. After some hours of painfully sad work, we had scraps of bodies. There was a shout from further down the hillside, and in company with the fire section flight sergeant, I walked down the slope. There, an ashen-faced corporal produced a pair of flying boots with the lower legs and feet still in them. Crying, he pointed out that the bootlaces were tied together. 'They died because some idiot played a joke on the pilot,' he sobbed. Regrettably, it was true. Someone, probably the navigator when he manned the bombsight from a prone position beneath the pilot's feet, had tied the laces together. The aircraft had suffered an engine failure at low altitude, and the Pilot, with the laces tied together, had inadequate rudder control. I don't know whether or not that was revealed to the families but there would have been little point in doing so.

The Canberra squadrons suffered a series of crashes in the early fifties attributed to run away electrically driven tail planes. There were many fatalities. Military funerals are solemn affairs conducted with dramatic flair, and they require good training, timing and, ideally, good weather. One dreadful funeral was conducted in the Binbrook village church cemetery. It was a doleful grey day, as we formed up to march down the hill to the village. The guard of honour assembled outside the Plough Inn and awaited the coffins. We marched from the church service to the graveside and the committals began. It was still raining hard. Firstly, one of the pallbearers slipped into the grave onto the coffin. This unnerved the trumpeter who blew many wrong notes. Finally, the firing party, distracted by the sobs of one young widow, produced a ragged volley. It was a dreadful unhappy day.

Modifications to the aircraft were carried out and the run of largely inexplicable crashes stopped. The modification comprised an unbroken cable run from cockpit switch to tail plane control relays. It was a long job. Reg and I became very familiar with tail planes. On one occasion, we were changing the upper and lower stop micro switches under the tail plane. We had switched the external electrical power off, and hung a No Power sign upon the generator. We had a printed sign in the cockpit, which warned others not to move the control column or tail plane switches. The aircraft batteries were disconnected, and a sign displayed to that effect. With the two of us working with our arms inside the tail plane, movement would slice off our arms like a guillotine. The tail plane motor began to run down – fast, carrying a forty-five-foot, twin-sparred tail plane with it. With both arms inside the fairing I had no time to get out. Chiddick, as usual faster in his work than I was, made no attempt to extricate himself. Instead he pressed the down stop switch that he had just finished wiring. The tail plane stopped with both our arms gently held fast. We screamed blue murder. There was an investigation and the NCO concerned left the squadron by nightfall. The Boss was heard to say that anyone who could totally ignore so many warning signs had no place on his squadron. To this day I am convinced that Reg has no idea that his action saved my hands.

The Station Warrant Officer (SWO) was a man of power in those days. This particular chap was a large genial man who enjoyed his beer. Usually a pleasant man, he wielded great power, and it was a hard Squadron commander who refused to supply manpower when asked to do so. The SWO favoured the Marquis of Granby public house in the village with his custom, and usually enjoyed a game of dominoes in the snug. On several occasions his pleasure was disrupted by a very small, middle-aged man, who would stand behind him muttering that he'd played the wrong stone, or that he would be better to do something different. Finally the warrant officer stood up, towering over the little man. 'You're too small to hit,' he said, 'but I've had just about enough, for I've stood your comments all night.' Picking the man up by the scruff of his neck he took him to the entrance hall where he hung him by his raincoat collar on a coat hook! The man hung there, suspended within his coat, legs dangling some inches from the floor. Without another word the SWO sat down to resume play. There was a good deal of laughter and the beer flowed in his direction for the remainder of the night. At closing time, he called for a taxi which arrived promptly, but the driver refused to take the fare claiming, quite justly, that he always threw up all over the cab. He had a fine reputation in such matters. Eventually, two of us decided that we'd better walk him up the hill. The SWO was a large man and it was about a mile to the married quarter area – uphill. Tired, and soaking wet because it was raining, we eventually got him home. We knocked on the door, which opened promptly. An arm shot out, grasped his collar and withdrew like a piston. The door slammed in our faces. Not a single word was spoken. As we left, we heard a tirade of angry words fall about his head. Little dogs have little fleas. Bigger dogs appear to have bigger fleas.

A few months later, the warrant officer completed his service and retired. We were dumbfounded when he appeared as one of the refuse collectors working for the local council. As the weeks passed, a change came over the collectors. Flying columns of men trotted ahead of the refuse truck, bringing dustbins to the side. The truck, which never came to a true halt, moved swiftly throughout the camp area. Later still, leaflets were inserted through letterboxes encouraging residents to put out their waste paper separately. A trailer was added to the refuse truck to collect the paper. Gradually over a period of about a year we noticed that he was no longer always present on dustbin day. Intrigued, I asked a bin man what had happened to him. 'He's a bloody star, mate,' he said. 'He's got us organised. He negotiated a productivity bonus for us and got us extra pay based on the sale of paper. We've a new work contract that has just about doubled our pay!'

I met the ex-SWO in a pub later that month. He looked prosperous and happy. He told me that he had taken the only job where he knew he could shine! Applying the techniques learnt over a lifetime in the service, he had changed the rubbish collection practices of the area. He now was a minor official and would shortly advise on the purchase of new refuse collecting equipment for that part of Lincolnshire. His teams had had their contract bought out by the council as it was too expensive and was distorting local council pay scales! Later still, he became the County Union representative. He was very popular with both men and management for he was a very good man manager. Where there's muck there's money.

Our new SWO was a red haired man of about fifty years of age. He had an uncertain temperament and there was little humour in the man. In short, he was a generally repressive spirit. A firm, fair and humorous SWO can do much to make a happy station. It was my turn to be Fire Piquet Corporal over the next weekend and it definitely was not convenient for me. One of my friends offered to stand in for me, but we needed the SWO's permission to swap duties. We went down to see him and he readily agreed to the change. As he said, 'No skin off my nose, lads as long as one of you is there.' You can imagine my consternation when on the following Monday I was charged for being absent from my place of duty. I did a quick check to see whether or not my friend had let me down. He had performed the duty as promised. I was 'arraigned' yet again and stood before the Boss to hear the SWO state that I had come whining to him on the previous Thursday asking for a change of duty that he had refused to grant. It was as if God himself had lied. I was dumbstruck and my face must have been a picture. I mumbled that the warrant officer must have mixed me up with someone else. Unknown to me, the squadron disciplinary sergeant Gilhooley was stood behind the witness and me. Signals were being passed to the Boss who was plainly disturbed. On one hand, even a Squadron Commander would not call the Warrant Officer a liar, nor could he ignore the frantic signals of his own Sergeant who was clearly objecting. The charge was adjourned. In the afternoon I was recalled informally to the Boss's office and asked if I would accept an 'Admonishment'. I declined this offer as that represented a punishment of sorts and I was not guilty. I said, brashily, that I'd take a court martial before I'd accept a punishment. The Boss was in a quandary, but the problem resolved itself a few days later when the SWO went absent without leave, taking the contents of his safe with him. The poor chap had suffered a nervous breakdown. I nearly had one myself when I heard his evidence to the Boss. It was as though God was lying to me.

In the village there was a central bus shelter, much used by 'young love'. Late one night I walked into the shelter to find it occupied by a young couple. Shortly after I arrived, a middle-aged pair joined us. Unknown to me, at least, there was a light switch, which was turned on by the man so that he could read the timetable located on the rear wall. To my surprise, the courting couple was frozen. He with his hand inside her blouse, she with her hand inside his open fly. His hand was swiftly removed, but the girl, no doubt fearing that if she took her hand rapidly away, it could be followed by some thing else, left her hand in place. The lover continued to sit motionless with a peculiar, desperate, look in his eyes. However, the girl seemed unperturbed. You might say that she had the situation well in hand.

A Meteor 7 aircraft crash-landed on the airfield and was to be repaired on site. The site was an old hangar on the far side of the airfield. I was chosen to work with the airframe Chief Technician because of my earlier experience on Meteor aircraft in Germany. The Chief was a gaunt almost emaciated man, who was known for the quality of his aircraft skin repairs. He was thought to be eccentric, but in truth he had been badly shell-shocked during the war. He worked entirely to his own timetable, and I found it more convenient to adapt to his erratic schedule. His behaviour was a trifle odd at times for he would without warning jerk his head up and utter whop wahopop ta do, quite loudly. After a few weeks of listening to this, I developed a habit of doing chicken imitations as a form of self-protection. This may not seem world shaking, but forty years later, with mind in neutral, I am still prone to cluck like a chicken. The two of us were once asked to get off a bus because of his whoops and my cluck. Many years later, stood waiting alone in the Commandant's office at Officer Cadet School, I walked aimlessly around the room, clucking away, quite unaware that the Commandant had returned. He was definitely not amused by such conduct in an officer cadet. It seemed pointless to try and explain. I didn't get much of a chance anyway.

I have been fortunate throughout my life in that others feel able to discuss their most personal feelings with me. I regard it as a great compliment. A Junior Technician asked if he could have a quiet word in private. After beating about the bush for five minutes, he blurted out that he was about to get married. I congratulated him and asked what the problem was. He prevaricated for some minutes before asking me if he was 'normal'. I was dumbstruck and asked for some time to think it over. Half an hour later I told him that there was no such thing as normal and that anything he and his girl got up to was fine, providing that it was pleasurable to them both. Anything that was not mutually pleasurable was not 'normal'. He brightened at this and was about to make off when I asked who the lucky girl was. Oddly enough, I had met this very attractive girl at a squadron function and said that he was a lucky chap and that he should send me a piece of the Christening cake. He blushed and went his way. I've lived many years since that particular conversation and even today with hindsight I would not change a word. Years later, when I was based in Aden, a small white box appeared, containing a piece of time expired cake. The box had been re-directed round the earth to find me.

CHAPTER SIX
THE MALAYAN DETACHMENT

It was now 1955, and although the squadron had deployed overseas on exercises several times we had never travelled to the Far East. The Malayan counter terrorist campaign was still going strong and the Canberra bomber squadrons from the station were deploying in rotation for three months at a time. I think that we replaced 617 Squadron.

Twelve Squadron was to be detached to Malaya where we would undertake operations in support of the army, who were attempting to defeat a communist group of insurgents led by Chin Peng, general secretary of the communist party of Malaya. The emergency had been declared in June 1948 and ended in August 1957, when independence was declared by the new country of Malaysia.

Life at the bottom

I was one of the most fortunate of the squadron ground crew, for I flew out in a Canberra B2 piloted by one of the last sergeant pilots. It was a fascinating journey, and I enjoyed the flights tremendously. We flew from Binbrook to Akrotiri (Cyprus) then on to Karachi (Pakistan), Negombo (Ceylon now Sri Lanka) and thence to Butterworth. Our first refuelling at Akrotiri was uneventful and we continued our flight the next day to Karachi. I'd never been there before, but was impressed by the line of Supermarine Attacker fighter aircraft that had obviously come from Britain. We were accommodated in an old and otherwise empty transit camp, complete with huge lines of thunder box toilets. The aircraft had a small oil leak and I was sent off to find a tin can, or anything that would hold a small amount of liquid. I hunted around the dispersal to no effect but suddenly I remembered where I had seen a can. It was in the ground crew toilet beside the big footprints that flanked a hole in the ground. I rushed off, picked up the can and headed back to our parked aircraft. 'Sahib, Sahib, the can! It is our can,' a technician cried. A few other Pakistani ground crew echoed this. I said that I was only borrowing it and would return it almost immediately. Another man came up and said,' Sahib, that is not just a can, that is *the* can. We are Muslim people and do different toilet to you.' Suddenly I realised that this indeed was *the* can and hurriedly returned it to its rightful owners. There was a great deal of laughter, I think mostly at the consternation on my face!

I had never flown at heights in excess of 45,000 feet and secondly I had never seen such clouds as those that towered above the Indian plains. I asked the Navigator why these clouds reached so high into the sky and aired my knowledge and ignorance by saying that I thought clouds never went higher than the troposphere, which was 36,000 feet. The Navigator laughed and said that I'd got everything half right. The troposphere was 36,000 feet but only if the ground temperature at sea level was plus 15 degrees C. He went on to say that the temperatures below us on the plain could be as high as 45 degrees C. and that the clouds that rose in towers above us were cumulus nimbus and could be up to 70,000 feet in height! Suitably impressed I lapsed into silence.

When the squadron deployed to Malaya, Reg could not come with us for he was due for discharge. He really did want to come, but the only way that he could do so was to extend his engagement. This gave him an unfortunate choice. He could not extend his service by less than three years. He was in love too, with a girl that he had met in Jersey while on holiday. Very reluctantly, Reg waved goodbye to us all. Most of the ground crew travelled by Hastings transport, but I went by Canberra. Reg and Jo have been happily married now for nearly forty years. (You get less for committing murder nowadays and there's no time off for good behaviour. Parole is rarely granted.) Captain Cole, USAF could not come with us either, for America took a dim view of its nationals fighting British wars while on detached duty.

I'm drifting away from the story again. Butterworth lay on the west coast of the Malayan archipelago opposite the island of Penang and was to be our home for the next six months. (I know that I said earlier that the detachment was planned to last three months. Plans can change in the military!) Our task was unusual, or at least I thought so. The idea was to keep the relatively small group of communist insurgents

Me on the ice-cream tricycle

on the move all of the time. The British had moved the villagers into large, fortified villages to prevent the bandits from stealing their food and extorting money. It was said that Penang Island alone was worth one million dollars in extortion each month. The terrorists could be extremely brutal and in one village the 10-year-old daughter of a headman was impaled through the anus on a bamboo stake and the villagers forced to watch her die. We were to see proof that Penang paid some form of protection money for, some two months later, the Malay customs officers stopped an elderly Chinese wheeling a bicycle from the ferryboat. He immediately jumped over the side of the boat and was never seen again. His bicycle proved to have a saddle made of gold. If asked very politely, the officers would show you the saddle.

617 Squadron left one of their aircraft standing alone and neglected on the old Japanese runway at Butterworth. The aircraft, we were told, had completed an outside "bunt" (loop-the-loop but starting off backwards) following a runaway tail plane actuator. This manoeuvre is not recommended, either for the integrity of the airframe, or for the continued good health of the crew. That the airframe had been badly strained was beyond dispute, but six months later there was still no interest in effecting repairs. It could still be there.

To perform our particular part in the master plan, the Air Force employed light aircraft, cameras and botanists. The light aircraft photographed the jungle looking for cultivation plots. When the botanist believed the crop ripe for harvesting, we bombed the area while the surrounding ground forces (pongoes) collected those terrorists escaping outwards from the cultivation plots. Sounds good doesn't it? It did work too, although we had a tragic accident, when an aircraft flying in on the bombing run opened the bomb doors and an electrical short in the weapon release button caused premature release of the bombs. The explosives fell onto our own troops resulting in the death and wounding of a group of Gurkha soldiers.

Life in Malaya for a group of extremely green young men was decidedly different to that enjoyed in Lincolnshire. Firstly, the sun shone and it was hot but not oppressively so. When it rained, it poured down in sheets. However, weather changes were extremely rapid. One moment the sun was shining and ten minutes later it had poured with rain and the sun had resumed its place of duty. The ground steamed.

On arrival at Butterworth the senior medical officer treated the entire ground crew of the squadron to the standard medical lectures on venereal and other diseases. At the end of his talk he introduced an Australian doctor who looked after the advance guard of airfield construction workers who were building a second runway in anticipation of the handover of the base to Australian forces. His approach was totally different and he started by quoting a saying I'd last heard on the American Forces Broadcasting in Germany. 'Easy for you, easy for others. If she's got it – you get it. If you get it, you've had it!'

He continued by telling us that he wasn't going to waste his breath telling us what could happen for he knew we wouldn't pay any attention. He told us we could come and see for ourselves in his small hospital area. One of the civilian workers of the construction company had contracted a bad infection. He left the airbase to live with his girl. She called the Air Force authorities after six months when it had become clear that he was seriously ill. The doctor said that he'd very little idea what he'd caught, but what he could say was that it was terminal and that the man was in a coma and dying. He was literally rotting to death and oblivious to the line of airmen who walked around his bed and out into the clear fresh smelling air and sunshine. I don't know how impressed the others were, but it cured me of any desire to chance my luck. The word 'chance' appeared to be a misnomer or understatement, for the statistics stated that a very high percentage of the local women that were prepared to put out for Europeans carried this or worse variants of venereal disease. That visit had a lasting effect on me. He continued by showing us dreadful looking instruments, and explained their use. I remember the catheter that was inserted into the penis. It was then expanded into an umbrella shaped thing that was then pulled slowly out of your private part, I was impressed, but there were others who swiftly forgot that part of the lecture.

Of course we were briefed on the insect and reptile dangers of the area, but the snake part of the talk was lost upon Smith with FFFFs. He was seen, only days later, poking a long snake out of the thatched roof of our workshop and chasing it through the long grass. I reflected that a limited vocabulary might not be all of his personal difficulties.

Within a few weeks the more testosterone driven were on the town. Georgetown, the main town of Penang was a delightful place and full of interest. There were two great dance halls that we favoured called the City Lights and the Piccadilly. Lots of very pretty girls frequented the place and one could enjoy a very pleasant night that could end any way that you chose. Some of the Chinese girls were very pretty indeed. They would stand so demurely, dressed in beautifully cut high collar cheongsam. Their coal black hair, almond eyes, and lively conversation made them pleasant companions. They were definitely not all prostitutes, and even if they were, this was Malaya, a country of different cultures.

Culturally, there was much to see on the island with great temples and all sorts of interesting sights. The beaches of Penang were incredibly clean and the sands seemed to extend forever. The island was very much larger than I had thought and once, when I was out cycling on a country road, a Green Line bus came around the corner! It was a number 406 and was heading for Guildford! I nearly fell off my bike. When I told the others, they just laughed and said that it belonged to a British Recreation Centre on the other side of the island. I didn't know that the centre existed and really was quite startled by the appearance of that bus.

Our accommodation was pleasant and was made up of long single storey buildings with wide verandas. Our rooms were for four persons and light and airy. And there were large electrical fans in each roof. We shared the services of two Indian bearers who had served with the British for many years. They both had families in India that they supported financially, but they seemed to prefer life for themselves in Malaya. I enjoyed talking to them both, for they remembered the days of the Raj and could spin a good yarn. We had mosquito nets, but curiously the insect life disliked my foul pipe. (I smoked a pipe from the age of eighteen years. I stopped many years later when the family stopped nagging me to throw the habit away.) Outside my room in a large tree lived a stone lizard that was about three feet in length. This lizard made a noise like two large stones being thumped loudly together. The little reptile would wait until I was on the verge of sleep before beginning to voice his love call. I hated that lizard, for I can't tell you how many times that pesky reptile disturbed my rest.

There was a large flying beetle, I believe that it was called a coconut beetle. This was an armoured beastie that could fly into a roof fan running at full speed, and emerge unhurt. When held tightly in the hand, it made a whimpering cry, not unlike that of a human child. A favourite practice was to place a beetle inside the bedclothes of the unsuspecting. Oh, very funny. One idiot put a dead snake in another's bed, with near tragic results. Whether or not it was the mate, I don't know, but a second very live snake appeared.

The humidity was such that our thick blue uniforms quickly became mouldy and we were advised to air them in the sun regularly. The idle amongst us hung their uniforms up to air, but omitted to either turn or remove them from the sun for days on end, if not longer. This had the result of producing an Oxford and Cambridge Blue effect on the tunic. It was not recommended, for a new uniform had to be bought.

There were station personnel who kept pet snakes, monkeys and the like. The snake man had found a six-foot boa constrictor, or perhaps it was a python, basking in the sun at the end of the runway. He had owned it for some months and it was growing well. He was showing off his pet to us, when he stepped too close to a tree. The snake swiftly anchored its tail end and proceeded to display great affection by attempting to squeeze him. We thought that this was part of his act, and did not react at all quickly to his yells for help. When we realised that he was not putting it on we forcibly unwound the anchor, and released him. He offered to sell the snake, but there were no takers.

An Instrument Fitter Corporal owned a dear little monkey. He called it Edwina, because of its principal habit. It passed water with a frequency that defied description. One day in the airman's club, a group of us were talking to the delightful mature WVS lady. We were enjoying our cups of tea, when the lady stood up, with a purpling face, and spat the contents of her mouth all over the place. 'That bloody monkey!' I'd never even heard her raise her voice before that day. The monkey, unseen, had peed in her cup!

While at Butterworth, a Scots lad asked me if I came from Colinsburgh, a village in Fife. Very surprised, I said that I had lived there until I was ten or eleven years old. 'I'm Jim Anderson, I used to be called "Big Jim", and we went to school together.' I instantly remembered him, despite the passage of years. He asked if I was likely to visit the village on return to the UK. I said that I doubted it, because I only had one surviving aunt left living there. 'Well, if you do go, remember that the Piccadilly and the City Lights are very respectable places, especially if you meet my Mum!' I did visit my aunt, and I did meet Jim's mother. In broad Scots, she confided to me that she had been very concerned when he was posted to Malaya, for although her son was a very nice boy, he was easily led astray. She was so relieved and pleased that he had found such respectable and comfortable places as the City Lights and Piccadilly to visit at weekends. I don't know how I kept a straight face, especially as she asked if I had been to these attractions myself I was grateful that he had warned me of any indiscretion. My aunt did ask later why I was always chuckling to myself, and I told her, and she laughed her head off when I swore her to secrecy.

I never did own a fingertip length drape jacket and stovepipe trousers, but 'Drug' Drury did. Drury was at that time going through the 'pimply stage'. Since he was slight and small, the overall effect was not impressive. I am small, but I was beautifully made, or so I thought. Drury was a complex character and he too was an aircraft electrician. If Drury was given a task, he stuck with it. It was necessary to ensure that he went to meals and stopped work with the rest of us. I won't say that he was engrossed in the job, but he was present in body if not always mind. He appeared to dream at times, but was competent in his work. He went to a tailor in Penang and ordered a bespoke suit. After several fittings he emerged in splendour, at least two inches taller, due to wearing suede leather, thick crepe soled shoes, known to us as brothel creepers. The drab colour of the suiting did not enhance his rather sallow features. On return to base, he missed the ferryboat and chartered a sampan. Mid stream the duty cloud appeared in the sky, and with nowhere to run to, he was forced to endure a pre-monsoon downpour. The suit did not like this change in the weather. By the time he reached the airbase the suit had dramatically shrunk. The buckram of the collar had twisted and distorted. One sleeve did not hang too well from a soggy shoulder pad and one leg of the trousers appeared to have shrunk more than the other leg. Despite protests, he neither took the suit back to its maker, nor did he throw it away. Instead he decided to wear it out. When he went out in this suit, he was usually alone, although Smith FFFF tagged along sometimes.

It was about this time that the squadron crew room was given a new coin-operated soft drinks dispensing machine. The representative of the firm was a large and opinionated individual, who told the assembled masses that this machine, unlike others, was thief proof. It was even, he sneered, airman proof.

Unlike machines of today, this was a horizontal metal cage rising from a table like base upon which some two hundred bottles stood on a cooled base. The top was open, but fitted with a metal grid, and a six to eight inch gap formed the part from which the purchased bottle could be lifted free. The mechanism then shoved a new bottle to the issue position. The heavy machine was bolted to the floor. When he left, there was considerable competition to be the first man to beat the machine. After a few weeks of failure, we lost interest. One afternoon, when taking a soft drink, I had an idea that worked. I emptied the entire machine, and had just finished stowing the last bottle into my locker, when the firm's representative arrived to catch me in the act. He read my nametag and rushed off to report me. I was, of course, placed on a charge. When brought before the Boss, the representative was the witness against me. The charge was read out and I was asked how I pleaded. 'Not guilty,' I said. The witness interrupted to say that he had caught me in the act of stealing. I had read the Manual of Air Force Law (a fine tome) and had determined that in order to prove theft, it was necessary for the prosecution to prove 'intent to permanently deprive' the owner of his property. When asked to explain myself I said how the representative had challenged not only 12 Squadron, but also the entire Royal Air Force, by telling the whole squadron ground crew that his machine was airman proof. I produced witnesses to this effect. The witness admitted to the challenge. I then quoted the relevant passage from the Manual of Air Force Law and told the court that there was not one single bottle unaccounted for, other than those for which money was held in the machine. The Boss demanded a bottle count, as the witness had neglected to make one. When everything was reconciled, the Boss threw the case out; saying that the witness had been ill advised to challenge technicians of his squadron and bade him a curt Good Afternoon. Five minutes after the departure of this gentleman, I was recalled, 'Don't *ever* presume to quote the Manual of Air Force Law to me again, Hayes. Oh, by the way,' he said, 'Flight Sergeant Brisbane never doubted that you were innocent, but he was very interested to hear how you would wriggle out of it! He said that you weren't the type to steal'. I didn't know quite how to respond, so I didn't.

    I haven't said much about work, but we did work doing our normal day and night flying training, interspersed with furious activity as those cultivation plots ripened. Our aircraft were usually lined up in a single row of ten or twelve aircraft, facing a 50-yard wide concrete hard standing, drained by a deep concrete monsoon ditch. One day a strange Canberra was diverted to Butterworth with a bomb 'Hang up'. The strange aircraft was marshalled into an empty space in our line as number five. I was walking down the hard standing in my little one piece, short trouser khaki overall ensemble with matching floppy hat, when I saw four armourers standing beside the stranger aircraft. They positioned themselves, holding a canvas stretcher beneath the bomb doors, and indicated to the marshaller that he should give the 'Bomb Doors Open' sign to the crew. I didn't pay a great deal of attention but, at the very extreme corner of my vision, I saw a large green bomb appear, lying on the opening bomb doors. I took three rapid, long strides and threw myself into the monsoon ditch. All I could hear were thumps as other bodies joined me in this haven. We lay hands over ears, waiting for the explosion that would destroy the entire line of aircraft. There was silence. Dead silence. Cautiously, we peered over the parapet of the ditch. It was like a scene from a tableau, for all the principals were stood still, each frozen into his position at the time that the 1000lb bomb had appeared. The only difference was that the armourers remained in the stretcher-holding position. The stretcher canvas was split and a large green bomb lay on the concrete. The marshaller had chosen to join us in the drain. Lesson one; 'Ask what size the bomb is before accepting strangers.' We had assumed the 'hang up' to be a 25lb practice bomb. In fact it was an iron bomb that required the bomb to be dropped from a height necessary to spin the fuse to the armed position. (Many Argentinean bombs did not explode in 1982 because they were dropped at low altitude.) We blamed Air Traffic Control for failing to elicit precise information from the aircraft before it landed.

Butterworth

More and more Australians began to appear at Butterworth as their airfield construction squadron arrived. They were to build a new runway for their Mirage fighters that would arrive sometime never. The runway utilised bits of the old Japanese runway and extended through the site of their wartime NCOs Mess. Five female skeletons were found there, or so we were told. The Australian airmen were usually bigger and older than we were, and I had the misfortune to work with them in the battery charging room and in some component areas. They were not subordinate to us, and were very definitely airmen of a different country.

Australians do not like to be told anything by anybody, especially

Poms. One day, an Australian officer told me to get his men out to him on the airfield. They were playing cards on the floor. Two of them were sitting on one leg with the other extended. I'd never previously seen people sit in such a style. They told me that they had been 'ringers' on cattle stations at one time and that they found it comfortable. Everybody sat like that at home. But I digress. The officer repeated his order to me,' Get 'em out'. 'We'll just finish the hand, Corporal,' said one with a knowing look of contempt. Something snapped in me, I'd had this treatment once too often. They would do anything that they were told to do – but only after a good twenty minutes of some kind of prevarication. I used to retire to the toilet nearly crying with rage and frustration. I heaved the speaker to his knees and belted him. The reaction was totally different to that expected. Man One said, ' You shoulda said you *meant* it, Corporal.' Man Two declared in broad Australian mournfulness, 'You didn't have to *hit* him, Corporal.' The victim of my attack, pulling at his front teeth said, 'Christ, the worm's turned.' Not another word was said. I had expected a load of 'aggro' coming my way. This was not the end of it though, for the group turned me into a mascot!

A large fat Australian storeman made life difficult for most of the Australian detachment. He was storeman, and a storeman stores. He didn't like to issue anything at all. When my group of reprobates encountered problems, they would threaten the storeman. 'Do we have to get the Pom Corporal, Fatso? You know, the one that dished Fred up.' Meanwhile I would be cornered and frog-marched to stores. Under the guise of holding me back, they would push me to the stores. 'Don't lose your rag, Corporal, but this fat slob won't give us what we want – and it's there on the shelf.' They then put their heads together as if in conference, muttered at each other, and apparently came to a decision. 'Give him one last chance, Fred, before we let the Pom go.' It always worked, and the bemused storeman would gracelessly hand over whatever they wanted. I'm five foot seven, and they were all six footers!

Airfield guard was a shared duty, and sometimes there would be Australian guards and a British Orderly Officer and Sergeant. The bomb dump was supposed to be patrolled by two groups of two guards. The dump was concealed within a plantation of coconut palms. The Aussies would know roughly the times at which the Duty Officer and Orderly Sergeant would do their evening and night inspection and plan accordingly. There were paths through the plantation, and one Australian would be apparently asleep under a tree, and his rifle, would be just outside his reach. The second guard was concealed in the undergrowth. Finding the guard 'asleep,' the officer said, 'Get his rifle, Sergeant.' At that precise moment, guard two would shout urgently from the darkness,' Halt, halt, halt or I fire,' and immediately blast off a few rounds. The sound of three or four rounds of .303 ammunition ricocheting down through the palm trees at night can be quite disconcerting. Quite naturally, the Duty Brits departed at high speed. The next day, the Aussies would be up to mischief again. 'You could tell that the officer was a public schoolboy, couldn't you, Jim?' said one. 'Nah can't say that I could, Fred,' drawled the second. 'Well,' the other stated with grave conviction, 'didn't you see how the officer pushed the Sergeant out of the way so that he could lead?' They were incorrigible, but I liked them, and their twisted sense of humour.

The toilet facilities down on the aircraft line were rudimentary and consisted of a canvas enclosure inside which was an elegant hole in the ground and a line of 45 gallon oil drums suitably cut down and bent to form a seat of sorts. Each day, a measure quantity of petrol was poured into each drum. Cleaning was affected by tossing in a match. As our numbers swelled with the arrival of the Australians, so did the number of oil drums. The Aussies improved the cleaning system by fitting a vent pipe, or chimney, to each drum. Later, they added a connecting pipe. There was now a long line of thunder boxes, probably about fifteen or twenty of them in total connected by piping. The Aussie duty bog man slopped in the fuel and moved, away, chatting to his mate on the other side of the canvas that screened off the area. Continuing his conversation, he flipped a match into Bog 1. The combustion swiftly spread up the line. There was a roar of agony as a 'passing peasant' rose vertically from Bog 20, clutching a badly scorched rear. I'm glad that he was another Australian.

Alas, one of the Australians was nearly the death of Dizzy. There was an engine change in progress using an Australian crane and driver. Dizzy had to interfere with an operation that was going quite well without him. 'Left a wee bit, right a wee bit, up a wee bit.' The Australian looked at his watch, dumped the engine back into the carriage cradle, wound in his jib and began to drive off. 'Where, the hell do youse think your going?' screamed Dizzy. The Aussie leant from his cab, smiling. 'Twelve o'clock, mate. Lunchtime. Thank God that I'm not in your lot.' He drove off, and poor Dizzy suffered a stroke on the spot. He made a marvellous recovery, but the old venom had gone. Strangely, the squadron regretted that part.

One day we were told that we would be staying for a further few months in Malaya and that replacement aircraft would arrive in the next week. The first pilot out of the replacement aircraft was a broadly smiling Captain Cole USAF. He couldn't fly missions, but he could fly in replacements!

Georgetown, the principal town of Penang Island, is a multi cultural port that is home to many ethnic groups. Malays, Straits Chinese and Asians lived together in virtual harmony. There were many differing religions, and each celebrated their individual Holy Days with processions and Feast Days. This particular celebration was Deepavali, a Hindu Festival. Led by a sacred white bull the procession contained devotees who had pierced their skin and faces with a network of decorated bamboo sticks. On some men the structure rose some two or three feet above their heads and extended left and right for about a foot beyond extended arms. The devotees appeared to be in a trance, and surrounded by their chanting followers the procession moved up the main street past the covered markets. The covered market had a second floor containing restaurants and eating places of all kinds and from one such vantage point I could see the whole parade. Something must have upset the sacred bull, probably a small Chinese boy with firecrackers, for it suddenly lunged free of the handler and tore off into the market area. It was unbelievably chaotic, for children took advantage of the turmoil to pinch a wallet or two from stalls. Hawk-eyed stallholders sent their minions off in hot pursuit. Hindu merchants appeared to hire little Chinese boys to whack the bull away from their premises. (They couldn't do it themselves for fear of a riot.) It didn't matter much about not having a riot because we enjoyed the next best thing. An Australian announced that he had always wanted to be a cowpuncher. He went down and did just that! There was outrage on one side, laughter on another, and indescribable chaos, in the midst of which the bamboo-spiked devotees came out of their trance as they were jostled on every side. It looked very dangerous for their continuing health. Safely away from the conflict, I settled down to my meal of steak and chips. No meal is complete without tomato sauce and a bottle was produced. Still watching the fracas beneath me, I shook the bottle vigorously. This was unfortunate because the waiter had removed the cap – everybody except me got a share. Even the walls and ceiling were dripping! I paid up and left the scene.

Young airmen are not always as nice or considerate as their Mothers might wish. Taxi drivers are judged by the same standard, especially if they are Straits Chinese. Stepping ashore at Mitchell Pier in Malaya from the ferryboat from Georgetown we asked the taxi driver if he knew where the main gate at Butterworth was located. A smiling face declared that indeed he did, and quoted an outlandish fare. Five of us leapt into the cab and off we went in the darkness. The main runway, at that time, ran at right angles to the road, which led along the coastline. As we reached this point we asked the driver to stop as one of us was going to be sick. This was certain to bring the cab to a halt, for no driver wants his cab to stink to high heaven for days thereafter. We leapt out, gave three cheers for the driver, and legged it across the airfield to our accommodation. Out of breath and panting like old warhorses, we were laughing together when we discovered that there were only four of us present. We had lost Dave Porter. We retraced our steps back across the airfield to find a softly moaning Porter. When he saw us, he spat nails of rage, for he had fallen down a drain hole from which the cover was missing. None of us had stopped to help him despite his cries for help. The taxi driver did come to help and, smiling broadly, announced, Your friends all gone, John – twenty dollar I help you out. No twenty dollar – you bloody stay.' With no small banknotes in his wallet. Dave paid a fifty-dollar fee for retrieval. His anger was compounded the following day when the Medical Officer told him that he had quite serious injuries to his knee. He was still limping around when we returned to Lincolnshire.

My younger daughter concedes that I was semi-presentable when young!

Memory is a funny thing. Sometimes you're absolutely sure of something, and the next day you are not so sure that it did actually happen. So I'll tell the story anyway. A very senior officer was to speak to all station personnel and their families. The young officer aide de camp introduced him and he began, 'Officers, Ladies, Senior NCOs and Wives, Airmen, Women.' At this point, an outraged shudder ran through the assembly. As one, every female in the place silently, but pointedly left. I recall the total consternation of that senior officer who had chosen to preface his talk with such an outmoded and insulting salutation. Those days are long gone, thank God.

It seemed that it was time to return to England. How did we know that? The local traders, usually anxious to extend credit, were now more than equally anxious to collect their outstanding debts. The local traders always knew before we did. How they know I've no idea, but I have been on detachments worldwide and know of no more reliable indicator of imminent change.

CHAPTER SEVEN
THE JOURNEY HOME

The Squadron was return to the UK, and once again I was allowed to fly back in a Canberra bomber.

At RAF Negombo, in what was Ceylon, I met an old friend from Boys' Service. He was a ginger haired lad called Byard. In the course of bringing each other up to date with our news, he said that he'd changed his name to Cockshead! I said immediately, that it would take a lot for me to change my name to something as daft. He smiled at me, and said that he'd been paid a lot to do just that. Apparently a childless neighbour had left Ginger, whose parents were dead, a considerable sum of money on condition that he legally took his name. There was no decent retort that I could think of, nor could I think of anything to add.

We continued on our journey home, landing at Karachi once again, but this time the row of Attacker fighters was sadly depleted. Either the Pakistanis were scrapping the aircraft, or they had crashed a considerable number of them. Wrecks were piled into an area of the hard standing. I believe that I saw fourteen aircraft on the outward journey, but now saw only six that superficially looked as though they could be in flying condition.

The mention of Karachi brings to mind another incident. The navigator, an officer, had bought himself a gold Rolex oyster watch, (The ultimate status symbol of the time). The toilet facility near to his accommodation was a long line of permanently mounted thunder boxes, reached by a short stairway. As he wiped his rear, his watch fell off his wrist and dropped into the darkness below. The watch was very expensive, and the Navigator no fool. Pulling out his pen, he carefully marked the hole and returned to his room to try and get a magnet from somewhere. He spent a pleasant afternoon fishing with the magnet on the end of a pole, attempting, without success, to attract the steel back plate of the watch. Finally, he spoke to some of the locals, offering a hundred rupees to the man who found his watch. The locals stared rather oddly at him before rising up and walking to the thunder box line. One opened a small door, walked up beneath the line, picked up the watch and handed it to a bemused, but grateful navigator. He paid the reward like a man should. Apparently, Karachi camp area had served as a staging area for up to thirty thousand troops during the war. The thunder boxes had not been used in years!

The following morning we took off for Habbaniya in Iraq and unfortunately suffered an electrical fault that would stop us continuing the flight (No 2 Inverter). It would be some time before spare parts could reach us so we joined in every activity with those stationed there. We spent I think two weeks living in a room that was tent topped and wooden walled. It was hot during the day, but it was bloody cold at night. The midday and midnight temperatures could differ by over thirty degrees! One night a pack of wild dogs tore through the encampment – there must have been hordes of them. They fought each other and barked and yelped like hell. Some of the airmen lived in tented accommodation and they didn't like the dogs at all. I learnt later that a good number of dogs were rabid and this helped to explain the sticks used to speed the dogs on their way. Their way? Yes, anywhere but in our camp area!

Shortly after this fracas, station personnel staged the great dog race, known as the Hab Stakes. Dogs were captured and fitted with rudimentary muzzles. A number was painted on their sides to identify the intended runners. We assembled the marshalls, who wore their pyjamas and green towels. The Chief Marshall wore a red towel above his tastefully cut service issue striped pyjamas and flip flops. The course of about a hundred metres was between the tented lines and marshalls, who stopped the premature exit of participants from the track, blocked the gap between tents. Each marshall carried a wet knotted towel. Dog handlers were assembled in pairs and at the order, 'Handlers to your dog', the hapless dog was helped to the start line. 'Prepare your dog.' At this order, the dog was held by the scruff of the neck with his tail lifted up, facing the start line. The chief marshall dropped his flag; a paraffin rag was applied to the dog's rear and the dogs were off. Some were away before the paraffin touched their rear, while others were disqualified for going up the course on their bottoms! It was obvious that many of the competing dogs were professional participants for I saw the remnants of previous numbering on their sides. I did feel sorry for the dogs, but these were the dogs that had terrified us in the darkness days earlier. The muzzles were definitely degradable and most dogs were free of them before they reached the end of the course. We were fifty miles from Baghdad, there was nowhere to go and nothing to do except go to the outdoor cinema. We made our own amusements and really enjoyable days were few and far between. It's not an excuse, but that was life.

To those of us who frequented the station cinemas on the bases all over the world I offer the introductory images for the Tom and Jerry cartoon series. Who of us now still does not cry, 'Good Old Fred!' when the Directors name of Fred Quimby is screened? I grant you that many of us will do so under our breath – but the thought's still there! I recall an amorous and far too long love scene that was screened at Gan, an island base in the Indian Ocean. There were a great number of raspberries and coarse comments from the front, when a stentorian baritone voice thundered from the back, 'Silence in the cheap seats!' The place broke up in laughter and derisory comment. It was a memorable moment – well, obviously it was.

The inverter arrived, was quickly fitted and we were off home. I was pleased to get home, although I had made a dreadful mistake when sending my Christmas cards from Butterworth. I bought a job lot of fifty identical cards, and as I was writing number thirty, I read the printed message inside. 'This is a card for you to say that a little gift is on the way!' Hell's Bells! I'd posted the lot off two days ago! Now I was deeply in the mire, for I couldn't tell everyone that I hadn't read the message. What could I buy that wouldn't cost me the earth? I had a stroke of genius – yes, another one! I would buy thirty pairs of straw slippers lined with toweling. They were cheap as chips and if I bought them in every size from four to ten I should be fireproof, especially if I bought more than one pair in the more popular sizes. In the event, all addressees expressed surprise and pleasure – genuine or not! I have meticulously read the printing in every Christmas card I've sent since then.

I did a night guard duty at Habbaniya wearing vest and pants, pyjamas, shirt, pullover and tie, topped off with working blue and a borrowed greatcoat and gloves. When the wind blew, I froze. Many years later, I warned friends off to the Gulf War to take their woollies. In the belief that I was exaggerating they ignored my advice – I do hope that they froze too. (35°c at midday - 10°c at night - too great a temperature differential for a European!)

CHAPTER EIGHT
MALTA AND THE SUEZ CAMPAIGN

Finally, the squadron personnel all got back to Binbrook. Reg had been discharged from the service and I missed him, not least because he was the provider of transport to Grimsby where my love of the time did live. I didn't stay long in England, for within weeks we were very suddenly scrambled away to Malta. The ill-fated Suez campaign was about to open. I had been to a Wednesday dance in Grimsby and returned on the late night bus. On arrival at Binbrook, I was told to pack my bag for an extended overseas stay. I was given forty-five minutes to return and board a squadron aircraft bound for Malta. A few hours later we touched down, not at Luqa the main airfield, but at the Royal Naval Air Station at Halfar. A grinning Sergeant Gilhooley handed me a printed map showing accommodation and cookhouse and told me to report to a place that he pointed out at five thirty the same morning. By the appointed hour the assembled squadron ground crew waited for a briefing. It was short and to the point. The squadron was split into four parties. One group was to paint all aircraft main planes with alternate black and white stripes. The second party was to service all aircraft and the next two groups were to manhandle bombs from lighters onto waiting bomb trolleys. I'm glad to say that I didn't get that latter job, for those who participated in this jolly outing were absolutely exhausted at the end of the day. There was, however, one bright spot in our day. The Royal Navy still issued rum! The good Brisbane announced to all that the first bloody airman who let the side down by appearing drunk would regret the day for the rest of his short life. The rum issue ceremony was quite splendid in its formality. Your name was called, and you saluted, or off capped if you were naval. On presentation of one's china pint pot, a measured quantity of diluted navy rum was poured in. In front of all, you had to drain the mug before the witnessing naval officer. We then returned to the mess for a meal. This was served in the then new fangled compartmentalised plastic trays. The airmen, to a man, never even saw what was on their tray. Glazed eyes stared into infinity as they shovelled their food down. Nobody got drunk, of course...

The naval personnel were a friendly bunch, but they definitely had different social habits. Aircraft carriers apparently do not enter harbour with their aircraft on board in time of conflict. Instead they fly off all aircraft and enter harbour with all their fuel tank vents open. Remember that I am no seadog and that I could be wrong. When all these aircraft arrived at Halfar, the naval duty crew comprised two WRENS. All the aircraft had to be parked into wind, their cockpit covers fitted and in many cases the aircraft had to be not only wheel chocked fore and aft but also tied down. It was a foul night and the wind was gusting spitefully, but the two girls did the lot. We were impressed.

This same night I joined some friends in the local bar called the First and Last. I know of several with that name on the island. The place was packed with the ground crew of three RAF Canberra squadrons and a considerable number of naval ratings from God knows where. At one end of the bar was a table upon which a naval girl was dancing a form of strip tease. She was singing a traditional ditty about 'This old shirt's been a good old shirt, but I don't need this any more.' There was a great deal of masculine, mostly naval, encouragement. A group of Wrens entered the bar. Assessing the situation, they formed a Leucrian Wedge formation led by a formidable female Petty Officer. 'If you take one more stitch off, Mabel Bloggs, we'll never speak to you again.' Fists flying, they forced their way through the obstructing mob to reach the table dancer as she prepared to discard the final shred of clothing. She was pulled down into the maw of the wedge and was seen no more by mere man. I enjoyed the whole thing tremendously.

I had never been to war and I watched in fascination as the bomber force went into action. The Canberra force had three squadrons at Luqa, more at Takali and three squadrons at Halfar. In addition, there were at least three further squadrons based at Akrotiri in Cyprus. The Valiant force was based, I think, in Cyprus too. Day and night an endless stream of aircraft took off or landed at all three airfields. The runway at Halfar was not very long and a fully fuelled and bomb loaded aircraft appeared to scrape the wall at the far end of the runway on take off. I believe that after the operation ended some bright spark worked out from the data manuals that they should never have even tried.

Almost as suddenly as the operation had begun, the war came to an abrupt halt. America did not share our concerns for the future of the Suez Canal and the Hungarian revolution was in progress. The Russians too were displaced and offered to start World War Three if the British and French did not cease hostile action. There was, of course, a lot more to the situation than that, but the effect was that we stopped bombing missions. The bomber force had worked up to become a truly efficient force based on the Herculean efforts of both air and ground crew. Now, there was a tremendous sense of betrayal and anti-climax and we had little to do. Idle hands make mischief, so the adage goes – and we did make mischief.

How the big fight started I don't really know, but surely it was not a wise move to permit the US Sixth Fleet to put into Malta for rest and recreation at this particular time. I was told that the fight started in the Gut (a lower section of Valetta known for its dens of iniquity and much else). I remember the area as possessing one of the foulest toilets on earth. At the top of the Gut, not far from the Egyptian Queen pub was this corner toilet. Any prospective user of the 'comfort' facility could be seen working his lungs prior to entry in the vain hope that he could rush in, pass water and return to the outer atmosphere before having to take a second breath. The air within reeked with harsh ammonia gases with a rich bouquet of sour urine enriching the gases. Alas, there was none of the wine taster's piquant undertones – here only true sewer overtones attacked the throat. It has all been changed now, but the workers must have enjoyed the renovation. Enough – back to the fight.

The Naval Air Station at Halfar during the Suez campaign

Grand Harbour, Malta

Legend has it that an altercation began between a large Bosun's mate from the USS *Forrestal*, a large aircraft carrier that had put into Grand Harbour with its escort vessels, and a Sergeant of 45 Commando Base Unit. The troops deeply resented the lack of American support for our Suez operation and reacted badly to any form of American criticism. Each rallied his own to the Colours and a jolly good punch up started. I suppose that it must have been well after midday when all this occurred. The British had ready access to reinforcements and the fight was on. Firstly it expanded throughout the Gut, and quickly spread up Old Bakery Street. The American Shore Patrol arrived and left the field in disarray when all united to send them on their way. The off duty personnel of seven bomber squadrons slowly joined in the fight, as did the crew of the USS *Spiegel Grove*. They in turn called for help from other US warships. The British Military, learning of a larger than usual fracas, sent in the whole of 9 Provost from RAF Takali. The Army weighed in with, I think, the East Anglian Regiment. It was not immediately clear whose side they were on. Their instruction, we found out later, was to end the fighting. The Maltese Police, with similar instructions, joined in strength when the fight spilt over into Valetta proper. There were 1002 policemen, including the mounted branch. Castile Square became a turbulent mass of fighting men. I was caught up in this outer fringe of activity, in Old Bakery Street, and earnestly punched any who reeled away from the inner circle of combat. I felt quite safe in this until some ruffians did me over. I retired to bleed in a safe corner.

The fight, which had now lasted many hours, came to a crescendo, when the entire crew of the *USS Boston*, a guided missile cruiser, was deputised as Shore Patrol and landed in force at the bottom of the Barracca lift. This lift climbed the ramparts of the harbour to the level of the road entering Valetta. American Shore Patrols are neither questioning nor gentle. With batons swinging they tapped every American seaman that they could find smartly on the head and removed his carcass to the waiting lift. From there he was hustled half, or even fully, unconscious, to a waiting boat, which sailed him off to the *Forrestal*. I suppose that at its height the battle involved about a thousand American seamen, about five hundred airmen, eight hundred police, four hundred soldiers, and two hundred Air Force or Army policemen. That of course does not take account of the Maltese volunteer forces that must have greatly swelled the number of combatants.

When the dust and the bleeding stopped it was rumoured that the casualties exceeded those of the Suez campaign. The Courts Martial went on for quite some time on all sides. Valetta shops were relatively unharmed, but some wondrous black eyes and split lips were to be seen everywhere. They were worn with pride, rather like the wounds gained on St Crispin's Day.

One Court Martial was special, in that nine Marines had held the upper floor of the Egyptian Queen (known as the Gyppo Queen) against all comers for the entire duration of the event. The premises of the establishment lay at the top of the Gut. They apparently had reserved their defence in lesser courts of justice and now faced the legal might of the Royal Navy in the old court martial rooms once used in Nelson's time. Friends had tipped us off that this was likely to be an interesting case. With due pomp and circumstance the President, Judge Advocate and lesser minions filled the lower levels of the courtroom. The accused were arraigned and the charges against the Marines read to the crowded courtroom. They were asked how they pleaded. The answers came, one after the other, 'Not guilty.'

The prosecution presented their case, stating that the interior of the public house had been utterly destroyed and vast quantities of liquor had been consumed or removed to the upper floor of the building. Several plain-clothes policemen had been badly manhandled, as had many others. Some had been in uniform; others had been less clearly identifiable. Indeed the witnesses went on to state that a pile of bodies had frequently filled the stairwell throughout the day. Ultimately, the Marines had surrendered to a posse from the Royal Navy Shore Patrol. The moment we had all waited for came at last when a spokesman for the Marines spoke in their defence. All the accused, when serious fighting had broken out elsewhere, had sprung to the defence of the ladies. Thinking that they could more easily defend the girls from the upper floor, they had taken them upstairs and guarded the stairwell! Their only motive had been to ensure their safety. Obviously they had had to drink some fluids throughout the long day and night, thus accounting for at least some of the missing liquor. There was a tremendous cheer from peasants in the courtroom, and the defence was quickly passed to those outside who had been unable to get in. The cheers and laughter at this clever defence from the courtroom quickly spread throughout the town. It was clever because of many factors. Firstly, the Naval Legal people could not deny the lady status of the Maltese girls trapped in the Gyppo Queen. It was political suicide to do so – for the Maltese had not been too keen at Britain using the airfields as a base from which to bomb Egypt. To name their womenfolk prostitutes would not be a good move at all. Moreover, the Maltese press was present in the courtroom in force. The *Times of Malta* could have a field day. The uproar continued for some time, despite efforts by the court officials to obtain silence. Finally, the President adjourned the Court for an hour. When it reconvened, the Court amid jubilant cheers ruled that there was no case to answer.

We were planning our return to the UK and one of the Squadrons found that on arrival home they were to begin a month long high intensity flying exercise. This new task was deeply resented, for they had worked day and night at full stretch for weeks. There was great muttering in the ranks, for they felt that such an exercise was unnecessary following their efforts in Malta. Firstly, the ground crew worked a protracted go-slow, the effects of which were offset by the diligence of the NCOs. However, despite their best efforts they could not sustain the workload. This problem was reported upwards and dramatic events followed. Suddenly the ground personnel were sent all over the place for a few days of change. Some went to work at the local brewery, a lucky few joined naval ships, while others visited different stations and the like. To my surprise, my squadron was included in this recreational activity and I was sent to join HMS *Totem*, a super T Class submarine lying off Sliema. I had never been on a submarine before and was quite anxious because I could feel uncomfortable and vaguely claustrophobic in the rear of a closed-in truck. I was the only airman of my squadron to board this boat. As I climbed down through the conning tower a bewhiskered face said,' I know you, I belted hell out of you in the ring at Dartmouth.' Hidden behind a 'full set,' I had no idea who he was, but I had no recollection of any matelot beating hell out of me at Dartmouth, or anywhere else for that matter. I told him that if I could see what kind of animal lived behind his nest of hair etc. My dread moment of claustrophobia passed and I followed him through to the mess deck. I was made most welcome by all ranks; all of them were keen to tell me of their strange life underwater.

One young man sticks in my memory. He was a would-be submariner who had volunteered for 'boats'. His present ship was a destroyer. I was told that the Navy had no selection process other than a trial week. Apparently the Admiralty, in their wisdom, placed a volunteer aboard a boat and, at the end of the trial period, asked the mess deck if he was compatible. Only then did the Navy conduct the selection process. I swiftly saw the wisdom of this move, for if it was possible to be in the wrong place at the wrong time, then this lad could do it. He trod on fingers as he came down off his bunk, he knocked over cups with regularity and worst of all, he was a moaner. I doubt that he became a submariner.

On the surface the motion of the boat was uncomfortable, but once submerged to a decent depth, the boat just slid through the water with no pitch or roll. I had thought that a submarine was easy prey to specialist aircraft, but the First Lieutenant educated me in the mysterious ways of submarine warfare. First, he stated, you must find your submarine. Then, having found it, you must hold the submarine in your detection systems long enough to attack it. Submarine crews have a host of unknown tricks up their sleeve and he was kind enough to explain the simpler ploys to me.

After a week at sea we returned in the evening sunlight to Grand Harbour. The view of the harbour from Valetta is superb, but the view from the sea entering harbour is staggeringly beautiful. The crew lined the deck, as tradition demanded, as the trumpets called from St Angelo or St Elmo, I'm not sure which fort made the call. A Marine band, by coincidence, was playing 'Retreat' in Hastings Gardens high above us on the ramparts of Valetta. On that balmy evening there was a fabulous Mediterranean sunset, the intensity of the colours quite unusually bright I stood on deck overwhelmed by emotion, triggered no doubt by the realisation of how many generations of British seafarers had enjoyed such a moment. Now, with the traditions of the Senior Service uppermost in my mind, it seemed that I had a football in my throat. It was a very special and treasured moment of my life.

It was with a great sense of anticlimax that the bomber force returned to the UK. I didn't have much time to moon about though, for I was to be posted overseas. Where was I to go? Back to bloody Malta for three years!

CHAPTER NINE
MALTA AGAIN

Well I was no stranger to Malta, and in a perverse sort of way I looked forward to learning more about this famous little island group. Aha, you thought that Malta lies all on its own at the bottom of Sicily, didn't you? Well, it doesn't, for there are two islands that are inhabited, Malta and Gozo, a third small outcrop of rock Comino, and a large lump of rock called Fifla used for target practice by the armed forces. Holidaymakers make a beeline for the two bigger islands nowadays, for massive investment since the 1970s has totally changed the landscape. Nelson's seamen knew Malta as the island of yells, bells and smells and I saw no reason to change their view while I was there. I like to hear church bells, and to see churches with two clocks! One clock was a dummy designed to confuse the Devil. The population is devoutly Roman Catholic, but during my time I thought that the administration was about fifty years behind Catholicism elsewhere. I preferred the Methodist Church in Floriana for they were a jolly congregation who enjoyed their faith and social brotherhood. I joined the Malta Choral Society shortly after my arrival and thoroughly enjoyed singing my heart out throughout my stay on the island.

Malta has an incredible history, reaching back to the earliest seafarers of the Mediterranean region. Phoenicians, Greeks, Spartans, Romans, Carthaginians and Arabs landed and lived on the island. The Knights of St John of Jerusalem set up home here after being driven out of Rhodes by the Turks in 1544, and the French took the island during Napoleon's time for a short while before the British moved in. There is a strong Italian influence, but the Maltese themselves are unique. A quick look at their written language will confirm that view. There are lots of Js and Xs, with the letter H occurring unnaturally often. I don't think that there was a written language until the 1930s. They are, or they were in my time, a proud people who felt put upon by the British. This was in part true, for Britain had blocked various employment prospects for Maltese labour fearing that there would be an inadequate workforce for the Royal Naval dockyard. When I arrived in Malta there was considerable political friction between the two main political parties and the British government. Dom Mintoff, the Labour Party leader, reviled Borg Olivier the reigning premier. Mintoff's Malta wanted either to be a part of Great Britain – or to be independent. The Church, in the form of Archbishop Gonzi, did not care for the Mintoff vision nor did he sympathise with Mintoff supporters, most of whom he offered to ex-communicate. This reaction appeared to me to be a trifle drastic; particularly as most of the staunchly Roman Catholic island workforces were actually Mintoff supporters. I had the good fortune to have friends living in Pawla, just around the corner from the Mintoff home. I liked the man and respected his viewpoints as being in the best interests of the Maltese. Others hated his guts!

I came to like the Maltese people very much, particularly the women folk, who appeared to be the stronger characters. The men, especially the young ones, appeared to have a simple life credo. 'Why buy a book when you can join the library?' and if married, 'Why run after a bus when you've caught it?' The young male attitude towards the fair sex left much to be desired, especially if you were the father of nubile girls!

Corporal Hayes was set to work in the main aircraft-servicing hangar. RAF Luqa was not only a staging post for British aircraft transiting the Mediterranean, but the home of a squadron of Avro Shackleton maritime reconnaissance aircraft. In addition, Shackleton aircraft based at Khormaksar (Aden) were flown to the island for minor and major servicing. Minor is a title not a fact, for the work schedule involved a great deal of work.

I'm not sure that the other Corporal and myself actually had a Sergeant electrician in charge of us. If we did, I saw little of him. We two Corporals had three Maltese working with us. All three were good value and could be totally relied upon. One of the trio, Tony Triccas joined the Air Force in England some three years earlier only to be posted back to his homeland. He had applied for the Far East. He was always cheerful and hard working and was commissioned many years later. He completed his career as a Squadron Ldr ground engineer officer responsible for C130 Hercules transport aircraft.

We used to have all sorts of Air Forces. There was the Near East Air Force (NEAF), Middle East Air Force (MEAF) and FEAF, which was of course the Far East Air Force. Just to give you an idea of the changes wrought upon the Royal Air Force, I joined an Air Force that was 600,000 men strong, I believe we numbered 52,000 when I left the service, and numbers have dropped since then. In fairness, the capabilities of today's aircraft of today are much changed too.

After I had been in Malta for about a year the Shackleton was grounded worldwide for a major defect in the spars of the mainplane. Repairs would take a long time and we, the electricians, had little to do. One day, when I was reading the manuals, I realised that the aircraft could carry all sorts of weird things. It could, for instance, carry great racks of rocket projectiles, torpedoes, depth charges and even a lifeboat. The aircraft was fitted with a comprehensive bomb station, which was home to a great box of post office relays (a mode of technology long superseded by electronic devices), which allowed the bomb aimer to select a variety of options. Wiring plugs could be moved around to create other options. Some of the options had remained unused for years and few of the air and ground crew were familiar with anything other than conventional 12/24-way bomb selection. The Boss of 38 Squadron asked us if we could fit an aircraft up to fire rockets. Over confident as usual I said that we could, inferring by the tone of voice that the answer was, 'of course'. We beavered our way through the diagrams and very swiftly we showed off the working system using a series of lights to indicate the various firing sequences. You could fire pairs, two pairs or a bloody great broadside of sixteen rockets. Our greatest problem was to find the rocket rail assembly. After telephoning all over the island we were told of a great underground complex where they had everything – including the rocket rails. I think that the place was called Tal Handaq. The aircrew were impressed and asked if we could find a lifeboat that they could drop when the aircraft was airworthy. This time, I hedged my bets and replied, 'Maybe'. Still, with little to do we could roam the island's cubbyholes and unknown places. We found an airborne lifeboat – the last of its line, for they were never very effective in use. They could be dropped by parachute, but the boat tended to break its back on striking the water.

During the period of inactivity I moved about a bit working in all sorts of places. One of these tasks was to stand in for the electrical NCO from the visiting aircraft flight, which was at that time combined with personnel of Station Flight. They handled the odd aircraft that belonged to the station. One of the aircraft was a twin-engined fighter-bomber Beaufighter from WW2. I remember it particularly because I spent a morning looking for the second engine electrical generator – there was only one. Remember the adage, 'When all else fails – read the book!' One other event sticks in my mind. A Hastings aircraft, a four piston engine transport with a tail wheel arrived en route to Cyprus. The ground party refuelled the aircraft, which took off only to return within a very few minutes. The Flight Engineer complained that all four cylinder head temperatures had shot off the top of the instruments and that there had been reduced power available. I'm not sure whether or not it had actually taken off. It transpired that the plane had been fuelled with AVTUR, kerosene. This was not a trivial error, for the engines burnt petrol. There was great activity trying to find an empty fuel bowser to drain off the fuel. Bowsers are rarely left in an empty state. The crew was not amused, nor was the hierarchy. Heads would undoubtedly roll at some future time. I was relieved to find that I had had no part in this exercise. After a great deal of delay the fuel was drained and the correct fuel loaded. Once again the passengers and crew embarked. The engines turned and the aircraft departed for the runway. Ten minutes later the aircraft returned to dispersal with exactly the same symptoms. Heads were scratched, and great discussion took place. Finally, with a cry of 'Eureka' the airframe Sergeant announced the solution. This was an aircraft that sat on the ground with the tail down but flew with the tail horizontal. It follows, he said, that there must still be kerosene in the tanks, for we had not drained the aircraft with the tail up on trestles. Frantically the ground crew raised the tail; opened the drain valves and drew off the offending fuel. On the third attempt, and days behind schedule, the aircraft lurched off on its lawful duty.

Now this little event, with all the lessons learnt, proved very useful to me many years later. Now the Flight Engineer of a C130 Hercules, I was en route to Belize via Freeport in the Bahamas. Freeport was not a usual stop, but was used by Hercules aircraft on Caribbean training flights. The airfield was host to a large flying club and there were about fifty light aircraft of all sizes, shapes and colours parked about the airfield. Holding forth at the bar of the club was a large, deeply tanned man of about fifty years of age. By his manner he was important, and he was certainly forthright in complaining bitterly about his little single-engined aircraft. Apparently it would fly perfectly for about twenty minutes and then the engine would begin to splutter. That meant, of course, that he couldn't fly the thing over water and as the USA was across the water, he was not going far. I listened to the tirade and said, 'Water in the fuel.' The man spun round, his face reddening. 'Damm it, do you think that I'm a fool? I had the guys from Bendix check the aircraft out. There was no water whatsoever.' He turned away from me sneering, 'Bloody Brits think that they know everything.' I returned peacefully to my beer, but I did ask a man on my other side if he had seen the Bendix team do the job. The man, a friendly sort, muttered that it was probably finger trouble on the pilot's part. But yes, he had watched them drain the fuel system.

The plane was an older variant of a famous light plane that was equipped with a tail wheel, so I asked if the crew had lifted the tail into the flying position during the draining process. 'Nope,' he responded, 'I didn't see them do that. Why, is that important?' I said that it was, because the fuel collector tank would probably have quite a bit of water in it and if the aircraft was not held straight and level in the flying position it was unlikely that they could have drained it off completely. My fellow drinker abruptly left my side, and brushed past me to poke the stomach of the owner of the machine. 'Hank,' he explained swiftly, 'the Brit's probably right, let's go down and take a look.' The bar emptied as we all trooped down to a nearby hangar where a strangely forlorn looking aircraft rested upon two main wheels and a tail wheel. The tail was swiftly lifted up onto a trestle, and I was shown the collector tank with its neat little drain tap at bottom of the rear face. Cracking the tap gently open, I placed my finger underneath the tap. I closed the tap and sucked my finger. It was water all right. 'There you are,' I said smugly, 'water in the fuel.' The owner swore furiously, 'I paid those robbers $1000 to fix that airplane. I haven't been anywhere in it for two months!' 'Okay,' I said, 'get yourself a big glass jug from the bar and a camera.' 'A camera,' he spluttered, 'what the hell for?' 'Evidence, you fool, don't you want your money back?' I smiled smugly. There were howls of approval from the gathering drunks. To cut a long story short, we took a considerable quantity of what was indisputably water from the tank, and took many photographs and witness statements. I'm sure that he got his money back. He was mad enough to really try!

Later, as I drank his beer, he asked how I had known so certainly. I told him about the Hastings incident of long ago. Hercules crews of the RAF were always given a superior welcome at the Freeport flying club thereafter. The incident did my reputation no harm at all, for I had two newly qualified flight engineer Sergeants with me at the time. I was pleased about that.

Ah dear, I've drifted from the point, for I am still in Malta. Tony Triccas bought himself a harpoon gun, a snorkel and a pair of blue rubber flipper fins. All were highly desirable items usually beyond the financial reach of young airmen and he had saved for some months to pay for them. He was therefore determined that he was going to catch something – anything in fact. There are some lovely beaches on the island and Tony headed for Hajn Tuffieha with all his kit. He scrambled down the steep pathway to the beach and prepared to display his prowess. I was not present, so I can only recount the tale as told to me. Apparently, after some hour of failure, he saw a flutter of a bottom fish in the sand. Swimming down to a depth of about ten feet, he speared the fish. Rising jubilantly to the surface, fish on harpoon, he held the lance aloft with a triumphant yell. This was followed immediately by an agonised yell, as the fish slid down the harpoon onto his hand. Sensing that all was not well, the others swam out to him and dragged him ashore. He was in considerable pain, and his hand began to swell up. His companions, with unusual presence of mind, poked the fish into a rolled up towel, and helped Tony up the steep path to the car. By this time his hand was about two inches thick and his elbow had become swollen too. Taking the quickest route, they rushed him to Sick Quarters where an almost unconscious Triccas weakly greeted the doctor. The offending fish was displayed, the ambulance was immediately called and Tony was driven off to the David Bruce Military Hospital at Mdina. The fish was either a lionfish or a stonefish, but whatever it was, the delicate little frilly bits were highly poisonous. Tony emerged from hospital, none the worse for his adventure, but even twenty years later the affected hand was appreciably thicker than the other hand. I am not sure whether or not he used the harpoon again.

It was about this time that we encountered sabotage. Sabotage, especially when conducted against aircraft electrical systems, is a most serious matter. The first wire found cut was very obvious and easily found and rectified, but you could not be sure that this was the only damage. I received the most idiotic of orders; I was to check the single Shackleton undergoing major servicing in the hangar twice daily for signs of sabotage, and sign in a special ledger that no act of vandalism had taken place! There are many miles of cables running through an aircraft of that size and a hundred or so panels behind which there could be all sorts of mayhem. I pointed this out to the Senior Engineer Officer, who merely replied that I should do my best. I totally refused to sign anything – on the grounds that it was impossible. In the weeks that followed we endured further little snips of cables here and there. The Special Investigation Branch (SIB) arrived and I swiftly discovered that Corporal Gee and myself were the chief suspects. Our tools and wire cutters were removed for forensic testing and for matching against the affected wire endings. A feeling of great gloom spread over the entire ground staff. The Maltese workers felt that suspicion would fall on them and they too were unhappy. Once a superior official of the SIB suggested to me that I had cut the cables of a 150 man hour modification that I had just completed. Furious, I dragged him to the aircraft. I dragged him along the tail section, into the bomb bay. I walked him up the length of the bay then showed him how difficult it was to lead the cables through into the cockpit section before threading them through into the nose section. I was livid. 'Do you think that I'm going to cut my own cables in the certain knowledge that I'm going to have to do it all again? Don't be bloody stupid.' Surprised at my outburst and a little disconcerted by the violence of my reactions, he left. After about three months there was no more sabotage. However, the very close inspection of the aircraft wiring revealed that another aircraft, recently brought into the hangar, had been damaged by sabotage in the distant past. The repair had been appalling. Some idiot had said to himself that in one hand he had 100 cables and in the other he also had 100 cables. He just joined them, and tested each system to see if it worked. If the galley light fuse was removed, then the lights in the nose went out. Nose light fuse out, then the instrument lighting on one side failed. It was unbelievable. We removed the bomb doors to gain proper access to the 'repair' to find that even the cable joins were below any standard whatsoever. The damage had been caused at Ballykelly in Northern Ireland three years earlier. There's supposed to be four inches between every in-line crimp cable repair, but here there were 300 repairs within a foot. We were asked to repair the aircraft in two days by a young Electrical Officer. Pulling out one cable, I asked him if he knew where it came from, and then taking the other end, I asked if he knew where it terminated. There were no identifying sleeves on any damaged cable. He then grasped the size of the job and asked how long would it take. We said that in all honesty, we didn't know, because we would have to follow every one of the cables through the aircraft. In the event it took a week.

Another unusual event happened under strange circumstances. Prior to the Second World War the Dutch had a colonial empire in the east. During the war the Japanese invaded and occupied that empire and although Dutch forces and former colonists returned to the colonies they found considerable opposition to their return. I suppose that to be an understatement for by 1957 refugees were pouring out of the former Dutch East Indies. Among those who fled by air was a group who got hold of an old Martin Mariner flying boat. I believe that several of these aircraft operated between Sumatra and the Netherlands, although I know of one that crashed at Asbadan in southern Iran in 1958. However, despite the condition of their aircraft they managed to reach Malta. The aircraft was an amphibian and equipped with landing gear that still worked so they landed at the main airport of Luqa. Apparently they were unable to continue due to problems with the main safety circuits. I was told that the engine fire system didn't work by the Electrical Officer, and that I was to do the minimum work on the aircraft necessary for the safety systems to work.

Taking my Maltese colleague Sam Sammut with me I walked across the dispersal area to the huge twin-engine aircraft with its cranked wing, twin tail and four bladed propellers. I had never seen a flying boat of this size before, nor had I ever seen any wiring diagrams for an American aircraft! Sam and I agreed that without diagrams this was likely to be a long job. Mercifully, we found that most of the aircraft books were with the aircraft, safely nestling in their proper stowage. What was equally pleasing was that the books were written in English for the aircraft had belonged to the US Navy in its youth, as the dark blue paintwork attested. We were astounded by this find, for the aircraft looked to be in a bad state if the flaking paintwork was anything to go by.

It was a pleasant summer day and Sam and I sat in the cockpit (old speak for flight deck) with the side windows open, reading up on how the systems worked and trying to establish where the major components of the engine fire system were located. We continued our research until rudely interrupted by the Electrical Officer who asked if we were finished. I didn't like the man very much under normal conditions, but this was a bit much. I told him that we were reading up on the problem and suggested that the job might take some time. This did not please him, nor did my comment that until we knew where the bits and pieces were, we couldn't fix anything. However, when I showed him over the various unfamiliar panels and components of an American built aircraft, he began to understand. I was glad that he was present when I dismantled a large plug and socket, because it fell apart in my hands spilling pillars of rust where electrical pin connectors should have been. The aircraft was horribly corroded. God only knows how it had functioned thus far. Everything electrical was a mess. By agreement we repaired everything that fell apart while finding the fault, because we could not do any less. Finally, at the end of a week, Sam and I could truthfully record that the fire system now worked. We repaired a lot of other systems too. The civilian crew was very grateful for our efforts, as were the women and children who had been packed into the aircraft galley and sleep area. I explained that I could not sign the paperwork associated with anything other than the fire system, but they could not have cared less. If we had not had the books and the diagrams, I doubt that we could have done the job. Looking back I probably gained a lot of confidence in my ability to fault find on unfamiliar aircraft from this episode.

One of the difficulties faced by any technician, tradesman – call him what you will, is that non-technical people assume that everything you do is either easy, or that you caused the fault in the first place. Then there is the problem caused by the elapsed time necessary to complete any piece of work, I learnt very early in my career that a nut and bolt were designed to fit together. I have seen absolutely no evidence that they were designed to come apart, particularly if they are located in a practically inaccessible position. Faced by a fault and asked how long it will take to rectify, it is far better to say that it will take an hour, when in fact the job takes only ten minutes. Tell authority ten minutes when it actually takes an hour you become an instant shit. Reverse the numbers and you can actually become well thought of – if only for a few fleeting moments.

This leads me to the only work that I ever did on a Vickers Valetta, known affectionately as the 'pig'. As far as I know there was only one such aircraft based in Malta and we, Aircraft Servicing Flight (ASF) had just finished a 'Minor Inspection'. As mentioned earlier, the word minor is a misnomer, for the inspection involved a great deal of work by all aircraft trades. I had worked extensively on the aircraft that was about to fly the mandatory air test following such work.

The aircrew like to see that the ground crew get an opportunity to fly on occasions like this, feeling that if the ground staff are willing to fly in the aircraft that they have worked on, there can't be much wrong with it. I was more than happy to fly, for I knew that I'd get the opportunity to see the island from the air. Malta is only fifteen miles by eight miles and the air test would take some time. As always, I took my tool bag and multimeter with me. Reaching the threshold of the runway, the engines were checked and with kind permission from the tower, we trundled into the air. After some minutes of flying around the island at about a thousand feet, all the ground crew were glued to the windows as we entered the turn over Grand Harbour. The flight deck door opened and the co-pilot emerged to ask if there was an electrician on board. I owned up to this and was told that the main undercarriage was stuck in the mid position and would go neither up nor down. It would be deeply appreciated if I could persuade the gear to move either fully up, or better still fully down! Now there's not a lot that you can get at whilst airborne, and I thought that I might well be forced to panic. However, I remembered that I had worked on the micro switch inside the throttle quadrant, but to get at that meant removing the co-pilot's seat and taking the side panel off the throttle box. This sort of thing could take time and I didn't know how long we could stay airborne. Anxiously, I asked the crew how long I had to do the job, to be told that I'd a couple of hours and no more. The seat was removed; the panel whipped off and the micro switch revealed. I pulled the fuses and checked the wiring. (In those days cables carried identification.) I replaced the bad connection, refitted the micro switch and replaced the fuse.

To my intense satisfaction the gear moved swiftly to the fully up position. After a few moments, after adjusting the airspeed, the gear was selected down – and it moved down and locked! I waited for the applause, but it did not come so I refitted the side panel and seat before returning to the passenger section. With the air test complete we made an uneventful landing and taxied into dispersal where we all dispersed to our various sections. I was quite disappointed when the co-pilot expressed the views of all on board by saying that I had found the fault so quickly that it must have been my fault in the first place! What a bunch of bloody ingrates.

My social life underwent change when I did the shopping at the local grocers. He passed me the bill and reading it I began to protest. 'Allura, you English are all the same – you want something for nothing,' he spluttered in bad temper. Other Maltese in the shop nodded sullen agreement. 'Hang on Tony,' I yelled when an opportunity presented itself, 'you've *undercharged* me by a pound!' The atmosphere totally changed in an instant. I never carried another shopping bag. I was invited to feast days, to weddings and to the inevitable firework display. They really are a most hospitable and friendly people. The fireworks, or the manufacture of them, accounted for at least several deaths and minor injuries each year. I once found a group of youngsters steaming the explosive from the shell of a wartime bomb! However, I digress, yet again, from the main point.

The recently published Defence Council Instruction (DCI) really interested me. There was to be an essay competition, open to all, which could earn the winner a place at university. I spoke with the educators and decided that I would write a thesis on Maltese history. I began my research and writing, but was disappointed with my efforts. I told Tony the grocer who sent me to his cousin, a lecturer at the Royal Malta

University. He scanned my effort and suggested that I concentrated on one part at a time and sent me on to the curator of a major museum. He spent hours telling of Roman, Carthaginian and Greek involvement. In turn, he passed me to the curator of a museum specialising in the period of the Knights of St John. I was passed around from expert to expert and my work was thoroughly vetted. Eventually, it was typed and a few photographs, taken by another of Tony's cousins were added to the bound final edition. Unsurprisingly, with help from the most erudite of Maltese society, I was advised that 'my' effort was of great interest to the judges. They noted with concern that I wished to take a BA degree, whereas the scheme was intended for those who wished to take a Bachelor of Science degree. Would I change my ambitions? In Chapter One I described my mathematical abilities as zero. I explained this unfortunate fact to the committee, who then offered a six-week preparatory course. Thinking for a few brief moments of my total bewilderment with the abstract I declined. I went back to read the DCI, where no mention whatsoever was made of BSc degrees – or any other specific degree for that matter. I then complained bitterly to those who should have known better. I must give the Command Education Officer his due – he did fight on my behalf, but with no avail. I used to know a lot about Maltese history, and I certainly met a great number of interesting people during my research. It was not time wasted.

The political life in Malta was in a state of flux for there was great indecision among the political leaders. There were great strikes of the naval dockyard workers called by the unions, and reviled by the Church. There were many who favoured independence and an equal number who would prefer to remain in close association with Britain. The world was changing and the Maltese knew that the British were reducing their forces dramatically. There was a real need for the Maltese people to look after their own interests. The strikes extended to other areas and even the Police withdrew their labour. I was knocked off my bicycle by a car in Pawla Square right under the nose of a Maltese policeman who did not even acknowledge the fact that the car did not stop. On another occasion an Air Force Sergeant drove past a group of strikers in his new car. Giving them a vigorous Vee sign he eventually drove on with not a single piece of glass left in his car and with new design bespoke bodywork, created when a hail of stones descended on the vehicle!

The American Sixth Fleet continued to visit Malta for rest and recreation and it was a fine sight to see those enormous vessels in Grand Harbour. The carrier *Forrestal* lay in the harbour surrounded by other ships of the battle group. The guided missile cruiser *Boston* was the largest escort, but there were smaller vessels of many kinds including the USS *Speigel Grove*, which was an assault ship. Some ten of us from RAF Luqa were invited aboard. American ships are 'dry', but what they lacked in alcoholic drink they made up by offering us enormous meals served American style. I was not accustomed to such lavish meals. An assault ship carries a large contingent of marines – the so-called' leathernecks'. (Apparently they are called this because they used to wear uniform collars lined on the inside with leather – I thought that I should air that gem.) They are a pretty tough bunch and once ashore would set out to thoroughly enjoy themselves. If this meant the occasional violent dispute, then they were ready to oblige. I saw perhaps the most brutal fight that I have ever seen between a very large Maltese waiter and a Marine Sergeant of equivalent build. The fight took place in a Castile Square bar. How it started I don't know, but they stood toe to toe slugging it out. Teeth and blood flew everywhere and the spectators both Maltese and American did not attempt to interfere. I certainly had no such intention for a little lad can get hurt – badly hurt – interfering in a gentleman's dispute. The fight continued with little advantage to either man until a large and competent looking Maltese waitress picked up a large metal tray and felled her countryman. Both combatants were dragged to chairs and the cleanup task began. As the waiter recovered consciousness he stared across at the battered marine whose eyes were rapidly closing above split cheeks. 'Who won?' he asked. The American smiled through split lips at his equally battered opponent and said,' She did!'

There were other distractions too. In the perverse manner of airmen we could both enjoy the distress of an American aircraft carrier pilot landing his fighter on the main runway and commiserate with him at the same time. The runway has a hump in the middle and the unfortunate pilot thought that he was about to run out of runway and retracted his undercarriage! The airline traffic too had its mishaps, when a Vickers Viscount taxied smartly into the Air Traffic Control tower, causing major damage to the aircraft. The aircraft was towed away to a deserted area where airline passengers could not readily see the wreck. The aircraft was declared beyond economic repair, but the airline technicians decided that the more valuable and re-useable components should be removed and returned to the UK. Their bean counters balked at the price of sending their own technicians and we literally fought to present ourselves as the logical personnel to conduct the aircraft strip down.

Eventually, a team from one of the squadrons got the contract, but I did earn a bit of extra money stripping out electrical and instrument components.

Valetta is a charming city built on a peninsula and entered through a single gateway that leads onto the main street. There are delightful cafes serving delectable pastries both savoury and sweet. The coffee served in Valetta is of a distinctive, rather sharp tasting bean. I believe it is the Victoria bean, but I'm not sure of that. The cafe extended onto the pavement and I particularly liked to sit there watching the daily promenade. There would be pretty girls with their boy friends, trailed by chaperones who showed various degrees of disinterest in their charges. There would be other girls more closely chaperoned by their smart mothers who were determined that no undesirables would engage their daughter's interest. Groups of young lads would parade up and down the street offering noisy compliment or insult.

There was a very nice modern Italian cafe at the bottom of the street adjacent to St John's Cathedral that served that bitter coffee so popular on the island. To this Victoria bean coffee add the delightful cheese pastries and the spectacle of the nightly promenade up and down the main street and the true spirit of Mediterranean life is revealed. Of course I was merely a spectator, but one can look. In the earlier hours of an evening the more mature and smarter ladies of Maltese society would frequent the Cafe, I particularly remember a striking buxom, if slightly overblown, lady who was known to the Brits as 'Lambretta' because her long black hair was styled into an enormous wheel-like bun worn high on the back of her head.

It is the small happenings in life that combine to illuminate our existence and without them life could become very dull. It had rained and the sky was overcast when I looked out of my friend's front window of his first floor apartment. A small black and white Jack Russell terrier approached a pole carrying electricity along the road and into the houses. The dog had a purposeful air about him and he moved in the confident cocky way that so endears the breed to us. The dog paused by the pole, lifted his right leg and peed, as was his usual habit when passing this spot. As I idly watched, the dog yelped and sprang backwards away from the pole. Mystified, I continued to watch, as the little dog walked around the pole with a puzzled look, resolutely returning to continue passing his urine. A second strangled yap alerted me to the fact that all was not quite right. The dog now moved away from the pole and sat down, possibly to cool his injured parts. Gazing at the pole, the little dog cocked his head first one way and then another in contemplation, before gathering himself for a third attempt. He *always* urinated here and was not about to stop now. With jaunty step he reached the pole, lifted his leg and sent a copious stream of liquid towards the pole. A pained yelp of despair came from the little dog and he shot off up the road with his normally perpendicular tail firmly clenched around his buttocks. What made the incident so very funny was the air of outraged dignity emanating from the little dog throughout the incident and the totality of his defeat. The insulation values for electrical supplies that existed in Malta at that time probably meant that the dog got an 80-volt shock each time he relieved himself! Much more would have killed him.

On a lighter note, a new carillon of bells had been mounted in Pawla church and the Archbishop was to conduct the opening ceremony. The church faces the square, which was packed with the population. Most of those present were workers from the dockyard and their families. These people were among those that the Archbishop had threatened to excommunicate because they had voted for Mintoff in the recent elections. The dais had been built up to a height of about ten feet and was sited at the front of the church. The various dignitaries were assembled on that dais from which Archbishop Gonzi would ring the first of the new bells. Dressed in his robes and wearing his official red hat he pulled the rope of the bell. The bell tolled, and the diminutive cleric neglected to let go of the bell rope. He rose into the air, hanging on for dear life, with his robes fluttering about him. There was silence as the elderly gentleman soared upwards, followed by guffaws of laughter from the vulgar throng. A quick thinking junior cleric grabbed the bell rope and heaved the archbishop back onto the dais. The crowd applauded enthusiastically and, I must say that the old gentleman looked quite pleased at this unexpected approval from what he knew to be a hostile audience.

I felt that I should be promoted to Sergeant and made appropriate inquiries through the General Office to determine my place on the promotion list. You can imagine my indignation when I discovered that I had moved from fifth on the list eighteen months earlier to three hundred and tenth! There was weeping and gnashing of teeth. I knew that my annual assessments had been good and I had been awarded a commendation by the Air Officer Commanding for doing my bit during the last year. What had happened to scupper my chances? Had I been credited with the sabotage? I asked to see the Air Marshal. This kind of interview is, or certainly was, granted once per year at the time of the Annual Inspection conducted by him of all facilities under his command.

Smartly attired, as one is for such occasions, I stood before the great man. I remember that he had a ten-inch spotted china cow on his desk that bore a legend informing all that 'his cow did not need their bull'. He told me that I lacked the appropriate educational qualification for promotion. I protested that this was impossible, for I had taken the Education Prize in Boys Service. He reviewed my records and stated that although this was so, I had not taken one of the exams for some reason or other. I countered this by saying that I had taken the exam separately and that I had captained the RAF Boys Boxing Team at the time that this particular exam had been scheduled. I added that it was surely impossible to win the prize if I had truly not taken one of the seven exams. He considered this, and said that he would have the matter investigated. Three weeks later I again stood before him, to be told that no additional records could be found and that this closed the matter. He then asked me to sit down. I needed to do just that. After chatting generally for a few minutes he produced two envelopes. 'Take this one to the Senior Medical Officer (SMO) and if he says, "Yes" you are to take the second envelope to the Education Officer at RAF Takali. Good afternoon and good luck.' Mystified and pretty downhearted, I left.

I presented envelope one to the SMO, who read the contents without any explanation to me. 'Come back at two o'clock,' he grunted. I arrived at the appointed hour to be given a rigorous medical examination by various people on his staff. Eventually, I ended up once more before the SMO. Unsmilingly he said, 'Yes'. Again he offered no explanation, ignoring my request to be told what was going on. The next day I pedalled off to Takali, arriving all hot and sweaty. Entering the education section I asked where the Education Officer could be found. The man turned out to be a young national service officer who, when he read the contents of the envelope, went red with rage. 'Do you know what this says?' he demanded. Truthfully I said that I had no idea. 'It says,' and he ground out the words in fury, 'this man has been fingered by the system – he needs 5 O levels in a great hurry – help him. Signed Uncle Fred!'

After asking who I was and where I was based he wandered around the room, obviously thinking fast. 'I'll do it, but I'm not doing all that work for just one person. Find at least another three people who want to learn in a hurry.' To cut a long story short, I found others and all four of us gained five O levels in six months. In another three months I gained one A level in Ancient History (Flying Officer Higgs, or was it Hicks, was a Classics Scholar). With the arrival of the certificates I was summoned to the Air Marshal's presence once again. He told me how pleased he was, and that I was going back to the UK to the Aircrew Selection Centre with the aim of becoming aircrew. He suggested that I try for Flight Engineer! Until this point I had not even guessed what authority had in mind – but it sounded good. I thanked him for his interest and retired, pleased and bemused.

CHAPTER TEN
DECISION TIME AND AN INTERLUDE WITH VULCAN BOMBERS

I returned to England to attend the Aircrew Selection Centre at Hornchurch, a place I dimly remembered from my Boy Entrant selection. A comprehensive medical inspection was followed by curious aptitude tests that left me confused. There followed various team leadership tasks and a variety of paper problems that had to be solved by small syndicates. Throughout the selection process we all wore overalls and displayed a candidate number upon our person. This apparently smoothed out any advantage possibly gained by the sartorially elegant. I passed the selection and some weeks later I was offered training as a Flight Engineer. However, I was still due to be discharged from the Air Force in some eight months' time. I really did not know whether to stay with the devil I knew, rather than venture out to meet the devil that I did not know. I decided to look at job prospects.

Firstly, I was offered the post of production manager in the embryo Birdseye frozen food factory in Grimsby. Two brothers who, most unexpectedly, hung on my every word, conducted my interview. They loved to hear Service yarns and they really seemed to be very pleasant people trying to make a name in a new industry. The salary wasn't up to much but there were good prospects. I lost that position because I dithered, unable to decide what I wanted. Secondly, I could go to Antarctica with the whaling fleet helicopters. Throughout this period of indecision I was stationed at Scampton and worked on Vulcan bombers.

Despite my impending release from the Service I was sent on a course at RAF Waddington, on the southern side of Lincoln, to learn all about this fascinating new aircraft. The Vulcan MK2 was the first truly alternating current generating aircraft operated by our Air Force. There were all sorts of new equipment. Constant speed drives controlled by magnetic amplifiers, transformer rectifiers etc etc. This was a new era, promising quantum leaps in the production and use of electrical power. I enjoyed the course immensely. The aircraft itself could be a nightmare to work on, but life could have its amusing moments too.

I have not met a single member of Vulcan aircrew who did not love that aircraft for its brilliant performance. I was at the Farnborough Air Show when the Avro test pilot, Roly Falk, lifted that huge delta shaped bomber into the air and immediately rolled the aircraft through 360 degrees! Yes, we all knew that the aircraft carried no load and had only minimum fuel on board, but who had ever seen a medium bomber rolled at take off into a near vertical climb? The perspective of the ground crew was somewhat different to those who actually flew the machine. It was an absolute pig to work on as an electrician. Access to components was not a strong design feature, particularly in the earliest versions.

Once, when we were attempting to parallel the alternators I had a minor accident. The aircraft engines were alight and running at medium power and I was about to enter the aircraft hatch situated midway under the fuselage. I was stood on a stepladder and, as usual, had shed some of my protective clothing so that I would be able to actually move around when inside the hatch. I had earlier removed the cover from some relays. As I moved my head into the hatchway, I struck the back of my head on a projection. As I swiftly removed my head, I placed my nose on the electrical contactor. This hurt, so I removed my head to once again strike the projection. In turn, I returned my nose to the contactor and did a sort of woody woodpecker act before falling off the steps. At this moment I 'threw a wobbly' and had a sense of humour failure. The nose took ages to heal – and it hurt!

CHAPTER ELEVEN
AIRCREW TRAINING

I had to make a decision regarding my future. I knew only the Air Force – and now I had a chance to better myself within that service by becoming aircrew. I felt sure that I could pass all the technical examinations, which would face me during the next eighteen months. I decided to stay with the devil that I knew.

My fellow students were a pretty mixed bunch of people. The majority were either ex Boy Entrants or Apprentices from the first four aircraft trade groups. (Airframe, Engine, Electrical, and Instrument technicians in the rank of Corporal and above). Later, the Air Force was to realise that they were selecting the best of their technicians who had been trained at considerable expense – only to expensively retrain them to do another job. Future generations of bean counters would bring a halt to this practice. I believe that there were originally nineteen of us and fortnightly phase examinations quickly placed us in what appeared to me to be an unchanging order of merit. I worked like hell, and was always placed between fifth and ninth – even when I accidentally found the examination paper prior to the exam! Those above me did no work at all and simply 'swanned' through the course. As in all courses, we lost a few of the course members. One was brought to court for having carnal knowledge of a minor, but the demure, pig tailed, slim schoolgirl we saw in court bore absolutely no resemblance to the young woman who had virtually seduced our colleague. The affair cost him dearly. Another seemed to be congenitally economic with the truth and he too left our group. In total, we lost six of our number during the period of the course.

I think that I remember Blackpool best of all the training schools. We were based at RAF Watton and enjoyed our trips out to the seaside resort. Of course we went to the Tower Ballroom. Most of my colleagues were taller than I was. (Unkind souls would say that everyone was taller than me – but that's not true.) One by one they had congregated at the bar where a full bosomed brassy blonde barmaid held court. She had apparently asked one of our number what they did for a living.

A tall dark haired lad, known as the Bishop for his habit of blessing a girl before attempting to remove her knickers, replied that they were in the 'Force'. She took that to mean the Police, and the size of their drinks measurably increased. However, my arrival at the bar looked likely to prejudice this perk. Without turning a hair, Jim introduced me as Eric Hayes, up from London to review the security arrangements of Mullards, a large electronics factory nearby. I never flicked an eyelid, and she seemed impressed.

This happy state endured for a few weeks until there was a major fight in the ballroom. The manager appeared at the bar and told the barmaid to call the Police. Inflating her not inconsiderable lungs, she bellowed over the noise, 'It's all right, They're here already!' I must say that I admired my colleagues, for moving into an extended line across the width of the ballroom they cleared the dance floor saying, 'Move along there'. We cleared the floor without incident and returned to the bar to find the manager and barmaid laughing their heads off. The barmaid had been aware of our true profession for weeks! Nevertheless, the ballroom staff was most impressed by the ease in which we had defused a potential riot.

Just prior to leaving Watton I was witness to an unusual incident. Our Engine Phase instructor was a Maurice La Haye who also taught a group of Sudani ground tradesmen. They had all but completed their courses in our country and on this particular afternoon were scheduled to conduct engine runs on a twin-engine transport. The engines, Alvis Leonides radials, had been stripped and re-assembled by the Sudani group. Maurice, wearing his mud brown jacket of authority, addressed the group in his usual breezy manner. He outlined the procedures to be followed and detailed the tasks for various individuals. Then he asked the time-honoured question: ' Okay, before we run them – Do you have any bits of engine over?' There was an uncomfortable pause before two of them each produced some piston rings! Maurice froze, as did we trainee Flight Engineers, as he gazed in disbelief at a number of oil control rings. Speechless, Maurice began to walk around the internal perimeter of the hangar. He did about three laps, during which time he did great damage to the remains of his thinning hair. He then told the Sudanis to take the engines out again. They were to get a meal and return to the hangar. There he would meet them and there they would all stay until the engines were stripped and reassembled correctly. This incident had a marked effect upon Maurice. He volunteered for aircrew the next day, saying that even if he was a lousy instructor he was at least the equal of any of us.

Our next training school was RAF Melksham in Wiltshire. We quickly found that the Station Commander did not like our free wheeling group. He placed quite a few irksome restrictions upon us and we didn't like that. When an opportunity to revenge ourselves was presented, we worked all night on a new camp building scheme, carefully walling his car inside blind walls of the partially constructed building. It was some weeks before a hawk-eyed representative of the Ministry of Public Buildings and Works (MPBW) realised that although the external dimensions of the building were as specified, there appeared to be a room missing. About fifteen years later, an older gentleman from the security services, who was conducting various screening interviews of airmen aircrew, asked me whether I had trained at Melksham. I answered and told him when I'd been there. He looked at me very strangely, saying that he had been the Station Commander at that time, and then asked if I had been one of those responsible for walling up his car. I never said a word, I just smiled and so eventually did he.

When we finished our ground training, we found that the flying training school at Thorney Island near Portsmouth was not ready to accept us for some months. We were sent to 'hold' at RAF Colerne near Bath. This unit operated some four squadrons of Hastings piston engined transport aircraft and was sited at the top of a hill – where else? We had a simply lovely time, for we went as supernumerary crew (bag carrier) everywhere the Hastings went. The Hastings was at that time the only medium range transport that the Air Force possessed. We had the Beverley C Mk1 complete with fixed undercarriage - a flying Dutch barn that cruised at 9000ft at the incredible speed of 135kts. The turbo prop Argosy had not yet entered service, and I believe that was about it. The Britannia, Comet and other exotic aircraft were some way off. I flew with the Engineer Leader of 24 Squadron, a Welshman, who spoke each day to his wife in Wales on the telephone. He spoke in Welsh, and he spoke for at least an hour at a time. I was allowed to carry his tool-kit, which was so heavy that it was as much as I was capable of. Taff Owen truly was an engineer and he thought nothing of the odd propeller change and completely stripping the Claudel Hobson fuel injector. What always surprised me was that he could put it together again and that it worked. Some of my surprise was due to the fact that his hands shook quite badly. Curiously the hands did not shake during flight. He carved bardic chairs in solid oak for the winners of Eisteddfod as a hobby and the standard of carving was that of Grinling Gibbons. Was he Welsh too?

My arrival interview on 24 Squadron was, well, unusual. 'Warmonger' Wolsey was the Boss, and his opening question was, 'behind me has appeared an atomic cloud. There has just been an enormous flash. What would you do now?' I said that I would immediately dive under his desk, then work my way still covered where possible to the window wall. I would rely on top cover by being underneath his body, as he would have to push his chair back before protecting himself. He threw me out, and ignored me thereafter.

The squadron crew rooms lay on the opposite side of the runway to the domestic site and it was irksome to have to wait for transport to cross the active runway. I needed an airfield-driving permit that required an eyesight test for colour blindness. I failed it! Now if I owned up, then I would have wasted over a year of my life. I couldn't understand this colour blindness at all, for I had been an aircraft electrician. After about three months, all of the student Flight Engineers were preparing to leave for Thorney Island and we were discussing the new unit. One said, 'We won't need an airfield driving permit there, for everything is all on the same side of the airfield.' Gradually it emerged that most of us had applied for an airfield driving certificate and that we had all failed the test. The idiot administering the test was colour blind! I also learnt that you cannot become colour blind. You either are colour blind – or you are not. We were all so scared of being thrown off the course that we had all maintained a fearful silence.

One day all student engineers were instructed to report to the General Office where we were told to complete two passport applications and to report that afternoon to the Photographic section to have our photographs taken. We were to have two passports because it was likely that we would need visas authorising our travels. The possession of two passports was an effort to ensure that we always had one in our possession. If you had a passport with an Egyptian visa the Israelis would not grant entry and vice versa.

One student, Al Howson, was a full-blooded Burmese and his family circumstances were to produce problems. The new passports arrived for everyone except Howson. A letter accompanying the passports noted that UK authorities had no record of his birth, naturalisation or indeed any record at all. He was advised to contact the Burmese Embassy. After many anxious weeks the embassy declared that they too could find no record of his birth. Howson was distraught and inquired of authority what he should do now. Al Howson had joined the Air Force just after me and his presence in Her Majesty's forces had never been questioned during the last nine years. The Passport Office magnanimously stated, that under the circumstances, they would issue him a passport at a cost of £150. That was a great deal of money in 1962 and Al was, shall we say 'peeved'. Talking with him in the crew room I said that he should not pay and that since he was not British that he could claim immediate discharge from the Service. He looked aghast and asked why he should do that. As we talked, I convinced him that the Service had spent a great deal of money training him and that for £150 they would not wish to lose him. I pointed out that any airline would be pleased to employ him especially in Burma! He couldn't agree to that however, for he spoke no Burmese. Howson's Mother had been a widow at the time his Father passed through the region during the war. They had married and returned to England where his Father ultimately became a Yeoman Warder at the Tower of London. Years later that Warder gave my family a very good tour of the Tower. Taking my advice, young Howson offered to retire from the Air Force! A week later his free passports arrived.

I had secretly hoped that those colleagues who never worked at nights and at the weekends and who always produced better exam results than me would fall flat on their faces during the flying phases. Wrong, wrong – almost everybody was better than me. You see the Engineer faces towards the back of a Hastings aircraft. Engines are referred to by number and No 1 is the left hand outer engine, when looking forward to the nose of the aircraft, and No 2 the left inboard engine and so on. My difficulty was that when I was told to shut down No 1 engine, my left hand twitched. This tendency towards shutting down the wrong engine I countered by twitching the left arm, tapping it with the right hand before shutting the correct engine down. It looked a messy technique, but it was safe. Well, in my view it was safe. Unfortunately, it was not deemed safe by my instructor who visibly flinched each time I corrected myself. I'll gloss over the next bit by saying that there were four student engineers surplus to requirements. To those in authority with weak hearts, I seemed an obvious choice to be dropped from the Hastings course. – Therefore I was dropped. Happily, I did not drop far, and found to my delight that I was to be retained on flying duties and would join the Beverley course the following Monday. The other three students were not so fortunate. Happily for all concerned, this time my seat on the flight deck faced forward. The aircraft was huge and not a thing of beauty. It was capable of short take off and landings and needed about 450 yards to reach a height of fifty feet at ISA temperature (plus 15 degrees C at sea level) The airplane was nearly a hundred feet long with a wingspan of 162ft. It could carry 44000lbs for 200 miles or 58 passengers in the freight bay and a further 30 in the tail boom.

The ground school was comparatively easy, for the aircraft was robust and did not have many moving parts. Four Bristol Centaurus, twin bank radial, sleeve valve engines powered the aircraft. The crankshaft vibrations were dampened by Saloman Dampers (known as Solomon's Balls) and the fuel injection system provided accurately metered fuel for all conditions of flight to the cylinders through 'Miss Shilling's Orifice'. Just who this lady was I don't know, but she probably worked at one time or other for Hobson Carburettors. These engines unfortunately made a great deal of noise, and there was little, if any, soundproofing. My ability to perform any mathematical calculation died as soon as the mighty roar began. To combat this, I would visit the ground staff when any engine running was in progress and attempt to add columns of figures and to use that delightful mechanical calculator, the Dalton Computer. In reality this was a rotary slide rule, and just as difficult to read, especially in the restricted lighting conditions so beloved of pilots during night operations. As my mathematical ability improved so another problem reared its head. When we had climbed the aircraft to height and the engines had been set up to economic cruise boost (ECB) and life on the flight deck settled down, I would slip gently into sleep. There are still some lumps under my hair to remind me of the love taps administered by an exasperated instructor!

We flew constituted crews at this time. This means that the same people always flew together as a crew. We were crewed up on arrival and we divided into crew-sized groups in the various rooms of the school. My Captain was a young Flight Lieutenant who introduced himself by saying that he had been a Cranwell Cadet (crème de la crème of the officer world) who had taken some prizes at Cranwell, had been selected as a flying instructor at an early stage, and had felt himself bound for greater things. He went on to say that he had then landed his pupil with the undercarriage firmly in the 'up' position. His reward had been eighteen months in a ground position that he had hated. He continued by saying that he was now some years behind his Cranwell classmates. He then displayed an astonishing knowledge of his new crew. The co-pilot had failed the fast jet course, the navigator was considered marginal, the engineer had been removed from the Hastings course, and the signaller had twice failed the Morse examination. The loadmaster, sorry air quartermaster at that time, was alone in having no visible defect. The captain went on to say that as drongoes went, we were the cream, but that we, under his relentless drive, would become the best crew of the course. Did he make himself clear? He softened this a little by saying that each of us needed the others if we were to graduate and that he needed our very best efforts and asked for our cooperation. When, at last, we flew unsupervised he doubled the work rate and we drilled ferociously both in the air and on the ground. The man was utterly determined to make good his damaged career. He laid down some ground rules for our behaviour. We were not to leave the flying school without his permission and we were to report our presence personally on arrival back from weekend passes. He would then inform the Chief Instructor that we were available or no longer available. He did not 'creep'. Some two years later he was promoted and I received a postcard in Aden that just said 'promoted – thank you Eric' Few careerists exhibit such courtesy.

Flying was fraught with danger, far more than nowadays, especially for student crews, and we lost nearly a whole crew from an aircraft that landed in the mud flats of Chichester harbour. They all survived the crash, but two were lost trying to reach land in the darkness. I had practised the dinghy drills with the engineer the previous evening. The engineer was not a particular friend of mine, but he was one of us. I was most upset, especially as the young widow came unaccompanied from the West Country for the military funerals. Trains were not frequent and the girl was left alone in the Sergeants' Mess to wait for four hours before she could catch a train home. A more experienced lady would have left the Mess and waited elsewhere. She looked so terribly alone, and so terribly unhappy. The other students were somehow so embarrassed to be alive that they could not approach her. At her request, I took her to an aircraft and showed her around, and then took her on a short local tour to while the time away. She badly needed someone to talk to. After a pretty strained and mentally exhausting afternoon I popped her onto the train and waved goodbye. Many years later, an officer present that funeral day remembered the occasion and said coarsely and casually, 'I remember that, didn't you have an affair with her?' I told this now senior officer that I had most certainly not had any affair and that he had a mind like a sewer. Why is it that people must think the worst of others?

The course finally finished and we all passed in our crew. Now came the big moment when we would find our new postings. There were Beverley squadrons in the Far East, Kenya and Aden as well as a couple of UK based squadron. I knew it! I knew it! Bloody Aden, the hellhole of the world. One hundred degrees every day and 98% humidity and, as if that was not enough, we were fighting a war there. Verily, my cup over-flowed.

CHAPTER TWELVE
ADEN AND THE BLACKBURN BEVERLEY

I'd been to Aden twice before as ground crew during the time that I had served on 12 Squadron at Binbrook. Then, I'd been the electrician of a specialist servicing team sent out from Bomber Command to repair Canberra aircraft that had become unserviceable worldwide. The Canberra was comparatively new at that time and technicians stationed abroad had little or no knowledge of the type. All that I could remember of Aden was that it was very hot and humid and that we were supposed to take a salt tablet at every mealtime. I remembered too, the admonition that I must not lie on my bed with my stomach uncovered beneath a large roof fan. There was no air conditioning except in 131 Maintenance Unit. I'm not quite sure why.

The principal reason for discontent among military personnel lay in the availability or rather the lack of married quarters and hirings in the Aden area. To try and make military sense of the situation, authority had arbitrarily divided the various military tasks into 'key' and 'non key' posts. Tour length varied from two to three years. Only personnel designated as 'key' could expect to bring their families to Aden. The speed at which families were united was dependent upon quite a complex point system derived from length of service, rank and the time periods of family separation previously endured within a specified time interval. Those who were designated 'non key' spent their entire tour in Aden without their families. A mid-tour leave in the UK was granted to this group. This system was not well received by the other ranks, nor was the body of NCOs supportive. In short, it was bloody unpopular. Generally speaking, the aircrews were far too busy and worked such long hours that their protests were muted. Squadron ground crew of every squadron based in the area were exhausted by the long hours and physical effort necessary to support the aircrew task. Everybody else at Khormaksar moaned like hell. There were innumerable guard tasks – for periodically a grenade would come over the screen of the open-air cinema (nobody sat in the cheap seats for that reason), and occasionally a flutter of mortar shells would fall in the aircraft parking area. I was sergeant of the parking area guard on just such a night. Five shells landed with thuds but no explosions – not that I complained. We did however, lose a guard during this incident and the search for him involved the Duty Officer who found him asleep in an aircraft wheel well. Dazed and half asleep, the unfortunate airman juggled with his rifle and torch. He dropped the weapon which spat out a single round causing considerable concern to the officer and very great concern to everybody the next day as we tried to find out just where that round had gone. There were many aircraft parked in the vicinity. The guard departed Aden in company with two very nice policemen bound for an invigorating action packed holiday at Colchester or Shepton Mallett, (locations of two well loved military prisons).

There was a limited but unpredictable danger from urban terrorists who, on one occasion, bombed a school children's bus. There were deaths and injuries among the children and this kind of incident did not thrill any section of the military community.

Khormaksar was not a terribly happy place for a variety of reasons. The climate of course did not suit everyone and the heat that built up in parked aircraft was unbelievable. The Hunter aircraft had canvas canopies erected over their cockpits but the Beverley, with the flight deck high in the sky, had no such luxury. Removing the signal pistol from its stowage above the navigator and inserting a bent metal tube created what passed for air conditioning on a Beverley. The tube extended into the airflow and faced forward; the flight deck end was flattened into a fan shape. Forward motion of the aircraft forced air into the tube cooling the flight deck. Those pilots who flew fighters had to get airborne as quickly as possible after engine start before the stifling heat destroyed their ability to think. Later some forms of ventilated or water-cooled suits arrived for the jet jockeys.

The Sergeant's Mess was very large, for there were lots of NCO aircrew serving on Beverley, Shackleton and Argosy Squadrons. The Maintenance Unit and ground crew from the squadrons brought the numbers up to about six hundred. The Mess was an enclosed square bounded by the dining rooms, the main lounge and accommodation blocks. The rooms were open to a deep verandah and usually were occupied by at least two persons. There were no gardens to speak of, because the soil was dark, volcanic sand mixed with just sand. There was definitely sand – everywhere. It very rarely rained in Aden and little dust storms were frequent. There was one sergeant who grew wonderful flowers in the most improbable soil, but it was said that he watered them twice daily if not more often. The officers enjoyed a Swimming Club at Tarshine near Steamer Point Hospital. The gardens there were beautiful, especially the traffic round about. Air Marshal Johnny Johnson our AOC had ruled that every transport aircraft leaving Nairobi empty was to return to Aden with as much fertile soil as possible. It is wonderful what a warm climate can do with fertile soil.

The Air Officer commanding the Air Forces in the region was Johnny Johnson the Second World War fighter ace. His arrival in Aden was marked by an informal personal walk around of the area and, of course, the annual inspection with the normal parade of all personnel. I was in Bahrain on detachment when the airfield at Muharraq was inspected. Aircrew members of the squadron detachment were instructed to line up beside their aircraft. We wore the Aden variety of Khaki drill (KD). The issue KD was a sandy colour and the shorts reached mid knee. The matching stockings were worn over black shoes. That was the issue kit. We wore stone coloured KD very short shorts and desert boots. Those on the station parade ground wore a wide variety of fashion wear. Those who had served in the Far East affected the Changi look of well-cut shirts and shorts in a light khaki, quite different to the issue material. They too wore desert boots of a sort. There were crepe soles, rubber soles and there were thick-soled soft rubber soles. Those personnel who had served in Cyprus wore the Cypriot styled KD of yet another shade of khaki. The Air Marshal viewed the assembled parade from afar and informed the Station Commander that he would return when the men were in uniform! He flew up to Bahrain some three weeks later to review the now uniformed parade.

The Commander in Chief received an official complaint from a Chief Technician (C/T) serving on our squadron who had been offered promotion to the rank of Flight Sergeant (FSgt) subject to successfully passing an examination. The technician pointed out that he had been promoted to FSgt in 1944 and that he held that rank until 1957 when he had taken an examination to become a Chief Technician. Why was he now supposed to take an examination to qualify for a rank that he had held for thirteen years? He also pointed out that he had even taken a promotion exam to become a Chief Technician. Was he now to be effectively demoted if he took and passed the new examination? The Air Marshal heartily agreed with the arguments of the SNCO and did his very best to sort the matter out. He even raised the matter with his own superiors in London. Much to the surprise of the Air Marshal and the Chief Technician there appeared to be no resolution. The pay, allowances and pension of the two ranks were identical and the C/T remained a C/T. After all, it costs money to change ranks on uniforms.

The climate had varying and often unpredictable effects upon Europeans. The occasional skinny, spotty faced child could positively blossom in the heat, whereas the virile fit young man could be returned to England quite unwell. Mentally it could be debilitating too.

There were some very odd bods in the Mess as a start. Next door to me in the Mess lived an aged irascible and largely silent warrant officer. His principle hobby was shooting cats with his large catapult. He would spend most evenings sitting on the verandah with a group of beer cans on one side and a pile of pellets stuffed with explosive cap gun pads. The large dustbins of the kitchens, sited some 20 yards away, provided a popular venue for a variety of scrawny, vicious and half-starved cats. Khormaksar was home to a great number of cats many of whose ancestors had jumped ship during the last hundred years. They were not lovable or even nice cats, but did they deserve a high-speed pellet up the rear when trying to survive in what was a hostile environment? The warrant officer was a crack shot and his reload speed quite remarkable. I suppose that was down to practice.

The Mess Ball was in full progress; the pipers were playing a reel (Yes the Brits are mad enough to over-exert themselves even in that climate.) The Air Officer Commanding the area and his party had just taken their seats with the Chairman of our Mess Committee and all was going swimmingly until ... ...there was an explosive crack, followed by a feline shriek of pain and anger.

Then a particularly scrawny object rolled off the single storey roof into the enclosed square of the crowded dance floor. The cat landed on all four feet and looked for a way out and screeched up to the dining room end. The way was blocked. The cat turned and streaked through the dancers, heading for the opposite end. Blocked again, the cat had near hysterics before leaping on a table and from there, claws at maximum extension, to the shoulder of a convenient male dancer before clawing its way via the guttering onto the relative safety of the roof. Recalling earlier attacks on its person, the hapless moggie went to minimum profile holding its body low to avoid silhouetting itself on the ridge of the roof and remaining on the safe side of the accommodation block roof. That cat truly caused chaos among the lightly clad dancers. We were in 'Red Sea' rig of just open shirt, trousers and cummerbund while the ladies were in their light dresses. When the cat sprang to the dancer's shoulders, women shrieked, tables overturned and there was general mayhem. There were not many of us 'livers in' present who did not know who to blame.

I joined an 84 Squadron that had been based abroad for many years. The squadron had operated the Beverley for about four years I think. They were very proud of their ability to operate this very large aircraft from desert strips and rough fields up in the Hadramut Mountains. Many of the airfields lay in the middle of nowhere and others served medieval forts that had existed from, it seemed, the beginning of time. We also served the coastal regions and we regularly flew to Bahrain. At that time we were forced through diplomatic difficulties to fly the long way around skirting the South Yemen coast turning left at Ras al Had passing Muscat on our way to the narrow Straits of Hormuz. At Oman we would then turn across the Persian Gulf to Qatar before landing at Muharraq the airfield at Bahrain. That journey took about eight and a half hours at 135kts indicated airspeed at 9000 ft. I found it a very pleasant run, for most of the activity in Aden was in support of the army and we made many flights of very short duration that made for long working days, but generated few flying hours for the newly qualified engineer.

There were odd bods among our crews too. I single out one Hamish Raynham as a case in point. He favoured an old wooden police truncheon, which he carried on every flight and he was not averse to prodding and 'tapping' other crew members with that weapon. I was the recipient of one such love tap and I was very sore – in most senses of the word. Nevertheless, he was a likeable if eccentric character. I enjoyed a very pleasant detachment in Kenya with him in later years. I believe that when he left the RAF, he flew Short Skyvans transport aircraft for the Sultan of Oman's Air Force.

My first route check in Aden was made in company with a very pleasant aircraft captain. He was the perfect pilot to fly the aircraft on my first check flight. To the intense annoyance of the checker he would say, 'In a couple of minutes Eng, when you've done your fuel figures, have a look around the freight bay'. In this manner he prompted me throughout the entire flight. I was most grateful.

There was a story attached to this officer – I don't really know if it's pukka but here we go. Barry was a pilot in the Fleet Air Arm returning to the UK just as the Korean War broke out. The carrier's aircraft were airborne on a radio silence exercise. The carrier received news of the outbreak of war and was given orders to turn around and head back to where it had come from. The aircraft were recalled, but the radio of Barry's aircraft was unserviceable. I think that the aircraft was a Wyvern turbo prop job. The exercise complete, he turned the aircraft back to where the carrier should have been, but was not. There was insufficient fuel aboard to make a landfall in any direction. Climbing to a higher altitude, the two crew peered around – no ship. The radar showed the possibility of some ships at extreme range so they immediately turned towards the radar trace. Reaching the carrier and escort vessels they attempted to rejoin the ship, which was steaming out of wind. On approaching the carrier they were waved off by the deck officer and red flares were fired. The Navigator/ observer told his companion that he was greatly afraid of ditching, and since Barry believed that he could contrive a safe landing he ignored signal flares and landed safely on the crowded flight deck. It was rumoured that M'Luds of the Admiralty advised him that there was no future in Her Majesty's Navy for an officer who disobeyed orders. On conclusion of the war Barry transferred to the Royal Air Force. Good story – but is it true?

Piston engined aircraft hate the three Hs. Heat, Height and Humidity, for they all affect engine performance and therefore the ability of the aircraft to carry meaningful loads in and out of rudimentary airfields. To my horror I found that it was the engineer's responsibility to calculate the performance. The captain would ask what was the maximum load that we could safely carry out of a very short strip with a seven and a half degree uphill section and a moderate sized hill some three quarters of a mile from the runway exit point. To determine the magic weight we used The Operating Data Manual (ODM), Although I could use the graphs and calculate for most conditions I was uncertain as to my ability to calculate the accelerate stop distance. That's when you accelerate up the runway, suffer an engine failure, and come to a safe stop without running out of airfield, using only the two symmetric engines in reverse. I could use the book, but that's a very long way from being certain that you would bet lives on your calculation – especially when one of them was yours. It was thanks to Master Engineer Billie Binfield's coaching that I survived. I was not over confident as to my abilities, for Boy Entrants were brainwashed into believing officers to be godlike and in my subsequent work I had had little to do with officers. The function of an engineer is, not only to operate aircraft systems, but to look after the aircraft despite every effort by other aircrew to damage or misuse it. There are specific speeds at which flaps can be lowered, landing lamps extended, autopilots engaged etc. It was part of my job to ensure such limitations were adhered to. That meant speaking to officers, even criticizing the blighters, and I was diffident. Gradually it dawned upon me that if I did not speak up I would be a waste of space and useless even to myself. Now I'm difficult to shut up!

I had been in Aden some three months and was flying during darkness from Bahrain to Sharjah when, quite suddenly, the port inner engine lost a relatively small amount of torque. The aircraft was empty and I asked the taciturn Scots captain, Jim McTurk, to shut the affected engine down, as a precautionary measure. He grunted and asked for my reasons. I explained that this particular power loss could be an ignition fault, or we could have lost a cylinder head. His grunt of, 'Rubbish – it's ignition' galled me. I explained that I had carefully inspected as much of the engine as I could from the freight bay and could see nothing, but that I had a feeling that all was not well. Because the aircraft was empty we could easily do without the engine. Peevishly, he turned and repeated 'Bloody rubbish'. Very much put out, I lapsed into silence.

Two minutes or so later he asked what would happen if I were correct in my fear that we had lost a single cylinder head. I replied that if the cylinder head had blown, and the sleeve of the cylinder was stuck with both inlet and exhaust valves open, then we would have an engine fire when he pulled the power lever back. With a sneer of exasperation he lapsed into disbelieving silence. An air of scepticism hung on the flight deck. My confidence took yet another dive. The 'Field Approach Checks' were called and power was reduced for our descent. Number 2 engine immediately streamed flame and the fire alarm sounded loudly. Without any comment the fire drill was safely completed and the fire went out. We landed, taxied to the dispersal and shut down in silence. I completed my shut down procedures and went out to find one cylinder head poking through the outboard side of the cowling. The Captain and the rest of the crew joined me in staring upwards. Sourly, Jim asked how I had known. I replied that I had not known for certain but that I had somehow felt it. Striding off into the darkness he grunted that maybe he'd trust my 'water' next time. Something in me snapped and I tore after him. I told him what his grunts and disbelief did to me, a very inexperienced sergeant. I told him how much someone like him could teach me if only he would be more approachable, and what a miserable face he presented to the world. 'What rubbish,' he exploded. I'm one of the most relaxed and cheerful men you'll find and I'm certainly not unhelpful or inconsiderate.' Behind me there was a roar of derision and denial from the rest of the crew. Jim became a helpful, but still externally miserable, tutor. Perhaps squadron members should have judged his temperament by the splendid white cummerbund with huge blue spots he wore over his modest paunch at Mess functions. Through this and other incidents my confidence began to grow, but it did not come overnight.

Confidence can be so easily destroyed by the unthinking superior. After six months in Aden I was to be 'route checked' by the boss engineer. This is a complete oversight of engineer activities throughout the course of the complete flight. The checker observes, but rarely interferes, for he wants to see how each individual engineer performs. An adverse report can be injurious. Jerry Hatt was a most experienced Flight Lieutenant Engineer who had flown during WW2. He was generally well thought of, and no more a 'Trapper' than others in his job. It was an easy day, and everything that I did went well. Gradually though, I became aware that Jerry was looking into the middle distance and frowning. I looked up to check the fuel contents gauges and noted the contents for my log. Jerry wrote furiously for some minutes. I adjusted the oil cooler shutter position and Jerry wrote again, this time with a strange look on his face. Every time I touched anything during the next hour, Jerry wrote at least six lines into his notebook. Suddenly I had had enough. I packed all my things away, tapped him on the shoulder and said off intercom, 'You have control – I've had enough'. Jerry rose to his feet, spluttering, 'Why, are you not well?' 'No, I've just had enough. All I have to do is to touch absolutely anything and you write forever. I can't take it anymore.' Jerry hung his head and handed over his notebook. He was composing poetry! I didn't know whether to laugh or cry with relief. He looked ruefully at me and said that he would continue his composition in the freight bay out of my sight. I was happy to see him go. When he reappeared later to ask some questions and to watch the descent and landing, he wore a broad smile and did not have a notebook in his hand.

Early in my tour of duty, I flew to the desert strip at Ataq situated on the first plateau of the Hadramut Mountains where the air was fresh and cool and invigorating after the heat and humidity of the coast. There I watched spellbound as the Audhali tribe salt train arrived. Hundreds of camels trudged in single file across the dusty flat plain framed by the backcloth of the higher mountain ridges. The train, accompanied by tribal and Federal Arab Army guards, passed the adobe houses of the town dwellers and the eight storey tower home of the Sheikh and his sons, skirting the immaculately laid out tented lines of the Federal Army.

It was a spectacular tableau set against the background of mountains and cloudless sky. I was entranced too by the contrasts of ancient and modern. Later, speaking with a British SNCO in the Mess tent I said how lucky he was to work in such a unique environment. Smiling gently over the rim of his beer glass, he murmured that prior to our arrival he had had his armoured cars running up and down the landing area. I inquired why this was done and his reply of, 'Mines, Sonny Jim', appalled me. Apparently the local dissidents had developed the friendly habit of placing mines on the runway and taxi track. He went on to say that if the mines were of the smaller variety his drivers got a nasty jolt, but if the mines were larger he and his men would collect up the bits. I must have visibly paled, for he inquired if he had spoilt my day. I replied in the negative and added that he had spoilt my entire tour in Aden. Most of the mines apparently came from Egypt's Canal Zone where we had left vast stocks in the storage at Tel el Kebir. Those who planted the unfriendly mines had apparently been told that if when planting the mine they covered the mine with mealy porridge, a mine detector would not work! I was happy with that for mines could be seen by noting the discoloured patches in the sand – sometimes.

A proud soldier of the Federal Arab Army

The weaponry found in the Aden Protectorate was diverse, to say the least. The most common weapons were 1878 Ecole Etienne French cavalry-carbines; Egyptian copies of the Garand rifle and a few Kalashnikov sub machine guns. The latter were highly sought after and comparatively rare at the time. There was an astonishing variety of camel guns, flintlock muskets and I even saw a matchlock musket. Pistols of every size and shape could be seen everywhere, for tribesmen were invariably armed to the teeth. Magnificent curved daggers on one side of the belt, a pistol thrust into the other side, and a rifle of some description on the shoulder. The stories of hawk-eyed Arab marksmen did not check out. Firstly, many of the locals suffered from eye disease, and my observation of their marksmanship (at the wrong end of the weapon) showed that they couldn't hit a barn door at ten yards. I'm not complaining, I'm just giving my opinion. The marksmanship of trained soldiers of the Federal army equipped with decent weapons was completely different.

One day up country, a British Army Sergeant, serving with the Arab army, came up and asked if I would send a telegram for him to Sotheby's in London. I agreed and he showed me the contents. He had bought a Manton duelling pistol in excellent condition in the local village, and was inquiring whether or not they might wish to buy it. Some days later I took the answer to him. They agreed to buy the pistol, offering what seemed to me a fortune. They regretted that he had not found the second pistol from the set. Some weeks later I sent another telegram for the Sergeant telling them that not only had he bought the second pistol from the original seller's brother, but also that he now had the case complete with all accessories in excellent condition. He paid much more for the second pistol and case!

One of the Armourers at Khormaksar had made a remarkable purchase of a Baker rifle. This was the first rifle issued to the British army. Initially restricted to members of the newly formed Rifle regiments, it came into use when the Horse Guards (now the Ministry of Defence) (MOD) noted the experiences of troops under rifle fire in the American War of independence. Skirmishers of the Rifle regiments used their new weapon to great effect in the Peninsular War in Spain. Those who watched the television series *Sharpe* starring Sean Bean will have some interest in this. The weapon was designed and made by Ezekiel Baker, a London gunsmith. The barrel was 32' long and had seven groove, quarter turn rifling. Unusually, it was fully stocked and had a cheek rest, and the brass patch box cover was fitted to the butt. In the hands of a trained rifleman it was accurate to 300 yards and in the hands of an expert to perhaps 500 yards. How such a weapon had found its way to Aden, God only knows.

On another occasion, with the aircraft shut down in the middle of nowhere we became conscious that we were being fired on from rocks about 200 yards away. The rate of fire was very slow, and each time the weapon was fired there was a great cloud of smoke. A soldier with us said that he thought the weapon in use was a flintlock musket. Borrowing some binoculars we could see that a very old man was apparently showing his grandsons how to shoot. The half-ounce slugs of lead zipped through the air but the shot fell no nearer than fifteen yards. Just as we had decided that we should return fire, the musket apparently blew up.

I came under fire a few days later at Beihan. Number one engine starter was unserviceable, and to reach the engine it was necessary to bring up an army truck and extend a ladder through the open cupola in the driver's cab. The co-pilot held the ladder while I opened the cowling to investigate. Although I didn't hear the first shot the co-pilot did and released the ladder. Since I was standing on the top rung, I wobbled and fell off, bouncing my way to the ground via the cab of the truck. The Captain told the co-pilot to get up and hold the !?! ladder. (It is the co-pilots job in such circumstances. You needed the Navigator, but the co-pilot was expendable.) Up I went again, and then when the next shots came, he once more let go the ladder and took cover. This time I was not so fortunate, for my wrist and hands were involved within the engine nacelle. The ladder fell away and I was left hanging painfully by one hand and a wrist. Mercifully, the others came quickly to help. They only came to shut me up they told me. Twenty minutes, later a young boy appeared with a small bouquet of desert flowers that he gravely presented to me. The other members, of the crew had near hysterics when the signaller declared that the flowers were an acknowledgment of my entertainment value!

Some weeks later I landed at Dhala and as we began to taxi to the dispersal point our way was blocked by a boy of about 12 years of age. He just would not move. The Captain told me to nip out and get the little 'wog' out of the way. When I got close to the lad, I could see that his feet were astride a substantial landmine that lay directly in line with our nose wheel. I gave him a great big hug and rushed back to the flight deck. 'That wog, my Captain, is stood astride a mine and he wishes to draw your attention to the danger!' The captain, unperturbed, responded with, 'I trust that you thanked the gentleman Eric.' We shut down the aircraft at that spot. We did indeed thank him.

Dhala strip was high up in the Hadramut Mountains and there was a 7.5% slope. One day an old woman walked her donkey laden with firewood across the runway causing a landing Beverley to overshoot the runway at the very last minute. The local sheikh was most displeased, and he had the poor woman chained outside the village for weeks. Justice was pretty harsh under Tribal Law. Nevertheless, the locals knew very clearly that the hand that stole too often was cut off and the

Up the ladder – it's a long way down.

eye that offended was put out. The hill tribesman who made his way to the town of Aden did not know the law of the city. The British failed to codify Tribal Law effectively and many a Hillman ended up in prison through ignorance. Beggars in Aden, and there were many, were not turned away with nothing. They got 99% of nothing on most occasions, but the Koran asks all to look after less well off brethren.

Little Arab boys were consummate beggars and once when walking with a friend in Crater (Aden had a large caldera in which lay a suburb of the main town) we were approached by a blind boy being led through the street by his little friend. David tossed a coin in the air – and the 'blind' boy's eyes followed the trajectory! We laughed, and so did they – the little devils.

I lived in Crater for some time, and from my balcony could look over the Arab Police barracks to the prison area. They held executions in the square of the prison and I was unfortunate enough to see one. I'm glad that I was some distance away. There were several very well stocked jewellers in Crater and a Jewish family owned one of the largest shops. I knew the son, Shimson Menachem, a very pleasant young man who had served in the Israeli Army for their form of national service. After some months of acquaintance, he invited me to his home. I went up a filthy street, through a filthy door, across a squalid square to reach an unpainted stairway. I knocked on the battered door. I was admitted through the outer door that led immediately to a second inner door. On the other side of the inner door was a very pleasant and luxurious home. His father dryly remarked. 'We Jews do not advertise'.

Shopping in the little shops of the town was a leisurely process. Many shops were not operator owned, but were commission agents selling goods for the best price that they could get. Obviously servicemen were considered easy meat, but we compensated by wearing the prices down throughout many visits. We did not attempt to shop when tour ships were in harbour. A very pretty American girl was about to enter a camera shop, when we saw that she was undoing the top three buttons of her blouse. Amazed, we watched her negotiate the price, bent over the counter displaying most of a very good pair of breasts. The shopkeeper was enthralled and throughout the bartering his eyes repeatedly dropped to this ample bosom. When his eyes dropped the girl would move sinuously and the shopkeeper would hurriedly avert his eyes. Eventually, the girl emerged with the camera, which she had bought at a price lower than weeks of our negotiation would have achieved. Outside the shop we congratulated her as she fastened her blouse. She gave us a very cheeky grin and told us that she was merely using her assets.

The local shopkeepers viewed their British customers with some skepticism, 'You aircrew. Wear two watches, one on ZULU!' This was because many of us kept a watch on Greenwich Mean Time, for it was easy to become confused when one flew between time zones. The shopkeepers in Malaya had a different view. 'I know you Air Force boys. Long shorts, white knees, all talk and no money!'

There were major political problems in the Aden Region and daily we found ourselves the target of several dissident groups. Among the British Army units based in Aden were soldiers of a Highland regiment. I believe that they were the Cameron Highlanders. I recall one splendid day when the Colonel at the head of his regiment marched through Crater with band playing and bayonets fixed. This gesture constituted an enormous risk – and the Colonel did not remain in the Army for very long after this event. He departed for a political career in the UK. Mad Mitch as he was known did a wonderful thing that day and I recall with great admiration the fact that the population of Crater – a hotbed of trouble makers – stood in their hundreds along the march route applauding as the pipes skirled and the regiment proudly marched on and over the Pass down towards Steamer Point. I was proud to be a Brit that day.

Two local chaps who provided tea and snacks throughout the day in addition to their cleaning task served our Squadron building at Khormaksar. Saif was a most cheerful and hard working man who lived with his family just off the Maidan in town. One day he very quietly asked to see the Boss privately. As a result of that meeting the Squadron staged a massive noisy explosion with ambulances, stretcher-bearers and fire engines everywhere. Smoke bombs completed the illusion of a major incident. Saif's family had been taken hostage and he had been given instructions to blow up the squadron accommodation or his family would die. The noisy ruse succeeded, Saif's family was freed and in the early hours of the following morning, we flew the whole family to Mukeiras so that they could travel out of the Protectorate. I believe that the contents of the Squadron Fund went with him. I hope that that bit's true not only because he had worked for us for some years but also that such loyalty would be rare.

Shortly after this I was helping to move one of the private armies of the region that Britain did not support from an old fort in the mountains to their base on the coast. Oddly enough the soldiers drove around in Ferret armoured cars and Commer trucks. The fort was old and there was even a cannon ball embedded into the outer wall. These were truly ancient forts and had supported the old slave and spice trade route. We were taken into the main courtyard and I was helping to move some equipment. The Arab officer sat at his desk and behind him on the wall hung the most beautiful flintlock musket I have ever seen. Actually it was a camel gun of about six feet in length and a ball of ebony inlaid with mother of pearl topped the ebony stock. The rifled barrel was both fluted and lightly belled. The hasps binding the ebony woodwork to the barrel were of chased silver. Into the stock, on one side was brass inlay writing which named the weapon 'the Father of all Noise'. Even the ramrod was chased and topped with silver. It was a very superior weapon indeed and obviously a valued heirloom. I then committed my greatest error to date by exclaiming, 'Wow, what a magnificent musket!' The musket was immediately taken off the wall and given to me! I flushed, for I knew then what I had done. Arab hospitality demanded that I be given the weapon. Equally, I could not give it back as this could be seen as insulting. I was horrified and not a little confused.

Our Squadron Commander, a navigator, hissed in disapproval at my stupidity. 'Give it back you bloody fool. I don't care how you do it – but give the bloody thing back. NOW.' I thought quickly and asked the interpreter if the Arab officer had a brother, a son, a cousin an aunt – anybody. Soon a shaven headed lad, about twelve years of age with a huge mouthful of betel stained teeth, stood before me grinning nervously. Shaking with relief, I told the interpreter to say that only a warrior, a soldier, should carry such a splendid weapon. I was an airman, and as such, did not deserve such honour. He went on to express my wish that he would carry it with the pride that it deserved. My Boss looked on with approval as the surrounding Arab soldiers applauded. Later, he said that I was bloody lucky not to have offended every Arab in the region. I agreed and I'll bet that the musket was back on the wall before we left.

A Beverley 'up country'

There were several of these peculiar Arab Army units and they appeared to rotate their positions with other equally peculiar units. When we moved such a group, we moved man woman and child. We were almost ready to start the engines, when a couple of Arab soldiers appeared driving a small herd of goats. Our quartermaster looked at the goats and the available space remaining and said, 'There's no bloody room. Tell them they'll each have to have a goat on their lap!' This was duly translated and the troops looked extremely doubtful, for they all knew that a goat would at best only urinate as soon as the engines started. After some more thought, it was decided that we would create a pen for the goats in the well of the clamshell doors of the freight bay. We cobbled baggage nets together with lashing tape and made quite a presentable pen for the animals. Smiling broadly as the goats were brought aboard the troops settled down for take-off. We roared down the runway and lifted off. As we climbed away we could hear strange noises above the engine note and the captain complained that the aircraft trim was all over the place. 'Nip down and see what's happening, Eng,' he instructed. I climbed down to the freight bay to be met by total chaos.

The Arabs had all been seated on canvas seating hanging from the sides of the freight bay with their boxes and heavy baggage secured down the central aisle. Now, nobody was seated for they were all chasing goats that had escaped from their net. True to their nature they had evacuated their bowels and soldiers were slipping and sliding in their evil smelling effluent. The quartermaster, stood on top of a large box holding the rear legs of a struggling goat, was desperately trying to keep his footing as the aircraft pitched and yawed. Tying the rear legs together with lashing tape, the two of us forced the soldiers to resume their seats and for the next half hour we entertained them right royally as we tried to catch and tie each goat in turn. At one stage we were forced to make deputies of four soldiers because two us had no chance against these agile animals that, under stress, could defy gravity. When I returned to the flight deck I was less than popular because I smelt strongly of goat.

Recruitment to the Federal Army was quite a spectacle and I was fortunate to view an attempt to recruit men from an isolated community living in the wilderness of the Hadramut. The aircraft carrying the recruiting team landed on a makeshift strip in a valley below the hilltop village. The hill itself had a single road looping upwards past the stone walls of the terraced farmland to the village perched atop the hill. The mud walls of the buildings formed the outer edge of what appeared to be at least three, or even as much as five storey buildings. From the air, the village had looked rather like a mud made Manhattan! The village, probably three hundred metres square, could be easily defended, for small windows commanded the difficult approaches to the area. Many villagers had rarely, if ever, seen a wheeled vehicle. Far less had they seen an aircraft on the ground, nor perhaps had even the headmen ever travelled by air. Some of the villagers, mostly women, had never left the area of the village and its farmland in their lives.

The recruiting party comprised one British Colonel and his Adeni counterpart, both in full uniform. Two Aden Protectorate scouts in full uniform completed the party, each carrying the newly delivered FN rifle. They made an impressive entrance to main square of the village the village seated in gleaming military vehicles that we had brought with us. There they met with the tribal leaders, before the men of the village were assembled to listen to the impassioned speeches of first the Headman and then the Adeni Colonel. They apparently extolled the virtue, conditions of service and pay of the Arab soldier, pointing frequently to the Scouts who brandished their weapons to emphasise the oratory. The Colonel closed his speech by inviting all who would wish to join the ranks to form a line across the dusty square.

I suppose it all reminded me of the film *Beau Geste*. The two Colonels, accompanied by the tribal leader, walked together down the line of expectant and eager would-be recruits, many of whom were patently too old or too young. With a dismissive wave of the hand, one or other of the trio would relegate an aspirant to leave the line. Occasionally they would stop to exchange a few words with a worthy applicant who would be directed to the shade of a tree, where the two doctors would give a seemingly cursory medical examination before either waving the man off or directing him to a slowly forming group of successful applicants squatting in shade on the opposite side of the square. Throughout this process the two Scouts acted as clerks recording the personal details of acceptable recruits. The leaders retired to the quarters of the Headman while we ferried the recruits to the aircraft where we sat them in the freight bay and provided drinks. After some time, the senior staff boarded the aircraft and we started the engines. The quartermaster was outraged for the engine noise appeared to have affected the bladders of some of the younger recruits! I made a note to have the area well washed down on arrival at Khormaksar! That night I reflected that many of the recruits had made little or no effort to say goodbye to loved ones. Perhaps they had said their farewells in anticipation of success.

The crewroom shared by all aircrew of the squadron was dowdy, and it was decided that we should paint the place. There were two difficulties; firstly getting some decent paint and then finding some people willing to paint. In the end John King a Flight Lieutenant navigator and myself carried out the painting. The only paint available to us was maroon gloss and half matt silver. Wince if you will, but that's all that we could lay our hands on. We were painting away when another navigator entered and sat down. Looking disparagingly about himself he criticised the colour, the quality of paint and the painters. John, wielding a two-inch brush, never missed a stroke as he thrice painted across the navigator's face! 'There are two types I listen to, Sport. Them as has brushes in their 'ands, and those who are likely to have brushes in their 'ands. You ain't in either group, so shut up and go.' I remember that incident so very well.

The local Commander was an unusual officer in that he had sustained major injuries in an aircraft crash that had left him badly bent. Known as 'Bent Fred', Air Marshal Sowerby was a man to be reckoned with. You don't get to that rank easily. Seated in an aircraft seat he looked perfectly normal. Like many senior officers, he liked to keep in flying practice and would very occasionally fly with our squadron. The Air Marshal needed spectacles and would change glasses on approach to the airfield. We were practising circuits at night and the Air Marshal was frightening me out of my mind as he laid the spare pair of glasses on the control console. This horizontal feature housed many important electrical switches and in particular was home to four engine shut down buttons. In near total darkness the pilot would put his hand back and down and flail around to locate the glasses with me desperately trying to keep his hands away from these particular buttons. I told him that I could hold the spare pair and hand them to him as required but he continued to pat the switch assemblies as he searched for the spectacles. Finally I took the glasses from his hands and told him that I'd hold them. I also said that I'd break his fingers if he continued to pat the area. It was all very amicable. Honestly.

The next day however the Squadron Commander wanted to know what had happened. Apparently the Air Marshal had told him that a fierce little Sergeant Engineer had promised to break his fingers if he touched the feathering buttons! I was relieved to hear that this had amused the great man.

Detachments to Bahrain were commonplace, because of the British paratroopers based there. Our task was to fly them and their equipment wherever they wished. We rarely worked at weekends while at Muharrag and once together with another SNCO I was walking along the beach when we saw that a small sailing dinghy had capsized a few yards out to sea. We pulled the young man to the shore and dragged his boat a few yards up the beach. We were profusely thanked in Public School tones of perfect English and he insisted in taking our names. Some few days later, we were called to see the Senior Admin Officer, who waved a letter before us. 'This letter says that the pair of you rescued the nephew of Sheikh .... and that he would like to invite you to tea on Sunday! He will send a car. Be at the Guardroom by 1500hrs on Sunday. Watch your manners and your step!'

We arrived at a pleasant villa to be greeted as minor heroes and presented with a magnificent English tea, served on Spode china! After tea, the Sheikh left us and the young man offered to show us his films. We agreed and tramped upstairs to a large circular air-conditioned room lined with what looked like large mirror-fronted wardrobes. Opening one door, he pressed a few buttons that caused a screen to come down the wall above the circular bed. Another button caused a wardrobe door to open and disgorge a large film projector on a stand. Deftly he selected a film, fitted it into the machine and invited us to sit. As the projector purred the screen was illuminated in colour and we realised that his films were actually of the young man in action! It quickly appeared that the young man had been doing his best to sexually satisfy as many of the Petroleum Company secretaries as possible. I can only say that he did well. The films were complete with a sound track and had obviously been taken in near darkness, and without the knowledge of his partners. When I commented on this, he told us that his very fast film was provided by NASA specialists! My friend asked what he did with all his films, to be told that he swapped them with his cousin in the Lebanon!

The presence of oil in the region was well known, but in the Aden Protectorate nobody knew where it was, or even if there was oil in the coastal plain. An American geophysical team was exploring the area under the protection of the Sultan of Socotra who was the feudal overlord of the coastal sheikhdoms. Socotra is an island in the Red Sea lying between Aden and Djibouti and there is an old WW2 airfield there with a useable strip. The Sultan had been paid a great deal of money by the Americans to guarantee the lives of the geophysicists and their attendants. The coastal sheikhs on whose land the explorations took place had received their instructions from above – but no money. The Sheikhs were not all friendly towards one another, but they shared one aim, and that was to get their share of the money. Acting in concert, probably for the first time, they chartered a Beverley from the Air Force and three rival leaders boarded the plane with their attendants at Khormaksar. There were blood feuds between two of the groups and we had been warned to keep them well apart if possible. The trouble began when the quartermaster attempted to make a tribal guard put the safety catch of his weapon to 'safe' prior to boarding and was rewarded by a swift clip across the head from the rifle butt.

Shortly after take off, I left the flight deck to carry out my checks. As I climbed down from the flight deck into the freight bay I could smell burning. Group one had placed a tin on the freight bay floor and were about to light a charcoal fire! When I had discouraged this, I moved through the curtain separating groups one and two and stopped to speak with the Quartermaster, asking how his head was. As we spoke I became aware of red fluid dropping from above the ramp. That's a funny place for hydraulic fluid to come from, I thought, smearing a specimen between my fingers. 'Oh God, it's blood,' I yelled to the quartermaster. We climbed up the side of the aircraft to reach the boom area where the last of the three groups had been seated. Hanging from the roof was a goat that had been neatly sawn through from nose to tail. Apparently they too had ideas of fires on board. It was not a pleasant flight. After some three hours of consultation with their island overlord, the groups returned sullen and silent and obviously without their share of any money. We were pleased and relieved to see them depart from Khormaksar in their beflagged and highly decorated trucks heading for Sheikh Othman and the coastal sand road.

Life had its lighter moments too. A quartermaster called Mick O'Reilly was, not unsurprisingly, Irish. He was a large cheerful and untidy man with a mouthful of buckteeth. We were scheduled to fly up country with supplies and had been asked to take a Colonel's wife and teenage daughter up to visit the regiment. When we reached our destination, the ladies in their light dresses climbed down the longerons that served as a ladder to/from the seating area in the boom. Mick appeared on the flight deck red with embarrassment and when asked the reason for this declared 'Sure there's not a pant between the pair of them!' He was a most unlikely man to be shocked at this!

Mick, who had his family with him in Aden, had five unruly children and a sharp-tongued wife of uneven temper. Nevertheless, she had a heart of gold and was well thought of. Sadly, she died quite suddenly and a very lonely and distressed Mick was left to bring up the children and carry on with his job. After nearly a year Mick remarried. Somehow he had met and wooed a slight and pretty air hostess. The unruly children apparently adored her and modified their behaviour and Mick's front teeth miraculously returned to the safe haven of his mouth. I liked flying with Mick, for, like most Irishmen, he could be extremely amusing.

I recall Mick's teeth because I had a most upsetting view of them. Three Beverley aircraft were to practise formation flying! Why, I have no idea. We took off from Sharjah and flew sedately around like elephants in formation. Then, we entered cloud. I believe that the procedure was that in the unlikely event of meeting cloud, number one aircraft was to climb, number two should continue at the same altitude and number three was to descend. I was in aircraft number two and we emerged from cloud with the nose of our aircraft six feet from the open freight bay of the first aircraft! We were actually flying under their boom. The first aircraft was in the 'Heavy Drop Role' and the clamshell doors of the freight bay had been removed. Standing in that freight bay hooked up to his safety harness was Mick O'Reilly. His mouth was wide open, and I could have counted his teeth! We pulled our engine power back, but we still hung in our position under the other aircraft. We put the flaps down without effect other than our nose crept even closer to the boom, and for at least a year we continued to stay where we were. Finally, to our intense relief, our aircraft fell away in a steep dive from which we recovered easily. I have never liked formation flying and have always thought that if God had wanted transport aircraft to fly in formation he would have provided a good reason for them to do so.

Operating from Bahrain we would conduct exercises with the Parachute Regiment, and then commanded by an officer who had made a name in Korea. He was later to reach the highest rank. We would fly with the paratroopers to the desert near Sharjah, drop them, and land at Sharjah. On the return flight, we would land in the desert to pick up the paratroops and return to Muharraq. The troops were about to embark when the Colonel noted that the pile of loosely rolled up parachutes had not been loaded. 'Staff Sergeant,' he said to Flight Sergeant O'Reilly, 'Get those parachutes on board first'. Mick looked round at the freight bay which was full floor to ceiling with boxes of all sizes and replied, 'Them parachutes is bein' left here sir'. The Colonel then looked around for the aircraft captain, but before he could find him, Mick continued in his thickest brogue,' You can ask the captain, sir, the next best thing to God himself, and he'll tell you the same thing, so and he will.' The Colonel glared across at the airplane commander who had just joined the protagonists. The Captain said mildly, that if the quartermaster said that the parachutes were not to be loaded on – then that decision stood. In fury, the Colonel ground his teeth and spat out,' Who runs this bloody Air Force?' He smashed his swagger cane into his palm and strode off. Mick was not finished. He trotted after the Colonel saying 'Fer yer good self sir, ye wouldn't be worried. But would yer kill all yer fine fellers as them parachutes jammed the control runs along the freight bay roof?' Turning in exasperation the Colonel snarled with deep feeling, 'God damn you bloody Irish, you didn't kiss the Blarney Stone, you bloody well swallowed it.'

We enjoyed a sort of love hate relationship with our army friends. They didn't understand us, and we didn't understand them – at times it seemed as though we didn't even speak the same language. There was an unserviceable army truck at a field up country, and I was asked if we would take it to Khormaksar for repair. I said that of course we would and inquired what it weighed. The Lieutenant looked amazed. 'It's a 3-ton truck,' he said. 'Yes, I agreed 'but what does it weigh?' I then explained that I needed to know what the truck weighed and not merely its load-carrying capacity. He then pointed out that there was plenty of space on the aircraft for his truck. I once more agreed, but pointed out that the weight of the load affected our ability to take off, and that I was responsible for that calculation. He looked like a spaniel that had just lost his ball and could not remember just where he had left it. We took the truck, because the quartermaster knew an approximate weight.

Propellers in reverse pitch – a dusty landing at Thumier

The war raged in the Radfan region and we regularly flew Army support missions to Thumier, a strip that lay in a bowl of the mountains. The Army sat up in the hills waiting for us to crash on take off or landing for the available strip was quite short. Our arrivals were quite spectacular for we would drop the aircraft in from 50ft and immediately reverse the propeller pitch to bring the aircraft to a rapid halt augmented by full wheel braking. The aircraft would emerge from an enormous dust cloud to swing smartly onto the hard standing.

I don't recall ever coming under fire at Thumier, but I went to the aircraft toilet in the rear of the tail boom one day when we were flying along the coast at low level. As I emerged from the toilet I heard a rattling noise. I reopened the lightweight door to find some holes in the side of the aircraft and that the metal screen between two toilets had been sort of rolled up. Closing the door, I returned to the flight deck and said that somebody had shot at us. I explained the damage to the toilets. The navigator said, quite casually, that it was a good job that I hadn't been on the flight deck, and pointed to my seat that looked a bit mangled. We all had a good laugh and carried on as normal. I had a good look around the aircraft on landing and reported the damage to the ground engineer officer. I lived in the Sergeants' Mess at the time and woke, crying my heart out shortly after midnight. I continued to cry for the entire night, despite my best efforts to stop. I had no idea why I was crying. I was grateful that my roommate was on detachment to Bahrain. I reported sick in the morning and explained all to the Senior Medical Officer. The doctor was not a young man, mercifully. He listened to me with great care and remarked that I was one of the very lucky people. (I didn't feel one.) My subconscious had not liked being shot at, he explained. It did not matter what conscious Hayes felt. Subconscious Hayes had not liked the experience, but had probably got it all of his system in one night. He then rose and handed me his office key saying. 'I'm away for an hour or two. Have a good cry again.' I mumbled something along the lines that I didn't want to now. He smiled as he departed and the tears flowed again. True to his word, he returned just before lunch, and looked closely at me. He said that he thought that I'd be OK and that I should now wash my face and go to work. I did and had no further ill effects. Years and years later, I was asked during a medical inspection if I had ever had any psychological problems, I answered that I'd never had any problems. Scrambling in my medical record file, the doctor produced a piece of paper like a conjuror producing a rabbit from a hat and asked about the incident above! There are no secrets – is nothing sacred?

About ten years ago at the national headquarters in Germany, I was stood talking of those Aden days to a Wing Commander friend. He had served with 1 Squadron flying Hunters. Adopting the familiar pilot pose, he demonstrated using his hands, (as pilots do), how they used to scream into attack positions in the Radfan at ground level. I said that I'd seen them perform this kind of attack and added how quickly their attack profile changed when the first of his colleagues returned to base with a hole in the aircraft. Sheepishly he admitted that this was true. It's not often that you can get the better of a pilot's story! George Lee can be seen today, incredibly smart and well-groomed, driving a BA 146 out of London City airport. I enjoyed that man. He once arrived at a fancy dress party in a convict outfit clutching a toilet roll and brush. The caption on his hat read, 'On the Run'.

When flying upcountry we carried weapons. My weapon was a Sten gun and I was issued with two taped up magazines of ammunition. A twin Pioneer aircraft had crashed on the disputed border between Yemen and the Protectorate. Actually there were three borders; our border, their border and the locally observed border. We carried a ground party to strip/move the aircraft. On the ridge behind the crashed aircraft appeared a dust cloud that moved in our direction. We produced our weapons and I attempted to load my sub machine gun. Frantically I tore at the black tape that prevented me from doing so. I stabbed away with my dinghy knife as the cloud approached. The dust cloud proved friendly, but it was some minutes later before I could finally load my weapon. The final insult came when I returned my weapon to the Armoury, for the Duty Armourer indignantly pointed out that I had removed the protective tape from the magazine.

Among the Pilots of 84 Squadron was a Polish officer who with many of his countrymen had chosen to remain in our Air Force at the end of the Second World War. He was a very well educated man and impressed all by his ability to complete the *Times* crossword during the lunch break. His name was unpronounceable to most Brits and it had been reduced and anglicised to 'Andrus', and that's how his name is written in my logbook. He spoke excellent English but retained a heavy accent. One night on continuation training the signaller told him that he was unable to understand the transmissions from the tower because of the heavy accent of the Czech controller. Andrus grunted and said that he would do the radio calls. The controller called again and even Andrus could not understand, after several requests for repetition. Finally, pressing the transmission button in a fury, Andrus yelled 'Vy don't you speak bloody English!' Every aircraft within radio range pressed the transmit button and the sky was full of laughter. A happy moment.

To those readers who have passed through Aden, the words 'Sheraz Corner' will conjure up a road junction defined by a round about with the Sheraz cinema on one corner. It was not a military cinema and everyone flocked to the place when a decent film was showing in the English language. Visions of lightly veiled Arab beauties attended such showings (heavily chaperoned) and we lads let our imaginations run riot. A veil can enhance the perceived beauty. However, that's not why the Sheraz corner was well known. At dawn, the camel carts trudged in endless columns from Sheikh Othman some fifteen miles up the coast, bringing vegetables, supplies and wood into the city. The camels had plodded through the night along the beach road and their drivers had long gone to sleep high up on their loads. The camels knew the way, for this was their primary routine task. We would watch for a line of sleeping camel drivers and as the rubber-tyred carts entered the roundabout, we would gently guide the camels around to head them back to the coast! When the camel drivers awoke halfway back to Sheikh Othman there was hell to pay. I was never caught, but with the sympathy of old age, think the practice was a bit unkind.

Landing at Masirah, after a seven-hour flight from Khormaksar, I had eaten in the Sergeants' Mess and read the week old papers in the anteroom. In the evening I was wandering round the room looking at the pictures on the walls when I noticed that they had a door marked Television. I was impressed for no other units in the area had television at that time. I opened the door and fell two feet onto the desert floor! Residents of the Mess had a quiet snigger at my expense.

Although I was never fortunate enough to see the sight for myself, Masirah was famous for the turtle season. At a special time of year thousands of turtles would crawl up the beach to lay their eggs. My only knowledge of the beach was to prove painful. We had a night stop and had decided to walk along the glorious beach. The waves crested a few yards offshore before breaking and the water was so clear that we could see fish swimming parallel to the shore within that swell. None of us had bathing trunks, but we decided that bare arse would be the rig of the day. We didn't spend more than a couple of hours in the buff, but we certainly paid for it. I, for one, spent an uncomfortable night trying to sleep on my stomach. My bottom positively glowed in the darkness and the seven-hour flight back to Khormaksar was agony. I was grateful that the engineer could stand up on the flight deck and could legitimately walk about allowing the air to reach the afflicted area of the body.

Visiting aircrews were accommodated in large Nissen huts equipped with a large roof fan. One night, not quite sober, we had a competition to see if we could hold on to the rotating fan. Brian Cogger, an engineer who could get into more trouble in six weeks than most could achieve in a lifetime was a clear winner. As the fan reached top speed, he gave a yell of triumph and attempted to put out arm out. Centrifugal force now became dominant and he sailed, at high speed into the curved plasterboard wall. It was like a Tom and Jerry cartoon. His arched body penetrated the board and he hung for some seconds before slipping gracefully to the floor unconscious. We put him to bed and he woke none the worse. The wall didn't look too good though.

Brian was a likeable chap with a cheerful disposition, but he could be an absolute idiot. Emerging from 'Neddy's Bar', a small room beneath OC Flying's office where returning aircrew could get a quick beer, he hopped a lift with a quartermaster who owned a car. They weaved their way, and I mean weaved, out of the camp gate. A doubtful police vehicle had followed their erratic passage and that vehicle caught up with them. Brian leapt from the car, demanded that the policeman show his authority to operate out of camp and told the policeman that he would charge him for being in possession of a vehicle out of camp without permission! The happy pair then drove to their respective homes. Brian reconsidered his conduct and phoned the guardroom asking to speak to the police corporal involved. He then suggested that both parties drop their charges and call it 'quits'. The wily policeman however had put his superior on an extension phone. Brian was in trouble again. I don't know how many years of seniority he lost during the Aden tour. I believe that the Customs at Bahrain found him in possession of the Station Warrant Officer's silver topped cane too!

Brian's wife once told me that they met at a dance. He introduced himself as Mr Right! He distinguished himself on the first occasion that he was invited to the family home to share a meal by nervously cleaning his cutlery at the table on the serviette before use!! This lapse was understandable to an ex-Aircraft Apprentice, used only to his personal cutlery, but Mother was deeply unimpressed.

The Station Commander was a Group Captain Blythe who had a difficult job in a difficult climate at a difficult time. A Beverley co-pilot called Jones did not make his life easier. Jones had a precocious talent for the written word and he regularly published his version of Station Routine Orders. Deliveries of mail to Khormaksar, particularly to the units up country were uncertain and often delayed. Jones' orders would state, 'Station mail burning parties are to assemble at station headquarters at 0600hrs etc'. Another gem I remember was the warning to catering staff. 'Catering staff are to ensure that the bread rolls used in preparation for aircrew rations (known as Blytho Buns) are to be properly dried in the sun for a minimum of two hours prior to issue'. Jones's wit was always topical and if there was a local problem he could be relied upon to focus his wit on the unfortunate responsible. The Station Commander did not like the term Blytho Bun.

We suffered no transport aircraft losses during my tour other than the Argosy that landed in the sea 200 yards short of the runway. The captain was being route checked and had flown from Bahrain. It was a clear day and there was little wind. Half a mile from the runway threshold, the pilot route checker decided to enliven the day. Reaching down he shut down number three engine, but said, 'Engine failure number four'. The well trained crew launched into the engine shut down drill – and shut down number four engine. With two engines out on one side, and very little height to play with, the aircraft slowly, but irrevocably descended into the shallow waters. As the crew spluttered their way out of the aircraft, some one said, 'What are we going to tell the Inquiry?' Back came the answer – 'The bloody truth. Nobody will believe it!' Is this the whole truth? I doubt it, but it is what I remember. The aircraft was later salvaged and returned in pieces to the manufacturer. I'm not certain, but I believe that the Bishop to the Forces was a passenger aboard. He apparently was a good swimmer, but unable to walk on water.

A very large fighter ditched in almost the same position some months later. I think that it was a Scimitar. Happily the pilot was unhurt.

Our squadron aircraft suffered thirteen engine failures during a three-month period and this failure rate far exceeded the norm. The affected engines had been returned to the UK and the results of the manufacturer's investigations showed that there was very heavy wear on the cylinder sleeve. The Centaurus engine had no valves, but a reciprocating and oscillating tube, with two machined apertures that formed the inlet and outlet valves. There were deep grooves on the sleeve. Our problem turned out to be the stone crushing plant on the airfield and the 65 degrees overlap of the apertures in the sleeve. The engine was ingesting stone dust as it stood parked on the pan. I had one of those engine failures up country at Dhala. We had reported that we had lost an engine by telephone and explained the nature of the fault. The Squadron Ground Engineer said that he'd sent an engine. This arrived four hours later by Dakota aircraft. The big stand was manhandled out and a book of cards thrust into my hands. The Dakota took off and I was alone. Apparently, I was supposed to change the engine and the book of cards contained a DIY instruction! The Beverley had a mechanism which when fitted to the mounting points on the main plane could act as a crane. With the engine had come a big box of specialist tools and so, complete with cards, tools and engine, I began reluctantly to begin the job. It was very difficult to get the propeller off and to get it onto the ground, but the quartermaster and I managed this bit. Some army fitters who assumed that we were experts helped us. Flattering, but totally untrue. I telephoned the squadron, and received encouragement but little else. The days wore on and the new engine was in position with the propeller mounted. Now we had to run the new engine. My basic trade was electrical fitter and I had very little experience of conducting engine ground runs. I felt quite well when the engine was at low power, but as we increased to take off power the noise frightened me fartless. Finally we were satisfied that the engine did what it was supposed to and that the propeller would operate correctly at the right times. When all was tidied away and the Form 700 signed up we were ready to leave. I was petrified for we actually needed that fourth engine to make a safe departure. I have always hoped that my face did not show my lack of confidence in the adjustment of the engine control pantograph. We arrived in Aden and I screamed into the Engineer Officer's office demanding to know how he could possibly leave a new Flight Engineer to complete an engine change by himself. He looked blankly at me before saying that I was an Engine Fitter by trade, wasn't I? No I bloody well was not. I was an Electrical Fitter. He delved into his files and emerged to triumphantly state that his record showed me to be an E Fitt Air. I agreed that I was that designation and pointed out loudly and rudely that an Engine Fitter was Eng Fitt Air! He looked at me in an odd manner and asked if the aircraft was outside. Where else, I cried. I then asked him to have the whole job inspected very very carefully by his fitters – I cried with relief to be safely back. I suppose that I must be a bit of a wimp, but that's how I felt. Despite my Herculean efforts, devotion to duty and outstanding skills – not a word of praise was uttered by anybody. The next day the ground engineer officer muttered to me in passing that he'd only had to do minor adjustments to the engine controls and to relock some of the wire locking on the propeller studs. Did I care? No, I didn't.

There is a mutual respect between air and ground crew, but there is also professional pride and job satisfaction. Ground crew do not particularly like to be told how to rectify a fault. They like to be told what's wrong, but not how to do the job. The Ground Engineer Officer held just such views, particularly if there was an engine fault. He would declaim to all and sundry that the aircrew had called for yet another engine change. He would go personally to run the aircraft engine and there would be absolutely nothing wrong with it. Some time later I landed off route having shut an engine down and informed him that a new engine was required. We were standing in the aircrew crew room and there were about ten people present. The Warrant Officer looked confident, even smug, and said the magic words,' I'll go out there, drop the cowlings and run the engine and there'll be bugger all wrong with it'. He departed stiff with dignity. As he left, I produced from an oily bag a large piece of metal that was clearly an important piece of engine casing. Crouched with glee, I told the others that if he personally dropped the cowlings then he would receive a baptism of oil – lots of it. The warrant officer, dressed as usual in immaculately clean and pressed khaki drill did personally drop the cowling! He returned to the squadron offices looking like a drowned oily rat. I produced the crankcase part from my paper bag – and the crew room chanted, 'I'll go out there, drop the cowlings etc'. I don't think that he ever forgave me. On the other hand I never forgave him either for my engine change.

Although I was now comfortable in my role as Flight Engineer (at some point we became known as Air Engineers) I can't say that others saw me as anything other than a 'new boy.' In the next episode I grew up, both as a person and as a crewmember. The aircraft was at Eastleigh the former RAF base just outside Nairobi and we were to pick up our load at Embakase, the international airport on the other side of the city. The load consisted of a large number of wooden crates of various sizes and shapes. Filling the aircraft freight bay took the loading party some hours, and we planned take off for the early afternoon. The Air Quartermaster and the ground personnel prepared the weight and balance trim sheet. Incidentally, the Beverley freight bay was so 'slab sided' that it was necessary to calculate a vertical centre of gravity as well as a fore and aft job. If this calculation is not accurate, the aircraft flying controls will not have the desired effect upon flight. The airfield is some 6,000 feet above sea level and the runway is about 11,000 feet long. I tell you this because it will make the events that follow easier to understand. I completed my pre flight inspection, noting that the boxes, although piled high, cleared the control runs that ran along the roof of the freight bay by a decent margin. The quartermaster gave me details of the all up weight of the aircraft, and taking out the Operational Data Manual (ODM) I calculated the take off performance figures. The ODM is a large book containing diagrams and charts that allow take off performance to be accurately predicted. The remaining crew arrived and after engine start we taxied to the threshold of the main runway. Pre take off checks were completed and we obtained clearance to depart from the tower. With the engines at full power we roared down the runway. Part of the take off procedures is that the aircraft must attain a certain ground speed within a specified timescale. This is known as the acceleration check. Failure to reach this speed in the allotted time is followed by a mandatory abort call from the flight engineer. I had never before called an abort of take off 'for real'. There is or should be no argument on the flight deck or call for reason. The take off is aborted and when all is safe, the crewmember who called abort will present his reason. This abort procedure is a well-practised and mandatory training exercise.

I can't recall the speed at which I called, 'ABORT, ABORT, ABORT,' adding, 'acceleration check'. But I *do* remember with total bewilderment that the Captain ignored the call and continued down the runway saying that there was bags of runway left! There was as stunned silence on the flight deck as the aircraft lifted off just before the very end of the runway. There was an almost audible sigh of relief as the aircraft took to the air. However, the aircraft would not, or could not, climb out of ground effect! If the aircraft was climbing – then it was climbing unusually slowly. Now we faced a big problem for we needed to turn to make a landing into wind. If we lost height during the turn we would crash, for we had little in the way of height above ground. We successfully turned and made a safe landing. Only the essential words of the pre landing checks were spoken prior to that arrival. The co-pilot and the navigator studiously avoided eye contact with the pilot. The engines were shut down before I turned in incandescent fury on the pilot. 'When I call abort, you bloody well abort, or I'll see that you never have a crew to kill again. And I bloody well mean it.' Sergeant Hayes was a frightened and furious man. I went on to tell him that if he didn't listen to his engineer, he could bloody well do without one! I stomped off the aircraft and went to see the loading party, insisting that each box in the freight bay be removed from the aircraft and weighed.

With the Quartermaster and Navigator present, we discovered that we had attempted to take off 20,000lbs above our maximum take off weight from an airfield at 6000 feet and that the afternoon temperatures had further compounded the error. It was easy to see where the mistake had been made, for the boxes were clearly marked with a weight. That figure represented the empty weight of each box! When the contents were added, the calculations became rubbish. I had calculated the take off performance based on the weight given me, so it was little wonder that the acceleration was less than expected.

In due course the captain called us all together and apologised profusely. He attempted to save face by saying that he had continued the take off because he knew the runway was more than ample in length. A frosty silence greeted this effort. He then climbed down, apologised to each of us individually saying that he had learnt a hard lesson. I learnt as much as he did that day, and from that time nobody doubted my willingness to fight my corner when professionally in the right. Regrettably, I had a tendency to fight my corner when wrong too.

Back in Aden it started to rain! I had never seen rain in the Protectorate before. It rained and rained, and then it rained. The roads were awash. The paths were mud, but this was nothing to what was happening to the squatters' huts above the tenements of Maalla Straight. There was a dual carriageway through Maalla, on both sides of which were multi-storey flats occupied mostly by service families up to a steeply rising slope of the old volcano rim. On the slopes lived hundreds of Arabs in great poverty. The slope became saturated with water and the entire hillside began to slide taking the shanty town houses with them. It was, of course, dark when this began. Quickly teams of men from the Air Force and Army moved in, bringing mobile lighting to dig for survivors. We worked all night to save people but there were many casualties, most of whom were children. It was a sad night, lightened only by the unexpected applause of the locals for our efforts. I think that we were popular for a week and then it was back to normal. The rain had washed the skies and the following day we found ourselves able to clearly see some forty miles to the first ridges of the Hadramut and to just about see the second higher ridges. As the morning sun blazed down, the dust rose with it and visibility decreased to normal.

There were political problems with the Yemeni government who accused Britain of aggression. The truth from where I stood was that uniformed Yemeni, or uniformed troops operating from the Yemen, were crossing the Protectorate border and harassing local villages, mostly at night. When the Federal Army arrived, it was to find that the invaders had retired to their side of the border. It was very frustrating, especially as the Yemeni ambassador to the United Nations presented his side of events to the world. The Brits decided that 'something would have to be done'. With hindsight the plan was to let the Yemenis cross the border and then drop paratroops into the mountains behind them so that they would have to fight their way back to the Yemen. We would then clearly identify the site where the infiltrators died in battle with our troops and send photographs of everything to the United Nations. It didn't work out like that at all. A ground party of Special Forces was sent in to mark the dropping zones in the mountains and the squadron conducted night flying exercises for days before the operation in an effort to maintain secrecy. On the night of the operation we were conducting routine local night flying exercises. We landed, taxied up to a hangar, troops emerged and we took off with all navigation lights off. When we reached the approximate area for the drop we saw absolutely nothing on the ground. 'Flash the navigation lights once,' said the captain. I did, and the ground was immediately lit by pinpricks of light as hostile troops on the ground opened fire. There were a lot of pinpricks. We turned the aircraft away and told the paratroops, who had come especially from Bahrain, that there was a reception committee and that we were returning. There was no protest from the paras, many of whom were immediately sick. It's a brave man who will gear himself up to drop into mountains at night with a great heavy bag of equipment, and an even braver man who knows that if the descent doesn't kill him, the opposition will have another try. Later, we were to learn that the Special Forces had been seen and overwhelmed. Three days later there were some British heads on display in the Yemeni capital Saana.

The British fought in Aden under astounding political restraints. If, up country, you were fired on by rifle fire, then you could return fire, using rifles only! If you were attacked in earnest, it was necessary to obtain formal permission to respond. There was a story running in the area about an army major who when fired on by many riflemen was given permission to return fire using rifles only. He did, but used a 108mm recoilless rifle. There was no trouble for months in that region, but the newly demoted Captain was a bitter man.

There are many unusual ranks in the British Army. There are Corporals of Horse, who I believe to be sergeants, there are Pioneer Sergeants, Farrier Sergeants who carry ceremonial axes on parade and, among many other oddities, there is a Conductor of Ordnance. We flew a gentleman of this rank up country to visit artillery units and I had the opportunity to ask what this meant. Apparently his rank was one of the oldest in the army and was the equivalent of warrant officer grade one. His job was to visit artillery units and measure their weapons against the records of rounds fired, assess barrel wear and determine whether or not the troops looked after their weapons. He then reported back to Artillery HQ at Woolwich. On the basis of his reports, praise could be forthcoming or heads could roll. A group of young officers were there to greet him on arrival and he was quickly whisked away. Later, I was to learn that his duties took him all over the Gulf and I was to meet him again in Oman. He had been invited by the local Ruler to inspect the guns of his fort that controlled the harbour area. On inspection he had found that the guns were outside his expertise, for they were German Hotchkiss guns removed from a German destroyer beached during the First World War. However, he had carefully inspected the guns sited in the tower facing out over the harbour. His considered opinion was that the guns themselves had been carefully maintained, but that under no circumstances should they be fired with a full charge of explosive until the deep cracks in the tower plate had been repaired. Even when this work was carried out he would prefer to restrict the charge to a ceremonial 'pop'.

The Arab world is different and few Brits could get their heads around the concept of an absolute Ruler. A Major of the Royal Engineers was at the dockside to take delivery of the newly released Jaguar E-type sports car. The car, beautifully presented in lemon yellow and black leather upholstery, was greatly admired at the quayside. A Bahraini official arrived and led the Major to one side. Courteously he informed the Major that his Master, the Ruler had an identical car on order, but that it was not due to be delivered for some months. The Ruler, he went on to say, was anxious to be the first on the island to possess such a car. He asked that the Major sell him the car and that he in return would give not only the full price of the car, but would also give him the car on order. To this generous offer the Ruler had authorised the official to give the Major a brand new Cadillac limousine! Insanely the Major declined the offer.

The official withdrew and the Major set off to register the vehicle for use on the island. This was refused and he was informed that the vehicle could never be used on Bahraini roads! Some people learn the hard way. The Ruler's representatives made no further attempt to buy the car.

I liked the Ruler, then Sheikh Isa Bin Khaled, who enjoyed watching boxing matches. His attendance at the UK School Boxing Championships was erratic, but when he did come he generously gave both winners and losers a decent watch. Once when acting as Referee, I was given a beautifully cased Fabre Leuba dress watch. I've still got it and it is exceptionally slim, just about the thickness of an old one penny piece.

Our Section Leader reached the end of his tour of duty and returned to the UK. He was replaced by a Ground School Instructor from Thorney Island who had been particularly difficult to students. I phrased that very carefully. He was a nit picking Sod!

Prior to his arrival, the Flight Engineers agreed to help this chap only if he asked for help. Knowing the man we doubted that this would happen. He had never operated in a desert environment and he had never had the responsibility of calculating take off performance under very difficult conditions. Due to the heat and I hope worry, he lost nearly two stone in weight and had attempted, under the guise of standardisation, to pick the brains of newly arrived sergeants on the use of the Operating Data Manual. Finally he got us all together and asked for help!

Quite suddenly I was detached to Nairobi, one aircraft and one crew.

How I got the job I don't know. Until quite recently there had been a full squadron of Beverleys, based at Eastleigh just outside Nairobi, but 30 Squadron had moved to Bahrain. I didn't object at all, for the beautiful countryside and spectacular scenery of Kenya was infinitely preferable to the heat and dust of Aden.

CHAPTER THIRTEEN
KENYA

The British government decided, for reasons known only to them, to send one aircraft and one crew to Nairobi from 84 squadron based at Khormaksar to Kenya. The aircraft was to be at the disposal of the President's office and we were to be accommodated and based at the former Royal Air Force base at Eastleigh just outside the city. The newly formed Kenyan Air Force was in residence and training was in hand under a Squadron Leader Churchill. The old East African Federation, or Common Market, had collapsed and at the time I was there had recently separated from its two neighbours Uganda and Tanganyika.

In the past the three countries had formed the most successful Common Market in Africa. An East African Federation was in the planning stage and all the building blocks were present that would allow the creation of a viable cooperative. In my view the scheme was economically capable of stand-alone development. Alas, there were forces abroad that defied common sense and they led to the break up. I think that Obote failed Uganda and Julius Nyere Tanzania as it became known. Alas, the talks at the Nairobi Summit of July 1963 failed and by 1964 had led to the breakdown of the whole concept of Federation. I believe that a very real opportunity to achieve prosperity and stability was lost.

From my perspective I could see a pattern of development throughout what had been the British Empire. It seemed that it was prerequisite for any – and every – new Commonwealth leader to spend at least six months in a British jail. Without such qualification, a politician had no 'street cred'. Think about it for a while, India's Gandhi and Nehru, Kwame N'Kruma of Ghana, Kenyatta of Kenya and Hastings Banda and Nelson Mandela, they all spent time in a British jail. I could go on, but I won't.

The new Kenyan Air Force was equipped with twin turbo prop De Havilland Caribou aircraft and most crew were still in training. There were a few young Kenyan women also completing training on the base – just what they were going to be I don't know. I'm not even sure now that they were to form part of the Air Force. Kenyan officers at that time affected a black swagger cane with their No 1 uniforms and very smart they looked too. The young British officer of the Women's Royal Air Force who supervised the drill sessions for female entrants particularly liked those swagger sticks. In the thought that it might add a little panache to her own outfit she acquired a swagger stick. She would stand facing the ranks of the African trainees, holding her swagger stick in one hand while stroking it up and down the shaft with the other. I couldn't be sure from my nearby window, but I thought that the trainees were desperately trying not to laugh. The source of their amusement was unclear. Some days later, a kindly Kenyan told the young Englishwoman that the swagger cane was made from a bull's pizzle! Totally overwhelmed and puce with embarrassment as she remembered her hand movements, she departed at speed and was not seen in the Mess for some days! The swagger stick was never seen again.

Nairobi is a beautiful city and the legacy of the British was visible in the creation of the many traffic roundabouts. Each was made as an example of the flowers and scenery of various parts of the country. There were some inspired examples depicting the northern frontier districts and the Tsavo Plain. Some were displays of great rocks and plants that grew in the more arid regions. Beautiful flowerbeds abounded throughout the city and I particularly remember the displays of the crane flower and of the varieties of canna lilies. Blue flowered jacaranda trees flanked the main streets of the town, but there were also many flame trees, while bougainvillea draped over garden walls and climbed bushes. Nairobi was, and hopefully still is, a jewel of a capital city. I remember one Sunday on my way up to the Norfolk Hotel that lay on the hillside above the botanical gardens, visiting the Anglican cathedral where a major flower show was being held. The animals can be seen in zoos throughout the world, but the bird and flora cannot. I was standing before a magnificent display of lilies when I was buttonholed by middle aged lady with 'presence'. 'Do you know what you're looking at?' she demanded in a no nonsense voice. Turning, I said that I had very little idea, but that the flowers were quite beautiful. She smiled, and her face assumed a totally different aspect. When she smiled she was a different woman. Brooking little hesitance, she took me around the cathedral telling me what each plant was, where it grew and various experiences of her life. She was a midwife and her area of responsibility took in the nomadic Masai. In return for her kindness, I paid for our cream teas, seated in the elegant blue and white striped marquee erected for that purpose. – How frightfully British – I thought. She told stories of her lifetime spent in Kenya in a most entertaining manner, before driving off in her Morris Minor estate wagon with spear holes in the side. Masai husbands do not care to have their wife 'interfered' with!

There have always been great extroverts who present animal programmes on television. Among the first of these, long before David Attenborough, were Armand and Michaela Dennis. I recall with wonder the enormous American open topped car that cruised Nairobi with the pair lolling on zebra skin upholstery. Dressed in full cinematic safari suits and wearing wide brimmed hats, they created quite a stir.

The thought of television and cinema prompts two memories. The New Stanley Hotel boasts a world famous open-air cafe known as the Thorn Tree because an enormous thorn tree forms the centrepiece. Customers come from all over the world and the place is a most attractive meeting place located in the middle of town. The well heeled actually stay in the hotel and it was fun to watch the arrival of film stars and their entourages at the hotel. Most were dressed in brand new safari suits with empty ammunition pockets and wearing broad brimmed hats trimmed with leopard fur. Usually they were painfully white skinned, and surprisingly often, pimply faced. The women folk looked pretty good though. They would troop into the hotel foyer looking very self-conscious.

As a crew, we were seated in the cafe, when our captain noticed an Air India airline crew seated some fifteen feet away. The Captain was a grizzled veteran and wore his uniform proudly, sporting two rows of British medals. There was nothing grizzled about the two air hostesses. One, in particular was strikingly pretty. Our Captain recognised this and said that he would get a date with her. Resting his elbow on the table, he faced her, staring at her. As women do, she quickly noticed his attention and spoke animatedly to her colleagues. After a minute or two she rose, heading for the ladies toilet that lay behind our group. Pausing at our table, she suddenly asked our bemused pilot if he had a penny. Fumbling in his pockets he finally produced the required coin. The girl smiled broadly, threw back her thick plait of black hair and tossed the coin in the air before handing it back to an embarrassed man saying, 'I think that you've had your money's worth'. We laughed uproariously as she returned to her table to collect her winnings from her companions. The Air India captain rose from his seat and invited the losers to join his group! We did, but only after our pilot recovered his poise. We enjoyed his discomfiture.

Still at the Thorn Tree, I remember when a group of young women from the hospital were seated nearest to the pavement. A passing African reached down to grab a handbag before running off down the street. We looked on in total surprise. A large Danish girl rose, kicked off her high-heeled shoes and sprinted down the road. Her reactions were so quick that she came up to the thief within seconds. Swinging her fist she felled the young man. As he lay there seemingly stunned, she picked up her bag and returned to stand before the cafe. Feet astride, hands on hip, she screamed,' Well, are there no men here?' Admiringly, the entire custom of the cafe rose to give the blonde Amazon a standing ovation. Mollified, and more than a little embarrassed, she rejoined her group. We found it easy to sympathise with the young man for she was a powerfully built lass and she really hit him on the side of the head.

One evening, the crew was drinking in the bar of the Norfolk Hotel. It was my turn to buy (surprise, surprise). I was standing beside two young European women who were obviously nurses at the nearby hospital. I say obviously because their conversation was patient orientated. We spoke briefly, and the girls said that they found Nairobi a total bore. They were contracted to work there for a few years and that they were bored out of their skulls. Surprised, to say the least, I asked how this could be. Were they not outnumbered eight to one by European males? Didn't they get invitations anywhere and everywhere? Smiling ruefully, they said that this was not the case. They had days off and nowhere to go. They did not own cars and they had seen the Game Park. I returned to my colleagues and asked the skipper if it was possible to take the girls with us to Mombassa the next day. (Remember that we

Mombassa

were on our own in Kenya, and we could bend rules in ways that were impossible in the UK.) He looked across the room and smiled, 'Yeah, why not?' He went on to say that I'd better get them to the aircraft by seven in the morning. I returned to the girls asking if they wanted to come, and that if they did, I would pick them up at six thirty a.m. on the nose. Smiling widely they said that they would love to come.

I arrived fifteen minutes early before dawn at the nurse's accommodation and hammered on the door. The place was dead. No light showed and I was certain that they were still in bed. Angrily, I smashed on the door, adding the flat of my boot to increase the noise. Finally, a tousled head poked out of a window. Without war paint I was pushed to recognise her, but as she smiled at me, I presumed that she was one of the invited. Five minutes later the duo stood before me. They were still half asleep and if they had washed, then it had been a lick and a promise. We piled into the car and drove through the back gate to the aircraft. I led them up onto the flight deck, telling them that I must now do my pre flight inspection and that they must touch nothing, and I meant nothing!

Thirty minutes before take off, the rest of the crew arrived, introductions were made and we set off. The flight lasted just over an hour and a half. We flew at about 3000 feet above ground level and the visibility was superb. We could see on our right the glorious views of Mount Kilimanjaro. The mountain rises majestically from the Amboseli plain and the summit is rarely completely visible at that time of year. The summit is 19000ft above sea level and ringed with snow and ice. We flew on leaving the coolness and flora of the highlands to descend into another world. In reality Kenya has three completely different parts. The arid and rarely visited northern frontier district, the central highlands, of which Mount Kenya is the most northerly part, and the tropical area around the coastal regions. We landed at Mombassa airport and left the aircraft in the care of the Kenyan Movements staff. They would load the aircraft with the new vehicles in our absence. We began our look around the town by visiting the old Portuguese slaving fort. There we could see the slave quarters and imagine the dreadful scenes that must have taken place there. We stood on the ramparts, looking over the baobab trees on one side and staring out to sea on the other. We saw the small felucca rigged boats as they skimmed past the fish traps and along the beaches filled with the washing lines of the laundries. I found Fort Jesus to be most impressive.

We left the main rampart to have lunch at the Manor Hotel before strolling through the colourful street market where I bought a pair of carved bookends. I'm looking at them now and they remain prized possessions. Soon, too soon, it was time to return to the airfield for an uneventful flight back to Nairobi. The two nurses visibly enjoyed their day and were very taken with our pilot. I couldn't see why myself. Mark you, Hamish Raynham was a pleasant chap who carried a policeman's wooden truncheon around. Pilots, I've noted, often have strange foibles. The girls thanked us profusely for a wonderful day and then said something that caught our attention. They said that we were the first men that they had met in their three-year stay in Kenya who turned out to be what they said that they were! They went on to say that three weeks earlier, two nurses had been killed in a road accident together with their boyfriends. One of the young men was reputed to be a trainee white hunter with a leading Kenyan company, while the other was an instructor of cabin crew for East African Airways. In truth, the former was a bank clerk with Grindlays Bank and the second an airman from the UK Training Team Support Unit at Eastleigh. The girls said that although they were not exactly ready for marriage, it was not off their agenda. In their experience it was impossible to trust anybody. Giving us all a big hug they leapt into the vehicle for me to drive them back home.

My wife has read some of this chapter and remarked that we appeared to have had little time left for work between cafes and game parks! All right then, I'll do a bit on work.

I said earlier that the northern frontier district was arid and rarely visited. Some of the frontier ownership was disputed. In particular there was the matter of the Elemi Triangle, in the north east of the country. The Kenyan Army had a great interest in the northern frontier with Ethiopia and made sure that the locals knew of their presence. The Turkana tribe lived a nomadic life in the north moving with their herds to find pasture in this arid region. The Kenyan Army travelled extensively about the region and when we arrived with replacement soldiers, we found that all soldiers returning with us to Nairobi carried a string of up to four little, well labelled, canvas bags. It turned out that at every turn of a dried out creek or riverbed they would take soil samples for analysis. They were looking for gold! I thought that the soldiers, mainly from the King's African Rifles (They are now called the Kenya Rifles I think), seemed pretty effective, and some of the older SNCOs and officers wore British war ribbons. I was surprised to see that most of them had served in Burma. That was never widely publicised. Rather like the participation of the Indian Army in the trenches of the First World War.

Our work routine was no real routine at all. On Mondays we might fly troops north, landing on rough fields at Moyale, Wajir or Garissa. I remember Wajir best I think, because in the middle of absolutely nowhere was a hut bearing a sign marked' Royal Wajir Yacht Club'. I was mystified and it took time for me to realise that they were sand yachts. The sea was far away.

The wildlife too could cause difficulties. One day, looking ahead as we approached a rough strip airfield, I warned the crew that I thought there was something on the runway. The Captain elected to overshoot the strip and below us we could see an ostrich with young chicks. As we roared overhead the bird thrust its head down and extended her wings to cover and protect her chicks. There was no ground party that we could alert to shoo the bird away and we were forced to make three approaches to the airfield before the bird decided that the neighbourhood had become too noisy for family life. I was glad that the bird was unable to fly and thus presented a lesser danger to us.

Sometimes on a Tuesday we would fly a group of ministers and surveyors over and around the shores of Lake Victoria. On such days we would fly over the gold mine before landing at Kisumu. The people living there looked different to the mainly Kikuyu of Nairobi. These were wonderfully shining faced black people who quite dazzled you when smiling, for they had mouthfuls of tombstone sized white teeth! They were Kiji and Kipsigi tribes people.

Wednesday's work was fairly predictable for we would fly down to Mombassa to save driving new and expensive vehicles over the rather rough road from Mombassa to Nairobi. We usually flew most flights as low level cross-country as it was far more interesting, particularly as we disturbed vast herds of wildebeest and zebra.

Of course we had our own requirement to continue our own training flights during both day and night. One night, on continuation training (flying circuits and landings of various types) we became aware that the open-air cinema was showing *Flipper*, a film about a dolphin. We were all looking at the film as we turned on final approach to the runway. We gently descended, continuing the approach and saw the lights of the runway before us. Suddenly there was a scream/shout from the Loadmaster, ' Climb, climb, that's not the bloody runway. That's the Princess Elizabeth Highway!' We never watched films after that. I don't think that we could have been much more than a hundred to a hundred and fifty feet above that road.

Friday was spent rotating the Kenyan army teams or in taking government officials up to visit their constituents in the north. At Moyale we met groups of local people and again noted that their faces were very different from those people living in more southerly regions. The women hid their faces initially behind veils, but within a half an hour they did not bother. Their noses were finely formed, as were their thinner lips. Someone said that the faces were Nilotic, but perhaps Arab might be a better description. Borders in parts of Africa are somewhat vague, so people come and go without hindrance, but I believed that they were from Ethiopia.

Ladies of the Northern Frontier District

We had a change of airplane captain as an older officer arrived to replace Hamish. Dickie Livermore was a keen photographer who had to be restrained from flying off route from Mombassa to Nairobi. He wanted to stray as far as the Ngorongoro crater in Tanzania. We pointed out that we needed diplomatic clearance to fly into Tanzania. He was not impressed by our lack of a spirit of adventure. He wanted to equal the Christmas card published by 30 Squadron, equipped with Beverley aircraft, that had been based in Kenya. The card showed three Beverley transport aircraft in formation seemingly level with the 19000ft summit of Kilimanjaro. Nothing would convince him that it was the angle from which the photograph had been taken. Several of us were certain that it was a montage, for the service ceiling (the maximum height the plane could fly at) was nearer fourteen thousand feet. Nevertheless, we practised zoom climbs whenever we had an empty aircraft. Of course, the crew had to be on oxygen for such exercise. I don't believe that we ever came near to reaching 19000ft. I am most grateful for that, because

I'm sure that Dickie would have tried to photograph the interior of the crater, given half a chance!

At about the same time a new co-pilot arrived: Tom Sawyer. I liked Tom, for he had a great sense of humour and was always ready for a new adventure. We were given four and a half days off and decided that five of us would drive down to the Tsavo game reserve. I hired a large car while the others collected rations, tents etc. On the way down the quartermaster and signaller who had collected the tent, told of the experience of a couple of Air Force policemen. They had camped close to their landrover and were woken in the night by ferocious growls and the ripping of canvas. Terrified, they had managed to scramble out of the tent into the vehicle that they drove away at high speed. They returned in daylight to find that their campsite was totally destroyed. The tentage was in shreds. A local ranger told them later that it must have been some young lions! The storeman had showed them a metal service water bottle that was smashed flat with two deep score marks through the enamel. If you I and were to jump onto such a bottle, we would break our ankles and cause no damage.

I was most impressed by this story – especially when we decided to camp far too late in the day. In fact the light faded into total darkness quite extraordinarily quickly. The three-man tent turned out to sleep only two, and the car could also accommodate only two persons. Guess who drew the short straw? We ate our supper and carefully buried all the scraps. As a pre-condition of the agreement that I should sleep outside in my waterproof sleeping bag, the tent was to remain unzipped and the car doors were to be left unlocked. We retired for the night and soon we were all in the land of Nod. I woke in terror; something was sniffing at my face. I froze in panic. A hyena can take your face in a single bite! A tongue rasped across my face! Suddenly I could bear it no longer. I rose in a single leap still enclosed in the bag and ran – and I still maintain that I shouted and did not scream – as I raced for the tent like a man leading the school sack race. When I got to the tent it was firmly closed. Turning, I stumbled to the car, but the doors were locked! I stood paralysed waiting for the worst. I became aware through the mists of total dread that someone was laughing. Out of the total gloom came a man. He introduced himself as coming from an American Methodist Mission station, located just over the ridge and invisible to us at the time of making camp. The 'wild animal' manifested itself as a small over-friendly Scots terrier! It took the group ages to calm me down. When we finally settled down for sleep I inspected both car and tent before finally going to sleep. It bloody well poured with rain in the night too!

We enjoyed lots of adventures with Tom around. He was proud of his driving skills, we were never sure why. I remember driving at night in pouring rain down the foothills of Mount Meru on a murram road (murram is a red dust). The roads are usually ridged across the road and rutted along the track as well. When wet, the dust turns to a red mud that creates a driving surface as treacherous as snow. Never touch your brakes when slowly sliding down the camber towards the road edge, as this will accelerate the slide. As the roads frequently have high edges this can cause expensive damage. Where there is no edge to stop the vehicle there is often a substantial drop. This too can be expensive and injurious to life. Tom was faced by a new problem, for in the headlights he could see what appeared to be a ditch or deep rut running across the steeply descending road. The three of us in the back of the landrover were asleep amid piles of equipment and a large tea urn. I think that the captain was in the front with Tom. Tom made the decision that if he braked, then he could not stop before hitting the ditch. He also believed that as he braked, the vehicle would hit the ditch broadside on. He therefore accelerated in the hope of jumping the gap. We woke as Tom yelled that he was going to jump something, but we were not sufficiently alert to take in the situation.

The Landrover sailed over the gap, but the rear wheels struck the ledge. This was enough to throw the rear passengers and all equipment forward at high speed. When Tom finally stopped the vehicle we took stock. One near unconscious, dazed, signaller had tried to swallow the tea urn. He had chipped at least two of his front teeth and was spitting blood and curses. The Quartermaster and I were badly shocked and bruised, but otherwise we were unhurt. Something had, however, hit my ear lobe and that hurt. The captain was dazed. His head had struck the windscreen pretty hard. There were no seatbelts at this time and yet Tom was completely unscathed.

On another occasion, we decided to drive down to the Tsavo game park south of Nairobi. We decided to go there because we were fed up of searching for elephant. We followed ever-warmer piles of elephant dung in the hope of silencing the signaller who, alone among us, had not seen wild elephant. We tested for proximity by pushing the protesting signaller's finger into the dung pile! As we entered the Tsavo, the first of a series of mishaps occurred when the sidewall of a tyre was torn on a rock. I changed that wheel, but we had only one spare wheel and few tools. Later in the day we suffered another puncture Fortunately, I managed to take the split rim wheel apart and stuffed the tyre carcase with dry grass. I reassembled the wheel and we continued on at very slow speed. We found no village and saw not a single person. As we camped we could see no light, other than the brilliant stars in the heavens. Truly we were pretty nearly lost, and we had water for two, possibly three days. We had twenty gallons of fuel, but because of the tyres we were 'drinking' fuel. On top of all this, the engine was overheating necessitating frequent stops throughout the day. On the next day, late in the evening we were most relieved to hear the roar of an engine as a large Japanese landrover type vehicle heaved itself over a ridge on our right. Frantically we waved the all-wheel-drive vehicle down and were relieved to find the driver to be an English farmer who grinned broadly as we explained our predicament. He produced a large scale map and confirmed that we were absolutely miles from anywhere. Not merely miles from where we could make repairs and buy new tyres. We were miles from *anywhere*! Moreover, we now had only two full days in which to make repairs and return to Nairobi for our next military task.

To cut a long story short, he towed us for many, many hours non-stop. He recognised the urgency and importance of our return to Nairobi and allowed us to drive his vehicle in shifts. We made very slow progress, especially in darkness driving as closely as possible to a compass bearing. We were more than merely fortunate to find vehicle tracks leading in roughly the direction we wanted to take. We managed to have our vehicle repaired in a small township and made it back to Nairobi in time to have few hours sleep before reporting for duty. Fortunately, we had only a very short flight to make that day.

As we thanked our rescuer before he left, he dismissed our clumsy attempts to at least pay his fuel bill, adding that he lived on the border with Tanzania where he had a sisal farm. He saw very few Europeans and that if we felt that we owed him anything, he would settle for our presence for a weekend party. We agreed, silently promising that we would provide the means to hold the party.

About a month later, we phoned him telling that we were free for three days and that we would leave the airfield in an hour. He sounded pleased so we loaded the vehicle with duty free booze of all kinds. We included eight crates of Tuskers beer too. When we arrived, dusty and horribly thirsty in the early evening Jim's party was in full swing. Our friend's wife appeared and offered a choice of sandwich before dinner. Elephant tongue, zebra or giraffe! She said that on hearing that we were coming she had raided her deep freeze knowing that we would probably not have had the opportunity to try such delicacies. I enjoyed the elephant sandwich but not the zebra one. We were introduced to European neighbours, many of whom had travelled for hours to join the party. The night wore on as we sat chatting by an enormous fireplace. Flames flickered from the Meru log that lay in the hearth. It was fully seven feet in length and at least a foot in diameter. As it burnt down in the middle, you pushed the ends inwards. The room itself was unique. It was a large room with a ceiling made from reeds. The roof was formed into three domes and seemed almost cathedral like in construction.

The night wore on, and suddenly there was a tremendous crash. The double doors that led into the room flew open to reveal one of the largest men that I have ever seen. We froze as this black giant, who must have been well over six feet tall and at least twenty stone in weight, bellowed that he had not been invited to the party. Why was this? He strutted across the room, to confront our host, heaving him out of his chair and bringing his face up level with his own. Jim's feet dangled inches from the floor as the huge black roared in his face. I glanced nervously around the room and looked at Jim's wife who seemed unconcerned. 'How many times do I have to tell you, white boy, that you don't have a party without Frankie?' Then he released Jim, who fell to the floor clutching his throat. ' Listen you black ape, you were supposed to be away in Dar es Salaam until tomorrow, or at least that was what your wife said.' Frankie grinned, and hoisted Jim back onto his feet before hugging him breathless. Jim's wife grabbed a small piece of Frankie, saying that he'd startled her guests yet again! Turning to us all, she introduced Frankie as a very old friend who had been to school with Jim and who farmed on adjacent land. This dramatic entrance was their 'party piece'. A slight young African woman entered and was introduced as Frankie's wife. Unusually, she was well educated, and I don't mean that patronisingly, for in Kenya the politicians snaffled up the educated womenfolk. Incidentally 'bride price' was a practice still in force too. I was told that in rural areas the money or cattle compensated the father of the bride for the loss of her labour. Today the money was more likely to be held in trust by the parent against 'rainy days'. A parent who had spent a fortune educating his daughter might well see the bride price as some return on his investment. As the father of two girls, I see the bride price system as one that should be adopted here!

I needed a drink after this excitement. Today, this would all be considered racist – but the pair of them enjoyed their banter, each trying to outdo the other in imaginative verbiage.

Back to work again. The fuel contents gauges of a Beverley were unreliable and over the years, a series of dipsticks had been designed for each pair of main fuel tanks. The metre-long metal strips were carried up onto the top of the wings and the Flight Engineer would check each tank in turn. The dipstick method was very accurate indeed, but making the measurement could be a bit 'iffy'. I walked out onto the wing with four dipsticks in my hands, slipped on the dew laden surface, slid down the wing and flaps, hit the open clam shell doors of the freight bay before striking the ground in a horrible heap of dipsticks and flesh. I fell about fifteen feet in total, but my progress was slowed by the doors. I lay on the ground thinking that all was not well with me, but I could get up and I could walk. However, by the end of that day I was a very unhappy bear and was duly transported to the hospital. I had not broken my leg/legs, but I had a bad crack in a bone.

Sympathy is hard to come by when an injury inconveniences colleagues, I've noticed. It was as if I had deliberately thrown myself off the wing. The Captain said at the time that he had told me to check the engine oil tanks while I was on the wing! Had I done so? Why not? I don't know what they did with their time, but without me there was not a full crew. No full crew – no flying. They didn't come to see me either, although I was told that they had inquired as to my condition! I don't recall how long I spent in hospital, but it was not long. Complete with plaster, I was packed off to stay with a very kind family living near Nakuru about sixty miles away.

I enjoyed the scenery on my way to Nakuru, descending into the Rift Valley on the widely turning road that was built during the Second World War with help from Italian prisoners of war. We passed the beautiful hotel on the shores of Lake Naivasha before continuing towards Nakuru. The roadside was ablaze with flowers and bougainvillea decorated the landscape.

The great soda lake was near to the family's farmhouse, and I found out later that their eldest son had drowned some eighteen months earlier when he and friends had disturbed a group of hippo. The doctor who sent me to the family was aware of this, and thought that my presence might provide a welcome change of routine for the parents. As I hopped through the main door of the house, dripping mud from my one shoe, I had my ears boxed by the lady of the house! Later, she was greatly embarrassed by her reflex reaction to her muddy floor. Her husband had had his ears warmed too! However, this set the tone of my visit and we greatly enjoyed our time together.

The cows that searched for feed in the Rift Valley looked a bit odd to me, for they had wide horns and a humped back, rather like the Brahma bulls in India. The cows bred in Kenya are tsetse fly proof – I think. Herdsmen used to wear long sheepskin leather coats, for although the temperature could be 67-77 degrees F during the day in Nairobi, it could get very cold at night in the Rift Valley. I liked those coats and asked where I could buy one. 'Pooh,' she said, 'Buy one? We'll make a jacket ourselves and the Indian tailor can sew it all together, because my machine is not man enough to sew leather'. Together, we made a pattern and I lay on the floor, plastered leg outstretched, shearing the sheepskins until the pile was about a quarter of an inch deep all over. The tailor produced a very nice, but perhaps a little bulky jacket that was quickly liberated by my Father on my return to England. In truth, the job of making the jacket was very welcome, for it was the time of the short rains (mid November to mid December) and the weather was grim. Once you have seen the thousands of flamingo on the lake, you have seen all the flamingo of the lake – spectacular though the flight of ten thousand pink flamingos can be in the evening sun. After this very short interlude I returned to Eastleigh, for I found that I could do my job without much trouble or pain.

I did meet a most interesting lady in hospital through one of the doctors who told me that was a ninety-year-old lady in room X who had flown everywhere. I dragged myself to the room and knocked. A clear voice bellowed that I should enter. I looked at the lady and apologised for disturbing her. She asked who I was looking for and when told, laughed and said that I was in the right place. I grinned and said that I'd been told that she was ninety! She smiled unabashedly and said that she really was ninety years old. I was surprised for she looked no older than mid sixties with clear skin, good hair and teeth! We chatted together and she said that she had been one of the first to fly solo from Cairo to the Cape. She gave a regretful grin and added that she had been the first to *attempt* to fly the route in the twenties. She had engine failure due to a blocked fuel filter and had force landed in the foothills of Mount Meru near the Tanzanian border. She had been trapped in the wreckage of the little biplane for some hours, before being rescued by a group of young men who had seen the plane fall from the sky. I asked if she had tried again, but she grinned and said that her new husband was rather against the idea, as he did not want to cut her out of a second crash!

Her husband arrived to visit with their son and daughter. It was no exaggeration to say that it was difficult to say which was parent or child. They had spent a lifetime living at 6,000 feet above sea level and they all looked incredibly young and healthy. The Mother said that it was because they had never ever had time to be lazy or bored.

I asked the son if the family had lived in Kenya throughout the Mau Mau period and if the terrorist gangs had troubled them. He smiled wryly and said that their cattle had been attacked and the village where their work force lived had also suffered. The cattle had died through loss of blood when all four legs had been hacked off!

He continued by saying that his Mother had a great desire to educate all Africa, and from the day of her marriage had insisted that the children who lived or worked on the farm be educated. He laughed and said that half the politicians and a good number of teachers and lawyers in Kenya owed their education to his mother. Proof that this care was appreciated was demonstrated when a few bodies, presumed to be of those who had attacked the farm, were found laid out in a line on the edge of the farm. Smiling, he asked if I had read some of the labels on the flower arrangements that filled his Mother's room? I hadn't, but I did go and read the cards. A few were from members of the Kenyatta government, but there were more from business people throughout the city. There's proof that we can live together in friendship and peace, I thought.

There were a few members of the British Army in Kenya and two them were to fly to Nanyuki, where there was a Police Academy graduation parade. They were to be guests at the parade on Saturday. They asked if I would like to join them on their short flight. They flew a Beaver, high wing radial engined monoplane that had excellent short take off and landing characteristics. It also had a tail wheel, so that passengers sat low on the ground when the aircraft was at rest. My place on the flight deck of a Beverley was about 12-15 feet above ground. I recall coming into land in that Beaver, and as my rear descended through that 12 to 15 feet threshold, I could almost feel my rear end scraping on the tarmac! It was quite a disturbing sensation, with a high value 'pucker factor'.

Anyway, back to the parade. The Reviewing Officer was an elderly European in uniform of sorts. He wore two rows of British medals and in particular, he wore the General Service Medal before the Second World War group. To the initiated this means that he was most likely to have served in the Indian Army or one of the Colonial Police Forces. At the reception following the parade, I asked where he had earned the medal.

He replied that he'd been a Palestine Policeman. I told him that my Father had served there too and that he'd been there from 1936 to 1942. His interest was aroused and he asked if Dad had been based in Haifa. When I said that he had, he asked my surname. Seemingly stunned by my answer, he said that he had shared a room with my Father for three years! It's a small world. Later, having searched his memory, he asked if I was Jim or Eric! Calling his wife over, he introduced me as Terry Hayes' son. She was more than surprised for the couple had married in Palestine and Dad had acted as 'best man'. They asked if I could stay the night – and that if I could he would arrange transport back to Nairobi for me the following afternoon. I agreed and we spent hours in front of a log fire yarning away. To my astonishment he pooh poohed some of my Father's stories, but completely unprompted, confirmed the more unlikely. I'll give just one example. In the thirties the Palestine Police patrolled the Haifa-Iraq oil pipeline in armoured cars. They cruised up and down the pipeline, delivering food and mail to the many little fortified guard posts along the route of the pipeline. It was a boring and hot job, for there was no such thing as air-conditioning in the vehicle. Thoroughly bored, the two of them cut short their patrol and re entered Palestine. By a stroke of bad luck, they ran into their Superintendent who was not amused to find them absent from duty. As he turned away, a thought struck him and he pulled out a glass demijohn wrapped in a wicker covering from the boot of his car. ' If you pair drive back to the Jordan and fill this with river water and get it onto my desk by nine o'clock tomorrow morning – you're off the hook!'

It was a hot day, the Jordan was far away, but filling the bottle would get them out of trouble. Cursing under their breath, they headed back along the dusty road. Some miles later they spotted a roadside inn of sorts. Gratefully they turned into the driveway, past the small pond in which goldfish drifted aimlessly. There, they joined a group of fellow police officers and the day sped by, followed by most of the night. As they wandered unsteadily towards their vehicle, Dad remembered the bottle. He explained its purpose to the others, two of whom immediately peed into it. Dad topped it up with goldfish water and hammered the cork in. The flask was duly delivered to the superintendent. Some weeks later the pair asked where the water had gone, to be told that it was on its way to Westminster Abbey for the Christening of the newest member of a leading aristocratic family! This particular well-known chap has a receding chin and looks as though he had a strong smell under his nose!

Perhaps that's not surprising when one considers that he was christened in policeman's pee!

All too soon I was recalled to Aden. Back to dust, dreadful working hours and the possibility of booby traps and grenades again. Life had not improved in Aden, as I noted when I knocked on the door of a colleague who lived in a flat on the Maalla Straight. His pregnant wife answered the door pointing a 6.75mm pistol at my stomach! I had brought fresh strawberries back from Kenya at the request of her husband. She was a dangerous person to call on, for the safety catch was off.

Fortunately my tour of duty would end, in theory at least, in some three weeks' time. Then it would be back to England in January of all times to arrive after years in the heat. On schedule I departed Khormaksar. As I climbed the aircraft steps, I removed a shoe and shook the dust from it. I hoped never to return, but this was not to be.

CHAPTER FOURTEEN
WESSEX HELICOPTERS AT ODIHAM

It was now time for me to return to the UK and to my utter disgust, I found that I was to be employed as a helicopter crewman. This did most definitely not suit me – I was a flight engineer. However, I was to find that 95% of my colleagues returning from overseas were also to become crewmen, as the Hastings and Beverley aircraft were to be replaced by the Hercules C Mkl. The ministry were not replacing the earlier aircraft on a one to one basis (when do they ever?). As a result, until the new aircraft arrived in sufficient numbers we had been 'grabbed' to become crewmen on the twin jet engine Wessex helicopter force. I did not like helicopters, nor did I like the green flying suits that we were obliged to wear in place of our blue suits. Indeed, when visiting transport aircraft bases I would slink around the place in the hope that friends would not see me wearing 'pongo green'.

My arrival at Odiham provided considerable surprise. I entered Station Headquarters and sought out the General Office to announce my arrival and to obtain the blue 'arrival chit' that I would have signed by the various sections of the station that needed to know that the great Hayes had arrived. I spoke to a Corporal who was about to hand me the blue card, when the Warrant Officer in charge looked up from his desk. 'Flight Sergeant, you, Flight Sergeant. Why are you improperly dressed?' As I was a Sergeant, I did not react at all. The Warrant Officer rose and came to the long desk that separated staff from customer saying, 'Flight Sergeant, you are improperly dressed'. He was looking directly at me, and he didn't appear to have a squint. I turned to face the man who was grinning like a Cheshire cat. 'You've been improperly dressed for the last three years. You were previously ground crew on a six year tour of aircrew duty and you became permanent aircrew three years ago.' Astounded by this information, I managed to say that I was still a Sergeant. The Warrant Officer, clearly enjoying himself, continued telling me that airman aircrew at that time were automatically promoted on length of Air Force service and that three years ago I had become eligible for time promotion to Flight Sergeant! At the time, no one had thought to inform the authorities in Aden. I was bewildered, but clearly he was not joking. He told me where the camp tailor shop was and added that I should return to see him properly dressed that afternoon. In a state of shock, I departed for stores to obtain the brass crowns to insert above the three stripes of my uniforms. In a dream, I set out for the clothing store where I met an old friend who was now a Warrant Officer storeman. He heard my news with delight and searching through the drawers of his desk produced three pairs of the brass King's Crown. 'Wear these, Eric. They were mine and I know that you'd prefer these to the new ones.' He was right, and I was most grateful.

That afternoon, rather self-consciously wearing my new rank, I walked into the General Office to be greeted by a heartfelt 'That looks a bit better, Flight Sergeant!' He went on to say that Pay Accounts were calculating three years back pay and that they were also going through my documents to pay the additional allowances attributable to my new rank! Wow, thrice wow! The total sum payable was going to be substantial. Three years back pay! I could afford to ask Brigitte to marry me. I did, and she did! After years in the desert, I was attracted to the first woman I saw. Gitti (a diminutive of her name) came from Kiel in Germany and had come to England to learn English properly. She regularly called in to see my parents, who were well known to her family. I recalled seeing her as a teenager with her brother and sister cleaning headstones in the military cemetery with my Father. She seemed quite different now!

An inter service exercise was planned to take place in Libya for which the helicopter force was to fly there in loose formation. This transit would take about three days and involved night stops in France and Malta before the final leg to El Adem near Tobruk. An internal fuel tank was carried inside the cabin. The transit through France and Italy was uneventful but sitting on helicopter seats for long periods of time was uncomfortable and led to all of us feeling 'tall in the saddle'. As we flew down the Italian coast towards Malta, we were informed that Air Traffic Control refused us permission to fly the few miles over water from Sicily to Malta, claiming that we had no air sea rescue cover! The squadron had very recently stood in for the Whirlwind helicopters in the UK search and rescue organisation following an accident that had forced the grounding of that helicopter type. Most crews had qualified in that role. However, ours was not to reason why etc.

Somewhat disgruntled, we landed at Taormina to be met by the Italian representative of British Airways, or was it called BEA then?

As an Italian, he knew of only two ranks, officers and others. I was an 'other'. A tourist hotel was happy to take the officers, for it was 'off season'. All the others were sent off to what seemed to us to be a brothel in town. They didn't serve food so we ate at an establishment across the road. Rumour had it that it was a Salvation Army pizza house. Whatever it was, they made us most welcome; the food was good and the wine flowed. The building that 'others' occupied was home to a group of young women who found our presence hilarious. I was in the shower when a soft hand came in and soaped me down! I nearly died of fright until I realised that a group of squadron members were egging her on. Later, when we were all having a drink together, we told the girls about the more innocent and shy members of our group. In a quick reshuffle of chairs and seating positions we put the innocents in the middle of the girls. The evening was full of laughter on every side and I recall the popping eyeballs of the innocents as they were interfered with from under the table. At the end of the evening I was almost ashamed of my part in arranging this.

Our officers had not had a good night, for their hotel lay some miles out of town and it was expensive to hire taxis. Very few bars had been open and they were bored to death. Tales of our riotous night did nothing to improve their humour. While they were quite pleased that we had enjoyed our stay they definitely felt that we had the best part of the deal.

The Army units had deployed to their start positions some days earlier and now the helicopters moved out into the desert to establish their temporary base. We were equipped with new-fangled tentage (Type B shelters) and a host of new cooking stoves. Our rations were delivered, and off we flew. On landing we began to erect the shelters and to establish all the various tented communities such as the accommodation lines, cookhouse and Mess tents. The shelters could be linked in a wide variety of ways into Tee shapes or long lines. We found them to be a vast improvement on previous tentage. Each shelter had a groundsheet and a white inner lining. There were transparent windows that could be blacked out if necessary and the whole thing could be largely dust proofed too for there were double door flaps.

The new folding tables and chairs made us feel that we could be comfortable, especially as we had good lighting powered by petrol electric sets, complete with suitable back up for use in emergencies. All ranks were quite proud of our efforts as we sat down to eat our evening meal. I quite liked the contents of the D pack Compo Ration. Well, at that time I did.

Bright and early in the morning, the Boss took off for Exercise HQ and the rest of us straightened the tent lines, checked equipment and generally mooched around waiting for information and orders. The Boss returned after a few hours absence and summoned the flight commanders, in time and in turn, they summoned the next level of minion to brief us on the situation. We would not be required for the next two days, but thereafter we would each fly at least four sorties per day. That sounded OK to me. In passing, the briefing officer said that the Boss had told him that there was a tank unit bivouacked a mile or so from us. Waving his arm, he pointed out the general direction of the Army unit. That evening, we decided that we would walk across and say hello. It was a beautifully clear night and without any background light from towns as in Europe, the stars were unbelievably bright in the heavens. This was the time of the first satellites in orbit, and lying on the warm sands we could see the Russian satellite orbiting the earth.

We were warmly received by the Sergeants' Mess of the Royal Armoured Corps and spent some pleasant hours smoking and drinking before the Colonel entered and introduced the General commanding the exercise. The General was a large well built individual and clearly well known to the Squadron Sergeant Major who was chairman of the Mess. He told us that the General had served in the last war and had landed on D Day and fought through to the end of the war. We all settled down to chat and the subject of tank vulnerability to air attack was raised. All sorts of opinions were aired and the General chimed in with the statement that during the Second World War a tank in his unit had destroyed an aircraft using the main armament. One of our Flight Sergeants looked up from his one too many beers and said scornfully, 'What a lot of bullshit, who's ever heard of a tank shooting an aircraft down?' There was a ghastly pause of horror. An arm shot across the table, taking the man by the throat and slowly raising him up and across the table. 'If the General says that a tank of his unit shot an aircraft down using the main gun, He bloody well means it.' The General then put our man back in his seat to raucous cheers! The Squadron Sergeant Major was not amused, but the general had defused the situation beautifully. The talk moved on to anti tank and anti personnel mines left in Libya. Most agreed that there must still be tens of thousands left in the ground and that this had changed the habits of those who travelled the desert. In the past, before the war, an Arab would lead his family followed by the camel the children and then his wife. Now they claimed, the wife and children led the procession; the camel followed next, and then finally came the man! I'm not sure that I believed this. Anti personnel mines were mainly those that jumped into the air when stepped upon. The weight of the individual released a ratchet and a spring threw the mine upwards to explode at waist level. The use of booby traps had been quite widespread and I remembered my own experience at Idris outside Tripoli (once Castel Benito in Italian times) where, when we moved an old diesel electric power set, we found a large unexploded bomb underneath. I had worked on that power set!

It was time for us to leave, and thanking our hosts for a pleasant night we walked back across the desert. After the discussion on mines, we were self consciously careful in where we placed our feet. After a few hundred yards, there came a hoarse shout, 'I think that I've got a foot on a mine!' There was a patter of feet and then a voice from a good hundred metres away called, 'How do you knoooow?' It appeared that the man had trodden on something metallic that had 'clicked'. We told him to stand still and that we would return to get help from the Army. When we arrived at the Army lines the General asked who it was who was on top of the alleged mine, adding that he hoped that it was the unbeliever! When assured that it was, he gave a huge smile and told his people to take every precaution to avoid further accidents. What he meant was that they should not hurry – well, perhaps he didn't mean that at all! When the mine clearance group arrived, they found that our man had trodden on an aged and rusty tin can that had collapsed under his weight!

Some days later, I was a guest of the Sergeants' Mess of this unit and in daylight I could see that their encampment was vastly different to ours. The Army had the same tentage, but theirs were perfectly erected and sited with all the inners correctly secured. Their lighting and blackout were masterpieces of innovation. I mentioned this to my hosts, who commented that they ran around the countryside professionally and that any fool could be uncomfortable. Suitably chastened, I said no more, but noticed that the tables of the Officers' Mess were laid for a formal dinner celebrating some regimental battle honour. The tablecloths were pristine, the regimental silver and crystal ware gleamed and a regimental pennant (not the regimental standard – that doesn't normally go out on exercise!) stood in a place of honour. Turning to the Colonel, I asked how on earth the regiment managed to insure their silver in the field. 'Dear boy, we don't insure it. We have a thing called a subaltern in charge of all this,' he said waving his hand expansively. 'If anything is lost, broken or damaged we have his balls!' I found it in my heart to feel sorry for the unfortunate junior officer.

As the exercise developed we became fully employed, rarely returning to our temporary base until nightfall. The food provided had a certain sameness about it, but this was not surprising for we had been given three weeks of D pack compo. After enduring Irish stew *ad nauseam*, the boss went personally to obtain an exchange. He wanted to make absolutely certain that a change of diet was achieved.

In most exercises there are casualties, but rarely are those caused by stupidity. Two soldiers were constructing a toilet. The ground was remarkably hard and their entrenching tools were proving useless. They decided that the most effective way to create the necessary hole would be to use explosives. The soldiers placed their charge, retired to the safety distance and created a big bang, but only a very small hole. They then doubled the explosive charge, retired to a bit extra on the safety distance and made a bigger bang. There was very little difference in the size of the hole. Placing all the explosives that they carried into the hole they retired to the same safety distance and fired the charge. There was an enormous and satisfying bang, creating a suitable hole. Debris was flung into the air, and that debris fell on the two soldiers. Both soldiers suffered serious head injuries and one would die as a result.

In the later phases of the exercise we were 'umpired out'. That is to say we were considered by the umpire to have been killed off in an attack by passing fighter bomber aircraft. The instruction given by the umpire was that we should remain on the ground in the middle of nowhere for the next four hours. We were to remain in this position until given new orders. There were four helicopters in our group so there were enough of us to get out some canvas and make a semi decent kind of shade and brew up. Our position was militarily idiotic for we were grouped on a rise and outlined on the skyline. We drank our tea and ate those delightful oatmeal biscuits and 'dispossessed cheese' (tinned processed) from the ration packs, making ourselves, in general terms, pretty comfortable. The hours passed and although we kept a listening watch on the radio, no message was received. The umpire had said, however, that the new orders would be brought to us. As the day moved towards evening, and over six hours had passed, one of the crewmen said that the quality of exercise communication was such that any message delivered to us would be by a peasant carrying a cleft stick! That raised a good laugh, and when twenty minutes later a tall thin figure carrying a shepherd's crook appeared on the horizon there was general hysteria. The tall, thin perspiring Army Officer who had walked miles to deliver our orders was not amused by the comments, nor was he enthralled by the ribald cheers that greeted his arrival.

Back in England for the snow and rain we continued our support for army exercises. A favourite play park was Sennybridge in Wales, where generations of brownjobs have frolicked on the hills. I found the area to be totally depressing, but I've no doubt that others may not share this view. Perhaps they saw the place on the solitary day that it did not rain that year.

We landed on a ridge and we were immediately asked to put an umpire on the highest piece of land in the area. As we landed, it appeared that all was not well with the rotor brake system and the reservoir tank was nearly empty. The captain and I consulted each other and we were agreed that we could not restart the aircraft without repairing the system. It's a long time ago, but I think the problem had something to do with a phenomena called 'padding'. The aircraft rotors could flail around if there was insufficient engine power to spin them quickly up to speed. The engines started relatively slowly and there could be problems. The hydraulic oil was OM15 and we had no oil with us, and the army did not use this oil. What day was it? Friday, of course and the day was wearing on and we were most unlikely to get help in a hurry. I then had a brainwave (I had them more often than I was ever given credit for). I pulled out my little book on fuels and oils and read that there was another hydraulic oil called OM13 and that the army used this oil in gun recoil mechanisms. The oil had a lower freezing point and a higher flash point than OM15. I thought about the problems of mixing oils and whether the OM13 would affect our rubber seals. Then I remembered that the rotor brake was an entirely separate system from the main aircraft hydraulics. Things were looking better, but the question of the rubber seals remained. I carefully reread the specification of OM13 and found to my absolute delight that the oil was suitable for use where the seals were pure rubber or made of synthetics. Bingo! I could use the oil that the Army had in abundance. The leak was stopped, the tank refilled, this time with OM13 and we were on our way back to base, I had a virtuous feeling that I had earned my keep and that we had saved the unit time and money. We returned safely to Odiham where the Squadron Cdr said that we'd done well to complete the task and get the aircraft back to base.

On Monday morning the senior ground engineer officer sent for me. How dare I use non-standard oils in his aircraft? Did I know what damage I had done to the seals? He went on to say that he wished unqualified aircrew would stay away from things technical and leave the job to professionals. He was considering placing charges against me for criminal damage.

I am a peaceful man, but this was too much. Angrily, I told him that flight engineers were qualified in many technical areas, and in some cases were better qualified than his half trained technicians. I went on to say that I was not in the habit of mixing oils willy-nilly.

How could I possibly know what I was doing out in the field? he sneered. I produced the manual on fuels and oils and pointed out how eminently suitable OM13 was. I then reminded him that the system was independent of the main hydraulic system and that all that was required of his so called technicians was that they should flush out the system prior to replacing the hydraulic oil. I saluted smartly and left his presence. Back at the squadron crew room the Boss asked what had been said. When told, he swore, and said that he still thought that we had done well. Later in the morning, the Station Commander called into the squadron crew room and said how pleased he had been to see some initiative and common sense employed in the return of our helicopter. Later that afternoon, I was recalled to the Senior Engineer Officer's presence. He said witheringly that he didn't care what the Squadron Commander or the Station Commander said. 'Don't play with my aircraft!' I left in confusion, but felt that the approval of two out of three superiors wasn't too bad.

There was an accident involving the Whirlwind helicopters employed on Air Sea Rescue missions in which the rotor head became detached from the aircraft in flight. The Whirlwind force was immediately grounded pending an Inquiry and the tactical force of Wessex helicopters was instructed to take over the task. I must say that I thought that as we were accustomed to carrying under slung loads at low level and carried troops to all manner of places in all manner of ways, that we would take over the task quite easily. I was wrong, and I quickly became aware that Air Sea Rescue involved the acquisition of new skills. Daily, my respect for the crews of the Whirlwind grew as we practised to acquire some of their basic skills. We flew to the wreck of a substantial cargo vessel that had somehow in the distant past struck the coastline at right angles and practised lifting other crewmen from the deck. We lifted colleagues out of moving ships in moderate seas and learnt that the decks could both pitch and roll simultaneously; that masts and stays were dangerous and that it was all bloody dangerous, particularly in bad weather. The worst bit, I thought, was that most of the incidents we were training to meet would occur in bad weather. I was amazed at the number of wrecks around our shores and equally amazed by the stories of the Whirlwind crews.

We were to practise picking up survivors from the sea. I was in the water wearing flying suit, lifejacket and bone dome (helmet). The crewman lowered the hook into the water to discharge any static electricity before streaming it towards me. The hook struck me on the side of my face and I lost consciousness. A second crewman came down on the winch line and attempted to put a strop around me. When he had the strop around me, he must have extended his arms indicating that he was ready to be lifted, for the winch man aboard the helicopter operated the winch and when the two of us were some fifteen feet above the water we both fell out of the strop and into the sea. The second crewman struck his head on my bone dome and was knocked out. Happily, I recovered as I returned to the very cold water and was able to inflate his lifejacket. Turning him onto his back I struck out for a small outcrop of rock. Together, we sat on the rock and made Anglo Saxon gestures to the approaching helicopter. I was bleeding from a cheekbone and the other crewman had bitten his tongue when his head hit mine. Eventually, we relented and were winched up. We learnt a lot during the few weeks that we acted for the Whirlwind people, not least about our fellow man. We met the most ungrateful sods. We rescued a bloke and his girl from a capsized yacht in truly rotten conditions and when he discovered that we were not about to go back and retrieve his boat, he went mad with rage. He actually asked us why he paid taxes! I had heard stories of people saying, 'Thank you,' but in our short period of stardom it never happened to us. Of one thing I am certain. The crews of air sea rescue helicopters are genuine heroes, for every day they conduct rescues in appalling conditions both in the air and in or on the sea. Remember to say a prayer for them each night.

In the days before the problems of Northern Ireland worsened, we would take our aircraft to Ulster and exercise with the resident army units. On one occasion, I was the crewman of a helicopter carrying a pallet of fuel filled jerricans as an underslung load. We were flying over open countryside, when the load began to spin and swing. We tried all the usual tricks to stop this happening, but the straps holding the cans in a nice square shape started to slip. I told the pilot saying that he should turn towards a nearby lake, just in case we had to shed the load. There was one cow in the field below us and there was nobody to be seen in the lake and surrounding area. Frantically we turned the helicopter towards the lake as the first jerrican fell from the pallet. I watched this single can, as it fell, bomb like, from the skies. I watched the single beast in the field below as it ambled nonchalantly towards fresh grass. I watched as the jerrican and the beast converged and then in horror as the can struck the head of the cow! The load continued to disintegrate as we neared the shoreline of the lake, and just as the load totally fell apart, we saw a fishermen's punt close into the shoreline! Helplessly we watched as the shower of jerricans straddled the two fishermen just like a film of a World War Two bombing run! One moment they were sat quietly smoking and chatting and the next they were involved in World War Three as they were dive bombed from above. Mercifully, they were not hurt, but the body language and gestures were most indignant, and offensive.

In the course of the Inquiry, it was revealed that the unfortunate beast was a prize bull whose services at stud were greatly sought after. This would, of course, be reflected in the compensation claimed. It was a strange fact that if the military injured or killed an animal in Northern Ireland we had the uncanny – and unlikely – skill to always pick prize animals. We never ever killed a runt or sick beast.

As part of a counter insurgency scenario exercise we were to conduct a night assault upon an isolated farmhouse where the leaders of various insurgent groups were supposedly to be meeting at midnight. The station commander from Odiham was coming to lead the ten helicopters that would carry the assault group of soldiers. We made all the preparations at RAF Ballykelly and embarked the blacked up and well-armed troops. The 'choppers' took off, and headed in loose formation towards the exercise farmhouse. With the navigation and and collision lights off we checked the wind direction prior to landing. The wind had veered and, as we did not wish the engine noise to announce our presence, the decision was made to change landing sites. Our misfortunes began at this point, for we landed in a large area of bog. Fortunately, it was not a watery soft bog, but enough to sink the helicopter to the axle of our wheels. The troops silently departed into the night, cursing gently as their boots sank into the mire. The troops surrounded the farmhouse and the assault group entered the main house. Quickly fanning out within the building they entered the bedroom of a buxom forty-year-old woman who slept stark naked. She had been awakened to find a group of ten, blacked up, fully armed soldiers in her room! She screamed the place down. She'd have the Law on them. She'd write to Terence O'Neill (Prime Minister). She'd write to the bloody Queen, so she would! Half an hour later, the troops returned despondently. They had surrounded and forcibly entered the wrong farmhouse!

Disconsolate, we fired up the engines, dragged ourselves out of the mud and returned to Ballykelly. Throughout the return flight the soldiers exchanged their views on the debacle. One subject dominated the conversation, 'Did yer see them knockers – they wus 42 double D's!' I wonder how he knew that.

Months later, we heard that the lady had kept every single one of her promises and had written to everyone. The heavy file on her complaint contained 98 enclosures and the number continued rising in a new file!

I felt comfortable as a crewman now, perhaps too comfortable for I began to get a bit over confident. We were operating as a single aircraft in Norfolk and had landed, rotors turning, near a group of army vehicles. I was standing outside the helicopter, wearing my waist safety harness connected to the aircraft and listening to the radio and intercommunication system. Without any warning the pilot increased power and lifted off. I WAS STILL OUTSIDE! Later, I was to discover that we were urgently required in another location and that the pilot had been told this orally by a chap who had approached on the other side of the aircraft. The helicopter rose and as I began to stream in the airflow, I realised that my radio cable had pulled out of my helmet plug. The helicopter levelled at about 300 feet and accelerated forward. I managed to catch my flailing radio cable and scream that I was outside and couldn't get back in as I was below the cabin step height. The Pilot, shocked and fearful, bloody well stopped dead in the air! I DIDN'T, and passed the entrance door, reflecting that another of Newton's Laws of motion was true. I hit the top of the curving jet exhaust pipe and bounced back to hit the entrance step. I clawed my way into the cabin and lay, all limbs akimbo, clutching the floor like a Disney cartoon cat slipping down a mountainside. The pilot put the chopper down onto the ground, shut down the engines and raced round to the cabin. Sick with fright, for I had known that the locking pin of my safety belt harness was not in position throughout this incident, I reeled towards the bushes. I threw up several times and was sweating like a pig in my half-inch thick acrylan pile inner and bulky outer clothing. The pilot rushed to me, 'Eric, Eric did I frighten you?' It was at this point that I hit him! He should have called 'Lifting off' but I was solely responsible for the lack of a safety pin in my harness.

We had two delightful Polish officers on the squadron. Alex and Tom. The first was a tall slim blond rather aristocratic chap and the second a stocky dark haired individual. Both men wore the Polish war medal, but Tom apparently felt that Alex was not entitled to do so. Alex had trained first with the Russian Army, before being sent to England for pilot training. At the war's end Alex was in England. Tom, then a corporal pilot, escaped the Nazi invasion in a stolen aircraft and flew for the British throughout the war. The first Pole became very anglicised and would appear in smoking jacket and cravat at any time after seven in the evening. Tom retained his Polish character, contributed to several Polish language societies, despite changing his name on marriage to an English lady. On arrival in the UK he had to demonstrate his abilities by going through our flying training programme. His logbook showed that he won every single prize awarded to students in flying training. His name was then Francisco Tomchatsky! He and Alex didn't really get on together and their heated discussion were a joy to hear. I recall that Tom had a miniature poodle that he adored. The poor little dog broke his fore legs when he jumped out of the first floor crew room window to meet his returning master. Tom retained a heavy accent and would say, 'For why you kick my dog and call him F- off? That not his name!' I'm certain that this was Tom's idea of humour.

I had served at Odiham for some six months, when an officer on the squadron was offered a post with the Singapore Air Force. He was required at very short notice and there was no time for him to properly hand over his secondary duties. The Squadron Boss asked me to take over the squadron tool stores – on a handshake! I declined, for I had knowledge of great horror stories when handshake handovers had taken place. The Boss countered by asking if I would do this as a personal favour. What could I say to that?

I retired to the stores and began a 100 per cent stock check helped by a competent if somewhat alcoholic Sergeant storeman. Within days of the officer's departure for the Far East, it was painfully evident that there were major deficiencies. Furthermore, the annual inspection by the Air Officer Commanding was due in the near future! His inspection teams would arrive in a six weeks' time. In total, we were short of thousands of pounds worth of tools and the exercise store had far fewer tents and less equipment than shown in the records. I informed the Boss, saying that I would do my best....but. He was stricken and fervently hoped that I could do something – anything! I reminded him of my opposition to the handshake handover. He grimaced and I left.

The Sergeant storeman and I put our heads together and thought furiously. Storemen are devious souls, for it transpired that many of the tools that I had known throughout my service life as A and B stores (A = valuable and attractive, B stores are 'accountable') were not. Storemen had spread and perpetuated the myth as a form of protection. That meant that much of what was missing was considered as 'consumable'! We replaced the thousands of pounds worth of tools relatively easily by writing off stocks as lost during the many exercises of the last year or so. The tentage presented greater difficulty, but to avoid incriminating the innocent, I will say that odd strips of canvas obtained from other airbases were returned to the main stores as scrap. Three days prior to the arrival of the inspection team our stores holdings were on top line. The sergeant said that I should see the Boss and put his mind at rest. 'Oh no, Oh no,' I responded, telling him that I would tell the Boss on the morning of the inspection team's arrival. I added that we had had a great shock, and that it was only fair that the Boss should share the pain. After all, he had got me into this. There was palpable relief on his face when told that we were in every respect completely ready for the inspection team.

I was rather keen on researching the squadron history, and began to look at the Battle of Britain period. The squadron had moved south to re-inforce the battered fighter squadrons who had borne the brunt of the attacks. It was clear that the Luftwaffe were gathering for a mighty onslaught on the fighter airfields.

As my research developed and answers to my many letters returned, it became obvious that all was not as previously thought. The squadron involvement lasted only a few days, and it seemed as though the squadron had destroyed more friendly than enemy aircraft. There were many ground accidents and one or two aircraft so strained that they never flew again. Indeed the Spitfire in the London Science Museum was one such airplane; The pilot climbed to 20000 feet without wearing an oxygen mask. He lost consciousness and did not recover until he was at low altitude. In the struggle to survive the main spar of the wings were damaged. At the time that I wrote the history the pilot, now an Air Marshal, declined to have his photo taken in front of the museum piece. He said there were several reasons for this, one of which was that he would clearly no longer fit into the cockpit! My research appeared to be unbalanced and I had no time left in which to present more than one view. The Boss put my incomplete notes into his safe. They may well still be there.

It had been decided (who does decide these things?) that crewmen employed on the Wessex helicopter would be subject to examination, both oral and practical. At that time, I acted as Crewman Leader of the squadron and by common consent became the first of those to be examined.

I drove across the airfield to the Conversion Unit where the examination was to take place. After some difficulty, I managed to find the officer who was to conduct the examination. I'd never met him before, nor did I know of him. He was small, a little untidy and I'd no idea where his expertise on the Wessex helicopter had been gained.

We began by chatting briefly on the leading particulars of the helicopter (Size, weight, speed, load carrying capacity and the like). Throughout the morning phone calls and visitors constantly interrupted us. I became rather unsettled, for clearly he had done little to prepare for the oral examination. When he told me that my answers were coming too slowly, I revolted. Rising to my feet, I said that it was impossible to concentrate when subjected to nineteen interruptions and headed for the door, adding that when he could arrange privacy I would return. He went red with rage and asked who the hell I thought I was to be counting interruptions. I told him that I was Flight Sergeant Hayes, Crewman Leader of 72 Squadron. I continued towards the door, when he said with some acidity, 'If you're so bloody clever, why aren't you commissioned?' Quick as a flash I answered 'Because I thought that you had to be the ace of the base technically and a gentleman to boot! But, after looking and listening to you neither can be true!' I left, leaving him livid with rage.

I returned to the squadron buildings, grabbed a General Application Form; wrote a request that I be considered for a commission and slapped it on the Boss's desk. He was out. I left for lunch. When I returned after lunch my temper had cooled and I attempted to get my application back. This time the Boss was in and he refused to return the form, saying that it was a very good idea and that he would give it his blessing! He asked what had prompted the application and when told, smiled understandingly and said that I should not worry too much about my outburst, as it appeared to be fair criticism – if a bit rude.

Feeling better, I drove back to the examination shortly after lunch to find that my examiner was in a better mood too. He made no mention of our earlier clash and this time the 'do not disturb' sign was on the door and the telephone was off the hook.

Some weeks later I attended the officer cadet selection process. This time I knew what to expect and using low cunning contrived to pass.

CHAPTER FIFTEEN
OFFICER CADET HAYES

At last I had been instructed to report to RAF Henlow near Bedford for officer training. It had taken fifteen years for me to reach this point! Still, at least I'd got here. Gitti and I were now married and she had moved to Basingstoke near to RAF Odiham from her flat in Tewkesbury. It would not be much fun for her to be left alone in a strange place.

I had, of course made my usual blunder. If I had asked for this training to be deferred for six months, I would have been promoted to warrant officer prior to reaching the Officer Cadet Training Unit (OCTU). This, in turn would have meant that I would leave OCTU as a Flight Lieutenant rather than as a Flying Officer. It was typical of me at that time that I lacked the confidence to ask for deferment, because I was afraid that I might not be reassigned for officer training. This failure caused me to spend four years as a Flying Officer. However, back to school.

In the past, all RAF technical officers trained at Henlow and the decoration of the student officers' mess reflected this. Enormous Leonardo Da Vinci technical prints formed the dining room backcloth, I was deeply impressed but understood little.

The student body of No 196 Course assembled in the Mess anteroom for the arrival procedures and there seemed to be an age split amongst them. On one side were the golden oldies, people who had spent years in the ranks; Corporals, Sergeants, Flight Sergeants and even a few Warrant Officers. On the other side of the room a nervous group of younger people chatted carefully around one another, circling uneasily like wolves in a pack. A smaller group of rather pretty young women glanced nervously at one another and about the room, before slowly drifting in the direction of the oldies. In crystal tones a slim blonde expressed the views of her group 'Thank God for a friendly face, can we come and talk to you lot?' and plonked herself down on a nearby chair. I was not greatly flattered by the assumption that we, the oldies at 32 years of age, posed no threat. However, we chatted artlessly, looking about the room for familiar faces, and in my case finding none, before facing a barrage of introductory talks from various members of the Directing Staff (DS). Most were aircrew of one branch or another. A tall, mustachioed pilot was conspicuous as he wore the ribbon of the Distinguished Flying Cross. The others looked just like any other aircrew except that they were mainly professionally grim faced. A Squadron Leader and a drill instructor corporal represented the RAF regiment, while the Education branch fielded a wing commander, the most senior officer present. The briefings complete, the Regiment Officer warned the oldies about liaisons with the young women on the course. Later I was to learn the true meaning of the word hypocrisy.

The total student intake was divided into four or five groups and each had a member of the DS as Flight Commander responsible for all aspects of training and administrative matters. My chap was a pilot who had flown Vulcan bombers. He would keep a beady eye on my progress and write the all important reports throughout the course that would determine my future.

I found my new situation a little odd, if not artificial. I had been a senior NCO for many years and was not accustomed to the idiosyncrasies of officer training and character assessment. I had not very much idea of what to expect, nor had I a great understanding of what the directing staff were looking for either. In truth, I really did not have much idea about anything. I left school at age fifteen and had had few opportunities to express myself in either the spoken or written word. I knew a lot about the Air Force – but I had now joined a very different one! I learnt some hard lessons but I did my very best to conceal this fact.

Life at OCTU began on the square. Where else, one asks, would one start? Endless dress inspections and little cameos of drill where, one after the other, the ex-airmen could demonstrate their ability to give drill orders while the students by squadron would pound up and down the square. I was told to sound more like an officer than the 'drill pig' I had undoubtedly been. It's hard to sound couth when trying hard to be heard at a distance. Happily, there were others who gave their orders on the wrong foot, leading to vast confusion, especially when 'changing direction on the march'. It took the pressure off me, because as a Leading Boy Entrant in my youth I was well acquainted with drill, and the correct timing of the necessary orders.

There were lectures on all sorts of things that showed me another side of my chosen lifestyle. We studied Air Force Law, had our own

No 196 course, Officer Cadet Training Unit, Henlow, 1967. Author is third from right, third row from front

copies of Queen's Regulations and thoroughly immersed ourselves in the role-play of subordinate commanders acting as local magistrates. I enjoyed this immensely because I had personal experience of the 'wrong side' of the desk. Acting as the accused I could really play up. On one occasion, when not deprived of my hat before entry into the Flight Commander's office, I launched it straight at my fellow student's face, expecting him to duck. Dumbfounded, the fool tried to catch it with his teeth. He failed, but did manage to head the hat into a corner. The instructor was not amused despite my explanation that I had known this to happen and that this was the reason that the accused wore neither hat nor webbing belt when entering court. Damned now as a 'Smart Alec' I had to work harder than most to survive. I think that the course was four months in duration. Gradually our number diminished as the obvious misfit was removed. However, very often we students had absolutely no idea why X had disappeared.

As individuals we had to give a series of talks to our fellow students. I had been warned of this requirement and had assembled my photographic slides from Kenya. Hoping to impress, I offered very early on in training to speak on that country to my classmates. There were about ten or eleven Kenyans at the OCTU at this time. One of them, Peter Kagume was the first Kenyan to rise through the ranks. He was to become a technical officer. Peter was my classmate, while the other Kenyans were spread about the School. My offer was not apparently accepted, until I was informed that I was to speak to the entire student body in the presence of the Commandant and the entire Directing Staff in eight days' time. My God, My God. I could natter to my classmates – but the thought of standing before the Commandant, the Directing Staff and the whole student body appalled me.

What could I do, what could I do? I owned some good slides of wild life and the peoples of Kenya. I borrowed some lion slides from a chap called Hamilton. I mention this because I found, years later, that I didn't give them back! I asked the Kenyans for advice, and got none, for I had travelled far more extensively in their country than they had done. Did they own a record or tape of their national anthem? No! Where could I get one? God knows. I rang their embassy and explained my predicament. I needed to positively start and end my talk, and the best way was to find a slide of the Kenyan flag and to end by playing the national anthem. The Commandant would have little option but to stand while it played. A kind soul produced a record of the anthem and to this I added a record of East African drummers. I also found an excellent little handbook listing the principal tribes of Kenya and the regions in which they lived. I quickly read this and memorised the areas where the principal tribes lived.

I now needed an overall plan that would allow me to control events and decided that I would open by producing a map of East Africa by overhead projector and introduce my subject with a very brief spell of drumming. I would then explain that the East Africa of 1966 was very different to that depicted in popular fiction. Today, Kenya could become a key part of any East African Federation and in my opinion had the potential to become a model for African countries that had become independent of a colonial power. I would then say that I had been part of a Beverley crew lent to President Jomo Kenyatta by the British government for a period of six months. I then planned to say that I would speak on my travels within the country, the scenery, wildlife and peoples of Kenya, but that I would express no views on Kenyan politics or politicians. To make sure that I was asked the right questions, I would plant about six questions that would be posed by my classmates.

How did it go? Bloody awful in some ways, good in others. I opened with a good OHP slide of East Africa clearly showing the location of the country, and followed this with some drumming while showing a 35mm slide of the Kenyan flag. So far, so good. I then explained the construction of my short talk, told the audience the subjects I intended to speak on. I launched into the slides of the wildlife, scenery and flowers, and waited for the planted questions. The first of my classmates mistimed his questions and all the others 'lost their places' as I furiously improvised. However, I recovered and toiled on, before concluding my talk by showing the Kenyan flag and playing the national anthem. The audience rose, the band played and the anthem stilled all voices. Joy of Joys, I had survived!

As the last note of the anthem played, a loud, very loud voice, bellowed that the audience should sit down again. The Commandant rose and said that my interesting talk prompted many questions. He noted that I had done my very best to avoid questioning. To start the ball rolling he asked what would happen in Kenyan politics if Kenyatta should die. I pointed out that I did not wish to comment, largely because of the sensitivities of the Kenyan students who came from widely different ethnic groups. Totally ignoring this excuse, he demanded a response. Reluctantly, I pointed out that Tom Mboya the leading opposition leader had recently been assassinated, and that the opposition was in disarray. There were leaders from most of the larger tribes of the country who had aspirations of power, but none of these leaders could attract much support outside of their own tribal areas. His next question was also barbed. What did I think of the Deputy President? The man in question was a nationalist who apparently detested whites, all whites. Odinga Odinga was an articulate and virulent speaker and his outbursts frequently formed the front-page articles of the East African press. What was I to say? I had flown him and other ministers on several occasions around the shores of Lake Victoria to view flood damage and had taken him on tours of inspection of the Northern Frontier District where he met tribal leaders. On all of these occasions he had totally ignored the entire crew, barely nodding to us as he left in his official car.

Another voice asked if I knew anything about Odinga Odinga describing the Caledonian Society as racist in Parliament. I said that I had heard of the incident and attempted to close off the subject. Pressed by the Directing Staff (DS) I spoke of the East African press response that had been to widely publicise the verbal attack, not only in Kenya, but throughout Uganda and Tanzania as well. The following day in Parliament the Kikuyu deputy Minister for Agriculture had risen to say that the Honourable Minister was mistaken, and that the Caledonian Society was definitely not racist. The only prerequisite for membership of the Caledonian Society was that full membership was limited to those who had been born in Scotland. He went on to say that it might interest the Minister to know that he himself was a member and that he took great pleasure in attending functions such as Burns Night. He added that he really must ask his parents how he came to be born in Edinburgh! The press of the erstwhile East African Federation reported this rebuttal with the same enthusiasm that they had given the earlier report. Odinga Odinga was not amused, but his countrymen were.

Mercifully, the awkward questions faded and there followed some 45 minutes of general questions which were easily answered. The Commandant thanked me for an interesting evening and I slipped away, conscious that I had been a little too clever for my own good. This view was shared by my course commander, and was no doubt reflected in my final mark.

I remember many incidents from this important period of my life, but only a few are relevant to this chapter. I said earlier that I was to learn the true meaning of hypocrisy and I did so at half past two in the morning some ten weeks into the course. A timid knock on my door woke me and I opened it to find a very nice young thing in a very thin nightdress and sheer coat. I believe this outfit to be a 'peignoir'. 'Eric, please can you come to my room and get rid of the Regiment Officer – he won't leave.' Heaving my trousers on, and putting something on my feet, I duly trotted up the stairs to find a smiling Rock Ape (the affectionate term for those serving in the RAF Regiment). 'Ah,' he cried,' I thought that it would be you or young Deaman (my neighbour) who would ride to her rescue!' He then went on to say, while gently rocking in the armchair, that perhaps ten weeks ago I would have had his guts for garters. However, that was weeks ago. Perhaps, ten weeks from now I might just try to have his guts – but now, smiling broadly, he invited me to push off and mind my own business. The girl became distressed, but did not cry. Thinking furiously, I asked the girl to leave the room; after she had left, I asked if he knew who she was and how she was connected within the Air Force. With a rush of alcohol-fuelled bonhomie he declared that he knew only that she was a finely built nubile young lady for whom he had formed a deep attraction. I pointed out that his taste in young women was impeccable, but that she was the daughter of a very senior officer and the god-daughter of our own Air Officer Commanding all officer training (absolute fiction). I questioned that this attempted seduction was such a good idea. As the girl re-entered the room, I whispered in her ear that her visitor would probably leave within the next five minutes. (Preservation of dignity is most important to a chap.) He did in fact leave, after making a decent apology for his intrusion, which he attributed solely to her superior charms. He was that kind of man. The actress Pauline Collins, enjoying a seduction scene in *Shirley Valentine* spoke a wonderful aside that encapsulated her response to protestations of love in a single sentence. 'Don't men talk shit?' I'm told that we frequently do.

Part of the course was the presentation of a group project. Each of the four flights was divided into teams of five or six students. Each team was given a subject and the date upon which the presentation was to take place. We were given at least one month to prepare. In my group there were some very clever people, but none of us had any knowledge of China's 'Great Leap Forward!' We elected a leader and allocated the various research tasks. We discussed how best to present the subject and decided that we needed a backcloth and the means to use an overhead projector as a back projector. I owned a little six panel Chinese screen with rather a pretty but simple motif. This was laid on an epidiascope table, projected onto a wall and the motif of each panel traced on to a very large sheet of strong paper. Two of our group painted the tracings to create a most authentic looking backcloth that was attached to stiffened hardboard. The research began to bear fruit and we learnt a great deal about China, the people and their difficulties. Our presentation was very well received and I was proud of the means and manner of delivery. My brother at this time was a Colonial Office official in Hong Kong. Some years later, when we were discussing China together, and pondering the problems of the day, I was not flattered when he looked surprised that I knew anything at all about China. Charitably, I thought that perhaps he measured his judgment upon the mental capacity of his Army service colleagues.

I was informed that a parcel awaited my collection in the station mailroom and the only time for this was during the lunch hour. It was quite a walk to the building that housed the office and I had a brisk walk to reach it by their closing time. The young airman looked me square in the eye and told me that he was shut and that I should return in the afternoon. With that he pulled down the door of the hatch separating us. Six weeks earlier that little sod would never have dared to shut on me. In ten more weeks he would not dare – but that little shit knew that he was fireproof at that moment. The status of an officer cadet is no status at all and this was a reminder of that fact. As my wife Gitti would say 'Every dog has his day!'

A substantial number of course members had been to the cinema in Bedford. We returned to the Mess at about eleven in the evening and we were enjoying a three-legged race up the corridor of the Mess. As we raced past the Bar door, my Course Commander came out just in time to see my partner and me sprawl on the carpeted floor. We were not three legged but were playing hopscotch on the checked squares of the carpet. 'You seem determined to throw away those few officer quality marks you possess, Hayes.' Ex Flight Sergeant Hayes replied 'Balls,' and I continued on my way. Another nail in my coffin.

No 196 course was to undertake a series of outdoor leadership exercises and we were instructed to load up all the tentage and equipment necessary for us to ensure that the DS enjoyed decent meals and a comfortable existence for some days in the wilderness. On arrival in the camp area, a student commandant was nominated and he immediately detailed colleagues to undertake the duties of adjutant, catering officer, admin officer etc. All were required to regularly report to the student commandant. By common consent a sweet young thing called Fredina Heard (Fred) was elected permanent cook. Other aspirants for the job were discouraged for Fred was a Paris trained Cordon Bleu chef – God only knows why she joined the Air Force. Fred was not only good looking but could do wonders with the rations available. Most was tinned stock and had been extracted from emergency stores; to maintain such stock in an in-date condition, regular usage or turnover is essential. The ill formed palates of would be young officers offered the command catering staff an irresistible opportunity to get rid of the damned stuff. In recent years I have, however, changed my views on the old-fashioned 'compo' ration. In the hands of an imaginative cook it can be far more palatable than the modern MRE (meals ready to eat) that are currently provided.

The leadership exercises continued and although I can't remember which UK wilderness we camped in, I do remember a deep stream reminiscent of a canal and that it rained. I remember that river and the steep banks, because I was instructed to bridge it. Lining up my team of six and the equipment provided, I asked if any of the group had experience of bridging. Happily, an ex Boy Scout with a Duke of Edinburgh's award had experience in such matters. Retaining command, I instructed him to carry out the task. He succeeded brilliantly in a remarkably short time, while I acted the part of an informed Leader. I didn't know it at the time, but this was a shrewd move – using the expertise of the group. To me it was common sense, for I had never built a bridge. The Course Commander said snidely that I had been lucky. Stung, I asked how he knew that I knew nothing about bridge building. That provoked a negative response and I realised that once again I'd put my foot in it.

Some days into the exercises I was appointed Adjutant in support of a very young and inexperienced Commandant. I told him to leave absolutely everything to me. I promised to report regularly and that I would provide him with the best run camp possible and make him look good. I felt safe in saying this because I had picked all the camp officers for the day. All of them were ex SNCOs and could be relied upon to produce the goods. Our Rock Ape student Chris Shorrocks was in charge of catering with our faithful friend, Fred, cooking happily on the petrol stoves that only Chris could safely coax into perfect order. Another friend, Chalky White, ensured that there was hot water available all day (a first). I trotted around looking important, complete with clipboard. Every hour or so, I popped into the Commandant and brought him up to date, handing him sheets of paper. He was most disturbed when told that a stray dog had made off with the meat intended for the DS dinner! Fred's minions pursued this cur for a full fifteen minutes before cornering the animal and relieving it of the meat. Shorrocks sadly brought the well-chewed meat back to the cooking area in the knowledge that we had very little fresh meat left. Fred cast a knowledgeable eye upon the flesh. 'No great problem,' she said after professional consideration. 'Get me some vinegar.' She massaged the meat with vinegar before thoroughly washing it off and throwing it into a large bowl filled with a marinade guaranteed to cover any canine flavour. I advised the Commandant of this culinary solution, but he seemed far from happy as the evening mealtime approached.

In my capacity as Adjutant for the day, I felt free to amend with some of the camp domestic arrangements. Previous evening meals had been served on cold plates, and on bare tables. I detest hot meals served on cold plates and I like tablecloths and flowers on the table. Moreover, I had overheard DS mutterings about cold plates and the manner in which the meals were actually served. Wild flowers, gathered by artistic souls, were placed in various containers on the top table. As the DS arrived for dinner, I lined up the waiters and held an ostentatious hands and gloves inspection. Selected gloved waiters placed the redhot plates before the DS, warning them that the plates were hot only after half of them had burnt their fingers. My cup overflowed. Enter Fred with a beautifully decorated meat charger upon which the evenly sliced meat was perfectly arranged. The waiters hovering attentively ensured that even if the students remained hungry, the DS would have nothing to complain about. There was no dissent, for we all wanted to see the DS reaction to the meat. As the meal came to a close, the DS spokesman, Squadron Leader O'Dwyer-Russell (ODR to his mates) rose and thanked the cook for excelling herself and led the enthusiastic applause of the student body that was celebrating a quite different event!

The Directing Staff worked quite hard to find ways of determining the character of their students. Frequently these attempts would appear rather stupid in nature and it was difficult for students to see what they were trying to do – and why. In the middle of the night the duty student arrived with a message that my Course Commander required a quart of boiling seawater within one hour! I went to the kitchen tent and the duty cook and I prepared just over a quart of salty water. While this was in preparation I found a small hexamine stove pack that I could carry with the extremely hot salt water. I reached his tent, lit the hexamine cooker, restored the heat lost in transit and presented him with a quart measure of boiling salt water. 'Your salt water, sir,' I said in my best butler's voice. Gravely he said, 'Thank you Hayes,' and slowly poured the water on the ground in front of me while watching my face. Picking up the hexamine cooker, I inclined my head and said, 'Will there be anything further Sir?' With equal gravity, he replied that I could retire for the remainder of the night. I know that he was trying to see if he could destroy my composure but there must have been other methods. At graduation he told me that I was absolutely poker faced when he poured out the water, and that as I left, he knew that he was wasting his time. As Boris Becker would famously say years later, 'I have been here since yesterday'.

To my surprise and disappointment, I had problems with public speaking. The instructor laid out the guidelines of effective speech, warning of excessive movement, irritating mannerisms such as jingling coins in pockets and coughs, ahs, mmmms and inappropriate language. His guidelines were intended for those giving military briefings from a lectern. Each of us was to provide a two-minute speech, two five-minute speeches and a final 15-minute offering. The subject of all but the fifteen-minute talk was given to us. However, the subjects for the two and five minute talks were given five minutes prior to speaking. We were awarded marks by our fellow students and at the end of each marking session the DS would express their view. An average mark of four was a necessary pass mark. My average immediately prior to the final talk was three. I was desperate, and had tried talking into a tape recorder and analysing my effort. Slowly, I realised that I would never survive if I slavishly followed those guidelines. I was simply incapable of standing still and restraining all mannerisms. I knew that I was first to speak in the morning and arrived early to position all the classroom chairs into a horseshoe group. The class arrived and sat down expectantly, knowing that I had remained outside the room. With the arrival of the instructor, I entered the room, walking to the centre of the horseshoe. Patting my very small stomach (It was smaller then than now) I said that this was, or would become, a problem with the passage of time. One solution was to take up sports marching. More specifically, to march in Holland on the world famous Nijmegen March.

I went on to say that while serving as the crewman leader of 72 Squadron at RAF Odiham I had been invited (fingered) by my Station Commander to become administrative head of the 500 UK military entrants to the Nijmegen March. The Station Commander at Odiham had taken part in this sports march on many occasions. As a Sergeant Pilot, he had been shot down over Germany during the Second World War, and had walked to Switzerland where an over zealous Swiss border guard shot him in the knee. Undeterred, he had hidden while his leg healed before walking to Spain. In his most recent medical, he had been warned that he should not further strain his knee. He told me that he would like to enter the town on the final day at the head of as many British teams as possible. He went on to say that this would probably be the last time he would take part in the march.

The task of arranging all this proved quite a challenge for me, because teams started off as early as 0500hrs and departed at five minute intervals throughout the morning and there were many classes of entrant, each team walking a different course and distance. Mercifully, I had the help of a Warrant Officer friend, Doug Griffith, who spoke fluent Dutch. I went on to tell the class of the various military participants. Teams of Germans, Israelis, Swiss, Belgians, Americans, and Italians abounded, but there were many others too. About fifty thousand civilians marched in teams or as individuals throughout the three-day event. Three Dutch ladies in their eighties walked 10 km in clogs! There were many categories of marchers including schoolchildren. Military teams with weapons and equipment marched 25km per day. It was not a competition. Unexpectedly, four RAF Germany teams arrived and told me that I was now their liaison with the Dutch Army responsible for sleeping and bathing facilities. The linguistic capabilities of WO Griffith were invaluable to me. Just where Doug had learnt Dutch I don't know, but he was truly fluent in the language. He provided a great deal of amusement when he surfaced from his tent early one morning clad in a one piece-sleeping suit rather like a large baby-grow. Subsequently, a SNCO from RAF Germany arrived to enquire if 'Brer Rabbit' was available!

Realising that I had the full attention of the class, I completed my talk by mimicking the troops marching sixteen abreast down the streets of Nijmegen. It was 1966 – the year we won the football World Cup. The airmen, their rifles at the low port, slapped their rifle butts as they marched chanting the football cry of 'England' to emphasise their slapping. Group Captain Randle, walking as an individual, proudly led at least six British teams in behind the RAF Germany band that I had held outside the town for an hour and a half for just this event. The Dutch townspeople were ecstatic in their approval. I thanked the class for their attention and sat down.

I had broken every guideline. I had marched around the room, slapped imaginary rifle butts and provided sound effects where necessary to amplify my talk. In short, I could be in trouble – but not more than I had been in before speaking. The class voted my mark in the customary show of hands giving me an incredible average mark of eight. I waited anxiously for the instructor to speak. 'Well,' he said, 'most interesting, and I agree the mark.' My spirit leapt within me. At the end of the period I asked him how, when I had broken all his guidelines, I could get such a mark. I emphasised that I was not complaining. He said that guidelines were just that, and that while briefing style talks required a disciplined approach, my body language and speech on this occasion were appropriate to my subject. I felt like Freddy Fly in the Dandy Comic. 'Narrow squeak, my wings creak!' I know, I know – you've never heard of the comic, far less the fly!

The course came to an end and to my delight I became a gentleman by Act of Parliament and commissioned into Her Majesty's Royal Air Force. There was an unexpected financial bonus discovered when diligently reading Queens Regulation (QRs) – as one does! I was, apparently, '*discharged* to commission'. I found this fact interesting, for years earlier, at the time of the Korean War, I had extended my service by one year. A bounty of one hundred pounds sterling was payable – on discharge! A quick trip to the Accountant Officer confirmed my reading of the situation. A further effort to extract money from accounts was refused when the accountants agreed my reading of QRs, but pointed out that I was of the wrong sex to benefit on this occasion. My Flight Commander took these efforts as proof that I did actually read QRs.

Before I leave this period of my life I must describe the preparations for the Passing Out Parade. We knew that the weather would be good, for Sam Azikwe, our Nigerian student had 'thrown the bones' to determine the forecast. All wives and girl friends had put on their glad rags and self-consciously made their appearances. I was particularly proud to see that my wife of one year, Gitti, was both the prettiest and the best-dressed female present. Blonde and blessed with a good figure she looked superb in her pink dress and matching coat, as she held onto the blue picture hat that had been bought with money borrowed from my Kenyan colleague! Peter Kagume was staying with us in our Basingstoke flat for a weekend prior to our graduation. We were visiting Winchester when we saw 'the hat', I didn't have much money on me, but Peter offered to make up the shortfall. He got the money back when I collected my bounty money. I've often wondered what he thought at the time – for he had never been in the home of a European before. Did he think that it was standard practice to borrow money from guests?

Sam Azikwe brought a touch of colour to our parade for he was resplendent in his red tunic. I had never looked so slim. The evening dance was a splendid occasion marked by the arrival of the Catholic priest. Father O'Shea brought the dancing to an abrupt halt by standing in the middle of the dance floor brandishing his Bible. When the band had ground to an uneasy stillness, the good Father unscrewed the top of his Bible and offered a toast to the departing course members! He went on to tell us that the students of a Spanish seminary had given him the flask earlier in his career. He astounded all by leading the assembly in a series of Mess Games. I greatly enjoyed his input.

Gitti and I had taken a room in a local hotel and tired and excited we prepared for bed. However, there was a major difficulty. It had taken considerable time and effort to get the studs into my heavily starched dress shirt when dressing earlier in the evening. It was impossible to get out of the pesky thing in the early hours of the morning. Together we struggled for a good ten minutes. Finally, in exasperation, I said that I'd have to sleep in the damned thing. At that second the stud popped out and I was free. The next day we returned together to Basingstoke and a new life began for us both.

CHAPTER SIXTEEN
THE HERCULES TRANSPORT AIRCRAFT

The transport force of the RAF was in process of transformation. The first of sixty-six Hercules C Mk 1 had arrived in the UK to replace the Hastings and Beverley aircraft. The first UK conversion course was in progress at RAF Thorney Island near Portsmouth. I knew the place well for, in earlier years I had converted to both the Hastings and Beverley aircraft at Thorney. Unfortunately, the next (the second) Hercules course did not start for some weeks so I was sent up to RAF Topcliffe to help with an administrative task. I distinguished myself by becoming so interested in the task given me that I failed to turn up for an arrival interview with the Station Commander. Fifteen minutes late, I explained to an amused Group Captain that I had become immersed in the task. He accepted my apology with a broad smile saying that he had never heard this particular excuse before. He said that on such occasions when he had been late as a junior officer, he usually invented diarrhoea! I spent only a few weeks at Topcliffe before returning to Odiham where they were very short of crewmen. My flying category was still valid and I was delighted to be able to go home at night. However, the long awaited posting notice arrived and I was sent to RAF Lyneham near Swindon to await the availability of a conversion course.

My arrival at RAF Thorney Island evoked memories both pleasant and unhappy. I had been withdrawn from the Hastings course and moved to the Beverley aircraft and I had lost friends at Thorney when a Beverley crashed into the mud flats of Chichester harbour at night. Had the crew stayed with the aircraft they would have survived, for the water was not deep. Unfortunately, the navigator and flight engineer were lost only yards from safety. I had very mixed feelings as I drove onto the base.

It's unkind to recall some memories but I enjoyed the arrival of a more affluent and extrovert Air Engineer. Seated in his aged, open topped, Austin Healey sports car and dressed appropriately, he swept into the Sergeants' Mess car park, waving rude greetings to us all. The surface of the car park was very poor and had deep ridges and the spirited arrival of the said individual tore the two metal bands that supported his fuel tank. When the car stopped, the tank was some yards behind!

I arrived in all the sartorial elegance of a newly commissioned Flying Officer and made my way to the large crew room in which my course members were assembling. In the foreground as I entered were several Master Engineers, one of whom had been my mentor in Aden. I was delighted to see him and walked across saying how pleased I was to see him again. To my amazement, dismay and horror, he spurned my hand and said bitterly that he was sure that I was pleased to see him! I learnt later that he had applied for a commission and had been turned down. I had learnt a tremendous amount from this man and was more than upset by his reaction to my appearance as an officer. He had sustained me when I was under confident and inexperienced and I was truly grateful.

Characters abound among aircrew and one that I remember was a Canadian, Squadron Ldr Ben Boutain. Ben was a pilot instructor with considerable Canadian Air Force experience of the Hercules. He did not particularly care for the customs and habits of the RAF. He especially disliked the practice of 'arrival procedures' when joining a new unit. He attempted to visit all the sections listed on his blue arrival card, but was confounded when he read that Stores dealt with arrivals between 0800 and l000hrs and that the Safety Equipment section would sign arrival chits only between the hours of 0900 to l000hrs. He quickly established that, because of the lack of coordination between sections and the physical distances involved, that it was impossible to complete arrival procedures in one day. Three times he attempted to arrive at Pay Accounts, each time to be met by a different clerk who would not deal with his arrival. Once the reason was that his papers had not reached the unit, and on another occasion he was outside of the published hours of business. On the third occasion he was unable to resolve his queries. Ben then went on a form of strike and made no attempt to complete arrival procedures. Some weeks later he was telephoned by OC Admin, a Wing Commander, who inquired why he had not 'arrived'. Ben replied that he was unable to deal with the Wing Commander because he only dealt with such matters outside of 0800hrs on Mondays until 1700hrs on Fridays! Further discussion did take place on a head to head basis, but it was noticeable that arrival procedures underwent radical change.

My Hercules course was the first UK course, or was it the second? That means that the RAF personnel who had trained at Lockheed, Georgia where the aircraft was built, had supposedly learnt sufficient about the Hercules to become instructors to those joining the new squadrons. It all seemed to work out reasonably well, for there were very few, if any, 'totally new boys' among our number.

Curiously, I remember very little about the course, other than that I enjoyed it. The aircraft was a real jewel and capable of so very much more than the aircraft types it replaced. As with all modernisation programs that I have experienced, we got rid of hundreds of old aircraft and replaced them with far fewer new ones. That the new aircraft could do the work far more economically and far faster is beside the point. Taken to extremes, it is possible that in the future ten super transport aircraft could technically perform the transport task. However, it makes no military sense to have all your eggs in so very few baskets. The sixty-six Hercules that had replaced large numbers of Hastings and Beverley aircraft seemed to us to be a relatively small basket.

Oh, one thing I do remember, I was standing at the bar of the Mess listening to a discussion by a group of my superiors (almost everyone was my superior) when I was asked for my opinion on the subject. I said that they probably wouldn't want to hear it, but a Wing Commander insisted. I gave my opinion and he frigidly stated, 'Rubbish, who the hell do you think you are?' I knew that as a Flight Sergeant my opinion had been both asked for and respected. I now learnt that as a Flying Officer my opinion was not normally asked for and was most unlikely to be respected. Three months later that Wing Commander apologised for his comment. I thanked him, but said that it was a pity that he had not made the apology in front of the same group before whom he had so embarrassed me. It's hardly surprising that I never made senior rank, is it?

I joined 36 Squadron, commanded by Wing Commander Paling, known as the Chairman. The squadron had begun the Second World War equipped with Wildebeest biplanes based in Singapore. There they were no match for the Japanese invaders. Most of the squadron personnel became prisoners of war. The squadron had only just reformed with the aim of becoming operational in September 1967. I liked the squadron badge that showed a Malay eagle with the motto 'Rajamwali Raja Langit' King of the Skies. Certainly the new aircraft if not King of the Skies was undoubtedly Queen of the Skies!

The embryo squadron personnel trained at the Lockheed, Georgia factory and with the United States Air Force in the United States and had formed close friendships. Despite this, I was well received and I worked as deputy to a respected and well-known character Trevor

Peacock. Trevor was an ex-Halton Apprentice of the pre war vintage. He had become aircrew early in the Second World War and had been shot down while operating bi-planes in the defence of Singapore. He suffered burns and some other injuries and was in hospital when the Japanese entered the city. After some days, stories leaked of atrocities as the invaders advanced across the city. Trevor left his bed and attempted to find a way out with some Army men who had commandeered a small vessel. Less fortunate was the arrival at sea of a Japanese warship that rammed the boat and left them to drown. After some hours in the water he was picked up by a friendly boat, but not before some of his fellows had drowned, or been taken by sharks. They put ashore in Sumatra to be forced only weeks later into boats again as the Japanese invaded the Dutch colony. Trevor's luck was again pretty foul, for a Japanese destroyer shelled their craft, leaving the survivors once more to drown. By another miracle Trevor and most of his group were picked up by an Australian cruiser and transported to Australia. Trevor was reunited with Sandy, another ex-Halton Apprentice in hospital and together they convalesced in that most friendly and hospitable country. After nearly a year, a missive from above arrived, informing them of their impending return to the European war. Totally unimpressed by this news, the two boarded ship for Blighty. On return to Durban, South Africam, the two had a brilliant idea that they could pass themselves off as instructors at the nearby training airbase at Bloemfontein. Neither wished to desert, but felt that they had both already enjoyed an eventful war.

Marching boldly into the General Office in Station Headquarters they announced themselves as new Engine Instructors. The Senior Training Officer asked for their papers, but accepted their explanation of a total cock up. Together the trio walked around the training facilities where the pair could hardly control their glee. The power plants that they were supposed to instruct on were essentially the same as the engines they had trained on as Aircraft Apprentices at Halton. Trevor and his friend reorganised the engine training on the base and made many improvements to the course before the inevitable call to the Station Commander arrived. With the pair standing on a very small mat before his desk, he handed them a letter and asked for their comment. The paper, from the Air Staff, tersely instructed the Station Commander to hand both men over to the Provost Branch, and that the Station Commander was to personally ensure that they were returned under guard and restraint to the UK forthwith.

There was little that Trevor and Sandy could say except that they were not deserters. The South African Commandant agreed and went on to say that while he would agree to their return to the UK, it would not be under guard, nor would it be in disgrace, for he was delighted with the results of their efforts. Indeed, they would return with letters of commendation from both the South African Air Force as well as his personal recommendation that any punishment considered by UK authorities should be scrapped. It was indeed scrapped and Trevor went on to fly Lancaster bombers. I was delighted to be deputy to such a man and we worked in great harmony and friendship for years after my return from the Conversion Unit.

I completed all my squadron arrival procedures and met an older Squadron Leader Flight Engineer from the Tactical Staff who said that he would conduct my acceptance flight. He explained that unlike such flights in the past on older types of aircraft, there would be no trick questions and that no little traps would be set for the unwary. I was relieved to hear this, for there had been an absolutely ridiculous level of questioning on Beverley and Hastings aircraft. 'Does the propeller valve move forwards or rearwards when feathering?' Similar irrelevant questions could follow on most other subjects. My view had always been that if you had no control of the movement it didn't matter. It either worked or it did not. If there was nothing that you could do to mend it or mitigate the effects of the failure, then I didn't want to know. I did my external walk round inspection and moved into the aircraft to complete my other checks. When all my pre-flight checks were complete, one of the ground crew appeared and I asked if, on his return to see the aircraft off, he would bring a tyre inflation dust cap, as there was one missing from the starboard rear wheel. My screen engineer told the airman, 'Don't bother about the inflation cap, I've got it!' Turning to me cheerfully he cried 'Just wanted to see if you were observant.' Nothing had changed, absolutely bloody nothing, it was still a trapping exercise.

One of my first flights was as Engineer to our new Squadron Cdr. We had an uneventful flight, landed and taxied into dispersal. At this point the Boss turned on me – and bollocked me rigid, for what reason I don't know to this day. I had offended him in some way, but none of the rest of the crew could provide a reason.

Some three weeks later, he lent me to the new Commander of 24 Squadron, a unit that was in process of reforming. Wing Commander Tetley – of beer and tea family fame was to fly on a world trainer with me as his Engineer. We set off from Lyneham with a first stop at Akrotiri in Cyprus. The No3 oil shut off valve failed on shut down. The Station Visiting Aircraft Flight (Station Flight) was extremely busy and said regretfully that they would be unable to fix our aircraft in time for us to make our scheduled departure. I told the captain that I'd fix it. I was happily working away when an Army Major who was in charge of our Army passengers walked by on his constitutional. He was horrified to see me at work. He asked if I was qualified and why I didn't have a qualified SNCO. Deeply touched by his concern I told him that I was better qualified than most SNCOs and that I didn't need one, even if one had been available. Shaking his head in disbelief at this information and pondering the differences between Army and Air Force he said that in the Army, officers did not repair aircraft (I was not surprised at this statement).

I had a few hours' sleep before we took off on schedule for Bahrain, where, once again, a minor fault caused me to work through what was supposed to be sleeping time. At this time there were very few technicians on overseas bases who had any experience at all of Hercules aircraft. Often, it was necessary to demonstrate refuelling procedures. The flight continued through Gan, in the Maldives, to Changi where we had a welcome day off before flying back through Hawaii, Offutt and Gander. Throughout the entire trip I rarely enjoyed a full night's sleep. Years later, Air Marshal Tetley told me that when he chaired Flight Safety meetings on crew fatigue, he remembered our eventful journey with a deep sense of guilt.

After a couple of days rest at home, I returned to my own squadron buildings where I was told to report to the Boss immediately. With a sense of foreboding, I collected my hat and knocked on his door. To my surprise, the Chairman stood in front of his desk smiling, holding out his hand. 'I've just had John Tetley in here singing your praises to high heaven. He thinks that you're the best thing since sliced bread and a most competent engineer. You and I have obviously got off to a bad start. Shall we start again?' totally taken aback, I took his hand and stuttered, 'Thank you, I'd like that,' before leaving in a daze. There are few men that will admit to mistakes and even fewer who will apologise to their juniors.

After helicopters I was delighted to be flying fixed wing aircraft again. The performance of the 'Herky Bird' represented a quantum leap forward from that of the Hastings and Beverley aircraft that it replaced. In the most general of terms, the Hastings could take 10000lbs of freight and fly to Washington from Lyneham in three days, stopping at Reykjavik, in Iceland, and Gander in Newfoundland. One Hercules could carry 30000lbs and fly directly to Washington in eight hours. Only occasionally would the winds or weather force an interim stop in Gander. The Herk flew over the weather, while the two older aircraft forced their way through cloud and ice. In some ways the Hercules was so sophisticated that the older engineers quite missed their battle with continuously adjusting power, oil cooler shutters and all the manual controls that had now been made to operate automatically. Now we not only synchronised propellers, we interleaved the propeller blades by synchrophasing thereby reducing vibration and noise in the cabin. Ah, there be progress!

I must confess, at times, to a degree of confusion. When I joined the transport force it was called Transport Command, but became Air Support Command. I spent some time in 38 Group and I served in Middle East Air Force (MEAF) and Near East Air Force (NEAF). In truth, I don't quite know what the Transport force is called today.

The Hercules C130K became very popular, not just because it was a most competent transport aircraft, but also because it went to places that most of us had never been to before. It is reliable and is a most forgiving aircraft. I say is, because those same aircraft are still in service flying with crews that are almost all younger than the airframe. The systems redundancy, even in the earliest models, is wonderful. There are lots of ways to get the undercarriage and flaps down. There is a good asymmetric flap protection system. Braking is duplicated and, in addition, propeller braking can bring you to a halt too. A decent de-icing system – Oh, I could go on and on. I liked the bird, which was just as well, for I sat in it for more than 8000 hours. I once heard an Army officer describing flight in a Hercules to a younger colleague, 'Dear boy, it's the only aircraft that I know of where one can relieve oneself at the pee tube, while simultaneously entertaining the troops.' He went to say that female passengers would do well to 'water their horse' prior to departure! The elsan type toilet was released from its stowed position on the port wall to descend into what became a curtained cubicle.

Now what made aircrew life so fascinating at the time was not really the aircraft and/or the travel, but the people who surrounded me. This was the time when the last of the wartime aircrew were completing their service prior to retirement. Many were quite remarkable characters. They and their stories and idiosyncrasies were a constant source of interest and amusement. Few of the Poles and Czechs who had helped our country so much during the war remained, but the few who did continued to enliven our lives. Flight Lieutenant Andrus, from 84 Squadron in Aden, was now Squadron Ldr Andrus (even at Lyneham few could pronounce his full name. Another Pole who lived opposite us, Wenderokowski (Wen), flew Britannia aircraft with 511 Squadron and both pilots were remarkable. Andrus could do the Times crossword over the lunch break! I most certainly couldn't. Nevertheless, within my own section were two or three master aircrew, who could be guaranteed to keep the conversation going on a dull day. A signaller, about to retire, one Wampo Wharton, worked in Squadron operations, ate raw onions and took snuff. He swore that he'd never had a cold. We believed this because no self-respecting germ would go anywhere near him!

 I think that of all the storytellers that I heard, I enjoyed most those told by Bert Sutcliffe. Bert was a man of dry humour who told his tales with a minimum of words and a few gesticulations leaving all the detail to be filled in by the imaginations of his audience. Aged just 19 years and trained as a flight engineer he was taking part in a raid by some two hundred Lancaster bombers on a south German city during late 1943. There was heavy flak and Bert found himself swinging gently on the end of his parachute gazing into the black void below. He was unaware of quite how he got to this situation, but felt, with some justification, that this shouldn't have happened on his first mission.

 He landed safely on a wooded hillside decked with deep snow. At the Conversion Unit he had been taught the basics of survival and he now set about putting it all into practice. He buried his chute and made off into the forest where he hid for the next four days. During this time he saw and heard absolutely nobody, nor did he see a light. He was now very hungry, his little tin of goodies in the pocket of his flying suit had long been eaten, but he'd been told to evade capture. On the fifth day, he walked down the hill and knocked on the door of a farm worker who set his dogs on him. Bert left quickly and tried again that night at another farm. This time he announced himself as British. No dogs this time, but he was chased off by a pitchfork-wielding woman of very uncertain temper. On the seventh hungry day, a tired, well-bitten and prodded Bert stood disconsolate in the middle of an autobahn with his hands up. He halted a military convoy demanding to be taken prisoner. (Prisoners are usually fed and watered.) His captors were not unfriendly, but insisted on handing him over to Luftwaffe personnel who, after questioning him, sent him off under guard to a prison camp in Silesia.

Bert said that life there was not too bad, but it was cold and boring. Life in a prison camp for an active young man was irksome and he joined in most of the camp activities so famously depicted in British post-war films. Oh, did you know that the chalk marks made on railway wagons by professional railway men in this country are understood throughout Western Europe? I didn't, but Bert told of a couple of airmen prisoners, ex-railway men from Swindon employed in working parties, who regularly misdirected railway trucks and stores throughout their enforced stay. The mind boggles at the idea of wagons moving back and forth never delivering their cargo. However, I digress. The Russian forces advanced from the east, and by Christmas 1944 the inmates of the POW camp could hear gunfire as the heavy weapons of the Wehrmacht and Soviet forces exchanged fire. One day there were no guards to be seen about the camp area, and various brave, or foolhardy souls, tested this fact by climbing over the perimeter fence returning via the main entrance. No working parties were called out; there were no German troops anywhere to be seen, nor were there any Russians. Bert and his friend announced that they were leaving, despite the dire warnings of the British Commander and many friends. 'You're safer here,' they cried. 'Balls!' said Bert, 'What about those bloody friendly fighters that shot us up here last week?' Off the pair trotted, clad in their warmest clothes and determined to go somewhere – anywhere, as long as it was far away from the camp.

On the second day, they were crossing a field when they heard the sound of horses' hooves and the jingle of saddlery. Looking towards the source of the noise, they spotted a troop of cavalry who on seeing them, drew sabres and charged. Bert and his mate tore at their clothing, desperately trying to free their identity tags before the horsemen arrived. The Russians spoke no English and the pair of Brits no other language. There followed some anxious moments as the Russians, who had never seen a British prisoner of war before, agreed to accept their story. It was only after some pantomime that the Russian officer indicated that they should each mount up behind one of his troopers. Sick with relief, Bert heaved himself onto the horse, clutching the waist of a rather smelly Cossack. He was to share a horse for only a short time because a brief skirmish with German soldiers reduced the Russian numbers. Bert and friend were each allocated a horse, Bert hated that horse, for it always fed before he did and he was under no illusions as to his importance to the unit relative to the horse.

Amid jubilation and general celebration (by the Russians) the war ended, but Bert and friend dutifully trotted about eastern Germany and Poland fulfilling their duties as Cossack troopers. The year 1946 came and went, and it was not until February 1947 that Bert and friend entered the British zone of Germany near Bad Harzburg. Nearly speechless with emotion they grabbed the first British troops they met and poured out their story. The British Army loved the pair, but the RAF Provost heavies that finally came for them did not.

Bert and friend were treated as deserters! Unfair as previous events had seemed, this was the last straw. Sent for interview cum interrogation to some now long closed sub unit, the pair were repeatedly asked to write down their experiences of the last two years. Bert said that he was bloody well fed up of doing this, for he'd done it twice already. The days passed, and Bert and friend were informed that they were to receive their back pay! They looked forward greatly to this because neither had been paid since capture in 1943! Bert viewed the paltry amount stated on his nice new pay book and demanded justice from the paymasters. An affable middle-aged officer arrived from Command Accounts a week later to deal with their queries, and when asked about the paucity of the amount said smoothly, 'My understanding of your situation is that when you broke out of the prison camp you actually deserted His Majesty's Forces.' At this, there was a spate of bad language, but the imperturbable accountant continued by saying, 'Your defence to the charge of desertion is that you have spent the last two years as troopers in the Soviet army. As I understand the position today, the military authorities and legal branch now accept your story. The Soviet forces have no doubt paid you for your services and the sums entered into your pay books today reflect that position. Payment stopped on the day you joined the Russian Army, and resumed when you reported to authorities at Bad Harzburg.' He rose, and smilingly wished them good day. Bert concluded his story by saying that, if in his lifetime he never saw a horse, a Soviet soldier or even an accountant again, it would be too soon.

My immediate Boss, Trevor Peacock, was understandably not pro-Japanese, and when Master Engineer Mervyn Botwright said that he'd seen a Japanese hitchhiker on the roadside, Trevor asked if he had 'got him'. When told that Mervyn had given him a lift for a hundred miles, Trevor studiously ignored him for a month. By the way, Trevor, despite his position as Engineer Leader would not travel further east than Bahrain. He expressed the view to me that he wasn't sure if he could trust himself not to assault any Japanese he met. I was never very sure how much of his attitude was posturing, but nevertheless, he never went further east during the next four years. I went instead! The Changi Slip as it was known was a five-day event and always we enjoyed a free day in Singapore.

Singapore in the mid sixties was a delightful place, indeed it still is. We were about to hand over government to Lee Kwan Yew – peaceably. You have simply no idea how pleased I was that this would be the case. I liked the Malay and Chinese people who behaved as a mirror of what you were to them. I liked them and they liked me. Together we have had some entertaining fun. I wanted to buy myself one of the new fangled fibreglass suitcases. I had walked around town and ended up on Bridge Street where there was a very well stocked luggage shop. A smiling young man showed me the latest thing in lightweight cases. The Chinese shopkeeper told me that it was tremendously strong and that I should jump on it. I declined, but he persisted bringing a few of his colleagues into the persuasive argument. Finally, to please the audience, I jumped on the case. There was a cracking noise beneath my sandals, and I found myself pinned by shards of fibreglass into the innards of the case. There was stunned silence followed by hoots and roars of glee as tens of young Chinese crowded into the shop to witness the discomfiture of their friend. His discomfiture was as nothing to mine, for I was bleeding profusely from both ankles – we had to cut me out! I don't jump on cases now, despite the knowledge that cases are no longer made of this material. I visited Singapore once every six weeks or so for years and usually popped in for a cup of tea and a laugh. Alas, the shop's long gone in the redevelopment of the city.

The frequency of my trips to Singapore did not go unnoticed by others. I enjoyed walking around and shopping, whereas few aircrew did. However, their wives would ask for things to be brought home, and I was quite happy to do the shopping provided that I stayed with the aircraft. In other words, I didn't have to load/unload parcels and carry them to hotels etc.

On one of my first trips to Changi (Singapore) I was part of a group walking through the evening market in Changi village. Quite suddenly a pretty Chinese girl, in her late teens, approached us. Turning to me, she said, 'Excuse me, but you are Mr Hayes aren't you? Please say that you are, you must be, you look just like him!' Totally stunned, for to the best of my knowledge I'd never seen her before, I stuttered that I was. A chorus from the rest of my crew confirmed this! And a few ribald but polite comments followed. She dragged me into a shop and triumphantly introduced me to her Father. I recognised him immediately, for we had spent many hours chatting to each other some ten years earlier when I served at Changi during a detachment. I used to swing his young son on an improvised chest expander swing hanging from the door lintel while we talked. The poor little lad had something wrong with his stomach and required constant attention. The doctors planned to operate on him when he was five years old. A long-nosed foreign devil provided respite for the rest of the family and the boy would stare in fascination at me for hours. Still puzzled as to how the girl clearly remembered me, and that I had no recollection of her at all, I asked her Father why this was so. He smiled, showing his two gold teeth, and said, 'Ah, it was her job to look after her little brother, and it was only when you came that she could play with her friends! That's why she remembers you so well and that you saw very little of her!'

There were some beautiful cedar and camphor wood chests available from a shop in Changi village. An acquaintance, serving on another squadron, offered me a cheque and asked if I would buy him a decent sized cedarwood box, preferably lightly carved on the front face. I agreed and duly bought the box and returned to the UK where I dumped the box off at his squadron headquarters. Returning to my own office, I discovered that with two engineers down with flu, I would have to go back to Singapore the following week. On arrival in Changi I went for the pre-sleep walk that I found so essential to my sleep pattern, turning down from the main gate to the village. I popped my head into my friend's shop with a friendly comment that I was surprised to find him out of bed. He smiled a greeting and after a few moments of pleasantries said diffidently that the cheque for the chest had 'bounced'. Horrified, I said,' My cheque bounced?' 'No, No,' he said, 'the one from your friend for the chest.' Fortunately, he had kept the cheque, and had not handed it over to the RAF authorities, who were not keen on rubber cheques. I say fortunately, because I, as the last to touch that cheque, would have been held responsible. The shopkeeper accepted my personal cheque and I took the reject back to base with me. I tried to contact the officer concerned, but he was off en route in America. I rang his bank, which was my bank too, and asked the manager what had happened about the cheque. He told me that the cheque had been stopped. Relieved, I asked if the bloke had lost his chequebook, to be told that only that cheque had been stopped. He went on to tell me the date and time when this had been done. Two hours after it had been given to me! Weeks later, I recovered my money from him, and asked why he had set me up in this way. 'Nah, don't take it to heart, it's just a

Chink shopkeeper.' Regrettably, his mouth healed before my knuckles did. The dentist spent some time on him though. There are a few officers who are far from being gentlemen.

We were in Singapore and our return load would not become available for five days – unheard of and wonderful. Wonderful, because we were told to stay at Changi and return on the following Thursday. We enjoyed a day out as a crew sightseeing in town the following day, but thereafter we saw nothing of the co-pilot. Indeed we became quite worried as the days passed because none of us knew where he was. He did not turn up until Tuesday morning, and we were due to depart the following day. When asked where he had been, he smiled enigmatically saying that we would never believe him. He maintained this silence, and since it was really none of our business we did not press him. We returned to the UK, and shortly afterwards a crew from another Squadron returning from Singapore claimed to have seen our man starring in a blue movie with Chinese girls! On my next visit to Singapore, the navigator and I visited the same movie house (a rather grand overstatement) and sure enough, there was our co-pilot with a pair of Chinese twin girls – and didn't he do well!

On our return to the Squadron I spoke with the star of stage and screen saying that I now knew where he had spent his Singapore days. He smiled indulgently saying that we knew nothing. I described the house and gardens, the girls and the room furnishings. The assured façade fell away and he looked absolutely stricken. He asked how I could possibly know all this and when I told him he became distraught. 'I didn't know that we were filmed, I didn't, I swear that I didn't,' he moaned. Looking at his face, I believed him.

He then asked what he could do. What could he possibly do? Perhaps the film would stay in the Singapore area, but perhaps it wouldn't. After a few weeks there were rumours that the film had reached Cyprus. The young man was at his wits' end and asked me what to do. He asked me because as a Flight Engineer I was, I suppose, a neutral. I had been thinking about the problem for some weeks and told him to report himself to the Security Services in London. In fact, he should go in person to their Shepherds Bush offices and confess. He wondered if he should see our Boss first, but I told him that it would be far better if he spoke first to Security for otherwise not only would he force the Boss's hand, it would mean that he would be *sent* to Security Services. He saw the sense in this and cheered up a little when I told him that they were unlikely to come down hard on him. That would create a precedent and stop others in trouble reporting themselves of their own volition. I said that they might even laugh at his predicament – I didn't believe that but it seemed to help him. He reported himself to London and returned a happier man, for they recorded his story; read him a long lecture and sent him back. He now went to see the Chairman (our Boss) who listened quietly to his story after which he said that he should inform Security Services. The Co-Pilot said immediately that he'd been already and that Hayes had said that I should report myself before seeing you. At this, the Boss bridled and asked what the hell did I have to with it. The young man explained that I had said that he would put him (the Boss) on the spot and would force him to take action. Furthermore, he would then be *sent* to Security Services and that would be a lot different to volunteering the information. The Boss agreed and said that he was grateful for such consideration for he had seen the film himself in Cyprus and had been looking for an opportunity to call for the co-pilot. He then dismissed the young man telling him to send me in to his office.

Very doubtfully, I knocked and entered. The Boss was leaning back in his chair and invited me to sit and tell him the whole story, as I knew it. He grimaced and said that the lad had style – and stamina! But since I was so bloody clever in dealing with the matter thus far, perhaps I'd be kind enough to tell him what to do now. The sarcasm and irony of the situation was not lost on me and I had had weeks to consider what I would do in the Boss's shoes.

'Look, Sir, he's a bloody idiot, he's married and he's posted to 48 Squadron based in Singapore in about three months' time. If he goes there someone is bound to tell his wife, and he could be open to blackmail as well.' The Boss nodded his head at that and said, 'What then? I could get his posting cancelled, but where should he go then?' I continued, by saying that from my perspective he was a promising pilot, and if the pilot leader agreed with that assessment, would it not be better to get him sent away from Lyneham to another unit, flying another aircraft type where his career would not be totally destroyed. After a period of reflection, the Boss agreed, and as I left the room he said,' What a devious little sod you are Eric. But I'm glad that he took your advice. But why did he ask you rather than his own Leader?' I said that I was a neutral and that he probably felt safe in talking to me.

Shortly after this the man was posted to Northolt where he would fly natty little twin jet aircraft capable of crossing the Atlantic. The matter closed with everyone happy – well, perhaps not everyone.

The British armed forces were to leave Malaya and Singapore, but as part of the defence agreements reached between the nations of the South East Asia Treaty Organisation (SEATO), Britain had to demonstrate a capability to put troops back into the region in a hurry. A defined number of troops and their equipment had to be transported by air within a specified time limit. The British components were to be flown west about through the United States to Malaya, simulating the loss of landing rights in Arab territories. The exercise was named Bersatu Padu and involved practically the whole of the British transport force of VC10, Britannia and Hercules aircraft. At that time we had a crew ratio of 3.8 to one aircraft and this meant that we could operate a full blown slip pattern. This, in turn, meant that the first aircraft to the States positioned crews down the route, so that subsequent aircraft spent only the time necessary to refuel and change crews – usually about an hour. The incoming crew went to bed awaiting the next scheduled aircraft arrival. This pattern of operation was repeated at Gander (Newfoundland), Offutt (Omaha), Hickam (Hawaii), and Wake Island before landing at Changi or at airfields in Malaya. I'm not certain, but we may also have landed in Guam. With most of the Hercules force involved in the exercise, it was no surprise to find myself positioned down route, initially tasked to fly from Gander to Offutt. It was very cold at Offutt, and when, after a brief sleep, we met the incoming aircraft to fly our leg to Hickam we found that the aircraft was unserviceable on engine start up. Due to an administrative error the ground crew had been released from work and thought that they had dealt with the last aircraft on their shift. When I got hold of them they were in no condition to work on aircraft. Donning my arctic parka, I set about changing a component in the nose wheel bay and radome. It took some hours, but my crew could not go back to bed, for the incoming crew were in possession. When I finally did finish the job, the planned itinerary was shot. We asked for advice from Upavon (our HQ) and were instructed to proceed to Hickam immediately and to await further instructions in Hawaii. With the prospect of an extended stay in view I have never been so popular!

The conclusion of exercise Bersatu Padu saw the return of the transport force to bring the troops home. I wasn't part of this because I was very ill indeed. I had some form of virulent influenza that really flattened me. I was one of the fortunate to survive this unusual variant, for four aircrew died in this epidemic. I spent my illness in my own bed at home and had the attention of my personal nurse. As I became better, my neighbour threw a large and noisy party to which I was not invited.

Since I couldn't sleep with the all the noise – my bed vibrated to the bass tones of the music – I put on a dressing gown and joined them. We lived in a semi-detached house and the walls were so thin that one could hear everything, and I mean everything. Oh yes, and I invested in a set of cold sores in a most inappropriate place that have plagued me for thirty years. I travelled from doctor to specialist and even on to Harley Street. Each time I was asked to swear on a bunch of bibles that this could not be venereal in nature. The Group Captain specialist asked if I was suicidal. Apparently the last person so afflicted had taken the easy way out! The specialist's name appropriately was Bellringer. Harley Street breezily shook my hand and said, 'Tough luck old son, we've no cure for this, but over the years it will diminish in intensity I promise you.' What he was paid for this opinion is unknown – but he was right, there's no bloody cure!

The captain of my crew was one William (Bill) Kemp, known to all as 'Whingeing Will'. I liked flying with Bill. His credentials were superb, for he was a Cranwell Cadet, the three-year kind of officer. Known as the crème de la crème, or in their own modest opinion as 'proper officers'. Bill was not smooth, Bill was not tact personified. Bill was an acid tongued extrovert who disliked authority. I enjoyed his patter as a training pilot. New co-pilots would be roundly cursed and told to turn when they saw the cress beds and to stop the turn when the scrap yard appeared below. Nobody was safe from his tongue. A navigator once guided him safely through a sky filled with minor cumulus nimbus into an extremely solid cloud. Once into smooth air, Bill, with a rolled up chart in his hand rounded on the Navigator, 'What's that?' he cried, pointing to the weather radar indicator. 'It's a bloody weather thingamajig. Using that, you're supposed to dodge not only clouds A, B and C, but also D, E and F.' punctuating his statement by thumping the unfortunate crewman over the head! Curiously, I never met anyone who didn't like him or respect his flying skills. To give an idea of his sense of humour let me tell of the time that we took our newly adopted baby daughter to the christening of his eldest daughter. Peering into the carrycot he said to my wife, 'Yea, not bad for a second hand kid!' I think that Gitti was a little startled by this remark but recognised the kindness behind his gruff exterior. Oh yes, and while I think of it another memory floods in. After leaving the Air Force, Bill flew for a minor airline. His Boss's secretary was a pleasant woman who couldn't spell – even with a spellchecker! Her name was Louise. Bill christened her 'Louse', a name that stuck!

My daughters asked once if flying aircraft for a living was dangerous and I have to say that while I have occasionally been apprehensive – code for shit scared – quite regularly, the frequency of such scares is about one a year. I can manage two frights a month driving my car. The answer to the question therefore is that it can be dangerous, but very rarely is – even for military aircrew. There have been notable occasions where I have almost died of fright – but manfully concealed the fact from others – I hope.

The Hercules crews are made up daily, and. we did not fly with the same individual crew members as a constituted crew. The procedures we followed were completely standardised to avoid mistakes and omissions. Strict adherence to the checklists produced standard audio responses understood by all. Aircrews were addressed by their crew position and the initiator identified himself by crew position. Thus a conversation might go, 'Eng Captain, No 4 Engine oil pressure fluctuating.' It was easy and efficient and avoided the problems of having three Peters aboard. The German Air Force is even more formal, addressing each other as 'Herr Major' and 'Herr Hauptman'. I flew with a Transall squadron from Lansdorf on several occasions and was quite surprised at the way they conversed with one another on the flight decks of their transport aircraft.

Very early on in my career on 36 Squadron I went to Singapore on my first major route-flying trip. As this was my first long trip since leaving the Conversion Unit, and I had the benefit of having a more experienced engineer as companion. The outbound journey to Singapore was uneventful, but the return was something else. Outbound from Changi, heading for the island of Gan in the Maldives, the No 4 engine began to progressively lose power, and while I was worrying about that, the No 3 engine also began to lose power. The captain said to open the cross feed cock between wings, but I wasn't having that for we could end up with all four engines affected. By a process of elimination, I managed to determine that the fault lay in the fuel heater strainer of each starboard engine. Something was progressively blocking up the fuel flow from the external fuel tank. The external tanks were nearly empty, but as the engines were still producing quite a lot of power, it seemed prudent, bearing in mind that Gan lay in the middle of the Indian Ocean, to use whatever fuel we could. To cover a few contingencies, I began to feed the starboard engines using the internal fuel tanks of the starboard wing. That didn't solve anything and the power continued to drop, if anything at a little faster rate. Clearly, the filter was continuing to block and the effects were compounded by the fact that the internal fuel tank pumps produced a lower pressure than the pumps in the external tank. The power loss accelerated, but the aircraft was becoming lighter as we used fuel. Gan was still a couple of hours away when the power loss became even more worrying. My more experienced companion had disappeared from the flight deck early on and was no help to me. I had an idea that if I could use the dump pumps of the internal tanks and re route the fuel to the starboard engines another way, I might improve the situation. The dump pumps are intended as emergency fuel jettison pumps and produce 55 lbs of pressure. Miraculously, this restored much of the power loss to both starboard engines. Nevertheless when we landed safely on Gan those starboard engines were producing less than half power.

The ground crew dropped the filters of the fuel heater strainer to find the thing was all of a dark brown slimy mess. Expert opinion was sought, but there were no bright ideas. We cleaned all filters and successfully ran the engines. The next day, after informing Changi and our HQ that we had suffered fuel contamination on one side of the aircraft, we said that we would press on to Muharraq airbase in Bahrain. To cut a long story short, we suffered the same difficulties on this flight. We cleaned filters and continued to the UK, making a precautionary landing at Lyon in France. The major investigation conducted at Lyneham showed that the cardboard packing surrounding the external tank fuel pumps had not been removed prior to installation. The cardboard had slowly decomposed leading to our problem. The Lockheed Company, the manufacturer, was unable to trace exactly where this had taken place. A likely story, I thought.

The mother and father of all frights came much later, when I was quite an experienced Hercules engineer. I was part of a crew detailed to practise three-engined take offs and landings. The day prior to the exercise was spent practising the necessary drills in the simulator. We were a relatively experienced crew. The pilot was an American Air Force Captain and he had about 7500 hrs of experience on type. The co-pilot had 2500 hrs and I had about the same. The navigator had 2000hrs and the loadmaster just over 1000hrs. We performed the simulator drills perfectly – as one would expect. The next day we flew to nearby RAF Fairford to make use of the very long and broad runway. The base was only in use for trial flying of the Concorde and there were very few other aircraft on the airfield. We lined up on the threshold of the runway, shut down the No. 1 engine and feathered the propeller. We then ran through all the pre-take off checks.

The captain, watched by both the co-pilot and myself, advanced the throttles and released the brakes. Accelerating rather more slowly than usual, we raced up the runway moving from the centre line to the left of the runway. We left the runway, heading hard left. We were mesmerised. The captain yelled, 'What's wrong Eng?' I looked at the speed indicator – 80kts. I looked at the engine instruments – all showing take off power. I looked at the position of the captain's feet – full opposite rudder (I'd been checking all of this all of the time). 'Nothing,' I said firmly. We were now heading directly towards three parked aircraft a few hundred yards away. The aircraft was accelerating, but had not reached a take off speed when the pilot heaved us into the air. As we climbed, desperately clawing for altitude, the co-pilot unfeathered the propeller of no. 1 engine!

He had not been instructed to do so, but he was the first of us to come out of shock. It was, of course, the wrong thing to do. Firstly, he had not been told to do so and secondly, as the unfeathering propeller went through the maximum drag position and the engine restarted, the port wing went down and we headed for the ground. We were only just above minimum control speed. The captain pulled the control column back hard, but we were still headed downwards in a dreadful attitude. I pushed the engine throttles fully forward and we skimmed the ground before zooming upwards. Just how close we actually were to the ground I don't know. I don't even care; I just know that we didn't hit it. We climbed into the 'hold' and levelled out in total silence. It was a minute or two before the captain said, 'What the hell happened there?' Again there was that awkward silence. The navigator said weakly that he was leaving the flight deck for a moment. He needed to change his trousers. In his absence, we racked our brains for a reason for our mishap. Suddenly, it dawned on me that what we had done was to advance three engine throttles to take off power and then released the brakes. The captain wore American flying gloves with large floppy wrist flaps that had obscured the throttle position. I am paid to notice such things, as is the co-pilot, but we had not! I doubt that any Court of Inquiry convened had we crashed would have considered that such an experienced crew could be so stupid.

What we should have done was to advance the throttles of the two symmetrical engines to take off power then release the brakes. As the aircraft accelerated up the runway and the speed rose to the point where the rudder would work (80 knots) the third engine's throttle should have been slowly advanced to take off power with the rudder keeping the aircraft on the runway centreline.

We made a further attempt at a three-engined take off, but despite having the fourth engine at flight idle rather than shut down, we still wandered about the runway during the take off run. The crew was badly shaken and the captain uncharacteristically nervous. When airborne he said that we would return to Lyneham and carry out the training on another day. Or, more truthfully, he said, 'Shit, it's back to the drawingboard troops. We're going home This ain't ma day!'

Survival courses were an important part of life for aircrew of all branches. I had completed the sea survival course three or four times in the past. Once at the Conversion Unit for Beverley aircraft, once in Aden and now I was to be flung into the English Channel in February (I had returned to the UK from Aden only weeks ago!). Winter survival courses would come later, but even this early in my flying career I had completed the desert survival course twice. Now I was to be sent to Bad Kohlgrub in Bavaria for the Winter Survival Course. We arrived by bus from the nearby railway station, to be met by the Bavarian host, Horst Schlittinger who was to teach us to ski. The town was all Schlittinger! Schule Schlittinger, Busse Schlittinger, Hotel Schlittinger, and even Ski Schule Schlittinger! Horst was indeed a well-connected fellow.

In the first week we had classroom lessons on survival and evasion in the mornings and we learnt to ski in the afternoons. We were a source of great amusement to the elderly, many of whom were taking a 'Kur' at the town Spa. They would slowly totter their way to the car park at the base of the hill in time to find a seat from where they could see the action. The action they looked for of course was the four o'clock arrival of the Brit students from the ski slopes. We would arrive in a tumbling heap, on our backs, on only one ski, indeed in every position other than upright. There was one exception to this, as a six-foot plus student arrived in the upright position to continue across the car park that had been swept of snow. He reached the far side of the park still on his skis that were totally ruined by the gravelled surfaced. Some of the old dears laughed so much that we were seriously worried about them. In many ways the action was reminiscent of scenes at Bad Harzburg where I learnt to ski.

The second week was totally different in that we were paired off and given one rudimentary map and a compass. We were to survive for some days and make our way to a grid reference by a certain time and date. Local Police and Army units would be looking for us. I was paired off with a very tall raw-boned Army corporal helicopter pilot who was clearly very fit and determined. The area was covered in thick snow and was heavily wooded, with few tracks. The rendezvous point was at least thirty kilometres distant. It didn't take long for the corporal and me to fall out. He took huge steps and I was totally unable to keep up with his pace – even if I had wanted to. I knew from experience that it was far better to move at a reasonable pace rather than to try and be the first at the meeting point. Clearly, the corporal was trying to make a point, either to me or to his superiors at base. We parted amicably, him with the map while I retained the compass.

A German Army unit captured me on the fourth day as I crossed a clearing, instead of keeping to the sides. Hastily I ate all my remaining rations and drank my water before the German soldiers reached me. I was eventually led to an armoured personnel carrier where four other erstwhile escapees were sitting. They were completely hooded and one made very rude comments about the Bundeswehr. The Lieutenant immediately ordered his driver to close all doors and instructed that he was to move off across rough country and to make sure that we enjoyed the experience. Within minutes I had thrown up my rations into my hood. I remained in this state until we arrived at a camp in Murnau some twenty kilometres away. We were stripped of our clothes while standing outside and were then washed down with fire hoses.

We were eventually given clothes and boots with no laces and were taken inside a shelter where we were told to sit on the ground with our hands on the ground beside us. We were hooded from behind. I sat there, shivering like a dog passing clothes pegs, in fact I shivered so much that my captors told me to put my hands on my head. I didn't stop shivering. Indeed, I was happy to shiver for that is a safety system of the body. I reflected that my captors had adhered to the Geneva Convention in that we were dirty and they had washed us. They had given us dry clean clothing with no zips or buttons, but only after some minutes had passed. Every few minutes, a guard would walk up behind us, pause and then move away to take another prisoner away for interrogation. (It's called disruption of expectation.) The guards would walk up behind and then urinate on the ground – or so it seemed, for I learnt later that they had a kettle of water! I think that they had a farting machine too. Or perhaps the guards were fed on diet of beans. After what seemed some hours, I was taken for interrogation by two guards who were not over careful that I didn't fall or bump into things. All that I could see was a clock on the wall, but at least it was a lot warmer in the office.

The interrogator asked the usual questions and was given number rank and name. He asked questions for some time before having me hooded, dragged out and returned to the cold, cold shelter. I turned inwards and mentally set out on flights that encompassed the world. At every stage I planned down to the tiniest detail. I created a separate world for myself that was only interrupted by my return to the office for further questioning. My interrogator made several mistakes. I remember with particular pleasure his face: when thrusting his face into mine he screamed that I stank. Inhaling a full lungful of air I breathed a week of eating near raw rabbit, vegetation and smoking my pipe directly into his face. He recoiled in absolute disgust. It quite made my day and I grinned maliciously inside the hood that was replaced prior to my return to the shed.

Back in the freezing cold of the shed, I resumed my world trip and concentrated on my memories of the base at Offutt, Omaha. I could almost smell the stench from the stock pens close to the huge abattoirs near the Base, while continuing to apparently uncontrollably shake.

Still on my world trip, I recalled the main bar of the Castle Harbour Hotel in Bermuda. One of my Flight Engineer colleagues from another squadron stood at the bar. He was a forty two year old Flying Officer with a large moustache, a receding hairline and a thick wedge of hair at the nape of his neck. Wally was quite an eyecatching figure with his large nose sheltering in the moustache, as he held his beer close to his lean body in the 'Limey Crouch'. This means that the beer glass is held close to the armpit with the hand turned inwards to prevent spillage.

A large, but short, American lady waddled up to Wally saying,' Gee Sir, Ah jist have ta tell yu that you look just like General Custer.' Wally turned and declaimed theatrically in his booming voice, 'Madam, I have not got long hair, nor have I had, I trust, my last stand!' Disconcerted by the laughter, the lady fled. A minute later an even larger short fat American came up to our group and addressed himself to Wally. 'Sir,' he said, grasping Wally's hand, 'I've been married to Alice for forty years and that's the first time Ah ever saw her with her mouth open and nothing coming out! What are you boys drinking?' We explained that there were fourteen of us and made to decline his offer. He would not take no for an answer saying that there was a *hundred* of them. All lying Chevrolet Dealers on a sales bonus award holiday with Chevrolet footing the bill. It was a good night. However, it was still bloody cold outside at Murnau!

The exercise came to a close and the post exercise debrief was conducted by the NATO team. They asked if I was OK, for some were worried that I had shivered so much. The Chief Interrogator asked me how much time had elapsed between capture and the end of the exercise. I thought 24 to 30 hours, but in fact nearly two days had passed. They asked what I had done with my time, and I replied that I had been around the world by Hercules aircraft! The staff then asked if they had made mistakes during interrogation. I thought that two mistakes had been made. Obviously, it was intended that I should see the wall clock. Equally obviously they had altered the time displayed, but not very cleverly, because I was aware that time had been 'doctored'. Secondly, my interrogator, who had been given my number, rank and name had not troubled himself to look me up in the Air Force List that was prominently displayed in a bookcase to the right of his desk. Throughout the questioning he believed me to be a navigator. Would I be a navigator? Never.

In another happy incident, I played Cupid to an unlikely couple. An older navigator in his late forties had been assiduously and unsuccessfully courting a widow for some considerable time. He worked in our Tactical Operations Centre, and rarely had the opportunity to go to exotic places. He asked if I would kindly bring a good-sized bouquet of Singapore orchids back for him. It was the lady's birthday, and he wanted to make a really good impression upon her. He asked me, because I could be relied upon to ensure that the orchids arrived in good condition. He went on to say that my crew would complete the whole trip on the same aircraft. He had checked this fact specially, for he'd bought – and paid for – a bouquet that had arrived as a few barren stalks from a previous flight! Pretty please, could I do my best, even if it meant watering them gently every hour on the hour? I bought the orchids, beautiful flowers most tastefully made up into a splendid bouquet. I personally placed them on the ramp of the aircraft and watered them sparingly on the hour every hour of our homeward journey. When we night stopped on the return flight, the flowers were carefully stored by the catering staff in a cool room and returned to the aircraft at the last minute before departure. No one could have taken more care to improve this idiot navigator's love life. The flowers were delivered to Tactical Operations personally and he was delighted at their condition. It was the day of her birthday and, ignoring all service commitments for the day, he set out for her home. The lady was overwhelmed with emotion. Her paramour had thought so highly of her etc etc etc. Six months later at a Mess Ball, he cornered me and accused me of complicity in his marriage to the lady. Married life was apparently not as harmonious as he had been led to believe!

Promotion from Flying Officer (Fg Off) to Flight Lieutenant (Flt Lieutenant) required a pass in the Officer's B examination. I studied hard, gained a pass to be told shortly afterwards that the requirement had been discontinued. A couple of years later, I studied for four hours a day for three months to take the C promotion examination to Squadron Leader. This examination was in several parts and included a specialist flight engineer paper. The first and mandatory question of this paper was on aircraft performance and involved the solution to a three-engine take off and climb out with ground obstacles! This subject had been specifically removed from the engineer syllabus some months earlier. However, thanks to years of practice with the Operating Data Manual of the Beverley aircraft in Aden, I was able to produce something of an answer. I actually drew the ground map, plotting the obstructions. I labelled each section of the diagram and left the question unfinished, as I knew no more. When the exam results were published I achieved an overall pass and a distinction for the engineer paper! Two years later the requirement for the C exam was discontinued! I was not a happy man.

I was SDO (Station Duty Officer), or was I OO (Orderly Officer)? In any case, I was the representative of the Station Commander outside of normal duty hours! I believe I had done the job once before – but as a Flying Officer the job came around quite often. It was Saturday morning, at about eleven thirty when I was handed a telegram addressed to a young airman in transit through the unit. The message had arrived the previous day, but duty staff couldn't find him. The man was part of a small group destined for Cyprus, and his flight was due to leave early the next day. The telegram read: 'Nan died peacefully this morning. Advise. Mum'. I set the Orderly Sergeant the task of finding the man, while I consulted the books in the duty officer's bag. I looked at the regulations telling me what I could do on such occasions. I could postpone the man's departure, or even after consultation with the Personnel Branch at RAF Innsworth authorise him to go home for a few days. I could issue a railway warrant to his home, and if the man needed money, I could arrange for a special payment. Armed with all this information, I telephoned RAF Innsworth and spoke to their duty personnel advising them that I had this compassionate case and might, just might need to ask for a delay.

The Orderly Sergeant rang to say that he could not find the man, but that an acquaintance had said that he had gone into town and would probably return for the evening meal. He went on to say that if I returned to the Officers' Mess he would tell me when he got back. I entered the Mess and placed my hat and armband on the centre table of the foyer and began to read the magazines in the anteroom. I was quite pleased to be able to read the *Flight* and the *Aeroplane* magazines in peace. At about seven in the evening, I was called to the telephone to be told that the man had returned and was waiting for me. I left immediately and entered the Transit area. I took the young man into a side room for privacy, and quietly told him that the Station had received a telegram addressed to him containing bad news. I handed him the telegram that he read in silence. He looked stunned. I sent for a cup of tea, and while this was coming, I told him that I could delay his draft. I continued by saying that if he wanted to go home immediately, I could issue a railway warrant, and if necessary arrange for a special issue of pay. Finally, I could arrange for a vehicle to speed him on his way to the railway station. The man looked baffled, and began to nervously sip his tea. In an attempt to relieve his anguish – pain – distress, I asked if he and his Grandmother had been especially close. There was a gasp of comprehension, and the young man blurted out, 'It's not my Grandmother; it's the bloody dog! She wants to know where in the garden to bury her.' Words failed me, but at least the duty staff at RAF Innsworth were amused.

As one grows older, it becomes apparent that all is not as it seems, and that some remarkably peculiar things happen, even in a so-called respectable society. I was unaware that I had lived a sheltered life, and that I was naive enough to believe that I lived a perfectly normal life and that my colleagues did too.

I had landed at Muharraq in Bahrain and was accommodated in the Air Force owned and operated Britannia House Hotel. As my crew left the airfield very late at night, I was handed a sealed envelope addressed to an officer of another squadron who was also staying at the hotel. I was instructed to personally ensure that he got the letter, and that this was essential if he was to return to the UK on a Britannia aircraft leaving in the morning. I asked the manager for the room number of the officer concerned and checked the room. It was completely empty and the bed not slept in. I returned to reception and asked the manager for his advice. I stressed the urgency of the matter and the instructions that I had been given. He looked very anxious, strangely so I thought, but he said that the only way at this time of the early morning was to knock on every door. He seemed most unhappy to give this advice, and he went on to say that he would permit this, only if I promised to see only the officer concerned and absolutely nothing else. Puzzled – I told you that I was a sheltered soul – I asked why. 'You will see situations of which you are unaware and that could seriously hurt marriages, careers etc,' he muttered. I agreed that I would see only the target chap, and off we went. To say that I was surprised was an understatement. The situation is best illustrated in a Goon Show when a cruise liner is crossing the Indian Ocean. Colonel Bloodnock rings the ship's bell vigorously in the middle of the night and in a stentorian voice announces over the ship's PA system,' Everybody back to their own beds!' There followed the noises of a vast rush of booted feet! The mixture of bedmates I found that night was educational, to say the least. Fortunately, I found my man after checking only fifteen to twenty rooms. What I would have found in the other rooms? God only knows and He is not saying anything either.

While I am on the subject of Sex and the Single Woman, I recall an attempt by the Air Force to curb the amoral and mostly nocturnal activities of aircrew. A decision had been made by somebody to discipline a WRAF flight sergeant loadmaster for extra curricular activities. The Hercules people were not involved because Britannia aircrew of 511 Squadron despised the Hercules lot and kept all their activities 'in house'. They were most protective of their female colleagues.

The Station Commander decided that before any disciplinary hearing took place, he should hear what the loadmaster had to say. His PA ensured that the intercom system was left on, and that his ear was glued to the box. Before the Station Commander could do more than exchange civilities, the young woman produced a diary. She said firmly, that if she was to face disciplinary charges for her love life, then it was only fair that her partners should do the same. She handed the bemused Group Captain a book, saying that she had made a copy, and that he could keep it. The diary, she said, contained details of all sexual activities conducted during the last two years and listed partner, time and place. She wished the Station Commander good morning and left. No more was heard about the matter, certainly not at my lowly level. The ladies of members of 511 Squadron were known, in moments of stress, to pointedly ask husbands if they featured 'in the book'.

Taff Warren was my neighbour at Lyneham. We lived at 89 and 90 Eider Avenue. My Father called it Eider Duck Hall. We had been on the same course at OCTU and were delighted to meet up again at Lyneham. He was Welsh, of course, as was Anne his delightful wife. Gitti and I had gone out shopping with Gitti's brother and his wife from

Germany, and somewhere and somehow we had lost our house keys. We scouted around the house unsuccessfully, looking for unlatched or open windows. The only unlatched windows were the upper small window of the ground floor toilet, and a small bedroom window upstairs. There was no possibility of reaching the upper window so we asked the Station firemen if they could help with a ladder. I was preparing to attempt entry through the lower window as Taff arrived home. 'No, no no,' he cried, 'you never will get through there. I'm a lot thinner than you.' Bloody Welsh dreamer, I thought. 'I'll get my body through and you can hang on to my legs,' he continued. Together, three of us hoisted him up and fed him through the aperture with his arms above his head. When his body was through, his belt caught on the vertical prong that held the window stay in position adjusting the degree of window opening. The belt was removed and Taff continued to enter the house, albeit face and head down, looking into the open toilet bowl. Still wriggling his way in, the fly of his trousers hooked on that same prong. Unfortunately, he was now well past his point of balance, and despite great entreaties to pull him back, he descended slowly into the toilet bowl as the crotch of his trousers ripped out! Mike, my brother in law, filmed the whole event on his cine camera, and the fire engine arrived just in time to see Taff's feet disappearing into the toilet room! There was a great deal of ribald humour as he eventually emerged through the front door clutching his parts. Gitti insisted on mending his trousers, that she has always maintained were cleaner than mine!

Hercules aircraft were involved in many strange tasks, and none was stranger than the rebellion of the Caribbean island of Anguilla. One Ronald Webster took charge of the executive island council and declared independence from Britain and the Caribbean Federation. The island was classified as a British Overseas Territory and had a population of about ten thousand persons. The island did have an airstrip, but only the first 60 metres were metalled. To control the situation, the Foreign Office arranged for a selection of British Policemen to travel by Hercules to the island. Most of the policemen were young London 'Bobbies', and unarmed they soon established a rapport with the locals. The operation became known as Operation Sheepskin, based on the nearby island of Antigua, and was immensely popular with those who had hopes of becoming 'Goldfinger', as the single liaison officer was known. There was considerable air traffic and the Antiguan hotels enjoyed a brisk out of season trade. Goldfinger, in addition to his other duties, was the billeting officer. He was so rarely in his hotel room that the hoteliers made no charge. His tour of duty lasted some two months and his accommodation was paid for by his allowances. Understandably, there was considerable competition for the job! Flight engineers had no chance against pilots and navigators!

It seemed sometimes that I 'lived' at Gander, Newfoundland. My logbook shows that I spent nearly a hundred night stops there. Gander airfield had been built to assist in the transit of US and Canadian warplanes to Europe during WW2, but became largely redundant with the advent of jet-powered aircraft and their improved range. At this particular time, the airfield was used largely by Eastern bloc airlines en route for Cuba and South America. The British used the place for all military transport operations in Canada, the US and Caribbean flights to Belize in Central America. The V bomber force was also a frequent visitor. The RAF crews usually stayed at the Albatross Hotel (known as the Albert Ross) while all communist crew members lived on the other side of the small town. I never saw or heard of any instruction forbidding contact between the groups, but it just happened. Sometimes we would meet Russians shopping in town. Just like us, they would have a rigid template of their children's feet and the measurements of each child. Together, we would rummage through the racks of anoraks and jumpers, exchanging smiles, but rarely speaking. On the rare occasions that we did speak, a second crewmember would call their colleagues away. I thought this a great pity in many ways.

Our take-off from Gander was scheduled for 0300 hrs and as I completed my pre-flight inspection I was told that we would delay our take-off by a further two hours. I shut all aircraft systems down and went to sit in the departure lounge where it was nice and warm and I could smoke my pipe. I'd been there for about twenty minutes when the crew of a Lot Airlines aircraft passed from the Customs Hall into the departure lounge. A pretty stewardess, who was followed by the Captain and the rest of her large crew, led the group. As the girl pushed open the glass double doors into the departure lounge, she stubbed her foot on the metal threshold bar set into the floor. She had both hands thrust deeply into the pockets of her greatcoat and was unable to check her fall. She landed very badly, splitting her cheek as her head struck the tiled floor. Her handbag spilled out its contents as it fell off her shoulder and some of the bits and pieces fell near my feet. I rose to pick them up, as anyone would, to be instantly charged away by two large men who raced forward from the straggling crew. I was absolutely furious, for nobody was in the least interested in the girl who was clearly hurt.

At this moment the Canadian police entered the room. The girl was still on the floor and I too am on the floor. The RCMP Corporal summoned colleagues who returned the Lot crew to the Customs area while the Duty Medic was summoned to see to the girl. The Customs and RCMP lectured the Lot Captain on what counted as acceptable behaviour in Canada and insisted that the 'heavies' apologise to me in person. Fortunately, the girl's face did not need stitches, but she was most upset at the incident. She said that her security people thought that she might have been passing information!

Later, in fact years later, as I was flying from Nairobi to Aswan in Egypt we were acting as a radio relay for a Russian transport aircraft. Radio reception was poor over Ethiopia. The Russian crewman completed his message and a. second voice cut in, 'Hi there Ascot 4896, any of you Brits been stationed at Khormaksar' (Aden). I asked the Captain if I could reply and when he consented said, 'Aeroflot 47934 this is Ascot 4896. I spent four years stationed there.' There was a whoosh of expelled air over the ether in either disbelief or sympathy as the Russian responded in thickly accented English,' Four years, four years – I been there since three days. Truly the arsehole of the world!' The conversation complete we each continued on our way. When the navigator asked if it had been so bad, I said that I never wanted to go there again. It was not just the climate, I did not like being shot at, nor did I like our schoolchildren to be targets of terrorism.

Anyway, as I said earlier, I seemed to spend a great deal of my time at Gander, Newfoundland. Here is another story. It was three in the morning and the weather was foul. Our take off had been delayed by some hours and I had elected to stay in the empty departure lounge where I could smoke my pipe. After a few minutes a small group entered the lounge area and I recognised King Hussein of Jordan. I saluted and extinguished my pipe and he courteously acknowledged my greeting and moving towards me with his guards, asked if I was in the Royal Air Force. We chatted and he remarked that he had spent some time at Sandhurst Military Academy. I asked if a certain Sergeant Major had been there during his time. He smiled broadly and said that was the case. He continued by saying that in any parade of his course, he was always in the centre because he was short. He continued saying that when marching in column he was at a disadvantage if the taller lead men took long paces. The Sergeant Major seeing him near skipping to keep up, would bellow,' You're a horrible little monarch Mr Hussein Sir. What are you?' I would reply, 'I'm a horrible little Monarch,

Sergeant Major!' Even now, years later at inappropriate moments, sometimes in discussions with government ministers, I remind myself that I am a horrible little monarch!' He seemed a most charming man and was most interested when I told him that my Father had been King Abdullah's Palestine Police bodyguard when visiting Jerusalem many years earlier.

My life as Deputy Engineer Leader was not difficult, but it was time consuming. Quite apart from my flying duties, I had my own simulator detail once a month; I was route checked once every six months and subject to a two day oral examination. To this must be added administrative responsibilities to the squadron and the preparation of statistics for Command, Under Trevor, I was responsible to the Squadron Commander for the continued training and improving categories of all Squadron engineers. In addition to these duties, we were responsible for the tasking of all Squadron engineers. Each planned flight required a crew suitable for the task. A new pilot did not fly with a new engineer. At intervals Trevor and I would fly with members of the section to check that standards were maintained. It was a decent and worthwhile job that I enjoyed. We, the officers, were involved in every aspect of the lives of our men. If there were problems at home, we would confidentially re-arrange the flying programme to help the man solve his problems. If there were difficulties of any kind we would do our best to help. Always such problems were handled in confidence. When one of us was absent on route we each left a sealed confidential letter detailing the up to date situation. We worked well together for years. The main task, however, was to provide crews to meet changing situations. It took but one aircraft to be unserviceable on the other side of the world, to change the month's programme for several men. This could happen twice or even three times in a day. Two added requirements were that each engineer should fly roughly the same number of hours per month and an unwritten rule that Trevor and I should balance out the most popular destinations in as fair a manner as each engineer's flying category would permit. I did have a home life, but there were times when Gitti doubted that fact. The phone always rang on my stand-down day. We learnt to go out together on such days.

Aircraft returning to Base were often rerouted, especially if our load was not particularly needed within a specified time frame. Usually the diversion would take place as we approached the toe of Italy on a return flight from Cyprus or Bahrain. Invariably our cases were stuffed with dirty underwear and we were looking forward to getting home to our families. 'Ascot 4856 this Upavon Control, do you read?'(Upavon was the HQ of Air Support Command.) We would acknowledge our presence and await the inevitable question. 'Ascot 4856, what is your fuel state?' There would be a moan on the flight deck, for we knew that a diversion to Malta or Gibraltar would follow. I used to dread that final leg home, for I can't tell you how often we were diverted.

A favourite trip of mine was to fly from Germany down to Decimomannu in Sardinia, where there was a NATO gun firing range used by fighter squadrons of the Alliance. The main attractions for the aircrew was that we lived in town and that the toys sold in the Base Shopping Centre were different and cheaper than elsewhere. In my role of Squadron Shopper I bought at least one Lima train set per trip and was often commissioned to buy the model cars and railway spares.

Parmesan cheese is expensive to buy anywhere and this statement includes both Italy and Sardinia. I bought a 2-kilo chunk at vast expense and spent the rest of the day fighting off my crew of hungry predators who attacked from all sides simultaneously breaking off and eating chunks of my cheese. I got home with a quarter of what I'd bought!

Later, when we had the children, I would return from a short flight away from base and prepare to bath the girls, then aged six and two years. 'I don't want you, I want Mummy!' was the cry from the eldest child. I could and did get quite downhearted and hurt when such rebuffs occurred. The children did like my little box of flying rations though and would watch anxiously to see if I was carrying a box as I walked up the drive. The rations weren't that good!

Aircrew life has its ups and downs and its moments of pure theatre. A co-pilot was to be elevated to sit in the left hand seat, but before he was allowed to sit there he had to complete the Captain's Course. The good news of his captaincy came at an inconvenient time, for he wanted to buy a special Hi Fi set in Singapore. The timing was inconvenient, for he wasn't sure that he could afford to buy the set and still have the money to pay the customs duty. He trotted down to the main servicing hangar where the customs had their offices. As he entered the building he saw the distinctive dark blue uniform of a customs officer on the opposite side of the hangar. He explained his position to this patient officer and asked what the customs would require in duty, telling the man the approximate purchase price. The upshot of this conversation was that the co-pilot was assured that the duty would be reasonable.

The co-pilot departed for Singapore where he bought the Hi Fi and returned to Lyneham, whereon entering the Customs Area he met Mr

Pearce the Senior Customs Officer. This particular gentleman was a Swindon Football Club fan, although some said that he was a director of the club. Suffice it to say, that his mood appeared to be dictated by the current success or failure of that team. The goods were produced and the sum of £80 was mentioned. Horrified at this, the victim cried out, questioning that such a sum was reasonable. 'I asked one of your officers about this Hi Fi, I even showed him the brochure of it. He said that any duty payable would be reasonable,' he nearly choked. Mr Pierce asked mildly if he could identify the customs officer that he'd spoken to. Looking wildly about him the co-pilot pointed triumphantly across the room, 'Him!' he cried. The Chief Customs Officer rarely showed emotion, but on this occasion his face cracked into almost a smile. Nodding to one of his men, he sent him off to bring the officer across to the customs area. The co-pilot, in an attempt to justify his outburst, reminded this officer of their conversation some ten days previously and accused the man of misrepresenting the duty payable. The blue uniformed officer drew himself up to his not inconsiderable height and stated that if the Air Force officer was unable to differentiate between a Lieutenant Commander RN which he was, and an officer of Her Majesty's Waterguard which he, pointing to Pierce, is, then you deserve to pay any duty, however unreasonable. He pointed to his anchor decorated buttons and then to the portcullis of the customs officer. The naval presence then moved off with great dignity. The customs officer was so moved by the incident that he reduced his duty assessment by a whole five pounds.

The Royal Navy has different customs and traditions to the Royal Air Force. We had landed at the naval airbase at Lossiemouth near Inverness and the loadmaster and I had gone to the guardroom to get something or other. We were told by the duty staff, 'Do you mind shoving off for a bit Sir? The Admiral's barge is due alongside!' What he meant was that the Admiral's car was due to arrive at any moment and that they would be fully occupied for a couple of minutes. We were on dry land!

CHAPTER SEVENTEEN
AN INTERLUDE AT GAN

A crisis had occurred at the Personnel Management Centre at RAF Innsworth, near Gloucester. Someone had found acceptable reasons why he should not be posted to Gan. Of course he had waited until the last possible moment to present his case and this resulted in a frantic scan of those deemed suitable to act as an Operations Officer. Apparently, rather like Abu ben Adam, my name was writ large on the wall as one who could be coerced into near immediate departure. Unfortunately, I was unable to produce an equally acceptable reason why I should not accept a gracious invitation to leave for Gan in the coming week. Of course, I knew where Gan was, for I landed there many times en route to places in the East. Gan is a small island of the Maldives group and is situated in the Indian Ocean. Some years ago, the Air Force built a runway there to enable aircraft with restricted range to refuel and to act as a staging post for aircraft flying to and from the Far East. I'm not sure if we still use the island, but I doubt it, because not only do transport aircraft have a greater range these days, but also we have fewer reasons for military aircraft to fly to points east. People now pay exorbitant prices to take their holidays in the Maldives. The posting was a short term temporary one and was likely to be of less than three months in duration. Underwhelmed with joy, I kissed Gitti goodbye and set off to become an Operations Officer.

I had never been an Operations Officer, but I had the assistance of a most experienced Air Traffic Control Corporal. With his advice and support I contrived to keep everything under control and kept out of trouble. Well, almost out of trouble! In the middle of the night we received an SOS from a ship in serious difficulties and in danger of sinking. The ship was located at the outer edge of our area of responsibility and was much nearer to Mauritius than to us. However, we could not contact Mauritius and had no means of telling whether any other agency closer to the ship had heard the distress call. The good corporal and I pondered whether we should act, and we also pondered over what was possible. A Hercules was in transit through Gan, and the crew had been in bed for some three or four hours. We found that the

Supply Squadron stocked an air sea rescue pack suitable for carriage by Hercules, and that it could be quickly readied for use. We decided that we would wake the captain and ask for his agreement to conduct a search and rescue flight. I already knew that we could do nothing without approval from Upavon (Air Support Command HQ). I woke the captain and outlined the problem. He agreed that he would fly the mission subject to approval from Upavon. I told him to go back to sleep and that we would wake him and his crew only if approval was given by Upavon. The Supply Squadron issued the rescue pack to the Safety Equipment people who began their checks. It would take the Movements team about one hour to unload the Hercules and a further half an hour to load the Rescue pack. The aircraft had been refueled on arrival at Gan, and could be ready for takeoff at a time that would allow the aircraft to reach the search area at first light. The good corporal and I decided that we had done all that was possible and I now signalled to Upavon outlining the situation and requesting their approval to use the aircraft. Minutes later we got our reply. Under no circumstances was the aircraft to be diverted from the primary task and utilised for a search and rescue mission. Approval was not, repeat not, given. A few sentences of censure followed. Chastened and a little dismayed at this brusque reaction we telephoned all the sections involved in planning to call off further effort. After a few hours we received a message from a French corvette saying that they had safely taken all crew off the ship, and that they were en route for Mauritius. Feeling that all was well that ends well, the two of us handed over the Ops Room to the incoming shift. I was seated in the Mess anteroom enjoying my pipe and a three-day-old newspaper after breakfast, when a steward told me that the Station Commander would like to see me. Since the steward had not said when I was required, I assumed correctly that he meant now.

  The Group Captain was a prudent man who insisted that every signal message into and out of Gan was copied to him. He had obviously read my signal and the response. As I entered his office, he indicated that I should sit and asked me to tell him the whole story from start to finish. Picking up the Upavon message, he asked if I would mind if he wrote the reply to Upavon. I said that I had no objections at all, but had not sent any reply thinking that I had asked a question and had received a reply. I had not thought any response by me was necessary. The Group Captain disagreed and said grimly that the tone of the Upavon response was uncalled for. He dismissed me, saying that a copy of his message would be sent to the Ops Room for me to read. Later, I was surprised to read that he considered that his staff had acted responsibly and with considerable initiative and that in his view we had performed our duties admirably. He continued, saying that while he understood the reason for refusal, we did not deserve such curt and dismissive lecture. Finally, at no time had there been any intention to divert the aircraft without their permission and that he hoped that Upavon duty staff faced with a similar problem would act with the same degree of competence and consideration! We may have lost a battle, but the Group Captain's support for his operations staff was total. The good corporal and I were quite 'chuffed'.

I had another scuffle with the HQ Ops staff some months later when a major exercise was to take place in the Indian Ocean involving air sea and land forces. The exercise was multi national and our South East Asia Treaty Organisation (SEATO) partners participated. The British component was controlled from HMS *Fearless* sailing in the Indian Ocean. Signals poured into Gan from every side although most gave information of activities, rather than requiring actions on our part. A large part of the exercise called for anti submarine patrols and for the movements of transport aircraft in quite surprising numbers. Detailed itineraries of ship and aircraft movements were received, and many aircraft were to move through Gan. In one multi page document it appeared that the planners had made mistakes and that the aircraft could not possibly meet their schedules. I signalled to HQ telling them of the mistake and in return received a message that stated, 'Reference your message etc obviously, repeat obviously, for 29th read 30th.' I loved my reply that read, 'But not so obviously, repeat not so obviously, all aircraft in transit that day now depart Gan before they arrive!' A further missive was received from HQ. 'I grovel, repeat, I grovel. Amended schedule in preparation to be sent when checked!' A naval information addressee of that message joined the pen pals by quoting a biblical reference that translated as, 'Then Jesus wept'.

It was the day of The Tour De Gan – a red-letter day in the Station calendar. A day in which all rank was put aside as everyone who could beg, borrow or steal a bicycle took part in the round the island race. I was not participating, as a few days earlier I had been injured taking part in the 'oldies' sprint race on station sports day. I had moved triumphantly into the lead when someone stole the earth and I fell down whilst at full speed. The ground at Gan is unbelievably hard and I managed to pinch a nerve in my shoulder and suffer abrasions various. I'm sure that the Station Commander must have had reservations about sporting activities at Gan for, as I arrived on the base, every engine fitter on the station was casevac-ed (casualty evacuated) home following a friendly rugby match. He must have known after the casualty list of sports day that there would be further reductions to his staff. The race went off pretty well and only four men were admitted to sick quarters suffering respectively from concussion, a broken leg, broken fingers and abrasions from the coral. The large fruit bats that inhabited the station flora were badly disturbed by all the activities and awkwardly staggered into the air to circle their roosting places anxiously waiting for the race to finish.

A story ran around the base that, some years earlier, a Russian submarine had covertly circled the island at periscope depth. Everybody on base had heard the story, but I have never met anyone who was actually there at the time. The submarine had been clearly visible to aircraft on approach to the runway, but no action was taken. Indeed what action could you or would you take? I'm told that station personnel turned out en-masse to wave to the periscope! The submarine continued observing the military activities of Gan until, most embarrassingly, it ran aground some short distance from the shore. The station commander courteously offered assistance that was equally courteously declined. The crew of the submarine in a successful attempt to lighten the boat threw out every thing not essential for their return to the deep. After some two days, the inhabitants of Gan woke to find that their inquisitive and uninvited visitor had departed. It's possible that the captain now commands a ferry boat on the Volga.

CHAPTER EIGHTEEN
ONCE A TRAPPER, NOW A FAILURE

Every good thing comes to an end and I received instruction that I was to become a Simulator Instructor and an Examiner. I was not overwhelmed with joy at this change of employment, but at least I would be at home more often and would enjoy a more settled and predictable life.

I was to instruct and examine many engineers that I had known at one stage or other of my life for over twenty years. Some were fellow officers and many of those men had instructed me on earlier aircraft types. A good number were personal friends of many years acquaintance. I quickly learnt that these very friends could be most awkward customers in the simulator. If they did not immediately see a fault on a panel, they would state that the fault had not shown on the instrument panel, or that the fault had been ignored because I had not presented it properly and was unrealistic. I was, however, born the day before yesterday, and learnt to nudge the pilot instructor as I injected faults. Armed with an indisputable witness we could more amicably continue with the exercise.

The aircraft simulators built at Lyneham in the very late sixties or early seventies were very sophisticated for the time. The simulated flight deck cabin was mounted on hydraulic jacks that could cause the cabin to move in all three axes. The terrain below the aircraft was a model over which a camera travelled recording the terrain and projecting this picture onto the pilot's windshields during take off and approach and landing. The aircraft noise was modulated by the engine power settings. Every aircraft system was simulated including the use of braking. Fuel usage was correctly adapted to the simulated situation. Aircraft flying controls and flight instruments mirrored the simulated flight conditions. From a pilot's point of view, I don't think that the simulation of flight was perfect, but from a flight engineer's viewpoint, the simulation was very good and when taxiing the aircraft would be sensitive to the expansion joints in the concrete taxiway. Of course, there were shortcomings, especially when the instructor engineer was feeding in the faults and developing the situation by inserting further symptoms. It's my opinion that by and large we presented a pretty reasonable picture of aircraft operations.

Crews scheduled for simulator training would attend a crew briefing for a detail of four hours spent in the simulator. It could be four hours of pure hell! Once seated and strapped in, the pre-start checks would be read. Sometimes, the electrical power could fail before even an engine could be started. If the first engine started correctly, you could be certain that the second wouldn't, and while the fourth was starting, a fault could occur on the first engine! When all was sorted out and with all engines operating, we would taxi out just in time for a brake failure. We then lined up out on the runway for take off, and one could be certain that some condition or another would cause the engineer to call out to abort the take off. Reset to the threshold for a further take-off, we would roar down the runway to suffer an engine failure at the point of take off. The secret here was not to attempt to shut the engine down before reaching a certain speed (137Kts?) if you did try, and the engine didn't shut down, the simulator would crash, complete with sound effects! I'm not going to bore you with the terrors of a full detail. Suffice it to say that there would be faults in the climb, in the cruise, descent, landing and taxi into dispersal. Life could be a real drag. I must emphasise that such activities were training, and intended as practice of dreadful events like engine fires, loss of pressurisation, flying control failures and the like in perfect safety. It was not intended as a rod for our backs – but boy, it seemed like it at times.

On one occasion I had a medical inspection planned for an hour after leaving the simulator. When my blood pressure was taken, the doctor went berserk and had me come back for a further check every day for a week. Apparently, my body didn't like the simulator either. Now the doctor was a specialist in aviation medicine – and still he was surprised. I was surprised that he was surprised. In conversation, I said that if he wanted to make a name for himself, he should take the blood pressure of those scheduled for simulator training on the day prior to the event, and then take the blood pressure of all the crew on completion of the detail. He did just that, and as a result of his visit had the sound levels of engine noise turned down!

A posting notice in my name advised that I was to join the Britannia squadron based now at RAF Brize Norton near Witney in Oxfordshire. I looked forward to the change. Gitti and I would not have to move house, for we had bought a bungalow at Lydiard Millicent near Swindon a few years earlier. Before we bought the house we drew a 15-mile radius circle around every transport base and headquarters. We then tried to find a house within a reasonable commuting distance of all of them. We failed, of course, but built the house 10 miles west of the ideal point. It would take an acceptable forty minutes to drive to Brize Norton.

In life there are always ups and downs. This next phase was to become a definite down. I came from Lyneham as an above average engineer, a simulator instructor and examiner and for a very short time a Route Checker. In short, I had been a 'wheel' on the Hercules.

I entered the Britannia ground school to begin learning about the aircraft. It was very different to the American built Hercules and there was little that was familiar from the earlier British built aircraft types that I had flown. I struggled a bit but managed to gain reasonably respectable marks at each phase of the groundschool.

To augment the training of the ground school, prior to beginning actual flying, each crew spent many hours in the aircraft simulator that was in poor order at the time. I was not happy in the simulator, although once again I achieved acceptable marks.

We entered the flying phase, and to cut the story very short, ended up as a very borderline student. We flew off to Hong Kong on our route training flight and yet again I was unhappy. When a student is unhappy it transmits to the staff, and they also become unhappy. 1 was not helped by a minor traffic accident in Kowloon. A taxi driver had the choice of hitting a jay walking young mother with a child in her arms or me, jay walking from the other side of the road. I was only just knocked to the ground, and was completely unhurt - but it added to my disquiet - especially when few believed that I had been hit at all.

At the end of the course I achieved the minimum possible pass in all areas. Clearly, this was unacceptable for a man who was intended to become engineer leader. I understood this and was prepared to stand down, for with the Britannia simulator off line for a year for major refurbishment, there was little chance that I could quickly improve. To my horror a report was filed that stated that I had failed at all levels. To this I added a sense of humour failure. I wrote in protest to the Station Commander. I wrote four pages! That gives an idea of two things: Firstly, that I hadn't grasped the point that brevity is not only helpful but necessary, and secondly that I was badly hurt, for although I had never tried to do an awful lot, I had never failed to achieve what I set out to do until now.

As a result of my interview, I returned to the staff of the Conversion unit and passed the Station Commander's message that the report should be rewritten -and should more closely reflect the facts. I produced my copy of all the ground school and simulator detail marks and pointed out that I had not failed any of the phases. I also told them that I recognized that I couldn't continue on to the squadron as leader. They wrote a second report that I didn't like either, but recognizing the inevitability of the outcome, I smiled and left.

I took some leave while authority considered what to do with me, and together Gitti and I went up to see my parents in Cheltenham. My mother, recognizing that all was not well, asked the reason behind the miserable face. I shall always remember her comment," Never mind son, its character forming!" Speechless, 1 lurched out of the room and circled the garden muttering to myself. Character forming! Character forming? What a bloody load of nonsense. Time proved her to be right.

You may think that this chapter is remarkably short, but do you want to remember your failures and unhappy parts of your life?

CHAPTER NINETEEN
RAF FINNINGLEY

The personnel management team at RAF Innsworth decided in their wisdom that I should have a tour of duty in a non-flying appointment. Apparently I was selected from a very small group to become a Flight Commander at the Air Engineer and Air Electronics School at RAF Finningley.

RAF Finningley is, or was, located just outside Doncaster and in my time was home to both the School of Navigation and the Air Engineer and Air Electronics Officer School and all their support staff.

The domestic area looked like most of the other units built during that enormous expansion immediately prior to the Second World War. The station had been home to a wide variety of aircraft types throughout its long history, and when the unit closed many years later, I believe that the buildings and facilities were modernised to become an open prison. It's a curious fact that a large number of redundant RAF bases were put to this use when no longer required. I read recently that Finningley has now been renovated and rebuilt to become Doncaster airport. The armed forces have continued to shrink in numbers from the 600,000 men strong RAF that I joined to the 52,000 men remaining when I left on retirement. The Army took over a good few bases too, for many units returned to the UK as overseas territories achieved independence and there was nowhere to put the returning formations. One such event was the closure of Little Rissington in the Cotswolds. The unit had been The Empire Test Pilot School and had provided pilot training for many over a long period of time. An infantry regiment took over the base. The airfield lay at the back of beyond and there was little for a large group of young soldiers to do save getting into some kind of trouble. The locals were appalled, and said that the Air Force had been with them for years without any of this trouble. Why was the Army different? Well, as most readers will know, it's a case of horses for courses. Just as a fighter pilot rarely makes a good transport pilot so the qualities required of a good infantryman do not make him the ideal gentle citizen.

Back to Finningley and my new job there. Among the smaller units that supported training was the Airman Aircrew Initial Training Course (AAITC) Commanded by a Squadron Leader, supported by four Flight Lieutenants, each acting as a Course Commander. The Flight Commanders in turn were assisted by a Master Loadmaster survival instructor, a WRAF Warrant Officer and a drill Sergeant. The task of this group was to take the product of the Aircrew Selection Centre and teach them something about the Air Force for five weeks, before taking them onto the Yorkshire moors for a joyous week of life on the moors. Once there, we would divide the course into improbable teams of five persons and conduct leadership exercises. Our intention was to get the student teams cold, tired, wet and hungry or hot, tired, wet and hungry. We didn't care which of the two, for we wanted to see the individual under pressure, and would go to great lengths to create that stress. We would then make a character assessment of each individual that would, in turn, determine whether or not that individual progressed to undertake very expensive aircrew training. To summarise: Biggin Hill said that the student had the health, education and aptitude, and we said that the student had the character to become a reliable member of an aircrew. The overall aim was to minimise the training failure rate.

It was into this wholly alien environment that I was thrust at the age of forty. The students in the main were aged from 19 to 30 years and the majority were as fit as fiddles. I had visions of being totally humiliated by fit young men racing past me on the moors and even offering to carry my pack! However, I was quickly to discover that youth, fitness and enthusiasm is no match for old age and cunning. My fellow Course Commanders, mere lads to me, were a devious lot. They were also very good at what they did, and all of them were happy to share their knowledge and expertise. The Staff was a mixed bunch of two Air Electronics Officers, and two older Air Engineer officers. The Loadmaster was in his mid thirties and the WRAF Warrant Officer a little older. The Boss was a navigator, young and no fool, for he was courting the Station Commander's daughter, a doctor working at the local hospital.

In the past, Air Engineers were recruited from junior and senior NCOs of the first four trade groups, Engine, Airframe, Electrical and Instrument fitters. Now, as such tradesmen cost a lot of money to train, the Air Force decided that they would recruit from the street. The recruit would have little or no technical background, but would not be expected to perform the same tasks as the older generation of Flight Engineers. To assist in the transitional period it was decided to augment the flight crew of a transport aircraft with a cross-trained multi-skilled crew chief. The crew chief had no airborne responsibility, but refuelled and serviced the aircraft when away from base. The presence of a crew chief allowed the planning staff to work on a 14-hour ground time. In the interests of flight safety, the air engineer was not to be involved in such rectification work. In the past, the service knew a great deal about the men that were recruited as air engineers, now they knew very little and the AAITC was necessary to gain an insight. Air Electronics and Loadmaster students had usually been recruited from within the service, but at a much earlier point in the individual's career. Thus the initial training course was to prove invaluable.

The value of the AAITC was two fold, in that there was a benefit to the Air Force, but perhaps an even greater benefit to the student. As my experience of the work grew, so did my ability to express myself. I told my courses at the outset that pass or fail they could only gain from the course. Never again would an employer pay for six weeks training during which a totally dispassionate and objective analysis of the strengths and weaknesses of their character would be made. Never again in their lifetime was someone likely to look at them as individuals and give an honest assessment of abilities and failings. What you will learn about yourselves here, and what you do with that knowledge will determine the course of your future. I told them that that statement might sound pompous, but that I would extend their physical limits, widen their mental horizons and improve their levels of confidence. I would also drive them at every turn to produce 100% of their capabilities. Failure to do so would lead to inevitable failure and return to their previous unit.

The joining instructions issued to each student were very carefully worded and stated that students were to present themselves for training in every way properly dressed and kitted out. On the first day of training, two uniform inspections were conducted. In the morning the working dress and in the afternoon 'best blue'. In preparation for taking over my own course, I was to work closely with a colleague and act in his support. Standing in the first floor corridor, looking down onto the square below where the students were paraded, he said, 'Eric, I'm going to conduct the two inspections, and I'm going to give you a sealed envelope at the end of the day containing the names of those who will fail, or be re-coursed. Put the envelope away and we will look at it at the end of the course!' I was astounded and very sceptical of this apparently arrogant and presumptuous statement.

The two inspections were completed and the Drill Sergeant conducted a half hour period, before handing over control to various students for a further half an hour of drill. With the departure of the Sergeant no member of the Directing Staff was visible to the students, some of whom visibly relaxed their effort. I've written all this; because it was at this point that the sealed envelope was handed to me. Six weeks later we opened the envelope, when the end of course reports had been written and filed. There were six names listed and four of these had failed to reach the required standard! The names of the other two students on the list featured at the very bottom of the order of merit pass list. The pass/fail list was not created by any one staff member, but was the product of group discussion between all members of the DS associated with the course.

Naturally, I asked what the secret was. This officer had noted that any student who was 'picked up' on both uniform inspections and noted as one of those students who noticeably reduced effort in the absence of staff was suspect. All had been warned during the arrival briefings that their view of 100% effort might not be good enough.

You'll have noticed that I used the word student rather than man or woman. We had quite a few young women Loadmaster candidates who had overcome a lot of competition just to get this far. All the women arrived at Finningley with regulation uniforms, skirts of the prescribed length, and wearing those dreadful flat-heeled shoes. Hair had been dragged back, or cut to regulation length to clear the collar. These young women were not terribly happy with their appearance.

I was about to begin my first course interviews. Those with young men presented no new problems, but I had not worked with women before. I decided that I would treat all students equally. The first of the women arrived for initial interview. Two of them stand out in my memory. The first marched firmly into the room and saluted. She stood there, spotty, hair scraped back, dressed in her regulation everything. She did not look like a young woman who had so impressed the selection board that she had beaten off the challenge of at least fifty others for very few places on the course.

I asked where she came from, and she gave a single word reply. I asked if she had any brothers or sisters and she answered in one word. Knowing that she had spent two years in Cyprus, I asked if she swam a lot. Again the single word answer defeated my attempt to draw her out. I asked if she had hobbies and once again she stonewalled. I was fast becoming irritated, for I knew perfectly well that she was aware of the reasons for an initial interview. I asked if she enjoyed walking, and finally an answer came. Yes, she enjoyed mountain walking. Had she walked in any of the military sports walks such as the Golden March through the Troodos Mountains? I knew that it had been very hot throughout the last march and asked if she had finished. She gave an emphatic single word answer to both questions. I threw her out, telling her to get her act together and return in five minutes. She re-appeared to say that yes, she'd completed the march and that she had walked a great deal in England. She had completed the Ten Tors and Three Peaks walks among many others. She climbed cliff faces as a hobby and enjoyed canoeing and abseiling. She then went on to say that 'I look so bloody awful because I fell in the mountains and put a rib into my lung, Sir.' I thanked her for finally answering my questions and she left.

The second memory concerns a buxom Scots girl from Dunfermline. A womanly figure, a pleasant face and platinum blonde angel cut hair completed the picture. She exuded a charm, and sympathetic good nature that I had good reason to doubt. I told her that I would be obliged if she dropped the act and acted her normal self. I went on to say that there was no such thing as a sweet good-natured Scots girl from Fife – and before the end of the course I would prove that to her. She looked outraged, with good reason. I went on to tell her that I came from Fife too, and that I knew from past experience that I was right. She spoke what fellow Scots would describe as 'Edinburgh Morningside' and those from Fife as 'Pan Loaf'. We parted amicably.

The AAITC provided some pretty basic instruction in Law, public speaking, administration, filing and physical training. On graduation, these young people became acting Sergeants and had to learn how to act as SNCOs. They learnt how difficult it was to clean an accommodation block to my satisfaction, and how to inspect a barrack block too. At every phase of their training, my support staff or I would be present, observing everything and every act. It was vital to obtain as much information on a student's behaviour as possible. If I was to fail a student, who may have cherished the idea of becoming aircrew from the age of fifteen years, then I had to be right to do so. It may interest you to know that I watched every physical training (PT) session. I needed to be able to recognise what each individual's 'best efforts' looked like. We are all different and 100% from a rawboned twenty-year-old man was different to that of a twenty two year old slight woman. Often the PT sessions revealed more than one might think. A volley ball game in progress might pause and an offender be told to do ten press-ups as the game continued. It was possible, in the excitement, to miscount once, but the same individual often did seven instead of ten. Each piece of information was part of a jigsaw that would in the course of time tell me something of the man. I needed to know when an individual was doing his very best. And for that judgment I needed first hand knowledge.

In the fifth week of training, the course travelled by bus up the A1 to Kettlewell on the Yorkshire Moors, where the Air Force had the use of a farmhouse at Hag Dyke. We used this house as a base from which to mount our orienteering and leadership exercises. There were basic cooking facilities and the students looked after the needs of the DS as well as themselves. Occasionally, the Physical Training Officer (P Ed O) would accompany us and his caustic inputs were both amusing and informative. On one occasion, a mug of tea was passed to him that he spat out immediately, crying that he'd been poisoned! The student cook refuted this and told him that it had been brought specially for the DS and was in fact Earl Grey Tea. The P Ed O looked darkly about him and stated unequivocally that it was Poofter's Tea! It's still known as Poofter's tea in my house after all these years, but Gitti and I both enjoy it.

I said earlier that youth and fitness was no match for old age and cunning and I'll now explain this anomaly. On arrival at Kettlewell, the students formed up into two groups carrying all their belongings. Although the majority of the DS continued on to the farmhouse, the Course Commander and the Warrant Officer remained with the students. Both carried substantial rucksacks and knew where they were going. The students did not know, nor how far they might travel. A student leader was appointed and told to move as quickly as possible while staying in a single group. Waving my walking stick, and bellowing that they should follow me, I shot off up the hillside. The hillside had many folds and from below the students could not see that I was lying behind a ridge panting furiously. As the teams approached I would reappear to bellow, 'Move, I told you to move!' All the students ever saw of the DS was figures on the horizon trotting uphill at speed. It quite demoralised them, for they had to move at the pace of the slowest.

A year or so later at a graduation lunch, an Air Commodore father of one of our students accosted me. 'Forgive me,' he said, 'I can't quite believe that you're the chap who broke my son's heart on the Yorkshire Moors. He said that each time he saw you, you were running up hill with a dirty great rucksack on.' I explained, and he laughed his head off. His wife chimed in to ask, 'How did you manage to make him tidy his clothes and everything away in just six weeks when I achieved absolutely nothing in nineteen years?' I explained that as a mother she held no useful cards, whereas I held them all. Her son wanted the chance to become aircrew and to achieve that he must first meet my standards. She was Mother, and at this particular moment of time had nothing that he wanted! I told her that this could change – her husband interjected to say that his own popularity often depended upon his son's financial situation. Little did I know at that time that as my girls grew older that I would become a mobile piggy bank!

I had promised the Scots girl that I would prove that there was no such thing as a sweet good-natured girl from Fife and now a situation presented itself where I could do just that. It was a pitch-black night on the moors. Two teams were very late to arrive at the rendezvous. As I considered my actions, a team marched in, soaked to the skin, tired but very glad to reach the meeting point. The rain was blowing horizontally and it truly was a dreadful night. A bit stupidly, I walked back alone along the line of probable approach to the rendezvous. I lay down on the hillside and listened for any clue that the missing team was in the vicinity. I heard the faint sound of voices, and a few minutes later the voices became clearer. The Scots girl had obviously fallen into yet another hole and treated her leader to a right earful. The team trudged, heads down, through the pouring rain, each with the hood of their anorak up. I slipped down the hill and joined the small team from the rear. The team leader led the group directly into yet another bog, and once more was rewarded by a relatively mild tirade from the rear. I 'snuck' in beside her and whispered in her ear, 'I told you, didn't I, that there is no such animal as a good natured girl from Fife?' Without another word I slipped away, off into the night. Weeks later, at the graduation party, she implored me to tell the others that I *had* been beside them on the moors! Incidentally, I make no apology for using the American word 'snuck' I feel that it is appropriate.

On another visit to the Yorkshire Moors it had been extremely hot weather throughout a day of long marches. I was conscious that the physically weaker members of the course were having great difficulties. One slight young woman in particular concerned me as the whites of her eyes were creamy and bloodshot and she was obviously very tired. I spoke with the WRAF warrant officer and she shared my view that we should take the girl out of the march. All the teams were now within three or four miles of the Hag Dyke farmhouse. It was night time and beginning to rain and I told the girl that I was pulling her out. Not as a failure, I emphasised, but because I felt that she had done enough to prove herself. Turning like an angry cat she spat, 'F-off, I'm finishing this.' There was a pause, 'Please, sir,' she entreated. The WRAF warrant officer looked askance at me, but I just grinned, and said that if she was so determined to finish, then she'd better get on with it. We kept a very careful eye on her, but finish under her own steam she did.

One beautiful sunny day we came across a large moustachioed man who looked just like a retired Army Colonel in his thorn-proof three-piece suit. He carried a large stick and was accompanied by a large and exuberant boxer dog. The five of us stopped to talk with the man, who was indeed a retired Army Officer, and unconsciously formed a sort of circle that appeared to move periodically in a clockwise direction drifting upwind. After the second move I realised that the reason was a disgusting smell. Nobody mentioned the smell, but we all shuffled away. After a few moves the Colonel kicked the dog away, saying, 'Bloody dog farts everywhere and people think that it's me.' The dog moved only a few yards and by the strained look on the dog's face it was obvious that he was prepared to issue more of the same! 'Too many bloody biscuits,' said the Colonel with feeling.

We had a new commander of the Airman Aircrew School, he was a Pilot and had come up to the farmhouse to see for himself how we lived and did our job. The staff officers had assembled in the main lounge of Hag Dyke farmhouse and were lounging around smoking and drinking tea. The farmhouse had a few old books in a cupboard, and one of us pulled out a tattered copy of a Biggles book by Capt W E Johns. We were chatting away saying that Biggles (the nickname of Captain Bigglesworth, a pilot) had become unacceptable due to his racist comments on 'natives' and the like. My colleague turned the book over to look at the dust jacket which showed Biggles, sat in an armchair, surrounded by Algy and Ginger, fellow officer characters from the story. Algy was sat on the arm of the chair. Noting that Biggles had his hand on Algy's knee, he said that he was not surprised that Biggles was no longer standard reading for the young British schoolboy, as Biggles was undoubtedly homosexual! Our new Boss, clearly a fan of all Biggles novels, had a sense of humour failure and stopped all conversation on the subject. That meant, of course, that we went around the place muttering, 'Biggles is a queer!' to one another. He didn't like that either.

I had walked all morning up hill and down dale, but I could not get rid of my 'stitch' on the right side. I stopped for a quick pee and discovered to my horror that my urine looked suspiciously like blood. I told my support officer to take over, and left with the Loadmaster to drive the hundred miles or so back to Finningley. Gitti looked totally stunned when told of this happening. I reported to the Medical staff. They sent me off to RAF Hospital Nocton Hall near Lincoln, where after a few tests the Chief Surgeon said that he would operate on my kidney stone in three weeks time! O Joy!

The Chief surgeon was posted to another unit at very short notice and his successor did not share the enthusiasm of his predecessor in wishing to operate at all. In pain, I continued my duties for nearly a year before I decided that if the Air Force would not do anything about the stone, then I would. I arranged to see a Professor at Sheffield Hospital who conducted tests, expressed puzzlement at the attitude of his colleague, and agreed to operate on me. He was also concerned that under certain circumstances, the Air Force could call my operation a self inflicted injury and deny me any pension rights should things go wrong. He advised a single premium payment to a Lloyds Insurance broker to guard against such an eventuality. Unknown to me, he then telephoned the RAF surgeon. What was said between them I don't know, other than that he said that he was going to operate upon me on the following Thursday. I was immediately informed that the RAF would operate on the Tuesday! On my arrival at Nocton Hall Hospital, the surgeon testily informed me that he did not care to have his 'arm twisted'. I responded by telling him that I didn't like being in constant pain; that I did not care to lose my flying pay and hard won professional career, and that I did not wish to defer surgery to a time far into the future when my physical condition might have deteriorated. We circled and stared at each other like fighting dogs, and I became conscious that this was the chap who was going to carve me up tomorrow! That night as I lay in the bath, delicately holding my part clear using thumb and finger as I shaved myself free of potentially germ carrying hair, I reflected that this surgical business might not be my finest hour.

The surgeon did a good job, although he obviously liked room to work for he made an enormous cut that extended from just off centre right to a similar position at the rear. The incision minimised the scars that might spoil my bikini line, for they cut was directly over an unsuccessful appendix operation, a second operation for peritonitis and a two-stitch knife slash from Aden. I thus would have only one combination scar, albeit a large one. With the removal of this largish stone that was jammed into one lobe of the kidney I made a good recovery, but it took time for my stamina to return. I did not enjoy jolting all over the Moors in a Land-rover, nor did I particularly enjoy walking over rough ground. However, as one colleague stated,' You shouldn't have joined if you can't take a joke.' To this I would give the equally standard response of, 'I don't mind a joke, but f— a pantomime'.

In a perverse way, I enjoyed my stay of four years at Finningley. I learnt a great deal, not only about the students, but also about myself. It's equally true to say that both Gitti and I developed as people, certainly in our ability to work with others. We enjoyed a good social life within the school, and returned the student hospitality by giving a supper party for each of my courses. We always invited Peter Dooling the Catholic Padre too, in the thought that his presence lent respectability to the gathering. Once a very young group confided that they had never eaten Italian food, but returned for seconds before Gitti and I had eaten firsts. 'Back, dogs,' I cried, 'After me, you're first!'

In my dealings with the course, I stressed the importance of information. If I was to be of any help in dealing with problems large or small, then I had to be told first. Gitti and I were reupholstering a settee and had worked past midnight, when there was a knock at the door. I opened the door to find four of my students standing decidedly dishevelled and downhearted on my doormat. They had driven back to camp, entered the turn into the entrance road rather late and had rolled the car through a small hedge onto the flowerbed. They contrived to complete this manoeuvre just outside the guardroom! Nobody was hurt, they hastened to add, but the car was hurt, as was the hedge and flowerbed. They had not been drinking, they claimed. They had been to the cinema and had only managed to squeeze in a pint before the pubs closed. The duty policeman was compiling his report for the morning.

I had said that I wanted to know of difficulties and problems first. Well, my bluff was called. I managed to convince the Flight Sergeant Policeman that no offence had been committed other than poor driving (we both avoided the word reckless). The owners of the hedge plants, the Ministry of Public Buildings and Works (MPBW) were less helpful and demanded that these slow growing and most difficult to find hedge plants be replaced by specimens of similar size. I trotted down to their offices and pleaded that my people were guilty on all counts, but that their vehicle was ruined, and gave a convincing 'free grovel'. By nightfall the following day, all was forgiven and no traces of the incident could be seen. The car, although drivable, had a neat crease across the roof at the mid point and a somewhat crumpled dog eared look at the starboard roofline.

I was most fortunate to enjoy the confidence of those of my students who remained at Finningley to complete the basic training of their branch. Air Engineer and Air Electronic Operators remained at Finningley while Loadmasters of both sexes continued on to Brize Norton. I retained administrative responsibility for students of each AAITC course that I had conducted. I was not, in any way, responsible for their technical training. I interviewed each student once a month and these meetings were usually relaxed chats. I would ask how things were going before asking who was having troubles. There was usually a long pause before an answer came, but I would be told that A or B was having trouble learning morse code and was driving himself mad into the small hours each day. I would thank the student and later take a walk up to the study areas of the Air Electronics School, where I would drink tea with the civilian morse instructor. Chatting away, I'd ask how such and such a course was doing and when the answer came, 'Fine, no problems with them at all,' I would tell him of A or B's difficulties. Very privately, the morse instructor would then feed the troubled student two or three test exercises at a slightly slower speed than before. Success at the slower speeds raised confidence levels and the problems disappeared. No AEO student of mine ever failed morse. I valued the confidences of the people more than I can say.

Two years ago, I received a letter, totally out of the blue, inviting me to a twenty fifth anniversary course reunion dinner to be held at a Waddington restaurant just outside Lincoln. I was surprised that they could even find me, for I had long retired from the Service and furthermore, had spent the final ten years of my career in Germany. As I drove up to Waddington, my mind wandered over the Finningley years and in particular to matters concerning these men. The organiser had been kind enough to send some up to date photographs of the course members, and I had looked back at the Graduation Parade programmes that I had kept for every one of my courses. Each programme contained a course photograph and the combination enabled me to see 'before and after' pictures. I believe that there were nine or ten ex-students present at the dinner, every single one of the Air Electronics Operators (AEOps). Two had left the service and both ran small shops in Scotland. Four had reached the rank of Master (Warrant Officer) and the remaining men had been commissioned. The most senior was a Squadron Leader, who was likely to be further promoted. This man amused me tremendously, for when standing before a board of officers deciding whether or not he should be allowed to attend an important course for which he was not eligible, his case had been described by the female president of the Board as 'plausible'. Unable to control his face, he was asked what had so amused him. He replied that he'd never heard the word plausible until I had so described him in his final report from AAITC, and that this was only the second time he'd heard the word used. The Board allowed him to attend the course.

The evening was a great success; I was touched to be asked to attend the dinner and more than flattered by the detail in which they remembered the antics of the course. Only damaging my nice new car when an airborne billboard was driven at me by high winds marred the event.

The accurate use of words was exceptionally important to the new commanding officer of the school. He presented his staff with a list of words appropriate for the description of student behaviour on a scale of one to ten. He listed acceptable adjectives and their suitability for each degree of ability. Thus, excellent, outstanding, exceptional and the like inferred the highest mark. He offered the staff word lists to meet each standard. He was particularly keen that he should be able to determine the order of merit within a group by reading the report and that he should not have to rely on the numeric system. This was a most unpopular if justifiable move to improve report writing throughout the school. Often the staff searched desperately for words to precisely express their observations. A Thesaurus became an essential tool of every course commander. On one occasion I was criticised for using the words 'mental turpitude.' I was called to the Presence and asked what the words meant. Fortunately, I could give him the dictionary definition. I was told, in acid tones, that reports should be written in readily recognisable and understood words and that he should not have to get out the dictionary to determine my meaning. (I meant that the student's thought processes were muddled and confused.) I was only trying to improve!

As a secondary duty, it was my task to organise the six weekly graduation parades held for Navigators, Air Engineers and Air Electronic Operators. I wrote all the orders and informed all interested parties. I organised course photographs and the arrangements for not only the parade but also the arrangements for luncheon and hosting of guests in both the Officers' and Sergeants' Messes. I sent out the orders under the signature of the Station Commander. Nobody wanted the job, so I became stuck with it.

After one particular graduation I was told to report to the new Boss of the Navigation School. When I got there, I found a sign on the door marked 'Do not disturb'. 'Mmmm,' I thought, 'In the shit again Hayes.' I knocked and entered to find the recently arrived Wing Commander seated at his cleared desk. His phone lay off the hook and I stood on what appeared to be a very small carpet! I saluted somewhat apprehensively and awaited the storm. 'This was my first attendance at a parade held to mark the graduation of my students, Hayes. I must tell you that I am wholly dissatisfied by the arrangements made to host guests within the Officers' Mess. They were not merely bad; they appeared to be non-existent. What have you to say for yourself?' I took a deep breath and asked if he was a recipient of the orders written in preparation for the graduation ceremonies. 'Of course,' he snapped. I went on to say that the persons responsible for the reception and hosting of guests within the Mess were detailed in the orders and this was because I could not be in two places at once. My students were all Sergeants and their luncheon was held in their own Mess. Irritated beyond measure, he searched for the orders in question asking furiously who actually was responsible. I looked him squarely in the eye without emotion and replied, 'You were, Sir.' I then asked if there was anything further that he required of me, and receiving no answer, I saluted and left. I got outside the door and was rubbing my hands with glee, when the door opened and a large horny hand hauled me back into the room. The navigator stood there red faced with embarrassment and accused me of enjoying the event. I couldn't lie, nor could I keep a straight face. I said that of course I'd enjoyed it. He had obviously set up his office to deliver a world-class bollocking and had fallen flat on his face (I didn't say that bit!). But he had failed to check the facts! Finally succumbing to my overwhelming glee he smiled ruefully and said that it would be all over the school by sun down! He was right of course, but we got on well after that.

His predecessor was a small stocky officer called Jean Claude Burton – known discreetly as 'Oddjob'. He was acting as Station Commander when some of his Navigator students were sailing in the English Channel aboard the Air Force yacht *Black Knight*. I was Station Duty Officer the night that the skipper called to say that the vessel had struck rocks off one of the Channel Islands and had sunk. There were no casualties and the students were now in an hotel. He gave a contact telephone number. Despite the hour, for it was nearly eleven in the evening, I phoned the Wing Commander. He arrived some minutes later asking if I had more information. I had none, but offered a comment on his supposition that the navigators would never again be allowed to use the Air Force yachts. I had heard that the boat was old and that the Air Force lacked the money to replace her. Perhaps, I suggested they might be thanked for the destruction of the yacht, for surely it would be insured! Brightening a little, he remarked that there appeared to be more to me than he had previously supposed. With this unflattering remark he shoved off to bed, relieved that there had been no loss of life or limb.

The big moment had come, and I was now off to London and the Central Medical Establishment (CME) for a medical examination to recover my aircrew medical category. The delay in operating upon my kidney stone cost me flying category (and flying pay) for a year. Statistically, I knew that only two out of every five kidney stone patients made total recovery. I hoped that I was to be one of them. Arriving punctually, I was shown into the Consultant's office by a most attractive young nurse. The Senior Consultant was a short man of about five feet four inches in height and girth.

After a brief welcome and a routine check to ensure that I actually was the expected individual (some people apparently send surrogates), I was led out to a series of rooms to complete the usual rituals of eye, ear, blood and urine tests. A small army of specialists prodded parts, took samples, and made X-ray pictures of me. They measured and weighed me and made a cardiographic inspection. I even blew up balloons before taking a long lunch break that would allow analysis of tests and samples. I returned at the appointed hour, to meet with the Senior Consultant for my final assessment and the decision. I lay on the examination table suitably unclothed as he pushed and prodded along my scar line, asking if this hurt. I said that it did when he leant on me. The doctor grunted and left, to return with a six foot twelve inch colleague. He too prodded and poked, and I conceded once again that it hurt; especially when this man by virtue of superior height and weight could provide more prod and poke. In silence the giant left, but perhaps he nodded to his colleague, and I was told to stand up. Armed with a sort of caliper, he squeezed the flesh around my waist and said that I was overweight. What followed was one of my greatest mistakes, and evidence of the misplaced sense of humour I am said to possess, for I said, 'Hell, that's a bit like the pot calling the kettle black, isn't it?' The man exploded into incandescent rage. I don't remember his exact words, but the gist of it was that his statement that I was overweight was a professional opinion directly linked to the examination in progress. My impertinent and totally uncalled for opinion was both irrelevant and offensive. Chastened, I put on my clothes and left the room. On the way out, I met the pretty nurse. She cocked her head inquiringly, noticing my red face and stunned look, and asked, 'Did you tell him he was fat?' I nodded weakly. 'He doesn't like that,' she said, totally superfluously. Fortunately for me, the Senior Consultant was a true professional and, overlooking my bad manners and lack of judgment, had passed me fit once more for flying duties.

CHAPTER TWENTY
RETURN TO FLYING

It was nice to return to our home at Lydiard Millicent. The house had been rented out for the majority of the time we had spent at Finningley, but my tour had been extended to allow me to recover my flying medical category – or was it because the incoming officer produced reasons why he shouldn't take post? Whatever the reasons, Gitti's parents came from Germany and stayed in the house for six months. We were most grateful to them, for short term rentals were hard to find. We brought a new member of the family back to Lydiard, Susanne Nicola Hayes. This diminutive little girl with bright red hair joined the family as sister to Sabina Antonia Hayes, now aged four, and was the most perfect little person. Despite the difference in age, they got along pretty well. I remember hearing early one morning a 'climb out course'. Susi slept in a cot and Bini said 'Put your foot here, and hold on to there. Move that foot here, and hold on to me!' Now that she could leave the cot at will, she never again slept there! The children brought us great happiness. Well, they made a great difference and certainly they enliven our lives even though they are now both in their thirties!

I returned to flying duties, but after such a long absence had to complete the Operational Conversion Unit (OCU) course again, including the ground school. I remembered quite a lot, but strangely and irritatingly, not enough to beat the marks of a Sergeant on the course. Colin consistently beat my marks by 3 to 5%. He must be clever, I thought! We graduated to the simulator phase and began to work through the checklist, learning where each individual switch and control was located. We learnt the responses to the checklist too. My instructor, an old friend, took the checklist book away from me and said, 'Let's see what you remember'. I wasn't word perfect, but I did remember a great deal more than I thought I would. We 'crewed up' for the Simulator and flying phase of the Conversion Course. My captain was an ex co-pilot who had joined us from the Queen's Flight. I had a good deal of experience from my earlier tours of duty flying the Hercules and I found his aptitude quite remarkable. He rarely repeated an error and learnt extraordinarily quickly. When we flew the real aircraft, he showed the skills of a natural pilot and had an easy, but precise, manner of captaincy. The end of course training flight was a good one. We departed Lyneham bound for Singapore to fly 'west about' through Canada and the USA. Our first stop was Gander, Newfoundland – where else? I put the aircraft to bed, helping the crew chief, and together we set off by taxi to join the rest of the crew at the Albatross Hotel. We enjoyed a good meal, as indeed we always did there, and congregated in the bar. Normally, I'm not a bar person. I drink very little, and in those situations where it becomes 'your round', I was permanently out of pocket. I did not consider it my place in life to subsidise the drinking class! At about eleven in the evening I retired to bed and was quickly asleep. I rose when called, breakfasted and joined the crew in the foyer to await the taxis. The co-pilot asked if I'd seen the captain. A quick check around the crew revealed that none of us had seen him since the previous night. I got his room number from the desk clerk and trotted off to get him. The door opened to show a bed that had not been slept in, and an unopened case on the bed. There was no sign of the man. I returned to the foyer and asked if the captain had been alone when last seen. All agreed that he had been alone and that he was still dressed in uniform. Puzzled, I returned to his room for a second look to see if there were any clues as to his whereabouts. As I turned to leave the room, I heard a sort of moaning/grunting noise coming from a wardrobe. I opened the wardrobe door to find my noble captain, dressed in full uniform, standing fast asleep, propped up by the sides, fly undone and a small pool of urine on the floor! He had enjoyed a good night's sleep though.

 Because this was a training flight, there was more than a single crew on board. My working legs of the journey were Gander to Offutt, and Hickam to Guam. Of course I flew other parts of the total journey, but for the moment I'm going to stop in Guam. I had last seen Andersen Air base at the time of the Vietnam war. Then, huge B52 bombers would line up in very considerable numbers for take off. Aircraft did not recover direct to Guam, but landed in Thailand to refuel. A fully fuelled and armed B52 taking off from Guam was quite a sight. Twenty or thirty of them, following one after another was an experience in itself. As the machines roared down the runway the wing tips would lift the tiny outrigger wheels clear of the ground. As speed increased, the wing tips would rise a further unbelievable ten feet as the wings began to take the weight of the aircraft. The end of the runway was signalled when the ground dropped away in a cliff face of hundreds of feet. From where we stood, aircraft disappeared for some agonising seconds before the monsters clawed their way into the air. I often thought of the crews and their feelings as they rushed at high speed heading for the big drop. An engine failure at take off would be disastrous. On the same runway a fully loaded Hercules was airborne in half the available distance.

During the Second World War Guam was the scene of some particularly nasty fighting between Japanese and American troops. Today this delightful island is home to a wide variety of splendid hotels catering for Japanese tour groups and in particular Japanese honeymoon couples.

The hotel selected for our use was such an establishment and catered for beach weddings and supporting functions. Situated some hundred yards from the beach, the elegant hotel was smothered in the most beautiful tropical flowers. The foyer was enormous and contained a most ornate fountain and water bowl containing a wide variety of water plants and specimen carp. Into this foyer came a bizarre couple. The man was about five feet four inches in height. His body size was out of proportion to his short, heavily muscled, bowlegs. His head sat on massive shoulders without the benefit of a discernable neck; his face was moon shaped and he had very little hair. His paunch was heroic in size. To dress this image, he favoured a colourful long shirt that even an American might not have the courage to wear. The shirt showed only two or three inches of the shorts, but the combination of colours screamed at one another. Short hairy legs led downwards to his bare feet that were clad in a pair of fluorescent green flip flops (thongs) decorated by a pink flower. He was truly a vision in himself.

His companion was quite different. Slim, beautifully proportioned and tanned to perfection, she was a truly beautiful young woman. Her long dark hair fell down her back nearly to her tiny waist and she moved in a most graceful manner. Nobody noticed what she was wearing, but all of the crew remembered that she clung to the arm of her companion and gazed at him in adoration. Beauty and the Beast had nothing on these two. The crew agreed that looks were not everything and that the man must have something in his favour! Some lewd suggestions were made, but I tend to believe that he had either personality or money.

Our training flight continued on to Singapore. The city-state had dramatically changed. Skyscrapers filled the skyline and the city streets teemed with people eagerly buying from the most modern of shopping areas. The road from Changi airport into town was lined by attractively styled three and four storey blocks set in small but neat garden areas.

The streets were clean – wonderfully clean and the pavements had been cleared of the blobs of chewing gum. I was astounded by what had been achieved by the government of Lee Kwan Yew. Moreover, the people appeared cheerful and prosperous. They certainly did not look like people living under the dictatorship that some accused the government of becoming.

I renewed my acquaintance with some of the shopkeepers that I had known in Changi village. There had been a bad fire, and this had destroyed a tailor's shop and the barber's place too. He used to give a good haircut and a most energising head massage. Everyone should enjoy a head massage, it's quite wonderful and you walk outside feeling quite euphoric.

Our flight back to base was relatively uneventful and I returned to Lyneham to become Engineer Leader of 70 Squadron. I had been Leader of a Hercules Squadron in the past and slipped fairly easily back into the routine. Many of the older engineers were well known to me. I may have said in an earlier chapter that the flight engineers of my age group had all been technicians before becoming aircrew. A glance at the nominal roll of the section showed that the 'old Guard' was composed of either ex Halton Apprentices or ex Boy Entrants. We either knew each other or knew of one another.

As winter approached, so our flights through Canada became more challenging. The Hercules has a pretty fair de-icing system and is an enormous improvement on what had previously been available on the Handley Page Hastings. Despite propeller de-icing, excellent leading edge de-icing of the wings, and radome ant-icing it was still possible to get into real difficulties in bad weather. Yes, we flew mainly above the weather, but the aircraft has to climb out above weather and must descend through weather to land. When the aircraft reaches the landing site, new problems may arise with snow or ice on runway and taxiways. Ice can form on the wing surfaces of the aircraft, destroying lift; ice can form on the whole airframe adding greatly to the aircraft weight and ice can jam controls.

During my time on Hercules I encountered severe icing only twice. On the worst occasion we had begun our descent at night from altitude to be told by Gander approach that due to a ground incident we were to enter the hold at 7500 feet. Prior to our descent, I had switched on all anti icing equipment, but a sharp rattle against the sides of the aircraft warned me that the propellers were throwing ice. I warned the Captain that we could be in pretty bad icing conditions and left the flight deck with a high-powered torch to view the mainplane and to have a general look around. I was appalled, for the whole aircraft reflected the light of my torch back at me. The aircraft was covered in ice and was picking up more. Rain ice, the worst of all icing, was accumulating quite rapidly. I returned to the flight deck and looked at the throttle positions and at the airspeed indicator. To maintain the required speed the throttles were well forward of the normal position. 'Captain,' I said as conversationally as possible, 'if you don't get this aircraft on the ground within the next few minutes, we are going to fall out of the sky and I mean it.' The co-pilot requested immediate landing from Gander tower and was told that there was heavy icing on the runway, but that we were clear for landing at pilot's discretion. That's another way of saying that it will be your fault if you crash on the runway.

We had no choice, for the diversion airfield lay about 30 minutes away and, in my opinion, we'd fall out of the sky long before then. Mercifully, a Hercules need not use wheel brakes to stop, and in addition to reversing the propellers to brake we could use asymmetric engine power to keep the aircraft on the runway. We landed safely and taxied through the avenues of steeply piled snow towards the terminal building. As we entered the well lit hard standing we could see for the first time the extent of the icing. It was horrendous, for the leading edges were distorted by packed rain ice and the whole aircraft was covered by about two inches of clear ice. By the time we had shut down the engines and left the airplane all four propellers dripped six-inch icicles and the engine nacelles dripped ice too. We said very little to one another, but we all knew that we had been very lucky to make any safe landing.

I spoke to the Canadian ground staff who worked for Allied, asking if they had seen any previous aircraft land that night in this condition. Their boss replied that he most certainly had not, and that on seeing the condition of our aircraft as we approached the terminal, he had telephoned the Approach Controller in the tower, telling him of the condition of our aircraft, stating that in his opinion the airport should be closed and warnings issued. The Controller was apparently happy to do this because no further aircraft were expected until morning.

The second of my icing experiences occurred over Northern Ireland as we descended to land at Ballykelly. During the descent we entered cloud and immediately the ice warning light illuminated I checked that all systems were operating before inspecting the leading edge of the mainplanes and engines. I was greatly surprised and advised the Captain that he should warn the Air Traffic Control of this patch of what quickly became 'severe icing'.

Over the years I had several experiences at Gander. In the first, I had an engine hydraulic leak. It was deep winter and extremely cold, and to work outside in such conditions it is necessary to wear the warmest of clothes and to establish a safety routine. My crew chief was laid low with chronic diarrhoea, but the repair was within my capabilities. I got kitted out and obtained the necessary stands from Allied, the airport handling company, to get me up to the necessary working height. I detailed off one of our airman passengers to act as safety man, stressing the importance that he brought me into the crew room every twenty minutes without fail. I stressed the importance of this, because I didn't want to get frostbite. After twenty minutes work I was relieved by the safety man and, after warming myself with a cup of tea, I returned to work. Even small jobs take a disproportionate time in very cold conditions. Unaware of the passage of time, I worked on. Suddenly a vehicle screeched to a halt beside my aircraft and a concerned and angry Canadian driver hauled me off the engine, down the ladders of the engine stand, and into his vehicle. Driving into the technical area, he dragged me into their crew room where one man ripped off my parka and began to pummel me as a second and third man examined my fingers, ears and nose. Only when they were convinced that I had come to no harm, did they explain that I had worked continuously for an hour and a half in sub zero conditions. 'Where was my safety man? Didn't I know any better than to work without a safety man? You English are all the same!' I protested that I did have a safety man, and that he was working, in fact he had relieved me once already. 'Where is he now?' they asked. Together we looked for the safety man to find him fast asleep in the warmth of the terminal building office. He too got the hard time lecture from the Canadians. When they had finished, I added my diatribe, for it was my fingers nose and ears that had been at risk. It was not this airman's night.

In Gander township is a remarkable drinking place called 'The Flyers' I hold the unenviable distinction of being one of the very few people who have been flung out of that establishment. Was I objectionable? Was I drunk? No, I was the only man sober – so out I went, sprawling in the snow with my parka following me out. I never did find out what prompted my ejection, but the stories told varied considerably depending upon whether I was liked or disliked. Some stories were libellous.

Flights that landed at Thule at the North Pole were rare, and I was particularly pleased to take part in a Cambridge University expedition to research the habits of the white-breasted goose. (Well, it was some kind of something breasted goose!) We were to fly the second part of the university team to Sondestrom in Greenland and to make an airdrop of food and specialist equipment to a location somewhere in the wilderness the following day. We were a single crew with the exception that a second captain was on board. The approach to the drop site in the tundra was conducted at low level and it was not long before the university people were all sick! Air is a bit lumpy at times and this was one of them. As we flew down valleys with high ramparts of hills on either side, I became uneasy, for they looked unusually close. Our flight path continued down the valley that was closed off by a small mountain, the summit of which was covered in cloud. When that too appeared uncomfortably close – for nobody in his right mind enters cloud when ignorant of the terrain – I turned to the second captain standing beside me. 'We're a bit bloody close to all this ground, aren't we?' Quietly, and off intercom he agreed a little nervously. I was about to voice my disquiet when I saw a bear on the ground and realised that in the absence of any feature on the ground I had totally lost my sense of scale and perspective. In truth there were several hundred metres of space on each side of the aircraft and we would turn down another valley long before we reached the mountain. The second pilot and I reached this decision simultaneously and grinned at each other – glad that we hadn't opened our mouths.

We made a superbly accurate equipment drop directed by the Loadmaster from the open rear doors to the university party on the ground before continuing to fly up the west coast towards the polar wastes. The glaciers and icebergs of the coastal region defy description. White as a clean sheet at the top and an incredible aquamarine as the bergs enter the water. Towering slabs of ice tilted towards the water and the sheer size of the glaciers was intimidating. Here and there we would see evidence of human habitation and once we saw a small group of locals riding skidoos across the ice and snow. They looked like black ants against the arctic backcloth.

When we were fifty miles out from Thule, the captain told all crew members to look out for the airfield. 'You should see it easily – the runway is painted white.' Oh Ho Ho, funny man I thought. However, he went on to say that this was to prevent the suns rays heating up the permafrost and causing the runway to sink. Wisely I kept my mouth shut – for this was indeed the truth.

Thule airbase belongs to Denmark and the American lease the place.

In the cold war period a large Army barracks was also built nearby. That base was maintained on a care and maintenance basis, whereas Thule airbase was surprisingly busy. Climbing out of the aircraft, I was fascinated to see that each hangar had huge pipes on the two longer sides of the building. I asked an American airman what was the idea behind the pipes. Pointing to a lop-sided building a half a mile away he said that it was to prevent just that happening! The pipes, a bit like those of a giant organ, carried a flow of air under the building keeping the permafrost from melting. The airflow was caused by the wind blowing across the top of the organ pipe creating a venturi effect that sucked air in. Because buildings in the arctic required heating, it was essential to maintain the permafrost, or face the costs of structures subsiding into the ground.

We reported our arrival to Station Operations and were each given a card that listed instructions should snow fall. We were to stay exactly where we were should the alarm siren sound. We were to report our presence to the building supervisor, who would inform operations of the names of everyone inside his building. In every building on the base there were stocks of food, additional heating devices and supplies of camp beds and bedding. Blizzards could last for days and only specialist teams with appropriate equipment would venture outside to search for any person unaccounted for. The search teams would be roped together and carry radios in duplicate. Sounded fair to me and when the siren did in fact sound, I found a good book. Sadly, the emergency lasted only three hours.

On the second day, the crew met together and we made for the Officers' Club for the evening meal. The manager politely turned us away, for the Base Commander was giving a private party to celebrate his birthday. We were directed to use one of three privately run restaurants! At the North Pole – three privately run restaurants? We chose the nearest, known as Francesco's. On arrival at the basement restaurant we were met by the Maitre D wearing a maroon outfit with a silver half moon disc hanging from his throat. Inquiring the number in our party, he directed us to a corner table in a room already more than half full of diners. When we were seated a wine waiter appeared followed by an equally smartly dressed waiter who took our order. Bemused, we sat relatively silently as a beautifully presented meal was placed before us. We asked the obvious questions. Those posted to Thule were mostly volunteers who served for one year. Those choosing to extend their tour were given tax breaks. Most of the people who chose to extend their stay were career airmen who wished to complete their studies without distractions and without paying taxes. Senior NCOs who purchased their food from Base Commissariats in the States appeared to own and run the restaurants. Deliveries to Thule were on an opportunity or availability basis and they were not billed for carriage. It was a good deal and the cost of eating out was not excessive. The steaks were wonderful, the sauce bearnaise remarkable, as were the crepes. The furniture and decor of the room was elegant and in the latest fashion, far removed from the Spartan military tables and chairs! We agreed that a fair amount of money had been invested in the restaurant. Apparently we had chosen the most exclusive of the eating-places, but were very glad to have done so. I can say that I have dined in a restaurant as near as dammit at the North Pole.

The following morning, almost ready for engine start, we were reminded of the base ownership. A Danish transport aircraft landed and taxied in to dispersal. All American ground personnel departed for the Danish aircraft, leaving us to manage our own departure!

All squadron members enjoyed route-training flights, especially those that allowed us to land at diversion airfields, rather than the normal route airfields. Thus, an aircraft that normally landed at Nassau in the Bahamas en route to Belize might fly from Freeport in the Bahamas to the Cayman Islands before landing at Belize. Alternatively, permission might be given to land at Merida in Mexico. In addition to the changes in destination airfields, permission was occasionally granted to fly low level through the island chains. To me, such changes were manna from heaven, for I might get one every two years. Even as Leader, or perhaps because you were Leader, you couldn't 'hog' the best flights. I particularly enjoyed Caribbean trainers that routed through the Cayman Islands. A fellow Scot ran a hotel on Nine Mile Beach and he was inordinately fond of Antiquary Whisky that he couldn't get for love nor money. We would bring a case or two out of bond from the UK, and in return, he would help us to throw a party. All route training flights carried two complete crews and together we would pay a few dollars to the two loadmasters who would buy soft drinks and beer in bulk at the most advantageous airfield en route. Each crew member would arrive with at least two bottles of spirits bought at duty free prices. In this way we could muster the makings of a party. A drink that I had not encountered called Pina Colada was popular and became known to us as 'Penis Collapser'.

On arrival in the Caymans we would post our invitations to a one-hour party by making a quick phone call to the managers of the local hotels. In this manner tourists would know that the Royal Air Force was throwing a one-hour free drinks deal. We felt that we could justly claim that we were participating in a successful public relations exercise on behalf of the Royal Air Force. Our hotel manager would have his staff set out the tables and provide a few crisps, biscuits and the like. At the end of the evening, his staff would clean up. Usually, about forty or fifty strangers would turn up, and when our drinks were gone, they would dig into their own pockets to prolong the evening. When all had gone home and the cleaning in progress we would all board the manager's yacht and cruise up and down the beach in the moonlight. The temperature was just right and the moonlight would be reflected in the fluorescence of the yacht's bow wave. It was the kind of moment that you would wish to share with your nearest and dearest but never could.

On the last occasion that I visited the Caymans, I flew with a pilot who was about to leave the Service to become a veterinary surgeon. After take off from the island, he asked the tower for permission to fly low level along the edge of Nine Mile Beach. The tower gave permission but added, 'not below 1000 feet'. Turning from the runway heading we descended to a very low altitude and roared along the beach line 100 metres offshore. As we climbed out, a call from the tower requested our altitude. Truthfully, we answered, '1000 feet AGL'. An aggrieved voice from the Tower said, 'But you weren't…' We were lucky not to have heard more of that, because the Governor's residence was on our climb out path and we must have flown directly over the house.

We had landed at McClellan airbase near Sacramento and our Loadmaster, Mike McLean, was laid low by a stomach bug. Clearly, he was unfit to fly and when we told Command of this, we were told to remain at McClellan for an additional 24 hours in the hope that he would be fit to fly. The crew chief and I put the aircraft to bed and retired to the hotel where the captain said that he'd heard that there was a cheap coach trip from town over the mountains to the gambling hell of Reno. The trip left in the evenings and returned to Sacramento by 4 a.m. He explained that we didn't have to get up early, nor did we have to fly until the following day. He would like to go, but would like some company. I pointed out that we couldn't really leave Mike alone, but the crew chief volunteered to stay behind, as he didn't like gambling. The crew agreed that they didn't like gambling either – but they'd go if the price was right! I was sent off to find out how we could get tickets and what the cost would be. Jubilantly, I came back with the news that $14 would buy us the return bus ticket to Reno, provide us with coffee and a sandwich on the way AND give us each $10 in chips to gamble! This was a true bargain, an irresistible bargain! On arrival in Reno we formed a syndicate and began to play the machines. Between us we soon got rid of the free chips, but our luck began to turn for the better. I must say at this point that I never ever played with *my* money. That is to say, I played with my monetary allowances for that particular route flight. Creating a crew syndicate we played only with the Queen's money. At the end of the evening we showed a profit of about $4 per man. We had been plied with free sandwiches and drinks while gambling and had enjoyed a pleasant evening in different surroundings. We slept all the way back to Sacramento in the warm bus.

Before I went to my room, I popped into Mike's room to see how he was feeling. I quietly opened the door and peeped in. The bedside lamp was on low, and there was enough light to see that Mike was breathing easily and quietly. Reassured, I turned away, before realising that there was a girl in bed beside him! Well, I thought he must feel better, I walked back to my own room, but curiously I didn't feel like sleep. I made myself a coffee, and as dawn broke, I walked back again to Mike's room. As I peered in, he stirred and woke smiling. I asked how he was, and he replied that at last his stomach had stopped churning. He told me that he had slept pretty well. I asked where the sleeping young woman had come from. Puzzled, he asked,' What young woman?' Pointing, I replied, 'That one, you lecherous sod!' Mike turned in bed and looked in genuine horror at the sleeping girl. 'Where the hell did she come from?'

Our voices woke the girl, who was clearly not with us at all. The pupils of her eyes were like pin heads and she was scarcely coherent. She had been to a party held in a room further up the hall and on leaving had got into a bed in the first room that she could open. Mike was quite upset about finding a girl in his bed – particularly an uninvited hopped up girl. His instinct and mine was to get rid of her as fast as possible. She said plaintively that she was hungry, so we took her to the coffee shop, gave her breakfast and then paid a taxi a big chunk of our cash. I maintained that Mike should pay the lot. After all, it was his bed that she had been in!

I liked flying with Mike as a crewmember, although I'm not sure that he would express the same feeling. A major NATO exercise was held in Norway and photo-reconnaissance aircraft of many nations were gathered on a single airbase. The exercise had terminated and the ground crews were out for a bit of recreation. There had been quite a bit of recreation that had got more than a little bit out of hand. Firstly, the American General who gave the initial exercise briefing lost his hat to a light-fingered lad, and was audibly not amused. Secondly, many of the other ranks had swapped uniforms with those from other NATO countries, making discipline 'difficult' to maintain, for many national units had been reinforced with reservists. Mike and I, still wearing flying suits, were walking along a very picturesque lakeside path on our way to join other transport aircrew at a local hotel. A large group of German, Danish and British airmen were skinny-dipping together with a few young women of considerable physical charm. The Germans shouted greetings that I returned and we spoke together for some minutes. We walked slowly on and I casually asked Mike if he could swim. 'Yeah, course I can. Why?' Still keeping my voice low, I said maliciously, 'Because the Germans are going to throw you into the lake'. At that moment, a group of shining wet and naked lads picked him up and launched him like a model aircraft into the lake. Just like a winged arrow he flew into the lake. As he clawed his way breathlessly out of the freezing cold water and up on to the bank he asked, 'Why didn't they throw you in?' I thought that you'd never ask, Mike,' I grinned. 'I told them that I couldn't swim, but that you could.' Knowledge of the German language can be most useful at times like this.

There is a physical phenomenon known as 'the Leans'. This is a condition in which the pilot believes that the aircraft is banking, while the instruments tell him that this is not the case. It is insidious and I became aware that there was a problem when I realised that the pilot was leaning hard to the left of his seat. The aircraft was in straight and level flight. After a few seconds, I nudged both pilots and suggested that the co-pilot take control. He did so and the pilot sat up straight in his seat again! Uncorrected such a condition can cause accidents and this was the first time that any of us had experienced the condition.

I have known of bizarre accidents in the air, but few can surely equal the incident on the Hercules flight deck. This event occurred when the crew could still smoke on the flight deck if no dangerous air cargo was on board. The navigator, Ron Tellis, was working away with his oxygen mask laid to one side of his desk. He was smoking a cigarette, when to our absolute astonishment and horror a blue flame sprang from the oxygen mask that lay on his desk. The flame was about a metre in length and could not be extinguished. We had no idea how the mask had caught fire, but now the rubber was melting and there was the prospect of a greater danger. Ron suddenly realised that he had left his dividers hanging from the oxygen supply lever and that the weight of the instrument had selected the emergency position. In the meantime, I had left the flight deck with permission to close the main oxygen supply knob on the rear of the flight deck bulkhead. When I returned to my seat the incident was over. Ron's mask was destroyed and all of us were quite shaken by the event. Some time later, Ron starred in a flight safety film depicting this event! Those of us who had seen it first hand did not attend the screening! Ron did not take kindly to those asking for his autograph.

Before I leave this part of my life I must tell the story of a transit flight to the Far East through Hawaii. The crew had flown fourteen hours a day during the last few days and we were to stay at a hotel in Honolulu for our rest period of 33 hours before continuing our flight. With the aircraft safely in the hands of our Staging Post personnel at Hickam, we sat at breakfast planning our day. I was sent off to hire a car while the others cajoled the hotel kitchen to produce a packed lunch. (Not a normal request, but the hotel management was compliant because their waitress had poured coffee all over us when the handle of the large pot fell off onto the table.) We set off and it became quickly apparent that the steering left much to be desired. The wheel was turned to the left but the car didn't quite respond as advertised. The captain criticised my driving and assumed control. We arrived at what was a world famous aquarium and drove into the enormous parking area that was delineated by large tree trunk sized logs chained together. The brakes too left something to be desired and we struck a log, rolling it under the huge chromed fenders of a very large American estate car. We headed for the entrance to buy our tickets as a very large family, large in every sense, emerged. The husband was cursing fluently. 'We come two thousand God damn miles to enjoy this damned holiday and what do I get? Moans bloody moans! What the hell *do* you want to do?' The obese family, of seven, muttering and bickering, departed to climb into that same estate car. The vehicle settled down under the considerable combined weight of the family. The engine sprang to life as Father gunned the motor and the angry man pushed the car into reverse gear and stamped furiously on the accelerator. With a dreadful sound of tearing metal the whole front bumper assembly was torn from the vehicle! It was time to leave.

In the thought that our presence was unnecessary and unwise, we quickly bought our tickets and entered the open-air part of the Aquarium from where we could clearly hear the bellows of the afflicted parent entreating God to tell him what had he done to deserve this on top of the shortcomings of his family! That man was upset and the world knew it.

The IRA Alert State was at high when once again it was my turn to be Station Duty Officer (SDO). I had attended the final parade of those under punishment with the Orderly Sergeant and was about to return to the Mess, when I asked what sort of a day the Sergeant had enjoyed. Smiling, he said 'Very quiet except for the last hour or so.' He went on to tell me that he had authorised the Transport Squadron to recover a bus full of Army sports people that had broken down on the motorway. I asked what progress had been made in repairing the bus and where the Army people were now. He said that they had moved into Transit accommodation and that the bus would be repaired in the morning. Turning away, I asked if he had checked the identities of the soldiers. When he said that he had not thought to do this, I had forty fits. ' Do you realise that you may have brought a bus load of terrorists and their weapons onto one of the biggest and best targets in the UK? You bloody idiot!'

I then asked where the coach had come from and telephoned that unit's Duty Officer. He rang back to say that the unit owned no bus of that registration. We checked the bedding issue register for the names of those on board the coach. Again that Duty Officer denied knowledge of bus and passengers. By now I was quite alarmed.

It was now after eleven and the various venues like the NAAFI, bowling alley etc were shut. We determined that the bus passengers were accommodated in Block X and that we should find out just who they actually were. If they were terrorists, this could be dangerous. You can't just walk up to a suspect and ask him to surrender himself! Thinking furiously I had an entire roomful of our own airmen woken up, taken to the Armoury and armed. The Duty Armourer refused to issue ammunition until I offered to put him into close arrest! Now suitably equipped we entered the Barrack block and placing armed guards strategically, we woke the suspects.

They very quickly established their identities and explained why the unit that they had said they had come from had denied them. They were in fact visitors to that unit and came from XXX. This was the second time that this coach had broken down forcing a night stop. A couple of telephone calls confirmed the stories and we made a graceful withdrawal.

The next morning after submitting my written report, I was called to the Station Commander's office. Blazing with rage he asked if I knew what authority was required to issue ammunition. I told him that I did, but said that the situation demanded no lesser action. 'Why, man, why?' He demanded. Pointing to the extended row of aircraft outside his window, I said, 'Because of those! You wouldn't be very happy now if you were looking at a line of blazing wreckage.' Silently he gestured that I should leave.

On reflection, I wondered if the Air Force really was psychologically prepared for terrorist warfare, and if the Service wanted officers who were prepared to stick their necks out when necessary. However, I heard no more on the matter.

All this stemmed from a man who, when taking up command, had assembled the entire officer cadre of the unit to declaim that he would not tolerate mediocrity in his officers. He required each and every officer to be a leader. To ensure that every officer on base heard this exhortation, it was repeated on three occasions at different venues. We went around accusing each other of being mediocrities for some weeks after the talks.

Every member of an aircrew knows that there is only one leader and that we called him 'captain' Any attempt by other officer crew members to usurp that authority would get pretty short shrift. Moreover, there were very few opportunities to lead others on the ground. The trend to having more chiefs than indians diminished the authority of the rank system.

I was due a posting, for it was unusual to remain in post for more than one duty tour of three years. I asked for Germany, because my hearing was deteriorating as I grew older. Ear defenders had not been available during my formative years and I had spent much time working on or near aircraft engine noise. In truth, I wanted to continue to draw flying pay and would not if I continued flying for much longer. Gratefully, Gitti and I left for the Fatherland.

CHAPTER TWENTY-ONE
A NATO APPOINTMENT

Rheindahlen was a popular posting for the British for it lay close to both the Dutch and Belgian borders. The HQ itself was built in 1956 and was a very substantial building. At the time that I was there it housed two national headquarters and two NATO headquarters. The British, then the largest contingent on base, had the HQ Royal Air Force Germany (RAFG) and the HQ of British Army on the Rhine (BAOR). The HQ of the Second Allied Tactical Air Force (2ATAF) and HQ Northern Army Group (NORTHAG) were co-located on the upper floor of the building. Sited near the town of Moenchengladbach it was possible to be in Holland or Belgium within a few minutes travel on the excellent autobahn system. We got cheap petrol too, through the issue of petrol coupons, and this allowed us to travel more cheaply throughout Europe. We travelled all over Europe during the years we spent in Germany.

Eberhardt Wille, German Air Force, commanded Plans and Policy Division of HQ2ATAF. Colonel Wille was without doubt one of the most unusual men that I have ever met, and definitely the finest leader that I encountered in 42 years service. His style of leadership was not 'British'. Wille was the senior Colonel of the German Air Force, and one of the very few Second World War Pilots to continue to serve. His logbook showed that he had flown 43 different aircraft types! He had been a Squadron Cdr at the end of the war, but he said that two aircraft, three Pilots, five ground crew and a dog was not much of a command! Although successful in business after the war, he had rejoined the German Air Force immediately it had reformed. On completion of the medical examinations and officer school he trained to fly once more in America, beginning on the F86 Sabre jet. Destined, I believe, for much higher rank he had suffered a heart attack while commanding an airbase in Schleswig Holstein. When I arrived in Germany he had held his NATO post of Assistant Chief of Staff (ACOS) Plans and Policy for some five years.

My predecessor conducted my introduction to him and we had to wait while he finished the last few words of an annual report in the

French language, which I was to learn was not his favourite occupation. Eberhardt was an austere, rather severe looking man, who glancing up from his papers, quite abruptly gave some sort of instruction. With mind in neutral I smashed my heels together and said, '*Auf Ihn Befehl, Herr Oberst.*' The colonel's eyebrows shot up and he looked closely at me. 'Where did you learn your German?' I told him of Gitti and he snarled, 'At least you'll know your place then.' What followed was a normal 'arrival' chat. Some three days later I heard a commotion in the corridor outside my office. I heard the colonel, speaking slowly in a stage whisper, warn an assembled group of German Air Force officers that they were to watch what they said in this corridor, for the Brits had posted another spy in! A head popped around the door and an impish looking Boss grinned at me. We got on very well together and I liked and admired the man.

He treated each member of the Division in exactly the same way and that included the British clerk and the German national serviceman. The division was composed of Lieutenant Colonels of Holland, Belgium and Germany assisted by an American Major and me as a Flight Lieutenant. When the Boss gave a party all were invited, and he and his wife Inge were gracious and thoughtful hosts. If a major task was in progress, such as the issue of a Plan or Supplan (supporting plan), he would gather all members of the division into his large office where we would check the documents to be sent to single addressees. Few Colonels would stoop to perform such tasks. Wille's logic was that by page checking individual documents intended for single adresses, he would not receive up to five hundred messages complaining of missing or unreadable pages! When all was well with the world, Wille would move about the Division in a most friendly and helpful manner, but if crossed, or if an error was made, he could create hell. He berated individuals irrespective of rank, and took no account of the presence of subordinates when doing so. Once, when the British Wing Commander was attacked, I tried to leave the room. A hand held my shoulder, '*Sie bleiben hier, Herr Hauptman.*' Later, he would assemble the Division and apologise saying that he was becoming a bad-tempered old man. His smile could charm a bird down from a tree. I don't know quite how he achieved it, but he led a Division of friends. His passing was deeply mourned when he died shortly after his retirement.

A major British live exercise was in progress. It had been a particularly warm day in the exercise area and it was now the middle of the night. Army exercises do not stop for darkness, indeed with the new equipment available activity may intensify. However, this was not to be the case. Radio silence was in force, meaning that the use of radio was prohibited. In the still of the night, a totally bored voice said over the radio,' I'm a bored bear'. A few seconds later, a second voice stated, 'I'm a tired bear'. Immediately, an authoritative voice barked, 'This is a radio silence exercise, report yourself immediately. Name, rank and unit'. There was a pause before the first voice said, 'I may be a bored bear, but I'm not a stupid bear!'

Among the many characters that it has been my pleasure to serve with was a British Wing Commander in the Plans and Policy Division at Rheindahlen. He specialised in the written practical joke and the advent of the word processor opened new areas of opportunity for him to torment his relatives and friends. If my memory serves me aright, he had *two* sisters, one married to a stockbroker and the other to an editor of some magazine or other. The husband of the elder sister was a chap who exercised regularly and was justifiably proud of his musculature and figure. It was against this chap that joke one was directed.

Taking the letterhead of the Royal Society for the Prevention of Cruelty to Birds together with the accompanying list of patrons that included the HM the Queen Mother, he amended the letterhead to become the Royal Regional Sperm Bank. The patrons remained unchanged save for the inclusion of a Dr Hans Christian Andersen.

The letter, directed to his brother-in-law, gave a most heart wrenching description of the problems faced by infertile would-be parents in two very well written paragraphs. The letter continued, that the establishment of the Royal Regional Sperm Bank now offered some hope to these unfortunates. It had been decided at the highest level, that sperm donors should be sought only from among those both physically and mentally above the average. An acquaintance had put forward his name as one who was eminently suitable for such purpose. The letter continued, saying that if he was interested in this, surely the most worthwhile of causes, he should ring the telephone number given at the top of this letter offering dates upon which he could attend a clinic to provide sperm samples.

The number given was that of a particularly acerbic and articulate retired Group Captain, now the Secretary to the Royal Air Force Club! He apparently, gave the well-meaning brother-in-law a real dressing down, particularly after he had been offered sperm samples. He delivered a memorable tirade culminating in 'Who and what the hell are you? A bloody pervert?' before slamming the phone down.

Any practical joker might have stopped at this point, but my man had two sisters. His next letter was directed to his younger sister who was married to a stockbroker. They lived in Surrey, and punctually each weekday morning at eight thirty a.m. he departed to catch the train to London. There had been a change in the postal delivery times due to changes in manpower and shift patterns causing the fortuitous delivery of post immediately prior to the morning departure of the husband.

The letters were placed beside the husband, who opened them all with his special knife before passing some to his wife. As his wife took the contents out of the envelopes a particular letterhead caught his eye. It was from 'The Scandinavian Fur Company' telex Otterwa. The directors of this company included Dr HC Andersen, but the name was in very small print.

The letter thanked Alice (the wife) for her most valued order for a full- length ranch mink coat that would be delivered for certainly not more than £3,500. The letter continued to say that many customers expressed great interest in the preparation of the skins and in the creation of the coat. Details of her coat, albeit in a very early stage, could be found in the enclosed brown envelope. The letter then continued with a few courtesies and a valediction. The husband tore the letter from the nerveless fingers of the wife. 'What the hell have you been buying? I can't talk now, we'll talk about this tonight'. With a face like thunder, he tore off at high speed to catch his train, returning in the same mood to discover that his wife claimed to know nothing. They were dining with friends that evening and arrived home quite late. Frostily, they said goodnight to one another, with Alice maintaining that she knew nothing about any order for any coat. She hated mink coats; she'd never wanted one. She disliked the use of animal skins and so on.

At breakfast the next day, they searched for and found the outer envelope which still contained the 'small brown envelope'. Opening it they found a cartoon picture of two minks. One, with an RAF roundel on his side was sexually assaulting a second mink decorated with a hammer and sickle insignia!

This officer was not completely sure that he would be a welcome guest in either home on his return to the UK. However, he was not finished yet – and this time I was the target.

At the time that I was posted to a NATO appointment. I was aged forty-seven years, and to my surprise the Security Services called me for interview. They advised me that because of my age and the nature of my particular appointment, that I should consider myself a potential target for Eastern Bloc intelligence gatherers. The 'Honey Trap' was the most likely method for chaps like me, I was told. Flattered, because I knew nothing of any interest, I took post at the Rheindahlen headquarters of the Second Allied Tactical Air Force (2ATAF). The months passed, and no approach was made by nubile young women offering their bodies, or indeed anything else. In fact there was very little interest shown in me by anybody. When I saw the written efforts of my Wing Commander, I decided that I would join in this new opportunity by writing a letter to the Director KGB (European Operations) in Moscow copied to the Commander 2ATAF.

I chose my words with care, emphasising that prior to my departure from the UK I had been advised that I should consider myself a potential target for Soviet or Eastern Bloc intelligence gatherers. I had now been in post for some eighteen months and no approach had been made. Was it possible that this was due to an oversight? I went on to say that I was rapidly approaching an age when I might be unable to enjoy such physical and mental activities to the full, and I asked for his personal intervention in this matter on humanitarian grounds.

I wrote the letter in May, put it into the locked drawer of my desk and completely forgot about it. Months later, I was walking through the top corridor of the HQ when the Military Assistant (MA) to Air Marshal Kennedy appeared like a jack in the box. 'Hayes, the Air Marshal will see you, NOW.' He turned back into his outer office and showed me, almost crowding me directly into the presence.

The Air Marshal adjusted his spectacles, stared at me and holding out a letter, demanded to know the meaning of this. Horrified, I recognised my letter to the KGB!

Frantically, I searched my brain trying to find out how he could possibly have got hold of the letter. 'You obviously don't have enough to do, Good Morning!' Dismissed, I turned, in confusion for the door, only to be called back. As I walked towards him, I became conscious that he was actually smiling! 'I like this letter, Eric, and I find it most courteous that you should forward a letter of this nature through me! – I liked that touch. My wife particularly liked the bit where you felt that they'd better hurry up the nubile women while you could still enjoy them.' Still smiling, he sent me off, to say as I reached the door yet again, 'The chap that you'll be looking for is a certain practical joker in your Division, I'm sure that you know him.' I did, I most certainly did.

I have many memories of 2ATAF, and in one our Colonel met our German conscript leaving early for home. When challenged, the airman airily replied,' 'Ah Colonel, you have an employer's watch, I have an employee's!' The Colonel told me that he was so surprised that he could think of nothing to say. He went on to say that he'd never been bereft of words before – old age had obviously blunted his wit and tongue, he added with a wry smile.

My family lived off base for the first few months in one of a few five storey apartment blocks at Waldniel, a village community some eight or ten minutes drive from the Headquarters. We lived on the fourth floor. My wife had gone shopping and I had gone downstairs to the basement to get something out of a box stored in the special wired cubicles that were individually locked. The two children aged seven and eleven were at home. I climbed the stairs and stopped outside our place. I realised that I had left the key to the front door in the kitchen, so I poked the flap of the letterbox in and cried' Little Pig, Little Pig, Let me come in.' There was a horrified shriek from within, and a red haired daughter with a smile from ear to ear called down from the stairwell above to tell me that I'd got the wrong house! This apartment was occupied by one of the female schoolteachers. I tried to apologise, but the door remained closed. When my wife arrived home, two daughters nearly fought to tell their mother what Daddy had done! Many months later, and long after we'd moved to a house at the Headquarters, my wife and I were sharing a table with some schoolteachers at a Mess function. I told them the story and the young woman teacher, blushing furiously, said that she had been alone in the apartment and had only recently moved in. She said that she had been badly frightened when the cry of 'Little Pig' came through the letterbox!

HQ 2ATAF would practise deployment into the field as part of its war role. I was responsible for the move of our division on exercises, and it was part of my task to write the orders, ensure that the office vehicles were available for use, and arrange transport etc. Our moves into the field were quite major operations because a war HQ, if it is to function properly, requires considerable support. Dedicated signals support and security are but two of the basic requirements of a working HQ. Moves from location A to location B always took place during darkness and transport was at a premium. On one such move, I was extremely short of vehicles, particularly buses and minibuses, and had to make do with trucks. I apologised for this inconvenience but was cornered by a German Lieutenant Colonel who loudly told me that officers of his rank did not travel by truck. I protested that there was absolutely nothing that I could do that would produce more suitable vehicles. The move of the HQ was called at 2 a.m., and of course it was raining and pitch black. No torches were permitted as blackout was enforced during moves. The truck arrived, and everyone piled on – including the belligerent Lieutenant Colonel. Colonel Wille jumped aboard to find that he was sat next to my favourite German officer.

Wille explained to his man that he should not threaten a course of action that he was unwilling to perform. Ordering him off the truck he said that the new location was not more than five km away and that it was not raining too hard! Finally, he told the unfortunate that he did not care to have officers of his Division spoken to in the manner that he had overheard. As the officer jumped down into the road, Wille called for the driver to depart for the new location leaving a less than happy Lieutenant Colonel in the road. When the truck was perhaps 80 metres up the road, Wille stopped the truck and called for the officer to get on the truck. He did and sat in frigid total silence.

I was surprised and somewhat disappointed at the attitudes of my fellow Britons towards NATO. I had begun my tour secure in the knowledge that I belonged to the best and most efficient Air Force in Europe. When I wrote to the staffs of ten nations, I knew that the response of the Brits would be the first to be received and that it would be well written and accurate. I knew that if I went as an observer with the international Tactical Evaluation Team (TACEVAL) I would clearly see the superiority of our equipment and training of our forces. In all of these assumptions I was wrong, for every one of the European Air Forces could excel at one activity and be bloody awful at another. No single Air Force was perfect, in fact far from it! The German equipment surprised me, as did the ability of the Belgians to achieve a great deal with very few resources. Moreover, the Dutch were streets ahead of anyone else in operating aircraft in nuclear, biological and chemical warfare conditions. I think what surprised me more than anything else was the British inability in at least paper exercises to recognise that they were part of an alliance. Frequently, senior commanders would bring expensive airborne refuelling assets to the front line from the UK, when there were a dozen NATO airfields where those aircraft could have been rearmed and refuelled. In the UK, I found my colleagues to be uninterested and apathetic in their attitudes towards NATO in general. Nevertheless, in my experience NATO staff worked very well together with a surprising level of friendship and cooperation.

As a staff officer of 2ATAF I was frequently the HQ's representative at various meetings. Sometimes I would meet with national superiors who had views that differed from those of the NATO HQ. On one occasion a Group Captain invited me to sit down and shut up. I told him that I represented a higher formation, and that I was not present as a junior officer. I would therefore be most grateful if he would sit down. The German, Belgian and Dutch officers, sensing a good old fashioned clash, cheered and clapped. Neither action soothed the ruffled feathers of the Group Captain. He complained to my superior, who after confirming that I had not been rude or disrespectful, supported me by saying that he did not send staff to meetings without good reason, and that my brief was to present the views of the HQ for discussion. Finally, he did not feel that it was appropriate for his representative to be told to sit down and shut up!

The German officers of the HQ were appalled to read a summary of Courts Martial conducted during the last six months on our national notice board. Was it not enough to court martial the man? Surely it was not legal to pillory the man twice for the same crime? In some cases they found our scale of punishments quite draconian and questioned the legality of a Commander's right to increase the punishments for prevalent offences. The German forces were not military; they were citizens in uniform and subject only to Civil Law, for there was no military law. I learnt that a civil servant of Colonel status received the same pay and pension as his military equivalent. The Germans found it odd to say the least that we paid our troops by the day, and that we received our pay monthly. They were paid 13 equal payments every four weeks, a practice that I found sensible. When the German forces were reformed after the Second World War, the government was determined that never again would they permit a state within a state to be formed. The glorious uniforms of the Third Reich were abandoned, and the uniforms of all three arms of the forces were 'de-glamourised'. One example is that of the Alpini. They used to have a wonderful dress uniform with yellow facings and edelweiss insignia. Today they dress in the uniform dress blues with only a very small flower on the back of the neckband to identity them as Alpini.

The German Air Force lost all decorative uniform art, and today only some wear identifying sleeve bands carrying the names of World War One aces indicating that they belong to fighter wings. In contrast, the dress uniforms of the British Army Regiments make a colourful show at any NATO reception. Officers from Highland Regiments have stockings decorated with little black bows. Gitti remembers that the kilt also had such decoration. Dragoons and Hussar officers looked absolutely splendid in their finery; infantry officers in their scarlet tunics looked pretty grand too. The Belgians wore tightly fitting high-collared frogged tunics with tight trousers. On one occasion, I saw a group of three Colonels talking to one another. They each wore three identical splendid enamelled medals suspended from watered silk ribbons. I asked one of the Colonels what the medals signified, and turning to my companion, one asked Paul de Brandt, a Belgian Captain, to tell me. 'The first is because he has been in the Army fifteen years and the second because he is a Colonel and the third because he has served for twenty years.' 'You are correct, Paul, but I must tell you that these medals were not presented to me – I was allowed to purchase them,' he grimaced. I laughed a little self consciously, but went on to ask the significance of what looked like little golden bicycle wheels attached to his high collar. 'Ah!' he cried, 'I am of the Carabinieri Bicyclette – we were formed as mechanized infantry in the first war.' He went on to say that his regiment staged a formal 'Cycle Past' each year. I looked at the ample form of all three Colonels, especially that of the speaker, and all three laughed uproariously. 'Alas, I only take the salute these days,' smiled the infantryman self deprecatingly.

Our Air Force dress uniforms were unexciting. International Receptions were always well attended, and Gitti and I enjoyed them tremendously. Our German General, Hans Ulrich Flade would greet his guest with old world charm, shaking the hands of the men and decorously sweeping up the arms of the ladies to kiss their hand in a truly elegant gesture. He had that off to a fine art!

The American Army Colonels had braid that ran all the way up the arm of their dress uniform and officers of some other US regiments wore French blue and red epaulets. The latter belonged to regiments formed at the time of the War of Independence and reflected the help of the French forces under Lafayette. All American officers wore at least three rows of miniature medals and a couple of us Brits set out to tease our allies. We grabbed our new Air Force major and pointing to his chest we asked what the nice medal was. It was a decoration for gallantry, and the second turned out to be an award for gallantry as well. Telling him that we had obviously got the wrong chap, we asked which medal was the one earned for going to the toilet twice in a day while in Vietnam! Nothing fazed Dan, he answered smoothly that this one, pointing to another of his medals, had been earned for killing cheeky Brits.

His decorations had been earned, I believe, when on returning to his base at the end of a fruitless fighter mission, he became aware that his base was under ground attack. At this moment he was about to taxi off the perimeter track into dispersal. He turned his aircraft to point at the horde that, after climbing the perimeter fence, were racing across the airfield, and fired off the total armament of a fully armed Phantom fighter bomber. This act so discouraged the attackers that the survivors hurried off. The authorities were most pleased with Dan's actions and showed it by decorating him.

Plans and Policy were very sorry that Colonel Wille was to retire. We all liked and respected the man and wondered who and what we would get to replace him. Enter Herman the German – no, I've missed a Colonel out! We had the pleasure of what was called a 'salon' commander. That is to say, we got a commander who had never been a subordinate! His understanding of daily life was confined to telling others what was required, giving a time frame for completion. He had gone from Officer School to become an ADC to a General and then on to a series of appointments as an Air Attaché followed by a period as Liaison Officer between an aircraft manufacturer and the German Air Force. He completely failed to realise that when he requested administrative assistance from units, his requests were dealt with as though God himself had presented them. All other unit tasks were set aside, rather as we would do when faced by an urgent parliamentary question. Frequently, my colleagues and myself were unable to complete jobs in an acceptable time frame and were called to task. I made the mistake of saying that to complete my task on schedule I would need the help of two other officers. Totally dismissing my statement he told me that he himself would help, and show me how it should be done. I was astounded, but he kept his word, but ultimately conceded that even the two of us could not possibly finish by his deadline.

The autumn exercises were upon us and the HQ was to deploy into the field. The detailed orders for the deployment were written by me and signed by the new Colonel. The orders were pretty standard, and there were no great changes from previous efforts. Accommodation for deployments was usually in disused barracks of which there were quite a few in northern Germany, while the mobile HQ could be sited anywhere, even in underground city car parks, old bunkers or in wooded areas. The office vehicles would trundle into whatever area they were going to and would then be wound out! Ah, you cry, you didn't say that they wound out! The vehicles did not extend, they were wound out laterally to make a pretty large office equipped with all manner of teleprinters and comms equipment. In addition the vehicles could be heated or cooled. I do not use the words air-conditioned or climate controlled – you either boiled or froze – there was no happy medium, but usually it didn't work anyway.

The Division deployed by mini bus crammed to the top with our bedding and military equipment. The Colonel, as befitted his rank, travelled by staff car. On arrival at the accommodation area, an old barracks, we set up our beds and in general got ourselves organised. At about six in the evening I was told that the Colonel was outside and would like to see me. A red-faced Colonel faced me indignantly. His room was totally bare. No bedding or blankets, in fact nothing. How was he to wake up in the morning, for he had no alarm clock? Where was his bed, his bedding etc? Aghast, I realised that he had not read the orders that he had personally signed. I produced a copy of the orders and handed them to him without a word. He read to the point where it stated that all officers irrespective of rank were responsible for providing their own bed and sleeping bag and then at the signature block. Now even redder in the face, he asked what he could do at this time of day. Straight faced, I told him that he should tell his Deployment Officer (me) to produce a bed and bedding and that the items should be delivered to his room within the hour! He gave me a long long stare and muttered that he supposed that I carried spares of all these items. I agreed and said that I had always found it prudent to carry a spare sleeping bag and bed. Yes, he burst out bitterly, because there's always some idiot who doesn't read his own bloody orders! Shaking his head despairingly he moved off into the gloom of dusk.

In the second of my two memories, the HQ was once more to deploy into the field for the autumn exercises and the mobile war HQ was being prepared for use. The vehicles were very old, possibly up to thirty years in age and had long shown signs of deterioration. On our last outing we had noted many defects in the wagons designated for our use and I was sent off to the transport section to make certain that all would be rectified in time for use during the exercise. I viewed the trucks, spoke with the engineer officers, and in general provided all the 'prodding' that could be made without antagonising everybody. I spoke to our new commander Herman the German (lately Defence attaché to the Arab world), on my return and said that they had promised to do their best. Grunting his dissatisfaction and disbelief, he strode off into his office. He did know, however, that I had visited the transport offices each week for the past six weeks in efforts to improve matters.

On return to base, after the exercise, he told me to write a letter of complaint to the British Colonel commanding the transport people for his signature. He looked at my draft and told me to write in stronger terms. I tried again, and was ejected from his office with the word that this was the letter of a courtesan. My experience was that rude letters are rarely exchanged at this level and that this was not the way to get things done. My third effort was dismissed with equal acidity and I spoke to a British Wing Commander colleague, showing him all three drafts and asking for his guidance (I wanted him to cool the Colonel down). His representations were ill received and I continued on draft four. It said, in clear language, that the condition of the vehicles was totally unsatisfactory to him and that he required the vehicles to be made available for his personal inspection by a specific date some six weeks away. Once again, I tried to tell him that this was not the way that things were done, but he reminded me that my weekly visits to the transport offices prior to the exercise, 'doing it my way', had produced no improvement whatsoever! Defeated, I had the letter typed for his signature.

Two days later a British Lieutenant Colonel stopped me in the corridor and demanded to know if I had written the letter to his Boss. I said that I had, and he created a veritable storm over me. When he had finished venting his spleen, I told him that although I had written it, my colonel had signed it. Did the Lieutenant Colonel believe that flight lieutenants wrote in such terms to colonels? Baffled, he departed saying that I would hear more of this matter. The following day, the British military assistant to the German Air Force general asked if I had drafted the letter and how had I allowed such letter to be sent. I told him that I had made several drafts but that I believed it to be more appropriate that he speak, with my Colonel. He looked at me a bit oddly, but let me go. Four weeks later I was summoned to our Colonel's office. He looked up from his papers and handed me a letter of some three or four pages. 'Sit down and read it,' he growled. I did, and noted that it came from the office of the transport colonel. I read that the author was both disappointed and saddened to receive a letter written in such terms from a fellow senior officer in an international HQ. He thought that a personal visit would have been more appropriate and might have had more effect. He went on to say that he enclosed a model letter illustrating the letter he would have expected to receive. The remaining pages contained details of work that would be carried out on the vehicles.

'Dear Frank,

The office vehicles earmarked for use by my division throughout exercise deployments of the mobile war headquarters are in a very poor state. I've had one of my officers speak with your chaps, but there would seem to be problems, perhaps in obtaining spare parts for these very old vehicles. I shall be most grateful if you will give the matter your personal attention.

Yours etc,
Herman the German'

'Well, Eric, it appears that you were right and my letter was not the proper way to get things done, but I *have* caught his attention. Put the letters with all enclosures on file and circulate it to every officer of the division.' I stood there absolutely astounded. 'Eric,' he explained, 'If I have to be humiliated in order to learn a lesson, then we must make sure that others do not have to make the same mistake!' He said, smiling wryly. I had no words, I simply did not believe that any British officer of his rank would care to advertise such an event, nor could I believe that he would choose to humble himself in this manner. Nevertheless, on reflection, I thought that it was a spectacular come back.

This brings to mind German 'Soldiers Day'. I don't know if this is the correct title, but it is a day upon which the soldiers of the German Army conduct a street collection in favour of their Army Benevolent Fund. In the town of Moenchengladbach near our Rheindahlen HQ, I saw the German Divisional Commander, a Major General in uniform, complete with his can. Recognising me, he smiled and said that he could not ask his officers and men to do things that he would not do himself. He went on to say that there were several unhappy colonels on similar duty! I don't think that COMNORTHAG (Commander Northern Army Group), a Brit of equal or senior rank would be seen on the streets rattling his can!

A lot of us snore from time to time, but probably the loudest snoring I have ever heard – or is at all possible – was made by Belgian artillery Major who contrived to snore on both inhalation and exhalation. He sounded like a cross between a trombone player and a sexually excited donkey. On exercise, three of us had the misfortune to share a room with the portly major. After an hour or so of trying to go to sleep we rose and carried the still sleeping – and snoring – man on to the disused parade square. There we left him, for it was a fine night. In the morning we were more than amused to see two other beds had been placed beside him, and all three were blissfully still asleep.

On my second tour at Rheindahlen, I lived in Douglas Way. My Welsh neighbour had his very Welsh parents as visitors and decided that they would all go to Venlo in Holland to buy vegetables and to buy coffee on the return run via Roermond at BFG Corner. It was so named because of the number of British Forces Germany customers. He left the car in Venlo parked behind a line of other vehicles in a side street and set off to do the shopping. The family spent a pleasant afternoon in the rain and finished off their day in one of the many good coffee houses. When they returned to the parking area, the car was gone! No other car was now parked in the street and there was some doubt as to whether this really was the street.

All members of the family fanned out into the immediate area looking for the car, to no avail. Finally, Stewart asked a passer-by where he could find the Police. Happily the Police Station was nearby and Stewart reported his loss. Where had he left the car? Stewart told them, for by now he had read the street sign. The policeman smiled and in perfect English told him that his car was perfectly safe. Stewart heaved a sigh of relief, until he heard the policeman continue, saying that his car had been illegally parked and that the car was now in the police compound. A 'modest sum' would release the vehicle. Stewart burst out that the whole bloody street had been full of parked cars and asked why he had been singled out. The policeman smiled broadly and said that if he went to the compound he would find all of the cars that had been parked in that street lined up, waiting for their owners! Stewart paid the fine that meant that his three bags of vegetables were probably the most expensive of his life! He later told me that he would not travel to Venlo again. I think that he kept to that promise too.

My neighbour had two young sons; the younger one was holding a pyjama party for his young friends who had gathered in fair number. It was Sunday afternoon and I had just had a bath so I secured all beneath and donned my pyjamas. Clutching an enormous toy polar bear that had been won in open competition by Susi, I popped across the five yards between our two front doors and knocked vigorously. It was answered by the boy's mother, who quickly grasped the situation and yelled above the din, 'Gareth, you've got a gatecrasher! Shall I let him in?' A five year old girl from up the road took my hand, led me into the party room and said,' You don't have to go away, Mr Hayes. You can stay and have a piece of cake!' They are all very grown up these days, but still remember my entrance. Nothing goes unnoticed in married quarters and weeks later, when I was telling this story, a lady who lived across the road said that she had seen me in pyjamas with the polar bear crossing the green between houses! She had wondered what on earth I was up to!

The IRA was active in Germany, but their intelligence gatherers were not too good. Firstly, they murdered two Australian tourists in Roermond, thinking the pair to be British. Then they murdered an Asian serviceman and his baby son. British servicemen in Germany stood out like sore thumbs despite every effort to make them less conspicuous. Military buses were alone in carrying no advertising and thus were clearly identifiable. I suggested that this be changed and that our buses should carry advertisements and the money raised credited to the various Benevolent Funds. This apparently, was too difficult.

One evening, watching television in my married quarter in Douglas Way, I heard an explosion nearby. Telling Gitti that I was off to see if there was anything that I could do, I walked in the direction of the explosion to find a couple of dazed army officers gazing at the remains of their Mess. A rescue group had formed under a major and all seemed under control. Suddenly I remembered previous bombings and told the major that it might be a good idea if he got all but essential rescue people back from the scene. A favourite ploy of bombers was to detonate a second bomb designed to catch the rescuers. He agreed with alacrity and took appropriate action. I got out of his way. Fortunately, on this occasion there was no bomb.

Once again, the bombers had blundered. Yes, it was the British Army Mess, but the Mess had been hired out to the German Army for a function. The bomb exploded against the Mess wall as the German General rose to speak. Incredibly, no one was killed, for a few minutes earlier the heavy curtains had been drawn for privacy and this minimised the casualties caused by flying glass. A German friend told me that he didn't know that he could get under a table so fast. There were ten casualties in total and the general was the worst injured for he was standing with his back to the window as the bomb exploded. All the injured returned to duty within a few days, although the general's injuries kept him in hospital for a little longer.

There is a happy side to this story, for this same General was the international host to the Duchess of Kent on the occasion of the Queen's Birthday Reception held in the Rheindahlen Rooms. The General rose and walked to the podium to make his speech of welcome. Speaking in accent free English, the General said, 'Your Royal Highness, I think that before I begin my speech of welcome I should warn you that the last time I spoke, I brought the house down!' There was stunned silence and then tumultuous applause. The Duchess burst out laughing. The German General was a very smooth customer indeed.

There were lots of parades at Rheindahlen and they were not always military in nature. One I remember particularly well, for it was the Church Parade of the Scouts, Guides, Beavers and Brownies, Cubs and Sea Scouts et al. The parade was led by a curious kilt clad figure who walked as though he was either monstrously well hung or had severe mumps. He strutted, wide legged, at the head of his troop with an unusual stiff shouldered gait, his jaw thrust aggressively out. Behind his Scout troop, the pouter pigeon figure of Brown Owl stalked, shoulders back to bear the weight of heavy breasts, heading a bevy of young girls who straggled in uneven formation. The Sea Scouts marched in a semblance of formation, hampered by the ill disciplined rabble of the Beaver group ahead of them. However, nothing could compare with a second Brownie group who brought up the rear. Something was irritating the bottom of the last little Brownie to pass the saluting base. With her right hand firmly up her skirt from behind, she shuffled awkwardly, attempting to regain the step of her companions. The irritation continued to trouble her and she marched for a hundred metres or so up the road scratching her bottom oblivious to all! Gitti and I nearly died laughing.

CHAPTER TWENTY-TWO
OPERATIONS OFFICER, BRIZE NORTON

As a short-term interim posting, for I was to return to Germany, I was sent to RAF Brize Norton. I was not terribly keen to be sent there, but the job would allow us to live in our own home at Lydiard Millicent again.

The job of Operations Officer itself involved competence in subjects that I knew little about and there was no formal instruction available. One thorn in my side was the Jet Plan Computer. This computer programme calculated the route and duration of flights between A and B, taking into consideration the en route weather. With additional information it would calculate the height to fly, the fuel usage and whether or not the flight was even possible. I didn't know how to use this machine but with lots of time available to me on the night shift, I learnt.

One officer and four airmen manned the Operations room at night and that staff was assisted by the Movements Section. All crews passed through the Operations room on their way to conduct their own planning. It was a revelation to me to find that colleagues previously known to be even-tempered and unflappable could become entirely unreasonable and ill mannered when subject to minor delays or omissions. It was necessary for me on one or two occasions to remind them that I'm Eric, old mate – doing my best on your behalf.

I had been in post for some months and it was six in the evening on a bright summer day. Outside on the tarmac stood a Boeing 747 aircraft on charter to the Air Force. The jumbo jet was carrying service personnel and a contractor's workforce to the Falkland Islands. The Operations room had two entrances, one of which led up steel steps from the airfield side. Through the airfield side door strode a tall dark blue suited pilot clearly in a bad mood. ' You,' he said, 'YES YOU', looking directly at me. I ignored him and waited for a different approach. ' I am scheduled to start engines in twenty minutes time. I have no charts; no NOTAMS and none of the aircraft planning documents. What have you got to say for yourself?' He demanded in a loud voice clearly audible throughout the Ops room. I turned, looked him up and down and said, 'Are you the captain of the Boeing 747 on charter to the Royal Air Force?' He contemptuously agreed that he was. 'Then,' I said, 'you should know that it is the responsibility of your company to supply you with everything you need. Please leave my Operations room, and if you require assistance I suggest that you ask for it politely. Good Evening.'

There was a stunned silence. The captain spun on his heel and walked out the airfield door. A minute or so later he returned, and said pleasantly, 'Good Evening, I'm the captain of the charter aircraft outside. I'm in a bit of a fix; for my company have not provided me with the charts and bits and pieces that I will need during the flight and I'm due to depart very soon. I wonder if you can you help?' Mollified by this change in manner, I played along with the new scenario. I rose from my seat saying, 'Certainly, Corporal Smith will take you to the flight planning room where he will ensure that you get everything you need. Should you have further difficulties, I'll do my best to help.' Smiling broadly he departed for Flight Planning. On his return, he thanked me and apologised for his previous behaviour. He spoilt the whole apology by saying that he'd forgotten that he was not with his own people. Unable to resist it, I told him that I was glad that I was not one of his people!

Civilian aircrew can be unthinking and discourteous in their dealings with Operations staff. One afternoon, I was talking with our Boss, when a British Airways chap walked through the Operations room totally ignoring our staff and us. He strode directly to our civilian telephone and dialled a number of at least twelve or fourteen digits in length. He then spoke to what was obviously a young woman on the other side of the earth for twenty-five minutes! The Boss observed the beginnings of this conversation and said that I was to send the gentleman to his office when he finished the call. He added that I was to time the call and inform him of the duration and to make sure that the man came directly to him.

As the man replaced the receiver, I asked him to see our Boss.'Oh,' he said, 'Do you know what he wants?' 'I'm not too sure', I replied, 'but I think that it will be something to do with marching in here, ignoring his presence and using our telephone to speak to your girl friend at our expense without as much as a by your leave.'

'Ooooh! What's he like, your Boss?' I smiled sweetly, with a sense of schadenfreude. 'Terrible, when roused.'

Ten minutes later a very red-faced man appeared. In a rather weak voice he told me that he had not been spoken to in this manner since his schooldays!

It was a winter's night, snow was falling but the runway and taxi ways were relatively free of snow. There were patches of mist over the airfield and the snow clearing equipment was on the runway. The Operations Staff knew this because we monitored the radio transmissions of Local (Airfield Site) Control situated in Air Traffic Control. A VC10 four-jet transport aircraft was beginning approach procedures to the airfield. Realising that we had heard nothing from the snow blowing equipment, my staff asked Local where the snow clearing equipment was. They replied that they had lost contact with the vehicles. I picked up a handset and called the aircraft to overshoot, telling them that contact had been lost with vehicles on the airfield. The aircraft was about a mile from touchdown, but overshot and landed at nearby Lyneham. I tell this story because the Operations Staff never heard a word on this matter. Operations Staff do not give instructions to approaching aircraft; it is not their job. However, if Local Control had not told the Controller that they had lost the snow clearing vehicles it was possible that a nasty accident could have taken place. Now if we were wrong to act, then the roof would have fallen in on us. As I said, we heard absolutely nothing. A few days later, the captain of that aircraft complained that I had left it a bit late telling him to overshoot. I expected one of two things. Firstly we would get a telling off, or secondly that we would be commended. Our action was totally ignored. I was quite hurt.

The security intelligence system had warned that there was likelihood that terrorist attacks would be conducted on the mainland. Accordingly, the base was on high alert. At just before midnight the Gate Guards rang to say that a middle-aged man in an old car had attempted to enter camp claiming to be a General Officer. He had no identification papers and claimed that he was on base to 'check his aircraft!' As they told me succinctly, Generals do not check aircraft! They had been unable to reach the Station Duty Officer to ask for guidance. What should they do now? I thought for a few minutes, recalled that the weather outdoors was dreadful and told them to bring the gentleman to Operations under escort.

A few minutes later a quietly distinguished looking man entered the Ops room with a service policeman. I smiled a greeting and asked if he could identify himself and explain his reasons for being on base at this time of night. He said,' I'm Major General X and I'm chief of staff to the New Zealand Army and I'm an indulgence passenger on the Australian Air Force Boeing 707 that is, I hope, still here. I hope to return home on it in two days' time.' I glanced at the movements board and told him that as far as I knew the aircraft would depart on schedule.

However, I needed to identify him properly. Where were his papers and didn't an officer of his rank have a military assistant or ADC? He agreed to all this and said that he had given his ADC permission to go to London two days earlier and had seen nothing of his briefcase or the ADC since then. This last was said with some depth of feeling and I had the idea that the ADC was likely to find big trouble on his return to the fold.

Thinking furiously, I asked if he was known to his High Commission staff in London and when he said that of course they knew him I found the telephone number and phoned their Duty Officer who was able to describe the General and to identify his voice. I was about to recall the policeman to drive him back to his car that had been safely parked well away from aircraft and other vehicles when I noticed that the General seemed most interested in the Operations room and in chatting with the staff. Clearly he was in no hurry to depart so we provided the coffee and he sat down to yarn with us. He said that he doubted that his countrymen could get their heads round the security threat posed by the IRA – or the precautions that had become a necessary part of our lives.

He spent a pleasant hour and a half with us before smilingly telling me that at last had a decent after dinner story to tell. How the Brits arrested me in the night! He was very much amused by the whole incident. The Station Commander was not and was not placated when I told him of the General's parting remark.

I found night duty tedious especially when there was little to do and made the mistake of telling the Boss one day that I was interested in history. That same day I was rewarded by the presentation of eleven months of incomplete F540. Every airbase and unit is required to complete a short résumé of the activities and events taking place on the base to form a history of the Air Force as a whole. Details are recorded on the Air Force form 540. Some officer had failed to complete his secondary duty and I was selected from a cast of thousands to complete the work! However, it kept me busy in quiet times. The moral of this story is to never give a superior an opening like I did. He'd probably had great difficulty in finding a 'volunteer'. Mugs like me are hard to find.

CHAPTER TWENTY-THREE
WINTEX AND MY FINAL TOUR OF DUTY

Gitti and I were absolutely delighted to return to Germany, this time to fill a national appointment in HQ Royal Air Force Germany (RAFG), located once again at Rheindahlen. I believe that we were allocated a married quarter on base relatively quickly. Gitti stayed with her parents in Buchholz just south of Hamburg for the few weeks before we moved into Douglas Way. I lived in the Mess for this period.

I reported myself into Air Plans, where I found that I was to become Mr Wintex. Wintex was a NATO wide paper exercise that took place once every two years. It was a most unpopular job, for it had no beginning and no end. The exercise area extended from Nord Kap in northern Norway to the southern borders of Turkey and from the inner German border (West Germany) to the west coast of the United States and involved the governments of all NATO countries from the Prime Minister and cabinet downwards. Every ministry within each national government took part, from the Medical authorities to the Department of Agriculture and Fisheries. The planning staff for such an exercise was enormous. I think that the staff writing the attack on NATO numbered about four hundred persons while the planners of the attacked numbered many hundreds more. Wintex was a 'paper war' that simulated the forces of the Warsaw Pact attacking the West. The men planning the Warsaw Pact attack used only the forces known to exist and the equipment held by those forces. Attacks were based upon the numbers of aircraft available and their ability to carry known weapons from known airfields. The tactics employed by the enemy forces were based upon known Soviet doctrine. Mobilisation of reserves and transport to areas of conflict were based on intelligence summaries. The exercise forces of the west included all three services on land, sea and air. To make life more interesting, the exercise scenario included exercise weather!

I was told that I was to write the exercise for the HQ and all UK air assets based in Germany and to exercise those plans that brought reinforcements of all kinds to the theatre of war. I was to exercise as many war plans as possible, and to liaise with German, Belgian Dutch and American forces. Additionally, I was to exercise 'Host Nation Support', whatever that was. A modest task, I thought, even for an Fit Lieutenant Air Engineer.

I didn't quite know where to start – and that's an understatement. I was given an office in the 'sheepdip' as the basement of the HQ was known, and I sat down to think. I arranged to see the Air Marshal to ask what areas of his command he would like me to concentrate on. I was told helpfully to exercise as many areas as possible. I then arranged to meet with the Deputy Commander with similar results. I worked my way down through the hierarchy to Heads of Branch, but there too, there was no direction, or advice. I then went to see Wg Cdr Air Plans, my Boss, if I had one. We chatted amicably. I told him of the lack of guidance and he smiled and said, 'Do it your way!'

I did do it my way and it was absolutely wonderful to do exactly what I wanted to do. If I hadn't been so frightened of failure. I decided what to do and if necessary I asked for the best way to do it. I wrote to the Stations (Airfields) in Germany and asked them to tell me what forces they would have on a given date, I wrote everywhere to get a start state for each UK air asset. The big cheese at the Ministry of Defence and the NATO exercise planners gave me the attack plans, numbers of aircraft by type and bomb load. The number of attacking aircraft that would be lost and the means of their destruction. This could be enroute to the target, over the target area or departing for home, with or without their bomb load. Of course I would have to exercise reciprocal agreements in which allies of all kinds could land, refuel and rearm on any NATO base. I was also tasked to ensure that UK aircraft operated from the bases of friendly nations. Wonderful stuff.

Now what did I know about the aircraft based in Germany? Absolutely nothing for, as you know, I had flown only transport aircraft. I knew nothing about Joint Theatre Plans (JTP), indeed I had never seen one, so I sat down in May and rose in August after reading as many plans as I was allowed to see. I then read the plans of the Army to meet certain situations and then the plans of PSA (Civilian works and bricks people) to meet the same contingencies. After reading them I began to believe that inter-departmental liaison was non-existent. Moreover, many plans called for assistance from long closed bases. The more that I read the more I realised that I could legitimately cause major mayhem – which was exactly why we exercised so that we could find and rectify such anomalies.

I now had to write the 'incidents' that would happen on each base.

The exercise was to last fourteen days, but it was quite possible, given the weight of the air attacks, that one or more main operating bases could be knocked out of operation for short or even long periods of time. Airfield runways might be littered with mini bombs, taxiways unusable, fuel or bomb stores destroyed. Where would new ordnance come from, how long would it take to create a useable runway? How could the unit replace crews and ground staff killed or injured? How and where could hundreds of casualties be treated?

Armed with basic maps of each main base I plotted the tactics of the attacker and marked the fall of the various weapons used, detailing their effect. Each Base received a daily map overlay that would help the base see the cumulative damage; calculate its effect on operations and facilities and submit their reports to HQ.

Each main unit formed a response cell that was equipped with all the necessary communications equipment. Staffed usually by a Squadron Leader, or Flight Lieutenant and four or five men per shift, they would man the cell for twenty-four hours a day throughout the exercise. The HQ response cells were located in their War Rooms and would man all positions of the HQ at war throughout the exercise. The NATO HQs of the alliance would deploy to their war locations and all communications networks would be established and maintained for at least two weeks. Yes, lovely isn't it? I can write all this now for every base has closed and HQRAFG has long ceased to exist.

We were just entering the electronic age and many officers of the HQ were not terribly electronically minded. I wasn't, for nobody would provide me with a computer. After consultation with the communications people, I arranged for courses to be available for officers to learn or to refresh their knowledge of some of the specialist equipment that would be available in the Ops rooms. I published a programme, telling of the training on offer by the Communications Branch some three months before the exercise was due to begin.

I travelled to London for meetings, and then I was off to Kaiserslautern, and Bonn. I did enjoy myself. All that was required of me was to present the Exercise Plan and the Incident List to my Group Captain three months before the exercise. Strictly on time, I laid on his table two beautifully presented books, one of two hundred pages and the Incident list of six hundred pages. I say beautiful because the Graphics Section made me some very smart covers for the books bearing the crest of RAF Germany. I knew that bullshit baffles brains – and all looked good! My Group Captain read for some days and made no changes. I was glad about that for I had worn my friends in neighbouring offices to a frazzle, asking that they proof read my drafts.

Nominally, my Group Captain was Exercise Director, but he chose to exercise himself in his war role leaving me and another junior officer to control the exercise from the Army Exercise HQ. To our astonishment there were over a hundred Army officers employed on this task. We installed our communications equipment and checked that we knew how to use secure telephones, the new electronic communications ASMA, and GASMA and all sorts of things. Two men in blue looked quite lonely amid the khaki throng.

The exercise took place, and from my planning point of view went reasonably well, although I was dissatisfied at the level of control that I could achieve. Quite complicated incidents were handled by 'Tick'. I spoke with the Dutch Army, 'Tick, there are no fuel difficulties, I replaced supplies from X.' Incidents that I had spent hours planning were dismissed by officers treating the incidents superficially – if at all! It was not sufficient to say that supplies had been restored. The incident required that the officer specified where the fuel would come from, how it would be transported and the time that would elapse before he got the fuel. Importantly, he was supposed to calculate the effect upon operations.

Every major exercise is followed by a post exercise report from which rectification of shortcomings are made. I found that the little job of compiling this report was mine too. When that had been fully staffed throughout the HQ I was summoned to the Air Marshal's office. He asked, 'What did you think of the performance of the HQ throughout the exercise? Come on, you planned quite carefully and in some areas there were problems, particularly in the early phases. Why did that happen?' I thought for a moment and said that more than half the staff could not use the electronic equipment of their war role. They were more than competent in their peacetime role but had not taken the trouble to learn about their task in war. 'Did you provide any training prior to the exercise?' 'Indeed I did, sir, and acting on advice from the Communications people I sent a copy of all classes available to Heads of Branch.' I went on to say that attendance had been less than 30% He looked up at me and asked who had signed the accompanying letter. I said that I had signed in his name! I left and heard nothing more for two or three weeks. When I did I was not thrilled, for the Commander wanted to know whether I could write a national exercise to take place in the following year and at the same time continue to prepare for the next Wintex! He called for me, I said my piece, I was only one man and that prior to my arrival in Germany two officers had written Wintex. Now he asked if that one man could complete double the task. He smiled engagingly, 'Haven't we just given you a beautiful new computer system? I hear that you can perform minor miracles on it and the incident list can be created and time sorted in a flash! I also hear that you've just had a two day course.' Cursing myself for over enthusiasm when I got the blasted computer, I had no option but to say that I would try my best!

Using the new computer system that had been delivered, boxed, to my office I was delighted to find that I could use CARDBOX, a computer software programme. That programme could complete in a fraction of time what had previously taken me many hours to accomplish. I used to pick up a thousand sheets of paper each representing an exercise 'incident' and walk to the main operations room where I had marked out a 24-hour matrix on the floor fourteen times, one for each day of the exercise. Then, walking around the room, I would place each sheet down in chronological order. That process not only took hours, but also required further checking to ensure that no mistakes had been made. The selection of 'Select All' followed by 'Sort in chronological order' on the computer accomplished the task with the certainty of first time accuracy in a second! When the boxes containing the computer were dumped in the office I asked when they would return to set the system up for me. They told me that it was dead easy and anyway the instructions were in the box! Some hours later I had it all connected up and apparently working. Now that I had a computer people assumed that I knew how to use it. Wrong, wrong and double wrong. I heard that some computer-training people had arrived on base and contrived to be taught Word Perfect, Excel and CARDBOX in a day! Armed with at least a glimmer of knowledge, I began to teach myself, pausing only to become a complete nuisance to the kind soul in the Communications Division. This chap was not a lover of IBM machines and bought himself a Macintosh 'Classic'.

Dominic Scott was a patient soul who not only helped me obtain a Classic for myself, but also spent a great deal of time teaching me to use it. At least one of my daughters has good reason to thank Dom, for I learnt enough to help her research during A level Business Studies. I was working well on the preparations for WINTEX after having convinced my superiors earlier in the year that my service should be extended beyond March 1989, my 55th birthday. I would be happy to continue my service in Germany to complete the current WINTEX and staff the post exercise report. Everyone was agreed and all parties were happy that I should continue until June 1992.

The Rheindahlen March was to take place in the next few days and I heard that the Air Staff intended to trot round as a team. The event was not a race, but a course of about six kilometres. The main idea was just to get staff officers out of their offices and into the fresh air for a bit of a change. I suppose that it was in 'modern speak' a team building bonding exercise. Entrants from every part of the HQ took part and there were teams and individuals running from all the nations represented in the local area. Families could take part and many of the wives and girlfriends took the opportunity to participate in this popular event. The rotters of the Air Staff said that I should not join them, as it was likely that I would be unable to keep up. They went on to say patronisingly that I shouldn't feel badly, for I was a good fifteen years older than they were. I waved a finger contemptuously and ran on my own. I let the Air Staff team run off ahead and started some minutes later. Running at a steady pace, I caught up with them about half a mile from the finish. As I passed them at speed, I asked what had happened and if I should wait for them before beginning to really run? I stood at the finish line as the panting group entered the finishing straight. Clapping enthusiastically I cried sarcastically 'Well done,' and had the satisfaction of hearing teeth grind!

All participants were presented with a medal on a long ribbon at the finish line. Sabina, my eldest daughter and her boyfriend were visiting home at this time and they set out with the throng running either the ten or the fifteen-kilometre course. Sabina is very pale skinned and as she ran round the course she met a team of young German soldiers who produced real laughter as one called out *'Mensch, ist die braun?'* (Gosh, isn't she brown.) Sabina flushed and ran on to catch up her boyfriend! I witnessed the moment and cherish it. Actually, I was very pleased to have Sabina and Mark, now married, see a little of our lifestyle and I believe that they both treasure their Rheindahlen medal.

Sabina was away at boarding school and Susi was just flexing her wings. Now aged twelve, she organised a raffle on behalf of 'Save the Children' Fund. Firstly, she had to ask permission from the Station Commander to hold the raffle, telling him when the prize draw would take place and who would oversee that draw. Susi pinned down the local lawyer who lived opposite us, who kindly agreed, knowing that if he refused there would be difficulties in finding a babysitter! She sold the tickets saying that twelve prizes would be available, giving the date, time and venue for the draw. In the early stages, she produced and sold a puzzle book and sold the raffle tickets at school, at church, and I was informed that I should sell the tickets in the HQ. The problem of suitable prizes was solved by donations, and through my visit to East Germany. Gitti was dragged off to buy a dinner for two at the Dalmatiner Restaurant. The Susi Hayes Aged Twelve Raffle was a great economic and social success, for she raised nearly five hundred marks for the Save the Children Fund. She presented the cheque to the Roman Catholic padres from the Army and Air Force. Father Tony Smith won the manicure set!

Each year a Church Fete was held at Rheindahlen in which all denominations participated. The proceeds were split between the three main groups. The Catholics were fortunate that their part was to provide a bottle stall. It was very easy for the Catholics and their drunken churchie mates to obtain donations of wines and spirits, for every house on the base had at least one spare bottle. One year we had a total of five thousand bottles or cans. The night prior to the event was spent in folding tickets. The task was shared among about four or five persons who were happily folding away when the Army padre arrived in the side office of the Church Hall clutching a huge jug of fruit juice into which he poured a bottle of Pyms. Continuing to fold tickets we drained the jug that was replaced by another container. Some hours later when we rose to go home, we found that the 'fruit juice' must have been very much more potent than advertised.

The Fete was always a success and our customers were more than happy with the number of winners. When business was slow I would grab an old school handbell and 'ring' custom in our direction, in this I was assisting a retired Parachute Regiment Major who had a voice like a foghorn. The Commander of the British Army Corps passed with his bodyguards, so I rang the bell and invited them to bring their lovely General over! I'm not certain that he was 'lovely' but he came with a smile. Attendance at such events was always overwhelming whatever the weather, for service people support their own.

Life in the 'Sheep Dip', as the basement offices of the Headquarters were known, had its moments, and one was painful to say the least.

While walking back to my office from the Operations room some twenty yards away I began to feel unwell. Quite remarkably unwell, so I called into the office opposite mine. Robb Wainwright, a large navigator, emerged. He took one look at me and barged into my office. He phoned for an ambulance and threw all the papers on my desk into a steel cupboard and locked it. Still talking to me, he slammed my window shut, breaking two panes, and then half helped and half dragged me up the stairs towards the side entrance to the ground floor where an ambulance arrived within a minute or two. By this time, I could scarcely stand or sit or indeed do anything – I just hurt like hell. I remember being loaded onto the ambulance and Robb yelling that he would phone my wife.

On arrival at Wegberg Hospital, some two or three kilometres distant, I was quickly examined; given painkillers that worked after two whole years and told that I probably had a kidney stone. This piece of information did not particularly thrill me for I knew that it could mean yet another operation on my side. Tucked up in bed, I could see that Gitti was deeply concerned as she entered at the trot. Robb had told her that I had collapsed at work but that it was not a heart problem! He offered no speculation as to any possible cause of my difficulties.

I think that I was discharged from hospital after a few days. The X-ray showed a few bits of grit in the system and these, I was told, would be passed in my urine. I was told to take plenty of fluids. What a euphemism the word 'passed' is. It conveys the impression that the stones would flow gently out in a generous flush of urine. Stones don't emerge like that at all. They block the flow; they hurt like hell and when they 'pass' it's like peeing razor blades! Still, they did pass and I should be grateful, I was told. (Always by someone that had never been so afflicted.)

A few weeks later, drama returned to the sheep dip when Tony Young got locked into the toilet! He entered the toilet and locked the door, but on completion of the necessary body function, he found that he could not get out. The toilet was located at the end of a corridor that was flanked on both sides by offices. The toilet was at one end of the offices and the door faced the doors linking corridors, and only my office shared a wall with the toilet room, and I was out! He yelled and thumped the inwards opening door to no effect. When I returned to my office I became aware of bangs and shouts, but they were muted and I paid no attention. It was not until I felt the call of nature myself that I discovered that Tony was trapped, I tried the door with no result and nearly broke my shoulder throwing myself against the door. Finally, I raised my foot and kicked the door in true movie star fashion. Tony's comment was that he wouldn't have minded a bit of peace and quiet, but he'd left his fags in his office!

Hugh Beattie was the Army Roman Catholic Padre at Rheindahlen. He was unusual in that he had been a serving member of the Parachute Regiment for some years before training in Rome as a priest. He was always well dressed and wore his black soutane and a brimmed black hat that he would swap with the ladies after Sunday Mass. He spoke with the lilting intonation of a Scot from the Western Isles and liked his wee dram or three; Hughie was quite a character and the children adored him.

Once Hughie was summoned to the office of a very senior officer, to be told that the General did not wish to see him touring the soldiers' bars and haunts. Hugh listened attentively to the General and then asked where else would he find his parishioners. He then gently said that he did not tell the General how to be a General as that was not his field of expertise, but that he would appreciate it if the General did not tell him how to be a priest! I know this to be true, for the General told the story at a barbecue long after Hughie had returned to the UK at the end of his tour in Germany.

I enjoyed the many stories told about this little priest, but none more than the story of his parachute jump at Bad Lippspringe, the home of German paratroop training. How Hugh had arranged to drop I don't know, but he was sixth in the stick of perhaps twelve men who would jump from each side door of a twin engined Transall aircraft. There was muttering in the ranks about the presence of the old Englishman who would surely hesitate in the door and force the remaining stick members to drop outside the dropping zone. The SNCO instructor then told the troops that the 'old man' had made more drops than half of the jump instructors put together, and that he had made combat drops into jungle etc. There was silence until the young soldier acting as the first man to leave the aircraft gave a half bow, saluted and said '*Bitte sehr, Herr Pfarrer*' waving an arm that indicated that Hugh should take his place. This was a very great compliment indeed, because if the first man hesitated in the door, it was almost certain that the last few men would drop outside the landing zone, and that could be very dangerous indeed.

Hughie's brother was visiting Rheindahlen and he too was a priest. He had just returned from a seminar, or meeting of hordes of catholic priests, held in Mexico. Enjoying a post Mass cup of coffee with us all, he told of the Mexican priest who complained of his difficulties in getting any work done in his parish. He continued by saying that his parishioner's attitudes to work of any description could best be described by the word 'Mañana, Mañana'(tomorrow). The Scots priest said that he had thought gravely of this difficulty, and had responded in his lilting voice by saying that in the Western Isles of Scotland he knew of no word in the Gaelic that conveyed such an air of urgency!

Hughie became Padre to the Guards at Chelsea Barracks some time later and was named as one of the priests who would conduct the televised Service of Remembrance that is broadcast to the nation each November. The Colonel of the Regiment detailed two young officers to stay with Hughie for two days prior to the event, in a way that closely resembled arrest! Their sole task was to present Hughie to the venue properly dressed, sober and on time!

Of all the unlikely places for there to be a NATO School, surely Oberammergau must be the most improbable. I had the good fortune to be sent there on two occasions, each time for a two-week course. I won't dwell on the first course but instead will describe a German Lieutenant Colonel who had the uncanny ability to get me into trouble. The Berlin Wall had fallen and the now obsolete course syllabus was replaced by a series of guest speakers who would speak on their vision of the future. The speakers were usually high-ranking officers from all three services and came from a number of nations. My German friend was something to do with air traffic control and was in charge of a group of Fledermaus radars that monitored allied aircraft flying in the designated low flying zones. His staff could produce photographic evidence of offenders flying below designated limits. The evidence was submitted to the national authorities for subsequent prosecution. Four of the radars under his command had been returned to Germany after they were captured from the Argentinean forces in the Falklands. (I add this for local colour!)

A German admiral gave his views on the future, to be interrupted by the Colonel who said, 'Admiral, surely your views are solely based on the assumption that the Russians will move out of Germany, I believe that may not be the case – and my English friend agrees with my views'. The admiral pondered and gave a reasoned reply. The next speaker was also interrupted and questioned. Once again, 'his English friend agreed with his views'. I had not uttered a syllable, far less a word. Throughout the next few days speaker after speaker was questioned and informed that 'his English friend agreed'. The amusement of the student body was such that my friend the Colonel had only to rise to make his point when the entire room would finish with, 'and his English friend agrees'. After four or five days, I was interviewed by the senior Brit. Who should it be but one of Directing Staff from Henlow. He was now Wing Commander O'Dwyer-Russell and he recognised me immediately. I told him the story and he laughed like hell, but told me to get a grip on Franz. Eventually, the joke wore off and we returned to listen attentively without interruption to the speakers.

One balmy evening as we, the Colonel and I, were walking down the path that led from the school into the small town, we passed a little 'Lokal' on the corner. It looked very pleasant, so we popped in for a beer. The lady who served was dressed in a beautiful dirndl and she was very friendly towards us. There was a rather nice zither on a table and I asked if she played. Taking up the instrument she sat down beside us at the window and began to play. After a few minutes, Franz asked if there was a guitar in the place that he could borrow and she left to bring down a guitar owned by her brother. She began to play a German folksong and Franz, after a few practice strums, joined in. I have never heard two people play together so beautifully. Each seemed to anticipate the timing of the other and they played together for a good twenty minutes before breaking to enjoy their drinks. I looked at the pair of them and said admiringly that they played as though they had played together all their lives. The two looked at each other and laughed. Franz grinned at me and said,' We played together throughout our entire schooling, right up to the time that I joined the Air Force. We lived practically next door to one another'. That night was a magical night for me. It was one of those special memories that so enrich life.

CHAPTER TWENTY-FOUR
MESS ENTERTAINMENT

I don't think that any account of life in Germany would be complete without mention of the many, many forms of recreation available. Quite apart from the international activities of the Church: barbecues, luncheon parties, fetes etc there were the more cultural activities of the Choral Society, The Rheindahlen Theatre Groups and the Operatic Society. There were sporting clubs of every kind. Andy Thomas and I helped form the Car Club, but more of that later. All the Messes, both Army and Air Force, held functions of all kinds, and many celebrated the main social events of the local area. Britons participated in every aspect of local life, quite unlike the Americans who seemed to live on their bases and to rarely mix with the locals. The Brits were enthusiastic 'mixers' and a good number of our young men and women married local people.

I suppose that Karneval could be considered the most important of the local celebrations, certainly it was the biggest. Karneval officially begins on the eleventh of the eleventh month at eleven minutes past eleven, and ends at midnight on Shrove Tuesday. Planning meetings, training sessions and parties take up the early days of Karneval leading on to a climax just prior to the Lenten period. Karneval is a tremendous generator of economic activity – many a small brewery might collapse if it were not for the sales of Karneval. It's hard to imagine the enormous amount of energy, time and money that generates the pleasures and spectacle of events. Dance teams, each led by their Tanz Mariechen, practice for months and many teams reach professional standards in both dance and costume. An elected Prince and Princess of Karneval tour the various Karneval parties, dressed in superb and costly costumes leading their entourage, including the dance groups from party to party.

The military units of male march teams are astoundingly dressed in the uniforms of the 1790s complete with appropriate weaponry. The uniforms are invariably well tailored and are decidedly not cheap. The companies of troops are often more than two hundred strong and march ten, twelve or even as many as sixteen abreast, led by mounted officers.

Troop formations do not straggle, but march and conduct arms drill with their muskets and are as proficient as many a military drill team. I have seen as many as five military teams in a single parade, a thousand men perhaps, each unit clad in a different coloured uniform, marching behind their brass bands! I tell you that such a sight amid the children's floats, the floats of many of the premier firms of the area, local band and dance groups and the innumerable troops of clowns and dwarfs present an entertaining spectacle that takes several hours to pass. The Band of Royal Air Force Germany always marched in the local Karneval Parade *Im Umzug* (Local walk around). This scene is duplicated throughout the Rheinland in every town and village to a greater or lesser extent. It is true that Koln and Dusseldorf dominated the Karneval scene in my area, but the parades and parties of towns like Aachen and Mainz were no less grand. Incidentally, Dennis Healey, one time UK Defence Minister, earned his Karneval hat (Nahrren Kappe) by giving a humorous speech in German in front of a Mainzer Karneval gathering! Karneval parades are watched by tens of thousands, perhaps even hundreds of thousands, of spectators many with their umbrellas at the ready. No they are not expecting rain but, when opened, the brollies could catch more of the 'goodies' thrown from the floats into the press of spectators. Children are very fond of the Karneval period for it can positively 'rain' sweets. On very cold days, those walking in the procession carry small bottles of Schnapps that they offer to spectators. One group had a Fass (little barrel) of Schnapps that replenished the stocks of donor! Of course the bigger firms use their support for Karneval to advertise their work and it was probably tax deductible, but nevertheless it was all quite wonderful. I have been hit by 4711 bottles, tissue packs, sweets and crisps, and every child goes home with a bag full of goodies.

It is against this backdrop, that my Mess would prepare a Karneval party to which the town's Prince and Princess would be invited. Our Mess Manager was Dutch and we benefitted from his ability to cut costs at every turn by accepting tenders for major expenditure from at least two countries. Our parties were always well attended, and often we had to restrict attendance because of fire and security risks. A feature of our life was the necessity for bomb dogs to inspect the place prior to parties and for armed security personnel to roam around the area. However, we got used to it all, and it certainly didn't stop our enjoyment.

Gitti and I enjoyed our life in Germany for we had a good social life. Mess functions were quite splendid and we joined many excursions into the surrounding area organised by the Mess. A trip down the Rhine to see 'The Rhine in Flames' was quite spectacular. I recall our Indian senior medical officer complete with one of the first video cameras. His two sons carried parts of the equipment while the girls each struggled with a heavy battery pack, and he manfully shouldered the enormous camera part! They were a lovely family who enjoyed a close relationship with each other. I was particularly pleased that my old friend Reg Chiddick and his wife Jo were able to come with us on the Rhine cruise.

I was into all sorts of things. I belonged to the Operatic Society and played minor roles in many productions and on a couple of occasions made up choir numbers when the Anglican Church presented *The Messiah*.

During my time in Germany the Operatic Society staged *Guys and Dolls, The Gypsy Baron, The Gondoliers* and *Cabaret*. My favourite show was *Die Fledermaus*, partly because the music was always fresh and a delight to sing. Individual performances were quite astounding and the Judge Advocate made a most convincing drunken Sgt Frosch! It was much more fun on stage though. On the final night of *Die Fledermaus* we drank real champagne - and were 'half-cut'.

Of course the scores of 'Schutzenfest' parties followed the end of the Karneval period almost immediately. The Shooting Clubs originated in the Middle Ages when the defence of town or village depended upon the will and skills of local musketeers. There was a requirement for the menfolk to be proficient in the use of their weapons, rather like the requirement that the English should practise archery in the earlier centuries. Today, the Schutzenfest is a shooting competition and an opportunity to party both in the street and in private. The winner of the competition is declared Schutzenkonig (King) and he will lead parades and partying. The title of Konig is a hotly contested competition, but many a crack shot inexplicably failed at the final shoot off, for to become Konig could become a very expensive exercise as much social activity was expected of him. There was a tale in circulation that some years earlier, an English navigator with a German wife had won the competition. The Englishman had decided to live in Germany following his retirement and winning the Schutzenfest was a very fine piece of publicity for the small business he had recently opened. Whatever the truth of the matter, we were warned not to win such competitions!

The celebration of the Oktoberfest was a great occasion in the Mess. The origins of the Oktoberfest lie in Bavaria, but most of Germany has adopted the idea as a great reason to hold a mega party. Great striped canvas tents were hired and erected outside the Mess, and vast stocks of beer were prepared. I was Wines Member at this time and there was plenty to do. I visited the local breweries to ensure that we had plenty of beer available and discussed the production of the Mess beer mug. Each year, the Mess produced a half litre stein bearing the Mess logo and some appropriate caption. In the past, such mugs had cost about eight marks and we usually sold about five hundred of the mugs at a price of nine marks. I mentioned this in talking with the director of the local Schlossbrau brewery. He cocked his head and said that we paid far too much for the mugs and that, if we promised to take a total of x beers from him throughout the next year, he would produce mugs for half the price. He produced a specimen mug that looked superior in quality to our last year's model. A quick phone call to my barman reassured me that the quantity requested was under that purchased from the brewery in the last year. With that job out of the way, on advantageous terms, I scuttled back to base to deal with the next problem.

The Mess and tents were filled with trestle tables and benches and scattered throughout the Mess were game stalls, coconut shies, all sort of activities usually found in a fairground, I particularly recall the American style electrically operated bucking bronco. The senior RAF Regiment officer, a well-known macho man, mounted the machine, but within minutes he lay in the remnants of his pride. Calling on Myfanwy, his diminutive wife, he cajoled her into mounting the machine. The machine pitched and rolled and then did both simultaneously with the lady clinging on for dear life. Gradually the spin speed increased, as did the violence of pitch and roll. Still Myfanwy held on grimly, until to her visible relief the machine stopped. Looking directly at her husband she made a familiar coarse gesture and smiled in derision! Macho man was impressed – as were the rest of us!

The party was officially opened by the tapping of a large barrel of beer (Pils) mounted on a trestle. The head barman formally handed the American General a large wooden mallet and held the great spigot in the correct position. The speeches over, the mallet swung, missing the spigot and smashed the fingers of the barman! Oh dear, what a furore that caused. The poor barman was rushed out to the Medical Centre while the Brigadier General was distraught with apology. I only hope that when the Army took over our Mess many years later they honoured the pension agreement made in settlement of the injury.

We tried to make this a Bavarian costume night, and to a great degree we did succeed. I can understand the reluctance of those with bony knees and bowlegs, for few of my colleagues were as beautifully formed and proportioned as me. Perhaps I am vertically challenged, but otherwise... I was going to wear my lederhosen, but Gitti refused to go with me if I did.

The oompah bands played throughout the night, sometimes conducted by the Air Marshal who thoroughly enjoyed the experience. In speeches, the Army Commander, also a Scot, would refer to our man as his 'musical friend' and not to be outdone, our man referred to his Army colleague as' his linguistic friend'. The Commander NORTHAG, Major General Gow, had no ear for German and his accent was atrocious! The Germans loved to hear him speak. I cannot comment on the quality of the conducting – but I think that the band ignored his batonwork.

Just as an aside, Major General Gow was the last British officer who had served in WW2 to retire from his Service. He would later claim to have been wounded at Waterloo! This was true, for he broke his ankle, I believe, alighting from a moving train at Waterloo station!

The Mess Draw was held at Christmas and the Draw prizes were unbelievable. Tickets were sold from summer onwards and many small bar raffle prize consisted of groups of Mess Draw tickets, in fact almost every small gathering that held a raffle throughout the autumn had Draw tickets among their prizes. Each cost one Deutschmark (remember? the coin before the Euro!) One year I held over four hundred tickets but won absolutely nothing. Many Dutch and German members spent their 'winnings' from the gaming machines in the bar on draw tickets. I say the Dutch and German officers because they were the main players on the machines that many of us were reluctant to have in the Mess. Nevertheless, the machines made a lot of money for the Mess despite paying out 97% of the takings. The star prizes, one Christmas Draw Night, included a Daihatsu Charade car, a holiday for two in Barbados and a complete computer system including printer. Lesser prizes at the same event were top of the range microwave ovens, exotic bicycles and posh health machines. The list was endless, but at the six Draws I went to in Germany, I won '*silch, gar nichts*, or absolutely bloody nothing!' In one year I know that over fifty thousand tickets were sold. Four major events held in the Sergeants' and Officers' Messes each year provide the Chefs with the resources to really show what they can do when the constraints of time and money are removed. I recall the most splendid butter sculpture of an eagle presiding over an equally luxurious buffet, while at the same Ball, a swan of equal stature, carved in ice, overlooked the fish bar. On such occasions the staff provided a display that many an international five star hotel would have been proud to present.

Christmas passed, and now it was time for the New Year's Party. Gitti and I were fortunate in obtaining two additional tickets that would allow our eldest daughter and partner, who were visiting, to come with us. I was particularly pleased that Sabina and Mark could see something of our lifestyle before my retirement from the Service early in the next year. Fortunately, dress for the occasion was black tie.

Among the surprises offered by the Dutch manager were the two white overall clad painters who were still at work on the main entrance doors when the Air Marshal and guests entered the foyer for the Ball. The painters courteously held the skirts of the ladies as they passed the apparently still wet doors. Quite unaware of the 'joke', the Boss sent for the Mess Manager, but in the interim, the dead pan faced painters sucked their paintbrushes like lollies! Silently cursing for falling for the prank, the Air Marshal and his guests entered the main anteroom. In fairness, I must say that all the people who passed through the main doors had shaken their heads in disbelief that the painters should be working at this time and in this place.

Once inside, and after the main meal, a team of table conjurors and pranksters toured the tables performing incredible tricks before our very eyes. The 'painters' still in overalls attempted to tie the Air Marshal to his chair and transport him out of the Mess. However, the close security squad moved in and stopped that idea dead! Despite a few hiccups – we initially had a table inside a loudspeaker – it was a wonderful night.

I think that the Summer Ball was the most prestigious entertainment event of the year. In the UK, the Ball presented the Station Commander with an opportunity to repay the hospitality he and his officers had enjoyed throughout the year. In Germany, the Ball allowed the really top brass (Anything above brigadier in rank) to invite senior figures of the local community to share our hospitality. Tickets were initially restricted to Mess members and their wives or partners, but a second list was created with ticket applications for additional family members or guests. The emphasis was that Mess members had priority over additional guests. The flower decorations were created by the ladies of the Flower Club. The Mess paid for the flowers, but the inspiration and hard work was carried out by the Flower Club members. The ladies surpassed themselves in creativity year after year, creating superb floral backdrops. I have pictures to prove this, for the event photographer usually chose to pose all his victims in front of the foyer display. The Summer Ball was a very expensive occasion for those attending, even after Mess funds had subsidised the event. Three bands and a disco played for those who wished to dance. A very suave German Army General and his wife showed us all how ballroom dancing could look like. There were many places where one could eat; a sea-food bar, an enormous buffet offering both hot and cold fares, and at least four bars were scattered throughout the Mess public rooms. Sabina's young man sidled up to me asking how he could buy a drink. I was pleased to tell him that he couldn't, but that he should just ask for what he wanted, as it was all paid for! We never saw any more of the pair all evening. Breakfast was served in the early hours!

There were a couple of Australian Army officers who had been seconded to the British Army in Germany. I liked them both, particularly the female officer, who was a great traveller. She informed Gitti that she was taking a couple of weeks off to walk through the Alps! Producing a map she showed her proposed route. That route took no account of physical geography and the planned time frame was more than optimistic. Gitti gently told her that straight line walking was impractical in Alpine regions because it was all ups and downs too.

The Australian male officer was quite a wit – well I thought him so. I recall him poking a finger into the paunch of a portly colleague saying,' Got yourself a bit of a verandah over the toyshop there, haven't you Fred?'

On 9 November 1989 a momentous and unexpected event took place – The Berlin Wall was torn down and the reunification of Germany began. That obscene structure, built in August 1961, divided the two Germanys and effectively imprisoned the East Germans in a time warp that has not even now been fully eradicated.

As the full implications of the changes that were about to take place sank in, I realised that all my work was now pointless, moreover, every single British air asset in Germany was in the wrong place and that the aircraft based in Germany would have no place in the new Europe. The military paused hesitantly, for as Clauswitz, or some other tactician, so succinctly put it, 'The military are the sharp end of the political arm'. In reality, that meant that we must wait for the politicians to reach decisions before we could act to either reduce or move our forces. Clearly vast changes must take place, but 386,000 Soviet troops were still based in Eastern Germany. What would happen to them, and where would they go? Just as we Brits had no place to base our troops returning after the handover of Empire, the Soviets were faced by the same difficulties, and it was winter on the steppes.

It was New Year's Eve at about seven in the evening when Pete Hinton, a Squadron Leader of Air Plans knocked on the door of my quarter. Seated and provided with a cup of coffee, he asked if I took the *Daily Telegraph*. A little puzzled, I said that I didn't, but that I usually read it in the Mess. He went on to say in rather an odd way that I should get a copy on the following day. Something didn't sound quite right so I asked him why it was so important. His response was that I might find my name in it. Puzzled, I thought that the Air Officer Commanding's Commendations (AOC's Commendations) were not published in the *Telegraph* and muttered something to that effect. Pete retorted that I was a dumb sod, and that I had been awarded the MBE! I was utterly dumbfounded and was totally overwhelmed. He reached behind him and slammed a bottle of champagne on the table saying that we'd need it tomorrow and left with a huge smile on his face. I nearly cried, and told Gitti much later that I had absolutely no idea why I had been so honoured, unless it was given for good looks, charm or modesty!

The following day, I helped my neighbours prepare the garage block at the end of the street for our New Year's Day barbecue, I put all the drink that I could lay my hands into a box and trundled it down the road in a wheelbarrow. We had a splendid day. Throughout the day some of my superiors came round, several bringing congratulatory letters from the AOC and Deputy Commander. All in all, it was a day to remember.

I was asked if I would like to go back to England for the presentation ceremony or if I would prefer to receive the award from the hands of the Ambassador in Bonn, I had absolutely no hesitation in saying that I'd prefer to go to Buckingham Palace.

The great day came, and Gitti, Susi and I drove to Calais and took the boat back to England where we met up with my eldest girl. Susi was still at Windsor School in Rheindahlen and I believe that Sabina got the day off from Dixon's in Bristol and came up to town by herself. I had booked rooms at the RAF Club in Piccadilly and had invited Trevor Peacock, my erstwhile boss on Hercules, and his wife to a small party to be held in the Club after the award ceremony. I was particularly pleased that two of my nieces could join us for the meal. I was bemused, I think that that is probably the right word, for there are not too many families in which both sons – leading quite different lives – are honoured by the Queen for their services. Some years earlier my brother was awarded the Imperial Service Order and he too came to England for his ceremony. My Mother would have been astounded had she lived to see her second son so honoured. She might reasonably have expected that James William Hayes might achieve honours, but certainly not me! I shared in that astonishment.

We gathered in a large and very grand room of the Palace where we were briefed on procedures by a very tall Guards Officer dressed in a high collared black frog coat. His briefing was short and clear. Those who were to receive awards were separated from their relatives, who then moved into their seats within the great reception hall. Recipients were divided into groups of those receiving similar awards and then each of these lined up in the order specified by the Directing Officer. Outside of the main hall, an orchestra from one of the Guards regiment played softly in the background, as the line slowly wound its way into the main chamber. Retired admirals appeared to be used as bollards, for several stood at strategic points directing the slowly moving snake. There was a tough looking kilted Highland Regiment officer ahead of me who was red-faced, bull-necked, and wore a fierce moustache. Clearly he was extremely nervous, for he must have wiped his hands on his kilt a hundred times before he reached the Queen at the end of the receiving line. I was impervious to all nervousness, for I was wonderfully happy, humming very quietly to myself as the musicians played extracts from *The Merry Widow*. I caught the eye of one of the bollards, who smiled broadly and stated the obvious by saying that I was clearly enjoying myself. I smiled agreement and floated towards Her Majesty who asked what I did in the Air Force. When told that I wrote paper wars, she murmured tactfully,' How fascinating!' before pinning the insignia to my tunic. I made a graceful withdrawal and joined the others in a separate room as the awards and investitures continued.

Susi's new suit, bought in Moenchengladbach, was appropriate for the Palace, but Sabina required something a little posher than she possessed. We toured Oxford Street, among many other streets, until finally she bought some new boots and a brown costume complete with very long skirt. I wasn't too sure that I liked it, but was told by all three of my ladies that this was unimportant. Later, after the ceremony, when all recipients of awards were having their photographs taken in the courtyard, a large, very smart lady, whose husband had been awarded the CBE, moved across to Sabina's side and said, 'My family said that I shouldn't do this, but I just have to tell you, my dear, how smart you look in that very elegant suit!' Sabina grew two inches on the spot! I can't say that Bini put her tongue out at me – but the look on her face clearly said, 'I told you so! You never believe in my good taste.'

The Air Force Club was an eminently suitable venue for my little celebration and offered a degree of comfort and privacy that I would have been hard pushed to find elsewhere. We enjoyed a good meal and an extremely pleasant and memorable evening before we all returned to 'old clothes and porridge' as my Father would say. That red and white striped ribbon looked very nice on my tunic, and might even look well on my pyjamas. Quite 'extinguished' as some might say!

Sabina, Gitti, me, and Susi, at the Palace

With the collapse of the Berlin Wall and the uncertainties that followed, the military were left in limbo. Clearly we would have to re-organise to meet some threat. What that threat might be was not clear. The Soviet Union was in distress and in danger of total collapse, but she still had control of a vast nuclear arsenal and a very powerful Army, Air Force and Navy. All the military forces of NATO countries figuratively held their breath, waiting for the politicians to reshuffle the pack of cards that made up the countries of Europe as a whole. Where would the political imperatives lead? Would the countries of the former Warsaw Pact form a new union with Russia, or would they decide that their future lay in closer ties with the West? Only time would tell, and for the present at least, my colleagues in the four HQs at Rheindahlen must wait and see.

With no instruction as to whether or not NATO would continue with the paper exercises, I continued to work in a very desultory way. My 'enemy' the Warsaw Pact forces had evaporated. My paper work was irrelevant and I really had nothing meaningful to do. I acted as secretary to some meetings held by the Air Staff, but I was of little practical use because I did not understand the abbreviations used by the speakers. 'ATM' to me was an air turbine motor, but something quite different to the speakers, and I was totally confused. I came from the Transport Force and knew little or nothing of the language of offensive or defensive operations. Mercifully, the chairman recognised my handicap and understood my inability to write minutes without comprehension. I was pleased about that until I got another full time task.

The Air Staff Registry was the heart of all paperwork associated with aircraft operations. It held the Top Secret Registry, the Secret Registry and the ordinary document registry. A WRAF officer had been in charge of it for the last year or so, but she had just left the HQ at fairly short notice. I don't know why, but I do know that she had done very little work for some time! I found out that the major periodic inspection of the entire registry by the RAF Police was due in some nine weeks, and that even on a cursory inspection things were not as they should be. Gratefully, I listened to the advice of the Sergeant who had run the place for the last two years. We sat together for some hours as he outlined what would be checked on the inspection. He was in the middle of checking all sorts of things himself, and would require my counter signature a million times! He continued to depress me by saying that the periodic page counts of all top secret documents was long overdue and that this task was mine and mine alone.

Truthfully, I had very little idea of how a very large Registry was run. My staff comprised the Sergeant, two male corporals, one female corporal four airmen and two airwomen. Additionally, eight positions of the registry were manned by ladies who were married to servicemen working in the HQs. Working together, the Sergeant and I divided the supervisory tasks and I did precisely what he told me to do, concentrating my efforts upon the Secret Registries. Gradually, I became aware that the Sergeant was a very knowledgeable man, who controlled his empire with firmness and tact. However, we faced an uphill battle, for so much had been neglected at the top, and there was so very little time.

Every document must be accounted for and be in the correct file; every page of a Confidential, or NATO Secret document must be accounted for. Inevitably, in the course of a year, documents are misfiled and it takes time to sort things out – and a great deal of patience. One day, the civilian ladies were all moaning to me about their jobs and pay. I laughed and said, 'It's not that bad, anyway it keeps you off the streets!' There was a stunned silence and a large lady rose to her feet. ''Get him, girls.' I ran for my life pursued by eight ladies baying for my blood. As I fled at high speed down the corridor, I ran into a group of very senior officers who parted ranks to allow the chase to continue. I was cornered and was being walloped by rolled up papers when asked by authority the reason for their actions. The explanation provoked the response that I was lucky to be hit by only magazines – and that the ladies should continue beating me!

Under the guidance of the good Sergeant, we made good progress and the entire staff worked exceptionally well as a team. The police inspection duo arrived and explained their function and I responded by saying that I would appreciate their advice as to where improvements could be made. The two policemen worked well with my staff and I made sure that we gave them instant cooperation. The inspection lasted six weeks, but at the end of that time, thanks to the tact and helpfulness of the inspectors we had very few outstanding problems. Their report on the Registry was more than satisfactory, but my report to the Police Inspectorate, submitted some week or so earlier, thanked the inspectors for their unexpected willingness to work as part of one team dedicated to giving their best efforts.

I was well aware that without the unstinting help of the Sergeant I could have fallen flat on my face and did my best before leaving the HQ to ensure his promotion to Flight Sergeant, for he richly deserved recognition. It is never enough in such circumstances to merely say thank you, for the second reporting officer needs something tangible to support recommendations for promotion. With many years experience of report writing behind me, I sat down and spent some considerable time writing an annual assessment report for the attention of the second reporting officer, a report that reflected my recognition of his abilities.

The turbulent times that followed the collapse of the Soviet Union saw many changes in personnel as the inevitable run down of forces took effect. Bases closed, units disbanded and the Headquarters staff was reduced to reflect the changes. Nobody was quite sure of what the ultimate size of British forces in Germany would be, but most certainly the change would be radical. The bases at Wildenrath, Gutersloh, Laarbruch and Bruggen were to close and the Army too closed many bases, returning their personnel to the UK. The disbandment of many Army units caused considerable pain to some of Britain's most famous formations. The Gulf War had depleted the resources of many units and the process of reduction and withdrawal continued to drain the forces based in Germany.

Gitti continued to work in the RAF Information Room that helped personnel and families cope with the new experiences posed by living in a foreign country. Importantly, she also helped them to explore and enjoy the continent of Europe more fully than they otherwise would. The *Rheindahlen Bulletin*, a monthly magazine containing details of entertainment and general information, was prepared and edited by a staff that at one time included a WRAF Education Officer, Maggie Fish. This publication helped publicise the delights of the Fatherland, and her monthly article, entitled 'Fish Tours' became especially popular reading among those who wished to travel about the country.

As the day of my departure from Germany approached, we were invited out to many dinner parties. The Army marked my departure by presenting me with my very own pick and fourteen pound sledge hammer! I was quite touched by this gesture for few Air Force officers are treated in this manner.

Gitti and I were 'dined out' by the staff of the Record Library and the Information Room and Gitti was most unexpectedly given a huge bouquet of flowers by the German officers of the HQ. That was not a normal practice and Gitti was delighted by this gesture. The Officers' Mess dined us out on a night that unfortunately saw larger number than usual leaving Germany. However, despite this we got a reasonable mention and were delighted that we had not been allowed to slip away unnoticed into retirement. Our friends too dined us out in many homes and when we ultimately drove away from Douglas Way, we felt that a wonderful chapter of our life had closed, but that we could happily face the future, as long as we were together.

Retirement was rapidly approaching and I had to return to England three months before my actual retirement date or the RAF would not pay my household removal costs. The reasoning behind this was that they would not pay me to leave the Air Force! I think that I've demonstrated that I really don't know quite why I had to return three months before retirement, but I can assure you that that was the advice given.

Gitti and I had owned our house at Lydiard Millicent for many years and we knew the physical measurements of every room. All was recorded in the little black book! For months we had been buying bits and pieces for the two bathrooms. We got some pretty strange looks from our neighbours when they realised that we had bought two toilets, a bath, bathroom fittings and one hundred and four square metres of tiles!

A hundred and four square metres of tiles is an awful lot and they weigh a great deal. I obtained a lot of boxes and packed five boxes each weighing 120lbs and tens of boxes each weighing eighty pounds. I borrowed the banding machine from stores and spent quite some time securing them. When the time came for our household goods to depart for the UK, I explained to the removals men that there were rather a lot of heavy, low volume boxes. The two workmen exchanged looks and smiled happily at one another. This was not the response that I expected so I told them again of the number and weight of the tile boxes. 'Ah,' said the removals team, 'We don't mind at all, because your stuff's going into store for a few weeks and our office staff are going to unload this van! The Boss has been telling us for months that putting household gear into large box storage containers isn't much of a job. I hope that he and that snotty clerk break their bloody backs on this!' With this compassionate remark he and his mate returned to work.

I'll fast forward in time to my telephone call to the removals firm requesting delivery after our return home. ' Good Afternoon. My name is Hayes ...' I got no further with my speech, because I was interrupted by the interjection of, '56 Chestnut Springs, Lydiard Millicent!' I was astounded, and complimented the man on his memory. He gave a short gruff laugh and said that he should bloody well remember, because he'd put his back out carrying all the heavy boxes! I'm afraid to say that I laughed at this, but did my utmost not to laugh down the phone. The pantechnicon arrived and the same duo that had packed our goods in Germany stood grinning at the doorway. I told them that their charitable wishes had come true and that the Boss and the clerk were suffering because of the tile boxes. We enjoyed a cup of tea and a good laugh before work started. The Germans have a word for pleasure at the pain of others – Schadenfreude! You may have noticed that I over-use the word!

Quite apart from the bath, Gitti and I had baggage that was awkward and bulky. The large vanity unit for the main bathroom and the leather suite were difficult to get into the house. The latter had to come in via the large sliding glass doors leading to the back garden The furniture for each of the children's bedrooms proved especially difficult to get into the house because of their height and the difficult turning entrances to their rooms. After trying for some time to gain entry, we had the main pane of double glazed glass removed from the windows of both their rooms! That little exercise was expensive, but at least we did not damage the newly decorated corridor in the process.

My resettlement course took the form of what is known as 'the Works and Bricks Course'. At the end of a month of hard work I was awarded a City and Guilds Certificate from the London Institute stating that I was competent in most of the building skills! I was particularly proud of my wall plastering skill and had completed my test piece. Using my float I polished up the final surface and called all within earshot to view my effort. About ten persons strolled slowly across just in time to watch my entire wall plaster slip slowly down the wall onto the floor! The laughter was unkind, I thought, for the surface had been truly perfect. My problem was that I should not have attempted the final wet polish. It was a most useful and instructive course that I should have done twenty years earlier. I must say that I lay a good tile – but the standard of grouting is one that reflects the lack of any real practice. I do all the right things, but the finish lacks that certain 'something'. But.... I do know *how* to do things!

I found that my departure from Germany was unreal. I found great difficulty in coming to terms with the fact that I was retiring. I would leave, not a job, but an environment in which I felt supremely comfortable. I knew who and what I was and the consequent limitations. I knew my income and expenditure and lived comfortably within those constraints. All was about to change. I had spent forty-two and a half years in the Royal Air Force and had some misgivings as to my future. Did I need to find work? Did I have enough money to retire without the necessity to work? We believed that only time would tell. I said we because Gitti and I enjoyed a relationship and a lifestyle that did not need vast sums of money to sustain. That was just as well, for there were no vast sums of money available. I had my pension as a Specialist Aircrew Flight Lieutenant and a small additional pension that I had bought into. This income would in time be augmented by my state pension and by Gitti's state pension. The house was just about paid for and we had brought back from Germany an array of new furniture. Our assessment was that with Bini gainfully employed and Susi about to finish her A levels at school, we were reasonably placed to face the future. Anyway, who would employ a fifty nine year old with absolutely no knowledge of civilian life? Smiling at each other over the coffee table, we agreed that life was still good.

On completion of my terminal leave I reported to RAF Lyneham. I had just less than three months left to complete my service before final retirement on 9 June. As I drove into camp, I noticed some change. The entry to the camp area had been altered to accommodate heightened security and a Comet 4 had been installed as a Gate Guard aircraft. Little did I know that the cost of maintaining Gate guard aircraft would occupy the bean counters for years, as they debated whose budget should pay! It all looked quite impressive I thought as I filled in all the necessary forms to obtain entry to the base for the car and me. Finally, I made my way into Station Headquarters and into the General Office. I approached the central work surface that formed an island separating staff from visitor and announced my presence.

When asked for an 'Arrival Form' the Corporal Clerk smiled diffidently and murmured that the Station would rather that I did not arrive! Somewhat puzzled, I asked why not as I had three months to serve. What did the Corporal want me to do for the three months? He responded by saying that I should consider the time to be 'Gardening Leave'. He continued, saying that I should go home. If my presence was required, they would call, but he did not think it likely, as they had no work for me to do! Stunned, I thought that this was some end to a lifetime career in the Royal Air Force. Reflecting bitterly that I could have remained in Germany, I turned to leave the office. However, I returned to the desk and asked the seated Warrant Officer why I should not formally arrive on the unit. He rose and explained that under the new accounting procedures a budget was fixed for all units and all activities. If I officially arrived on the unit, then my salary was deducted from available funds. Since there was nothing for me to do, I should return home. There, my salary would be paid from central funds. Suitably enlightened, I left for home. Nobody called and I did not hear another word from the Royal Air Force. The only way in which I knew that I had finally left the Service was that I received a final pay chit. I still have that slip of paper, for it shows the remarkable tenacity of the accountant staff in obtaining their pound of flesh. I was given a language award in 1989 that paid some sum in recognition of my German language skill. My final pay chit reclaimed a proportion of that award because I had not served three full years in Germany following the award! Yep!

That's my Air Force – don't say Goodbye, but claim the last penny back! I did not receive a single valedictory word from the Air Force in the UK, nor did I get a record of my service in any form or shape. I was so very grateful to my colleagues in Germany for they ensured that I did not fade into the gloom at the end of my service.

As I left the airbase, I reflected that in civilian life I might have been given a clock to mark my retirement. I, on the other hand, gave the Air Force a clock as I retired by handing back my aircrew watch!

I look back on my Service life with a great deal of pleasure, I have been to some remarkable places and seen some remarkable sights. I have flown over northern waters and watched incredulously as the master painter caused the sky to swirl in vivid colours. Deep emerald followed red and electric blue and the whole sky swirled like a kaleidoscope. I have watched the Pacific cloudbanks, visible as far as the eye could see from left to right, marching in serried ranks towards the infinitely distant horizon. I have flown through the Pacific night to be astounded as the sun rose, casting its rays like the Japanese national flag, before seemingly leaping off the morning horizon in a wondrous display of colour. I have seen desert and the old world and have enjoyed the wonders of the new. Through flying, I have been privileged to see much of this earth, always in good company. I have had my miseries, but these have been short lived. Above all, I have enjoyed the company of my colleagues whose kindness, wit and humour have sustained me when all was not quite perfect.

I believe that my retirement was timely for I don't think that I could cope with the changes to Service life. Everything has become budget driven and the Officers' Mess has changed and standards have changed beyond recognition. Many of the support activities have been civilianised, and try as I might I cannot see equal or improved standards. Money, or the lack of it, appears to drive operations and attitudes have changed at all levels. The Service appears to have fragmented and the team spirit that sustained me throughout my life appears to be a thing of the past. Nevertheless, I salute my companions at arms and wish them well in the hope that when the need comes they will have the correct equipment in appropriate numbers in the right place and be directed by unambiguous orders. God bless the lot of you.

Printed in the United Kingdom
by Lightning Source UK Ltd.
124566UK00001B/109-207/A